Systematic Theology for Gen X: A 1-, 10-, or 30-Minute Devotional

A Guided Walk Through Christian Doctrine, Key Bible Passages and Real-Life Discipleship-Deepen Your Faith Without Long Study Sessions

Matthew R. Caldwell

CONTENTS

Introduction — How to Use This Book

You are tired. YOU are tired of the hustle, tired of the culture wars, and tired of pretending you have it all together.

You probably didn't pick up a book on systematic theology because you have an abundance of free time. You picked it up because the faith that carried you through your twenties and thirties is suddenly feeling a little thin.

At twenty, a few inspiring quotes and an acoustic guitar were enough to keep you going. But now you are in midlife. You are managing a career, worrying about your kids, and navigating the physical decline of your aging parents. The stakes are higher. The tragedies are closer. The cultural noise is deafening. You don't need a religious cheerleader right now; you need a heavy anchor.

The phrase 'systematic theology' sounds intimidating, like a seminary exam you didn't study for. But at its core, it is simply the blueprints to the house. It is taking the time to organize exactly what you believe about God, humanity, and the universe so that when the storm hits on a random Tuesday, your roof doesn't cave in.

The problem is that most theology books are written by academics for other academics. They are nine hundred pages long, filled with Latin jargon, and completely disconnected from the reality of a Tuesday morning commute. On the other extreme, modern popular Christianity is often just shallow self-help advice with a Bible verse sprinkled on top.

This book is the middle ground. It is designed specifically for busy, cynical, exhausted adults who want the deep, historic, orthodox truth of the Christian faith, but who need it delivered without the fluff, the Christian-ese, or the culture-war outrage.

Here is how this book is built, and how you should use it.

The 52-Week Structure The book is divided into 52 chapters. You can read one a week for a year, or you can go at your own pace. Each chapter covers one massive piece of Christian doctrine (from the Trinity, to sin, to the end of the world).

Choose Your Lane We know you do not have the exact same amount of time or mental energy every single week. Some weeks you have an hour to read; some weeks you have exactly five minutes while sitting in a carline or a doctor's waiting room.

Because of that, every chapter is divided into "Lanes." You choose the lane that fits your bandwidth that week. There is zero guilt for staying in Lane 1. You don't get extra spiritual credit for reading every word, and skipping a section doesn't make you a bad Christian.

- **At a Glance (1 minute):** The absolute core truth of the chapter, stripped down to a single page. If you only read this, you will still know the doctrine.

- **Lane 1 — Clarity (10 minutes)**: The bottom line. It explains the concept simply, gives you the primary Scripture, and shows you why it matters.

- **Lane 2 — Depth (30 minutes):** The heavy lifting. This section breaks the doctrine down into its core components, defining the terms, and building the theology directly from the Bible.

- **Lane 3 — Deep Dive (Optional):** For when you have the time and desire to go further. This section tackles the hardest cultural objections to the doctrine, looks at how the church handled it historically, and applies it deeply to real life.

The Tuesday Payoff Theology is useless if it only works on Sunday morning when the music is playing. Real life happens on Tuesday afternoon when your boss yells at you, your transmission fails, or you get a terrifying medical diagnosis. Every chapter includes a "Tuesday Payoff" to show you exactly how this specific doctrine keeps you sane in the middle of a stressful week.

The Midlife Module Every chapter also includes a short section dedicated specifically to the psychology of midlife. Theology hits differently at 48 than it does at 18. These modules apply the ancient truths of Scripture directly to the very modern realities of aging, career ceilings, and shifting family dynamics.

The Posture of This Book This book is written from a "broad evangelical" perspective. That means it holds fiercely to the historic, foundational truths of the Christian faith (the authority of Scripture, the Trinity, the physical resurrection of Jesus, and salvation by grace alone).

However, we also know you are exhausted by theological tribalism. Christians have argued for two thousand years over secondary issues (like how exactly the end times will play out, or whether to baptize babies or adults). Where those disagreements happen, this book includes a "Where Christians Differ" box. We will state the different views fairly, without mocking the other side. You don't have to agree with every secondary conclusion to benefit from the primary truths.

The Goal The goal of this book is not to make you the smartest person in your Bible study so you can win arguments on the internet. Theology that only makes your head bigger has failed. True theology should make your heart burn.

The goal is to give you a clear, unshakeable view of who God actually is, so that you can finally stop performing, stop worrying if you are doing it all wrong, and simply rest in the hands of the King.

Turn the page. Let's start building the house.

– Matthew R. Caldwell

PART 1 — STARTING POINTS

Before you can drive anywhere, you need a map. Not a GPS voice gently guiding your every turn, but one of those massive, folded paper maps you had to read under the dome light of a car while someone yelled at you to figure out where the exit was. That is exactly what navigating modern spirituality feels like today… chaotic, confusing, and full of people yelling different directions.

In Part 1, we are establishing our starting points. We are looking at the nature of truth, the reliability of the Bible, and how God actually makes Himself known. Before we get to the heavy doctrines, we have to adjust the tracking on the VCR so the static clears and we can actually agree on what we are looking at.

Week 1 — Why Systematic Theology (When You're Busy and Tired)

Core Question: Why spend time studying heavy doctrine when real life is already overwhelming enough?

Why this matters: Because what you actually believe about God is the only thing that will hold your weight when Tuesday afternoon falls apart.

At a Glance (One Page)

Big Idea: Theology isn't an academic hobby for pastors; it is the load-bearing foundation for living a resilient life in a confusing world.

Anchor Text: Proverbs 2:1–6; Matthew 22:29

We believe…: The disciplined study of who God is and what He has done is necessary for a durable, mature faith.

Key Words (3): Theology - The study of God; thinking carefully about who He is. Doctrine - The specific, foundational truths taught in Scripture. Systematic - Organizing what the Bible says by topic so it makes sense as a whole.

The One Mistake People Make: Assuming theology is just head knowledge that distracts from having a real relationship with Jesus.

Choose Your Lane: Lane 1 / Lane 2 / Lane 3

This Week's Practice: The Input Audit.

This Week's Prayer: Father, I admit that my attention is fractured and I am often just trying to get through the week. The idea of studying doctrine feels like one more heavy thing to carry. But I also know that shallow roots won't hold up in the storms I'm facing. Give me the desire to know You as You actually are, not just as I assume You to be. Clear the fog from my mind. Help me to trade my assumptions for the truth of Your Word. Give me the patience to learn, the humility to be corrected, and the quiet confidence that comes from knowing exactly who is holding my life together. Amen.

Lane 1 — Clarity (10 minutes)

The Bottom Line Everyone is a theologian. The only question is whether you are a good one or a bad one. Systematic theology is simply taking the time to organize what you believe about God so that when life hits you hard, your faith doesn't collapse under the pressure.

Scripture Snapshot Matthew 22:29: "Jesus replied, 'You are in error because you do not know the Scriptures or the power of God.'"

Jesus said this to a group of highly religious leaders (the Sadducees) who were trying to trap him with a hypothetical question about the afterlife. They knew the religious rules, but Jesus bluntly told them they were completely wrong. Why? Because they didn't actually know the text, and they didn't understand who God was. They had built a massive religious system on top of bad theology. Jesus cuts straight to the point: error happens when we stop paying attention to what God has actually revealed about Himself.

Say It Out Loud (One Sentence) Good theology is the blueprint that keeps your faith from caving in when reality hits.

Common Confusions Confusion #1: Theology is for academics; normal Christians just need to read the Psalms and pray. Confusion #2: Studying doctrine just makes people arrogant and argumentative.

The Tuesday Payoff Imagine it's 2:15 PM on a Tuesday. You get an email from your boss implying your department is being restructured. Ten minutes later, your teenager's school calls. Your chest tightens. In that exact moment, what you *actually* believe about God's control, His goodness, and your identity steps up to the microphone in your head. If your theology is basically "God wants me to be happy and successful," that Tuesday will crush you. If your theology is anchored in the sovereign, sustaining God of the Bible, you will still be stressed, but you won't be destroyed. Doctrine isn't what you study in a library; it's what catches you on a Tuesday.

Lane 2 — Depth (30 minutes)

Define the Terms Theology - From the Greek words *theos* (God) and *logos* (word/study). It literally means words about God, or the study of God. Doctrine - A set of beliefs held and taught by the church. It is the agreed-upon truth drawn from Scripture. Systematic Theology - Taking everything the Bible says about a specific topic (like angels, sin, or salvation) and putting it together into a coherent whole.

Build the Doctrine (Scripture-forward)

You Already Have a Theology You don't get to opt out of theology. Every time you complain about how unfair the world is, you are doing theology (grappling with the problem of evil). Every time you comfort a grieving friend, you are doing theology (expressing what you believe about death and comfort). The question isn't whether you have a theology, but whether yours is built on the Bible or cobbled together from internet memes, childhood assumptions, and self-help books.

Key texts: Proverbs 2:1–5

The writer of Proverbs doesn't treat knowing God as something that happens accidentally. He uses words like *accept, store up, turn your ear, call out, cry aloud, look for it, search for it*. It requires the same energy you would use to find hidden treasure. We are happy to spend hours researching the best mortgage rate or the most reliable used car, but we often coast on a fourth-grade understanding of God and wonder why our faith feels weak in our forties.

Bad Theology Will Hurt You Ideas have consequences. If you believe God is essentially a cosmic vending machine whose job is to reward your good behavior, you will become incredibly bitter when you get sick or lose your job. If you believe God is an angry taskmaster waiting for you to mess up, you will live with chronic, low-grade spiritual anxiety.

Key texts: Matthew 22:29; Hosea 4:6

When Jesus told the religious leaders they were in error, He wasn't giving them a mild academic critique. He was warning them that their ignorance was dangerous. Hosea 4:6 says, "my people are destroyed from lack of knowledge." Not a lack of passion. Not a lack of sincerity. A lack of knowledge. A badly built bridge will collapse, no matter how sincerely you believe it will hold you. A badly built theology will do the same.

God Actually Wants to Be Known Studying doctrine can feel arrogant, as if we are trying to put God in a box or figure Him out completely. But systematic theology isn't about solving God like a math equation. It's about listening to what He has explicitly told us about Himself. God is not hiding. He gave us a book so that we could know Him accurately.

Key texts: Jeremiah 9:23–24; Deuteronomy 29:29

In Jeremiah, God explicitly states what we should brag about. Not wealth, not strength, not wisdom, but this: "that they have the understanding to know me." God delights in being known by His people. Yes, there are secret things that belong to the Lord (Deuteronomy 29:29), but the things He has revealed belong to us. We study theology to clearly see what He has placed right in front of us.

Doctrine is an Anchor, Not a Straitjacket A common Gen X experience is having grown up in rigid, rule-heavy church environments. For many, "doctrine" sounds like a list of boundaries designed to keep you trapped, bored, and judgmental. But biblical doctrine does the exact opposite. It anchors you.

Key texts: Ephesians 4:14

Paul writes that mature believers will no longer be "infants, tossed back and forth by the waves, and blown here and there by every wind of teaching." Without an anchor, you are at the mercy of the cultural weather. When the culture shifts, or a crisis hits, you will just drift. Good theology gives you the massive, heavy anchor required to stay steady in rough water. It gives you the freedom to face reality without panic.

It Leads to Worship, Not Just Information The goal of systematic theology is never just to make you smarter. If you read this book and all you get is a bigger vocabulary so you can win arguments on the internet, you have entirely missed the point. True theology always ends in worship.

Key texts: Romans 11:33–36

After spending eleven chapters laying out some of the most dense, complex, heavy systematic theology in the entire Bible, the Apostle Paul doesn't offer a final exam. He bursts into a song: "Oh, the depth of the riches of the wisdom and knowledge of God!" He studied the mechanics of salvation, and the result was awe. Knowing God better should always make you love Him more.

BOX - What This Is NOT Saying We are NOT saying you need a seminary degree or a high IQ to please God. We are NOT saying that having the right theological answers removes the pain of living in a broken world. We are NOT saying that the Bible is just a textbook or an encyclopedia. We are NOT saying we will ever understand everything about God; mystery will always remain.

BOX - Where Christians Differ Not a major point of disagreement this week. Across all orthodox Christian traditions, the necessity of knowing God through His revealed Word is universally affirmed.

Lane 3 — Deep Dive (Optional)

The Objection You're Already Thinking "I don't need theology or doctrine. I just need Jesus. All this heavy study just divides people and distracts from loving others."

The Best Answer This is a common, understandable reaction, especially if you've seen theology weaponized by angry people. "Just give me Jesus" sounds deeply spiritual and beautifully simple. But it falls apart the moment you ask one follow-up question: *Which Jesus?*

The Jesus who was just a good moral teacher? The Jesus who is your cosmic life coach? The Jesus who exists to endorse your political party? Or the Jesus of the Bible, who claimed to be God, forgave sins, demanded total allegiance, and rose from the dead?

You cannot separate Jesus from theology. The moment you say, "Jesus is the Son of God who died for my sins," you have just made a massive, deeply theological statement. You've waded into Christology (the study of Christ) and Soteriology (the study of salvation). The issue isn't whether we will use theology to understand Jesus; the issue is whether our theology is accurate. Relying on a vague, doctrine-free "relationship with Jesus" usually means we end up worshiping a Jesus we invented—one who coincidentally agrees with us on everything and never calls us out.

Historical Lens The early church didn't write the Nicene Creed because they were bored and liked arguing over Greek vocabulary. They wrote it because normal, everyday Christians needed to know exactly who they were trusting their eternal lives to. Precision mattered because their lives were on the line.

Real-Life Translation There is a massive difference between reading a romantic poem about the ocean and studying a nautical chart. If you are sitting on the beach with a coffee, the poem is great. But if you are commanding a ship in a storm at 2:00 AM, you need the chart. You need to know exactly where the rocks are.

Many of us try to navigate the hardest parts of life—the sudden death of a parent, a child's chronic illness, the collapse of a career—armed with nothing but Christian poetry and coffee-mug slogans. It isn't enough. When the storm hits, you need the heavy, unyielding realities of doctrine. You need to know exactly where the rocks are. You need a theology rugged enough to handle your grief, your doubts, and your fears without breaking.

Midlife Module - This Doctrine in Midlife You are sitting in your car in the driveway after work, staring blankly at the steering wheel. You are the classic sandwich generation right now: worrying about your teenager's mental health while also managing your aging parent's medical appointments. The faith that carried you in your twenties—youth group highs, acoustic guitars, and simple answers—feels dangerously thin right now. It's not that you don't believe in God anymore; it's just that you need a bigger, stronger God to carry the sheer weight of your midlife reality.

1. You have permission to trade in shallow answers for deep truth. You don't have to fake a smile.

2. The Bible was written for exhausted adults living in a hard world, not just for kids in Sunday School.

3. Studying theology now is how you reinforce the foundation of your house before the next storm hits.

Practice + Prayer

This Week's Practice (3–7 minutes) The Input Audit. Look at your phone and review the last five podcasts you listened to, or the last five articles you read. Evaluate your ratio of cultural commentary/news to actual Scripture or solid theology. For the next three days, replace 10 minutes of news or doomscrolling with reading one chapter of the book of Romans. It matters because what you feed your mind dictates the baseline anxiety of your soul.

Prayer (100–160 words) God, if I am being honest, my mind is full of noise. Between work, family, and the constant hum of the news, I don't have a lot of margin left. The thought of studying theology feels like adding heavy weights to an already full backpack. But I know my current foundation isn't strong enough. I want to know You. I want to know the real You, not the version of You I constructed to make my life comfortable. Tear down any false ideas I have about who You are. Build up a true, biblical understanding in my mind and in my heart. Give me the endurance to do the work of learning, and let the result of this study be a quiet, unshakeable confidence in Your goodness. Amen.

Reflection

Solo (3 prompts)

1. If you had to explain who God is to a stranger in exactly three sentences, what would you say?

2. Think about a recent time you were highly stressed or afraid. What did your reaction reveal about what you *actually* believed God was doing in that moment?

3. What is one piece of "bad theology" or a Christian cliché you used to believe, but have since discarded?

Small Group (3 prompts + 1 hard question)

1. When you hear the words "systematic theology," what is your immediate gut reaction? Intimidation? Boredom? Curiosity?

2. Read Matthew 22:29 together. How does not knowing the Scriptures lead directly to not understanding God's power?

3. We talked about how good theology is an anchor, not a straitjacket. Where do you feel like you are currently drifting and need an anchor?

Hard Question: Are you avoiding digging deeper into Scripture because you are secretly afraid of what God might ask you to change?

<u>**Close**</u>

One Sentence Recap: The disciplined study of who God is and what He has done is necessary for a durable, mature faith.

If You Only Remember One Thing: Doctrine isn't what you study in a library; it's what catches you when life falls apart on a Tuesday.

Next Week Preview: Next week we tackle how to know the truth without becoming an arrogant jerk about it.

Scripture References Used Deuteronomy 29:29 Proverbs 2:1–6 Jeremiah 9:23–24 Hosea 4:6 Matthew 22:29 Romans 11:33–36 Ephesians 4:14

<u>My Thoughts & Notes – What Did I Take From This?</u>

Week 2 — Truth Without Hype: What We Mean by Doctrine

Core Question: How do we know what is actually true when everyone claims to have the right answers, and why does "doctrine" sound so rigid?

Why this matters: Because living on borrowed truth or cultural assumptions will eventually leave you exhausted; you need a standard outside yourself to survive the spin.

At a Glance (One Page)

Big Idea: Truth isn't a marketing pitch or a weapon; it is the solid, objective reality of who God is, and sound doctrine is how we stay spiritually healthy in a confusing world.

Anchor Text: John 8:31–32; 2 Timothy 1:13

We believe…: Christian doctrine is the accurate articulation of reality as God has revealed it in Scripture, not a set of arbitrary rules meant to control us.

Key Words (3): Truth - That which perfectly aligns with reality as God created it and sees it. Orthodoxy - Right belief; the historic, agreed-upon core essentials of the Christian faith. Heresy - A belief that severely distorts or denies a core, foundational truth of Christianity.

The One Mistake People Make: Believing that truth is relative to our feelings, and that claiming to know the truth makes you arrogant.

Choose Your Lane: Lane 1 / Lane 2 / Lane 3

This Week's Practice: The "My Truth" Filter.

This Week's Prayer: Father, I am tired of the spin. I live in a world where everyone is shouting their version of reality, and frankly, it is exhausting trying to figure out who to trust. I confess that sometimes I prefer my own opinions to Your truth because it feels easier and demands less of me. Help me to love what is true more than what is comfortable. Strip away my cultural assumptions and the religious baggage I've picked up over the years. Ground me in the quiet, unshakeable reality of Your Word. Give me the humility to submit to it, and the grace to share it without being a jerk. Amen.

Lane 1 — Clarity (10 minutes)

The Bottom Line Truth is not a preference, a brand, or a political stance. Truth is simply what aligns with reality. Doctrine is the church's agreed-upon way of describing that reality based on the Bible. Good doctrine doesn't exist to make us argumentative; it exists to keep us sane, grounded, and spiritually healthy when the world loses its mind.

Scripture Snapshot John 8:31–32: "To the Jews who had believed him, Jesus said, 'If you hold to my teaching, you are really my disciples. Then you will know the truth, and the truth will set you free.'"

Context matters here. Jesus is talking to people who supposedly already believed in him. But He places a condition on their freedom: they have to hold to His teaching. He doesn't tell them to look inside themselves to find their authentic truth. He points them to an external standard—His actual words. Jesus equates knowing the truth with experiencing freedom. In God's economy, truth isn't a cage; it's the key that lets you out.

Say It Out Loud (One Sentence) Doctrine is the grammar of faith; without it, our beliefs are just noise.

Common Confusions Confusion #1: Truth changes based on my personal experience or the current decade. Confusion #2: Doctrine is just a list of dead traditions created by old men to control people.

The Tuesday Payoff It's Tuesday morning and you are scrolling through social media. You see three different influencers confidently stating entirely contradictory things about morality, justice, and how to raise your kids. If you believe truth is something you have to constantly curate for yourself—like a Spotify playlist of beliefs—this will produce low-grade panic. You will constantly wonder if you are doing life wrong. But if truth is an objective reality established by God, you don't have to invent it. You just have to learn it and lean your weight on it.

Lane 2 — Depth (30 minutes)

Define the Terms Truth - Objective reality. What is actually real, regardless of whether we understand it, agree with it, or like it. Orthodoxy - From the Greek *orthos* (right/straight) and *doxa* (belief/glory). Holding to the historic, foundational teachings of the Christian faith. Heresy - A belief that contradicts or undermines an essential doctrine (like denying the Trinity or the resurrection). It's not just "something I disagree with." Sound Doctrine - Teachings that are accurate, reliable, and produce spiritual health.

Build the Doctrine (Scripture-forward)

Truth Exists Outside of You We live in an era that worships subjective experience. Phrases like "speak your truth" or "live your truth" sound empowering, but they are a heavy burden. If truth is just personal experience, then nothing is universally real, and whoever has the loudest microphone wins. The Bible insists that truth is objective. It originates in the character of God, not the feelings of humans.

Key texts: John 14:6; John 17:17

When Jesus says, "I am the way and the truth and the life" (John 14:6), He is making an exclusive, objective claim. He doesn't say He is *a* truth. In His prayer in John 17, He asks the Father to sanctify His followers by the truth, adding, "your word is truth." Truth is an anchor dropped outside the boat. It holds you precisely because it is not attached to you.

Sound Doctrine is About Health, Not Arguments If you grew up in certain church subcultures, "doctrine" was often used as a weapon to prove who was in and who was out. It felt angry. But the New Testament writers use a fascinating word when they talk about doctrine: *sound*.

Key texts: 2 Timothy 1:13; Titus 1:9

When Paul tells Timothy to keep the pattern of "sound teaching," the Greek word is *hygiaino*. It's where we get the English word *hygiene*. It literally means healthy, whole, and free from disease. Biblical doctrine is medical, not just academic. False teaching is treated like an infection because it sickens the church and ruins lives. We study doctrine for the same reason a doctor studies anatomy: to promote life and treat disease.

Truth Without Grace is a Weapon It is entirely possible to have perfect theology and still be a terrible representative of Jesus. If our pursuit of truth makes us arrogant, cynical, and mean, we have missed the plot completely.

Key texts: Ephesians 4:15; 1 Corinthians 13:1–2

Paul tells the Ephesians to "speak the truth in love." These two things are not opposites; they are twin engines. Truth without love is brutality. Love without truth is hypocrisy. You can know all the mysteries and all the doctrines (1 Corinthians 13), but if you don't have love, you are just banging a gong. God does not need us to be His angry defense attorneys. He calls us to be His faithful witnesses.

Doctrine Requires Holding Tensions Because God is infinite and we are finite, good theology often requires holding two truths in tension without forcing them to resolve neatly. We want a simple math equation; God often gives us a paradox.

Key texts: Romans 11:22; Proverbs 26:4–5

Consider Romans 11:22: "Consider therefore the kindness and sternness of God." We have to hold both. If you only focus on His kindness, you get a harmless, enabling grandpa. If you only focus on His sternness, you get an abusive dictator. Orthodoxy requires the mental discipline to hold complex truths together—like Jesus being fully God and fully man, or God being completely sovereign while humans are completely responsible.

BOX - What This Is NOT Saying We are NOT saying that Christians never have doubts or struggle to understand what is true. We are NOT saying that having right doctrine earns you salvation; salvation is by grace. We are NOT saying that every minor theological opinion is a hill to die on. We are NOT saying that quoting Scripture is an excuse to be abrasive or unkind to people.

BOX - Where Christians Differ Evangelicals agree on the core definitions of truth and the necessity of sound doctrine (historic orthodoxy). Where Christians differ is on *secondary* doctrines—things like how the end times will play out, the exact nature of the bread and wine in communion, or how a local church should be governed. A healthy church defends the core fiercely but shows massive charity on the secondary issues.

Lane 3 — Deep Dive (Optional)

The Objection You're Already Thinking "Doesn't claiming you have the absolute 'truth' make you naturally arrogant and intolerant of other people?"

The Best Answer Historically, yes. Christians have absolutely weaponized the concept of truth to control, marginalize, and harm others. We have to own that failure.

However, the logic of **The Objection** falls apart upon **Close**r inspection. The statement "There is no absolute truth, and anyone who claims to have it is arrogant" is, itself, a claim of absolute truth. Everyone, secular or religious, operates based on a set of truth claims they believe align with reality.

More importantly, true Christian orthodoxy destroys arrogance at its root. If the core "truth" of Christianity is that I am a flawed, broken sinner who cannot save myself, and that God had to send His Son to die in my place to rescue me—where is the room for pride? If I truly believe that doctrine, I can't look down on anyone. I am just a beggar telling other beggars where I found bread. Arrogance isn't the result of believing Christian truth; arrogance is the result of forgetting it.

Historical Lens The early creeds of the church (like the Apostles' Creed and the Nicene Creed) weren't written by ivory-tower academics with too much free time. They were forged by pastors—many of whom had been tortured for their faith under the Roman Empire—who needed to summarize the core truths of Scripture so that everyday farmers, soldiers, and mothers wouldn't be led astray by slick, convincing cult leaders.

Real-Life Translation Navigating life by your feelings is like flying an airplane into a heavy fog without instruments. Your inner ear will lie to you. Pilots are trained in "instrument flying rules" (IFR) because when they lose visibility, their brain will tell them they are flying level when they are actually diving toward the ground.

When you lose a job, when a friendship ends, when you hit a wall of anxiety, your feelings will lie to you. Your brain will tell you that God is angry with you, or that you are worthless, or that you have to take unethical shortcuts to survive. Sound doctrine is your instrument panel. It is the objective readout of reality that you trust over your own disorientation. You look at the panel—what God has said is true—and you fly the plane by that, regardless of the vertigo.

Midlife Module - This Doctrine at 48 You are having lunch with a friend you've known since your twenties. Over the past five years, they have completely dismantled their faith. They are exhausted, frustrated with church politics, and tell you they are now just trying to "curate their own spiritual truth."

You feel a wave of fatigue. You understand their frustration with the church. You carry some of those same scars. But the idea of having to wake up every morning and manufacture your own moral compass from scratch sounds utterly exhausting. At 48, you don't want to invent a religion. You just want a reality that is strong enough to hold you. You realize that separating the cultural garbage of your past from the historic truth of the Nicene Creed isn't just an intellectual exercise; it is the only way to keep your faith intact without losing your mind.

Practice + Prayer

This Week's Practice (3–7 minutes) The "My Truth" Filter. This week, simply pay attention to how often the culture around you uses phrases like "my truth," "your truth," or "living my truth" in podcasts, meetings, or social media. Every time you hear it, mentally translate it to "my experience" or "my perspective." Notice how it changes the weight of what is being said. Experience is valid, but it is not truth.

Prayer (100–160 words) God, thank You for not leaving me to figure everything out on my own. If my reality was limited to my own feelings and experiences, I would be completely lost by now. Thank You for giving us Your Word as a clear, unbending standard of truth. When the culture around me demands that I compromise or adjust my beliefs to fit the moment, give me the quiet courage to stand firm. When I am tempted to use Your truth as a club to win arguments and make myself look smart, convict me and soften my heart. Help me to be a person who is relentlessly committed to truth, and overflowing with grace. Amen.

Reflection

Solo (3 prompts)

1. Where do you find yourself most tempted to compromise what you know is true just to keep the peace or avoid awkwardness?

2. Think of a time when someone spoke hard truth to you, but did it with so much love that you could actually receive it. What did they do right?

3. How do you practically distinguish between a core Christian truth (orthodoxy) and a secondary issue (preference or tradition)?

Small Group (3 prompts + 1 hard question)

1. Why do you think the culture is so attracted to the phrase "my truth"? What is appealing about it, and what is dangerous about it?

2. Read 2 Timothy 1:13 and Titus 1:9. How does viewing doctrine through a "medical/health" lens change the way we approach studying it?

3. Discuss the difference between defending the truth and just being defensive. How can we tell which one we are doing?

Hard Question: Are there any clear truths in the Bible that you secretly wish weren't there because they conflict with what you want to do?

Close

One Sentence Recap: Christian doctrine is the accurate articulation of reality as God has revealed it in Scripture.

If You Only Remember One Thing: Navigating life by your feelings is like flying in a fog without instruments; sound doctrine is the dashboard you trust when you lose your bearings.

Next Week Preview: Next week we look at Revelation—how God actually crossed the gap to make Himself known to us.

Scripture References Used Proverbs 26:4–5 John 8:31–32 John 14:6 John 17:17 Romans 11:22 1 Corinthians 13:1–2 Ephesians 4:15 2 Timothy 1:13 Titus 1:9

My Thoughts & Notes – What Did I Take From This?

Week 3 — Revelation: How God Makes Himself Known

Core Question: How do we actually know anything about God without just guessing or projecting our own ideas onto Him?

Why this matters: Because if God hasn't actively introduced Himself, all religion is just humans fumbling around in the dark trying to guess what the boss wants.

At a Glance (One Page)

Big Idea: We don't have to guess what God is like because He has broken the silence, showing His power in creation and revealing His heart specifically through Jesus and the Bible.

Anchor Text: Psalm 19; Hebrews 1:1–2

We believe...: God has revealed Himself universally through the natural world (general revelation) and specifically through Scripture and the person of Jesus Christ (special revelation).

Key Words (3): Revelation - God making Himself known to humanity; taking the lid off what was hidden. General Revelation - What God has shown everyone, everywhere, through creation and human conscience. Special Revelation - What God has specifically spoken through the prophets, the Bible, and ultimately Jesus Christ.

The One Mistake People Make: Thinking that a spiritual feeling in the woods is enough to know the specific character and demands of God.

Choose Your Lane: Lane 1 / Lane 2 / Lane 3

This Week's Practice: The Sky Audit.

This Week's Prayer: Father, I admit that I often treat You like a silent partner in my life, assuming You are quiet and distant. Thank You for not leaving me to figure this out on my own. Thank You for speaking. Forgive me for the times I have preferred a vague, mysterious God over the specific, demanding, and loving God You revealed Yourself to be in Jesus. Give me eyes to see Your power in the world You made, and give me the discipline to read the Word You wrote. Amen.

Lane 1 — Clarity (10 minutes)

The Bottom Line You can't know someone who refuses to speak to you. You can guess their personality based on what they wear or how they keep their yard, but until they open their mouth, you don't really know them. God did not leave us to guess. He left clues in the universe He built, and He spoke directly through the Bible and Jesus.

Scripture Snapshot Hebrews 1:1–2: "In the past God spoke to our ancestors through the prophets at many times and in various ways, but in these last days he has spoken to us by his Son."

The writer of Hebrews starts with a massive assumption: God speaks. He isn't a silent watchmaker who wound up the universe and walked away. Historically, He used prophets—spokesmen to deliver specific messages. But the climax of God's communication wasn't a book; it was a person. If you want to know exactly what God has to say, you look at Jesus.

Say It Out Loud (One Sentence) God is not hiding; He has clearly spoken through the world He made and the Word He gave.

Common Confusions Confusion #1: God only speaks to super-spiritual people or pastors. Confusion #2: The Bible is just man's search for God, not God's actual revelation to man.

The Tuesday Payoff It is Tuesday evening, and you are staring at a complex moral decision at work regarding a client contract. If God hasn't spoken clearly, your only option is to poll your friends, trust your gut, and hope for the best. But if God has provided specific revelation about honesty, justice, and human dignity, you don't have to invent the ethical wheel. You have an objective standard. Revelation means the pressure is off you to figure out the universe from scratch.

Lane 2 — Depth (30 minutes)

Define the Terms Revelation - Unveiling something that was previously hidden. General Revelation - The knowledge of God available to all people through observing nature and experiencing human conscience. Special Revelation - God's direct, specific communication through the Scriptures and the incarnation of Jesus Christ.

Build the Doctrine (Scripture-forward)

Creation Speaks Loudly Every human being has access to a basic level of knowledge about God just by walking outside. The complexity of the human eye, the massive scale of the universe, and the precision of physics all point to a designer. The universe isn't just matter; it is a broadcast.

Key texts: Psalm 19:1–4; Romans 1:20

David writes, "The heavens declare the glory of God; the skies proclaim the work of his hands" (Psalm 19). They pour forth speech without using words. Paul takes this further in Romans 1, stating that God's "invisible qualities—his eternal power and divine nature—have been clearly seen, being understood from what has been made." General revelation is loud enough that no one has an excuse for denying a Creator.

Nature Is Not Enough While a sunset can tell you God is an artist, and a thunderstorm can tell you God is powerful, a sunset cannot tell you how to have your sins forgiven. General revelation is sufficient to make us accountable, but it is insufficient to save us. For that, we need specifics.

Key texts: Psalm 19:7–11

Notice the pivot in Psalm 19. David goes from the sun and the stars (verses 1-6) straight to the law of the Lord (verses 7-11). The law is what "refreshes the soul" and "makes wise the simple." Nature shows us God's power; the Bible shows us God's character, His promises, and His redemptive plan.

Jesus is the Ultimate Microphone If you want to know what God sounds like, acts like, and cares about, you don't just look at nature or even just read the prophets. You look at Jesus. Jesus is not just a messenger of revelation; He is the message itself.

Key texts: John 1:14; Colossians 1:15

Jesus is "the image of the invisible God" (Colossians 1:15). In the incarnation, the Word became flesh and blood and moved into the neighborhood (John 1:14). If you want to know how God handles sick people, watch Jesus. If you want to know what God thinks of religious hypocrisy, listen to Jesus. He is the clearest articulation of God's reality that will ever exist.

BOX - What This Is NOT Saying We are NOT saying you can't feel **Close** to God in nature; you absolutely can. We are NOT saying God gives new, authoritative revelation today that overrides the Bible. We are NOT saying the Bible answers every scientific or historical curiosity we have.

BOX - Where Christians Differ Not a major point of disagreement this week. All broad evangelicals affirm that God reveals Himself generally in creation and specifically in Scripture and Christ. Some traditions differ slightly on how much weight to give modern "prophetic words," but all agree Scripture is the final, supreme standard.

Lane 3 — Deep Dive (Optional)

The Objection You're Already Thinking "I feel much **Close**r to God hiking in the mountains or fishing on a lake than I do in a church building or reading an ancient book. Isn't my connection with nature enough?"

The Best Answer Feeling peace in nature is a profoundly human and biblical experience. God designed the world to provoke awe. But awe is not the same thing as relationship.

If you admire a painting, you learn something about the painter's skill and style. But you don't know the painter's name, whether they are married, or what they demand of their friends. To know that, the painter has to introduce themselves. Nature gives you the painting. Scripture introduces you to the Painter.

More importantly, nature is broken. If you look to the natural world to tell you who God is, you have to account for both the beautiful sunset and the devastating tsunami. If nature is your only Bible, your theology will be incredibly confused. Special revelation—the Bible—explains *why* the world is both beautiful and broken, and tells us what God is doing to fix it.

Historical Lens During the Enlightenment, thinkers tried to strip away all "special revelation" (miracles, the Bible, Jesus as God) and rely purely on human reason and nature—a system called Deism. The church firmly pushed back, maintaining that a God who creates a world and then refuses to speak to it is not the God of Abraham, Isaac, and Jacob.

Real-Life Translation When you get a terrifying medical diagnosis, general revelation is useless to you. The trees cannot comfort you. The stars cannot promise you resurrection. A hike in the woods might lower your blood pressure for an hour, but it cannot secure your soul. In the darkest moments of life, you do not need the vague comfort of the cosmos; you need the specific, ironclad promises of a God who spoke. You need "I will never leave you nor forsake you" (Hebrews 13:5).

Midlife Module - This Doctrine at 52 You are sitting in a sterile hospital waiting room. Your dad is in surgery following a sudden heart attack. At 52, the illusion that you have total control over your life has officially evaporated. You feel incredibly small.

If God has not spoken, then you are just waiting for a biological machine to either restart or stop, and the universe is indifferent to your grief. But if revelation is true—if God actually broke through the silence to tell us that He cares for the brokenhearted, that death is a defeated enemy, and that Jesus wept at a tomb—then the sterile waiting room isn't empty. You aren't navigating this crisis on your own guesswork. You are resting on words that were spoken by the Author of life Himself.

Practice + Prayer

This Week's Practice (3–7 minutes) The Sky Audit. Walk outside tonight, leave your phone inside, and look up at the stars for exactly three minutes. Acknowledge the sheer scale of the universe (general revelation). Then, go inside, open your Bible to John 1, and read the first 14 verses (special revelation). Connect the God who made the stars with the God who became flesh.

Prayer (100–160 words) God, the universe You made is massive and intimidating, yet You did not leave us alone in it. Thank You for not remaining silent. When I am tempted to rely on my own intuition or the vague spirituality of our culture, ground me in the specific words You have spoken. Thank You for Jesus, who shows me exactly who You are. Teach me to listen to Your Word with the same attention I give to the noise of this world. Amen.

Reflection

Solo (3 prompts)

1. When in your life have you felt the strongest sense of awe at something in the natural world?

2. Why is it often more appealing to find God in nature than to read about Him in the Bible?

3. What specific promise from Scripture do you find yourself needing most right now?

Small Group (3 prompts + 1 hard question)

1. Discuss the difference between knowing *about* someone and actually *knowing* them. How does this relate to general vs. special revelation?

2. Read Hebrews 1:1–2 together. How does viewing Jesus as the final, ultimate message from God change how we read the rest of the Bible?

3. We talked about how nature cannot comfort you during a crisis. Have you found this to be true in your own life?

Hard Question: Are you relying on "general revelation" (just trying to be a good person who appreciates nature) to avoid submitting to the specific demands of Jesus?

Close

One Sentence Recap: God has revealed Himself universally through the natural world and specifically through Scripture and the person of Jesus Christ.

If You Only Remember One Thing: The stars can tell you God is powerful, but only the Bible can tell you that He loves you enough to save you.

Next Week Preview: Next week we tackle the Bible itself—why we trust an ancient book to dictate our modern lives.

Scripture References Used Psalm 19:1–11 John 1:14 Romans 1:20 Colossians 1:15 Hebrews 1:1–2 Hebrews 13:5

My Thoughts & Notes – What Did I Take From This?

Week 4 — Scripture: Inspiration, Authority, Trust

Core Question: Why should we trust a deeply ancient, complex book to have the final word on how we live today?

Why this matters: Because if the Bible is just an inspiring collection of human advice, you can ignore the parts you dislike; but if it is God-breathed, it is the only rock solid enough to build your life on.

At a Glance (One Page)

Big Idea: The Bible isn't just a historical record of people reaching for God; it is the supernaturally engineered, entirely reliable record of God reaching out to us.

Anchor Text: 2 Timothy 3:16–17; 2 Peter 1:20–21

We believe…: The Scriptures of the Old and New Testaments are inspired by God, completely reliable, and the supreme and final authority for all matters of faith and life.

Key Words (3): Inspiration - The process by which the Holy Spirit guided human authors to write exactly what God intended. Inerrancy - The belief that the original manuscripts of Scripture are completely true and without error in all they affirm. Authority - The right of Scripture to command our obedience and define our beliefs.

The One Mistake People Make: Treating the Bible like a buffet, where you take the comforting verses you like and leave the challenging moral commands you don't.

Choose Your Lane: Lane 1 / Lane 2 / Lane 3

This Week's Practice: The Submission Posture.

This Week's Prayer: Father, I live in an era that deeply distrusts authority, and I carry that same skepticism. I don't like being told what to do. I often want Your Bible to be an inspiring guidebook rather than an absolute authority. Forgive my pride. I ask that You would give me a high view of Your Word. Help me to trust that because You are perfectly good, Your commands are also perfectly good. Give me the courage to bend my life to fit the text, rather than bending the text to fit my life. Amen.

Lane 1 — Clarity (10 minutes)

The Bottom Line The core claim of Christianity is that the Bible is fundamentally different from every other book in history. It wasn't dictated by God to human robots, nor was it just a human brainstorming session about religion. It is a divine-human partnership where the Holy Spirit guided real people, with real personalities, to write down exactly what God wanted to communicate, making it our final authority.

Scripture Snapshot 2 Timothy 3:16–17: "All Scripture is God-breathed and is useful for teaching, rebuking, correcting and training in righteousness, so that the servant of God may be thoroughly equipped for every good work."

Paul wrote this to a younger pastor right before Paul was executed. He didn't tell Timothy to trust his gut or follow his heart. He pointed him to the text. "God-breathed" (the Greek word is *theopneustos*) means the words of Scripture originate from the very breath and mouth of God. Because it comes from God, it does heavy lifting: it teaches us reality, rebukes us when we drift, corrects our path, and trains us to live well.

Say It Out Loud (One Sentence) Because the Bible is breathed out by God, it holds the ultimate veto power over my opinions.

Common Confusions Confusion #1: Inspiration means God put the authors in a trance and took over their hands. Confusion #2: The Bible is outdated because culture has evolved past its ancient rules.

The Tuesday Payoff It's Tuesday morning and you are dealing with a deeply frustrating coworker who actively undermines you. Your intuition tells you to retaliate. Your culture tells you to "protect your peace" and cut them off completely. If your feelings are the ultimate authority, you will do whatever feels best in the moment. But if the Bible is your final authority, you are bound by Jesus' command to "love your enemies and pray for those who persecute you." Authority isn't just a theological concept; it dictates how you draft your next email.

Lane 2 — Depth (30 minutes)

Define the Terms Inspiration - Not the way a sunset "inspires" a poet. It is the supernatural influence of the Holy Spirit on the biblical writers. Inerrancy - The truth that the Bible tells the truth. When interpreted correctly, it does not affirm anything contrary to reality. Authority - Scripture possesses the right to govern our actions and shape our worldview because it is the voice of the Creator.

Build the Doctrine (Scripture-forward)

Men Wrote It, God Directed It The Bible was written by about 40 different authors—kings, fishermen, doctors, and poets—over 1,500 years, on three continents. You can clearly see their different personalities and vocabularies. Paul writes differently than John. Yet, behind the human authors was the direct guidance of the Spirit.

Key texts: 2 Peter 1:20–21

Peter explicitly states that prophecy "never had its origin in the human will, but prophets, though human, spoke from God as they were carried along by the Holy Spirit." Picture a sailboat. The human author is the boat, but the Holy Spirit is the wind filling the sails and determining the final destination. The boat is real, but the wind is in control.

Jesus Trusted the Scriptures The easiest way to determine your view of the Bible is to look at Jesus' view of the Bible. Jesus did not treat the Old Testament as a collection of helpful fables. He treated it as historically accurate, legally binding, and completely authoritative.

Key texts: Matthew 4:4; John 10:35

When Satan tempted Jesus in the wilderness, Jesus didn't defeat him with a display of divine magic; He quoted Deuteronomy three times, saying, "It is written." In John 10, Jesus casually drops the phrase "the Scripture cannot be broken." If you claim to follow Jesus, you cannot simultaneously disregard the book that Jesus staked His entire ministry and life upon.

Authority Means It Has Veto Power Everyone has a final authority. For some, it is science. For others, it is their political affiliation. For many today, it is their own internal feelings. Biblical authority means that when the Bible and my feelings disagree, the Bible wins.

Key texts: Psalm 119:105; Isaiah 40:8

"The grass withers and the flowers fall, but the word of our God endures forever" (Isaiah 40:8). Cultural norms wither. Human opinions fall. The Word endures. When we submit to biblical authority, we are admitting that we are flawed, biased, and often confused, and that we desperately need a steady light for our path (Psalm 119).

BOX - What This Is NOT Saying We are NOT saying the Bible is a science textbook meant to explain modern physics or biology. We are NOT saying you must read every passage literally (poetry is read as poetry; history as history). We are NOT saying we worship the Bible; we worship the God who gave us the Bible.

BOX - Where Christians Differ Evangelicals universally agree on the divine inspiration and ultimate authority of Scripture. However, there are debates around terms like "inerrancy" versus "infallibility." Some argue the Bible is perfectly accurate in every historical and scientific detail (inerrancy), while others argue it is perfectly reliable in all matters of faith and salvation without demanding modern scientific precision (infallibility).

Lane 3 — Deep Dive (Optional)

The Objection You're Already Thinking "But the Bible is full of horrible things like war, slavery, and harsh laws. How can I trust a book written by flawed men in barbaric times?"

The Best Answer It is undeniably true that the Bible describes barbaric events. But describing an event is not the same as endorsing it. Much of the Old Testament is descriptive (showing us how broken humanity is) rather than prescriptive (telling us to do the same).

Furthermore, when the Bible does address cultural realities like ancient servitude or patriarchal structures, it consistently introduces radical, subversive ethics that undermined those very institutions from the inside. Jesus elevates women to the status of primary witnesses. Paul tells masters to treat slaves as brothers, planting the seeds that eventually destroyed the institution.

If we judge the Bible strictly by modern 21st-century Western standards, we are making our current culture the supreme judge of the universe. But what happens in a hundred years when our current culture is viewed as flawed and barbaric? We don't need a book that perfectly echoes our modern sensibilities; we need a book that challenges every culture, in every era, calling us back to God's original design.

Historical Lens The Protestant Reformation hinged on the Latin phrase *Sola Scriptura*—Scripture alone. The Reformers (like Luther and Calvin) weren't saying that history, reason, or church tradition were useless. They were saying that when push comes to shove, Scripture is the only infallible rule of faith. Popes can err. Councils can err. The Word of God does not.

Real-Life Translation We are drowning in advice. You can open your phone right now and find five brilliant PhDs telling you how to fix your marriage, manage your money, and optimize your diet. But if you listen long enough, you realize they all contradict each other.

Living in an age of endless information creates profound anxiety because there is no solid ground. Everything is a "hack" or a "best practice." The authority of Scripture is the antidote to modern anxiety. It takes the burden of omniscience off your shoulders. You don't have to figure out the secret to human flourishing; it has been handed to you. You just have to obey it.

Midlife Module - This Doctrine at 47 You are lying in bed at 11:30 PM, unable to sleep. You've spent the last hour reading articles about the best way to handle your teenager's sudden withdrawal and poor grades. The "experts" are giving you ten different strategies, most of which contradict your own upbringing. You feel entirely inadequate.

At 47, you are realizing that human wisdom is a moving target. The parenting methods that were popular ten years ago are now heavily criticized. If your final authority is the latest bestseller, you will live in perpetual whiplash. The doctrine of biblical authority offers you a quiet, sturdy rock. It tells you to stop frantically searching for a new formula, and return to the ancient, enduring commands: pray without ceasing, love patiently, model repentance, and trust God with the results.

Practice + Prayer

This Week's Practice (3–7 minutes) The Submission Posture. Pick one clear command of Jesus that you currently find irritating or inconvenient (e.g., forgiving someone who hasn't apologized, giving money away, serving in secret). Instead of analyzing it, simply do it this week. Experience what it feels like to submit to an authority higher than your own preference.

Prayer (100–160 words) God, I confess that I like to be in charge. I like to be the editor of my own life, cutting out the parts of Your Word that challenge my lifestyle and keeping the parts that comfort my anxiety. Forgive my arrogance. Thank You for giving us a book that is true, pure, and enduring. Send Your Holy Spirit to illuminate my mind when I read it. Give me the humility to stand under Your Word, rather than standing in judgment over it. Make it a lamp to my feet in a very dark world. Amen.

Reflection

Solo (3 prompts)

1. Be honest: what is one teaching or command in the Bible that you wish you could just erase or ignore?

2. Think about how Jesus quoted Scripture when He was tempted or under pressure. What does your mind default to when you are under pressure?

3. How does knowing the Bible was written by dozens of real, flawed people actually make it more trustworthy, rather than less?

Small Group (3 prompts + 1 hard question)

1. We said, "Everyone has a final authority." What are the most common "final authorities" our culture relies on today instead of the Bible?

2. Read 2 Timothy 3:16–17. Discuss the progression: teaching (what is right), rebuking (what is wrong), correcting (how to get right), training (how to stay right).

3. How do we practically apply the authority of an ancient text to modern problems that aren't explicitly mentioned in the Bible (like social media or AI)?

Hard Question: Are you currently holding onto a belief or a habit that you know directly contradicts Scripture, simply because your culture approves of it?

Close

One Sentence Recap: The Scriptures are inspired by God, completely reliable, and the supreme and final authority for all matters of faith and life.

If You Only Remember One Thing: When the Bible and your feelings disagree, the Bible wins.

Next Week Preview: Next week we ask the skeptical question: How do we know the right books actually made it into the Bible in the first place?

Scripture References Used Deuteronomy 8:3 Psalm 119:105 Isaiah 40:8 Matthew 4:4 John 10:35 2 Timothy 3:16–17 2 Peter 1:20–21

My Thoughts & Notes – What Did I Take From This?

WEEK 5 — CANON & RELIABILITY: HOW DO WE KNOW?

CORE QUESTION: DIDN'T A bunch of powerful men in the fourth century just pick the books of the Bible that fit their political agenda?

Why this matters: Because if the Bible was manufactured by a corrupt institution, then Christianity is a massive scam and you have no reason to submit to it.

At a Glance (One Page)

Big Idea: The books of the Bible were not arbitrarily chosen by a powerful council centuries after the fact; they were recognized as authoritative by the early church because they were written by eyewitnesses and backed by the resurrection.

Anchor Text: Luke 1:1–4; 1 Corinthians 15:3–8

We believe...: The 66 books of the Old and New Testaments form the complete, **Close**d canon of Scripture, accurately transmitted through history and historically reliable.

Key Words (3): Canon - From a word meaning "measuring rod." The officially accepted list of books that make up the Bible. Apocrypha - Books written between the Old and New Testaments that provide helpful history but are not considered inspired Scripture by Protestants. Textual Criticism - The scholarly science of comparing thousands of ancient manuscripts to reconstruct the original text with incredible accuracy.

The One Mistake People Make: Believing internet memes and conspiracy theories that claim the Bible has been changed or edited like a massive game of telephone.

Choose Your Lane: Lane 1 / Lane 2 / Lane 3

This Week's Practice: The Eyewitness Check.

This Week's Prayer: Father, I live in a skeptical age. I know how human institutions operate, how power corrupts, and how narratives are spun. It is hard for me to trust that an ancient collection of books hasn't been tampered with. Give me intellectual honesty. Help me to look at the evidence of history without fear. Thank You for preserving Your Word through thousands of years, wars, and empires so that it could reach me today. Anchor my faith not in blind leaps, but in the reliable truth of what actually happened. Amen.

Lane 1 — Clarity (10 minutes)

The Bottom Line The idea that Emperor Constantine or a shadowy council sat around a table in 325 AD and voted on which books to put in the Bible makes for great fiction, but terrible history. The early church didn't *create* the canon; they *recognized* the canon. They universally accepted the books that were connected to the apostles, taught orthodox truth, and were already being widely used in the churches from the very beginning.

Scripture Snapshot Luke 1:1–4: "Many have undertaken to draw up an account of the things that have been fulfilled among us, just as they were handed down to us by those who from the first were eyewitnesses... I myself have carefully investigated everything from the beginning, I too decided to write an orderly account."

Luke was a doctor, not a mystic. He didn't write his Gospel by going into a cave and waiting for a vision. He acted like an investigative journalist. He interviewed the people who were actually there—the eyewitnesses to Jesus' life, death, and resurrection. The New Testament is not a collection of fairy tales; it is a collection of ancient historical documents based on eyewitness testimony.

Say It Out Loud (One Sentence) We can trust the Bible because the early church recognized books rooted in eyewitness history, and God preserved them through time.

Common Confusions Confusion #1: The Bible was translated so many times that the original meaning is lost (the "telephone game" myth). Confusion #2: There are "lost books" of the Bible (like the Gospel of Thomas) that the church hid to suppress the truth.

The Tuesday Payoff You are at a neighborhood barbecue and a friend casually mentions a documentary they watched claiming the Bible was heavily edited in the Middle Ages to control the masses. If you don't know how the Bible was put together, you will either get defensive or secretly worry they are right. Knowing the basics of how the canon was formed gives you calm confidence. You don't have to panic or argue. You know the foundation is historically rock solid.

Lane 2 — Depth (30 minutes)

Define the Terms Canon - The agreed-upon list of inspired books. Textual Criticism - The academic discipline of comparing surviving manuscript copies to determine the original wording. Apostolic Authority - The requirement that a New Testament book had to be written by an apostle or someone **Close**ly associated with one (like Luke with Paul, or Mark with Peter).

Build the Doctrine (Scripture-forward)

Not a Telephone Game The biggest myth about the Bible is that it was passed down like a game of telephone: translated from Greek to Latin to German to English, losing meaning every time. That is totally false. Modern Bibles are translated directly from the ancient Greek and Hebrew manuscripts.

Key texts: Isaiah 40:8; Matthew 24:35

Jesus said, "Heaven and earth will pass away, but my words will never pass away" (Matthew 24:35). Historically, this has proven true. We have over 5,800 Greek manuscripts of the New Testament. If you compare them, the variations are overwhelmingly minor (like spelling errors or word order) and none affect a single core doctrine. We know with over 99% accuracy what the original authors wrote.

Eyewitnesses, Not Myths The New Testament was written too early to be a myth. Legends take generations to develop because the people who were actually there have to die off before you can invent magical stories about them. The letters of Paul were written within 20 years of the resurrection.

Key texts: 1 Corinthians 15:3–8

In 1 Corinthians 15, written around 55 AD, Paul lists the people who saw the resurrected Jesus. He mentions Peter, the twelve, and then "more than five hundred of the brothers and sisters at the same time, most of whom are still living." Paul is essentially saying, "If you don't believe me, go ask them. They are still alive." You cannot write a document challenging people to cross-examine 500 living eyewitnesses if the event didn't happen.

The Criteria for the Canon The church didn't pick books out of a hat. They had a rigorous filter. For a book to be recognized as Scripture, it had to meet three basic tests:

1. Apostolicity: Was it written by an apostle or their **Close** associate?

2. Orthodoxy: Did it align with the established truth about Jesus?

3. Catholicity (Universal acceptance): Was it widely recognized and used by the early churches across the known world?

Key texts: 2 Peter 3:15–16

Even within the New Testament era, the apostles were recognizing each other's writings as Scripture. Peter refers to the letters of Paul and explicitly categorizes them alongside "the other Scriptures." The core canon was functioning as authority long before any council made a formal list.

BOX - What This Is NOT Saying We are NOT saying there are zero difficult passages or copyist errors in the ancient manuscripts; textual critics study these openly. We are NOT saying the "lost gospels" don't exist; they exist, but they were written centuries later by heretical groups, which is why the early church rejected them.

BOX - Where Christians Differ The main division here is between Protestants and Roman Catholics/Eastern Orthodox over the Apocrypha. Catholics include these 14 additional intertestamental books in their Old Testament. Protestants respect them as useful historical documents but do not consider them inspired Scripture, primarily because Jesus and the New Testament authors never quote them as authoritative Scripture, and the ancient Jewish community did not consider them inspired.

Lane 3 — Deep Dive (Optional)

The Objection You're Already Thinking "Didn't the Council of Nicaea just pick the books that gave the church power and burn the rest?"

The Best Answer Thanks to *The Da Vinci Code* and internet skeptics, this is a massively popular belief. It is also entirely fictional. The Council of Nicaea (325 AD) didn't even discuss the canon of Scripture. They met to discuss the nature of Christ (the Arian controversy) and to figure out the date of Easter.

The core of the New Testament (the four Gospels and Paul's letters) was already functioning as unquestioned authority by the middle of the second century, long before Constantine was born. The later councils that did officially list the canon (like Carthage in 397 AD) were simply ratifying what the church had already been practicing and believing for nearly three hundred years. They didn't make the books authoritative; they recognized the authority the books inherently possessed.

Historical Lens When the Emperor Diocletian heavily persecuted the church in 303 AD, one of his main tactics was to demand that Christians hand over their sacred texts to be burned. This forced the church to clarify exactly which books they were willing to die for. You don't get executed for a helpful newsletter; you only die for the Word of God. The persecution forced the canon into sharp focus.

Real-Life Translation We are living in an era defined by institutional cynicism. We know how corporate sausage is made. We assume every political narrative is spun, every news station has a bias, and every institution is just trying to consolidate power.

It is incredibly easy to project that 21st-century cynicism backward onto the early church and assume the Bible is just a political power play. But history doesn't support that. The men who wrote and preserved these books didn't gain wealth, power, or political leverage. They were tortured, impoverished, and executed for claiming that a crucified carpenter was the Lord of the world. You might doubt their sanity, but you cannot logically doubt their sincerity. They handed down a reliable text, paid for in blood.

Midlife Module - This Doctrine at 50 You are 50, and you are exhausted by the spin. You've seen corporate leaders lie, politicians backtrack, and maybe even pastors cover up scandals. Your default setting is now skepticism. When someone says, "The Bible is the absolute truth," your internal defense mechanism immediately raises its shields. "According to who?" you think.

But looking into the history of the canon is deeply grounding. It takes faith out of the realm of blind, naive trust and roots it in cold, hard history. You realize that trusting the Bible isn't about trusting modern institutional Christianity; it is about trusting the historical reality of the first-century eyewitnesses. You can keep your healthy skepticism about modern power structures while holding absolute confidence in the ancient text.

Practice + Prayer

This Week's Practice (3–7 minutes) The Eyewitness Check. Read 1 Corinthians 15:3–8. Imagine you are a lawyer cross-examining this document. Notice how Paul appeals to verifiable facts (died, buried, raised, appeared) rather than private, mystical feelings. Thank God that Christianity is a historically falsifiable faith that stood up to the test.

Prayer (100–160 words) God, thank You for the meticulous, brutal, and faithful history of the early church. Thank You to the men and women who hid these manuscripts, copied them by hand, and died rather than surrender them. When my mind wants to default to modern cynicism, anchor me in the historical reality of the resurrection. Give me a deep confidence that the Bible I hold in my hands today is exactly what You intended for me to have. Amen.

Reflection

Solo (3 prompts)

1. Before today, how did you assume the books of the Bible were selected?

2. Does knowing that the Bible is historically reliable make it easier or harder for you to submit to its moral commands? Why?

3. How does the "telephone game" myth affect the way unchurched people view the Bible?

Small Group (3 prompts + 1 hard question)

1. Discuss Luke 1:1–4. Why does it matter that Luke functioned more like an investigative journalist than a mystic?

2. How do we explain the difference between the Protestant Bible and the Catholic Bible to someone who asks?

3. Why is it significant that the early church had to decide which books they were literally willing to be executed for holding?

Hard Question: Do you use doubts about the Bible's historical reliability as a convenient excuse to avoid dealing with what it actually says?

Close

One Sentence Recap: The books of the Bible were recognized as authoritative by the early church because they were written by eyewitnesses, aligned with orthodoxy, and were backed by the resurrection.

If You Only Remember One Thing: The early church didn't create the Bible by voting on it; they recognized the Bible because the eyewitnesses proved it.

Next Week Preview: Next week, we look at the mechanics of actually reading this ancient book without taking things out of context and making a mess of your life.

Scripture References Used Isaiah 40:8 Matthew 24:35 Luke 1:1–4 1 Corinthians 15:3–8 2 Peter 3:15–16

My Thoughts & Notes – What Did I Take From This?

WEEK 6 — HOW TO READ THE BIBLE LIKE AN ADULT

CORE QUESTION: WHY IS the Bible so confusing, and how do I read it without taking things out of context and doing something crazy?

Why this matters: Because reading the Bible poorly is actually dangerous; bad interpretation leads to spiritual abuse, crippling anxiety, and arrogant religion.

At a Glance (One Page)

Big Idea: The Bible is not a magic 8-ball or a book of daily horoscopes; it is a complex, ancient library that demands to be read in context, with every book ultimately pointing to Jesus.

Anchor Text: Nehemiah 8:8; Luke 24:27

We believe...: Scripture must be interpreted carefully according to its historical context, literary genre, and authorial intent, with Christ as the interpretive key to the whole Bible.

Key Words (3): Exegesis - Drawing out the actual meaning of the text based on what the author intended. (Good). Eisegesis - Reading our own ideas, biases, or desired meanings *into* the text. (Bad). Context - The historical, cultural, and literary surrounding of a verse that determines its meaning.

The One Mistake People Make: Opening the Bible at random, pointing a finger at a verse, and assuming it is a direct, personalized instruction for what to do today.

Choose Your Lane: Lane 1 / Lane 2 / Lane 3

This Week's Practice: The Chapter Challenge.

This Week's Prayer: Father, I confess that I often want Your Word to be quick, easy, and entirely about me. I get frustrated when I have to do the hard work of understanding context and history. Keep me from twisting Your words to fit my preferences. Teach me how to read this ancient library with wisdom, patience, and humility. And above all, whether I am reading the law, the prophets, or the letters, help me to always find Jesus. Amen.

Lane 1 — Clarity (10 minutes)

The Bottom Line A text without a context is a pretext for a proof-text. If you isolate a Bible verse from its surrounding paragraph, chapter, and historical setting, you can make the Bible say almost anything. Reading the Bible like an adult means respecting the author's original intent rather than treating the book like a personalized fortune cookie.

Scripture Snapshot Nehemiah 8:8: "They read from the Book of the Law of God, making it clear and giving the meaning so that the people understood what was being read."

The Israelites had just returned from exile and were hearing the Bible read aloud for the first time in a generation. But the priests didn't just read it and walk away; they *explained the meaning*. They translated the language and provided the context. The biblical pattern isn't just "read the words"; it is "do the work to understand what the words mean."

Say It Out Loud (One Sentence) To understand what a Bible verse means for me today, I first have to understand what it meant to them back then.

Common Confusions Confusion #1: Every promise in the Bible applies directly to my specific situation right now. Confusion #2: The Old Testament is about an angry God of rules, and the New Testament is about a nice Jesus of love.

The Tuesday Payoff You are anxious about a massive financial risk you took with your small business. You open the Bible and read Jeremiah 29:11: "For I know the plans I have for you... plans to prosper you and not to harm you." If you read that as a personal guarantee of financial success, you will be devastated if your business fails. You might even blame God for breaking a promise. But if you do the work to see that this verse was written to a rebellious nation entering 70 years of grueling slavery in Babylon, you realize the promise is about ultimate spiritual restoration, not immediate comfort. Context protects your faith from collapsing when your circumstances drop.

Lane 2 — Depth (30 minutes)

Define the Terms Exegesis - From a Greek word meaning "to lead out." Extracting the true meaning out of the text. Eisegesis - "Leading into." Forcing your own preconceived ideas into the text. Hermeneutics - The science and art of biblical interpretation. Genre - The style of literature (poetry, history, letter, apocalyptic). You don't read a poem the same way you read a legal document.

Build the Doctrine (Scripture-forward)

The Bible is a Library, Not a Single Book You cannot read the Bible front-to-back like a novel. It is a library of 66 books spanning multiple genres. If you read the Psalms (poetry and hyperbole) the same way you read Romans (dense, logical argumentation), you will be incredibly confused.

Key texts: Proverbs 26:4–5

"Do not answer a fool according to his folly... Answer a fool according to his folly." These verses are back-to-back. If the Bible is a flat rulebook, this is a glaring contradiction. But if Proverbs is a book of general wisdom principles—knowing *when* to apply which proverb requires discernment—it makes perfect sense. Respect the genre.

Context is King The most dangerous thing you can do with the Bible is isolate one verse. Every verse lives in a paragraph, which lives in a chapter, which lives in a specific book, written to a specific audience, facing specific problems.

Key texts: Philippians 4:13

"I can do all this through him who gives me strength." This verse is tattooed on athletes and printed on coffee mugs as a slogan for personal victory. But look at the context (verses 11-12). Paul wrote this from a Roman prison, describing his ability to endure starvation, poverty, and suffering without abandoning Jesus. It isn't a promise that God will help you win a football game; it is a promise that God will sustain you when you lose everything.

It is All About Jesus If you read the Bible and it just makes you a more moral, rigid, rules-following person, you are reading it wrong. The entire library—from Genesis to Revelation—is ultimately pointing to one person.

Key texts: Luke 24:27; John 5:39

After the resurrection, Jesus is walking with two confused disciples on the road to Emmaus. Luke tells us, "And beginning with Moses and all the Prophets, he explained to them what was said in all the Scriptures concerning himself." Jesus is the interpretive key to the entire Bible. The Old Testament is the lock; Christ is the key.

BOX - What This Is NOT Saying We are NOT saying you need a theology degree to read the Bible; the main things are the plain things. We are NOT saying the Holy Spirit doesn't sometimes use a random verse to comfort you in a tough moment. We are NOT saying the Old Testament is useless; it is the essential foundation for understanding the New.

BOX - Where Christians Differ Not a major point of disagreement in broad evangelicalism, though traditions place different emphasis on how literal prophecy should be read (e.g., Revelation). All agree that sound exegesis, historical context, and a Christ-centered focus are mandatory for faithful reading.

Lane 3 — Deep Dive (Optional)

The Objection You're Already Thinking "If God wrote the Bible, why didn't He just make it a clear list of rules? Why hide the truth in weird historical stories and ancient letters?"

The Best Answer Because God isn't just trying to program our behavior; He is trying to form our character. A list of rules produces robots or Pharisees. A story requires you to engage your heart, mind, and imagination.

When you read the story of King David's massive moral failure with Bathsheba, you don't just get a sterile rule that says "Don't commit adultery." You see the slow, creeping nature of temptation, the devastating collateral damage of sin, the agonizing weight of guilt, and the breathtaking depth of God's grace upon repentance.

God gave us a messy, historically grounded, complex library because human life is messy and complex. We need wisdom, not just a spreadsheet. By forcing us to wrestle with the text, God shapes us in the process of reading it.

Historical Lens In the Middle Ages, the church often used "allegorical" interpretation, finding hidden, secret spiritual meanings behind every minor detail in the text (e.g., assuming the two coins the Good Samaritan paid meant the Father and the Son). The Protestant Reformers rejected this, insisting on the "literal-grammatical" method: figure out what the plain words meant to the original audience first.

Real-Life Translation There is a massive market for taking Bible verses out of context to sell you things. Televangelists will pull a verse from Malachi to promise you financial wealth if you "sow a seed" into their ministry. Politicians will pull a verse out of Romans to justify their policies.

Learning to read the Bible in context is how you protect yourself from spiritual manipulation. When you know how to do basic exegesis, you can listen to a charismatic speaker and quietly realize, "That is not what that text means." Good biblical interpretation is the ultimate defense against spiritual abuse.

Midlife Module - This Doctrine at 49 You've tried the "Bible in a Year" reading plan four times. Every January, you crush Genesis and Exodus. Then you hit Leviticus—with its ancient rules about skin diseases and animal sacrifices—and you quietly **Close** the app. You feel a lingering, low-grade guilt that you aren't a "good enough" Christian to understand the hard parts of the Bible.

At 49, you don't need guilt; you need a better strategy. You realize that you don't have to read Leviticus as a list of rules for your Tuesday. You read Leviticus to understand the absolute holiness of God and the desperate need for a perfect sacrifice—which makes the cross of Jesus Christ so much more powerful. Learning to read the Bible by genre, and seeing how it all connects to Jesus, removes the guilt and replaces it with awe.

Practice + Prayer

This Week's Practice (3–7 minutes) The Chapter Challenge. Stop reading single verses. This week, pick one of the shorter letters in the New Testament (like Philippians, Ephesians, or Colossians). Read the entire letter in one sitting. It takes about 15 minutes. Note how the paragraphs flow together to make a single, logical argument.

Prayer (100–160 words) God, thank You for the depth, beauty, and complexity of the Bible. Protect me from the laziness of wanting a quick spiritual fix without doing the hard work of understanding Your truth. Guard my mind against twisting Your words to justify my own behavior or opinions. When I read the hard parts of Scripture, give me patience. When I read the comforting parts, give me gratitude. Teach me to read the whole library through the lens of Jesus' life, death, and resurrection. Make me a careful, humble student of Your Word. Amen.

<u>**Reflection**</u>

Solo (3 prompts)

1. Have you ever misapplied a Bible verse (like Philippians 4:13 or Jeremiah 29:11) because you didn't know the context? What happened?

2. Which genre of the Bible do you find most difficult to read (prophets, poetry, history, letters)?

3. Why is it dangerous to read the Bible primarily looking for "what this means to me" instead of "what this says about God"?

Small Group (3 prompts + 1 hard question)

1. Discuss the difference between Exegesis and Eisegesis. What are some common cultural beliefs that people try to eisegete (force) into the Bible today?

2. Read Luke 24:27. How does knowing that the Old Testament is fundamentally about Jesus change the way you read ancient Israelite history?

3. Why do you think isolating single verses (proof-texting) is so popular in modern American Christianity?

Hard Question: Are you intimidated by the Bible, and are you using that intimidation as an excuse to avoid reading it altogether?

<u>**Close**</u>

One Sentence Recap: Scripture must be interpreted carefully according to its historical context, literary genre, and authorial intent, with Christ as the ultimate key.

If You Only Remember One Thing: A text without a context is a pretext for a proof-text; respect the author's original intent.

Next Week Preview: Next week, we wrap up Part 1 by dealing with the elephant in the room: doubt, deconstruction, and what to do when your faith feels fragile.

Scripture References Used Nehemiah 8:8 Proverbs 26:4–5 Jeremiah 29:11 Luke 24:27 John 5:39 Philippians 4:11–13

<u>**My Thoughts & Notes – What Did I Take From This?**</u>

Week 7 — Doubt, Deconstruction, and Staying Honest

Core Question: What do you do when the faith you grew up with suddenly feels fragile, confusing, or entirely inadequate for the pain of real life?

Why this matters: Because pretending everything is fine when you are secretly plagued by doubt will eventually lead to spiritual burnout or total collapse; God can handle your honesty.

At a Glance (One Page)

Big Idea: Having questions or doubts does not disqualify you from the kingdom of God; Jesus responds to honest doubt with staggering patience, but isolation and cynicism are the enemies of faith.

Anchor Text: Mark 9:22–24; Jude 22–23

We believe…: Honest doubt is a normal part of the Christian life in a broken world, and God invites us to bring our questions directly to Him within the safety of the church community.

Key Words (3): Doubt - Uncertainty or questioning; struggling to reconcile what you believe with what you are experiencing. Deconstruction - The process of dismantling the faith you inherited to see what is culturally assumed versus what is actually biblical. Deconversion - The final abandonment of the Christian faith.

The One Mistake People Make: Thinking that doubt is the opposite of faith. (Apathy is the opposite of faith. Doubt is faith struggling to breathe).

Choose Your Lane: Lane 1 / Lane 2 / Lane 3

This Week's Practice: The Honest Prayer.

This Week's Prayer: Father, I am tired of pretending. Sometimes the things I read in the Bible confuse me. Sometimes the pain I see in the world makes me question Your goodness. Sometimes the behavior of other Christians makes me want to walk away from it all. I bring my doubts to You because I don't know where else to go. Protect me from the arrogance of cynicism. Give me the courage of the man in the Gospel of Mark who said, "I do believe; help me overcome my unbelief." Meet me in the quiet, fragile places of my faith today. Amen.

Lane 1 — Clarity (10 minutes)

The Bottom Line The modern church has often treated doubt like a contagious disease, forcing people to hide their questions behind a smile. But the Bible treats doubt as a completely normal part of living in a deeply broken world. God is not panicked by your questions, offended by your confusion, or threatened by your deconstruction. He invites you to bring the mess directly to Him.

Scripture Snapshot Mark 9:22–24: " 'But if you can do anything, take pity on us and help us.' 'If you can'?' said Jesus. 'Everything is possible for one who believes.' Immediately the boy's father exclaimed, 'I do believe; help me overcome my unbelief!'"

A desperate father brings his demon-possessed son to Jesus. His theology is messy. His faith is hanging by a thread (*"If you can do anything…"*). Jesus challenges the "if," and the father's response is one of the most brutally honest prayers in the Bible:

I believe, and I don't believe. Help. Jesus doesn't scold him for his lack of perfect faith. He doesn't tell him to go read a theology book and come back when he is certain. Jesus heals the boy. He meets the man exactly where his faith is fraying.

Say It Out Loud (One Sentence) God prefers our messy, doubting honesty over our polished, religious pretending.

Common Confusions Confusion #1: Good Christians never have doubts or questions. Confusion #2: Deconstruction always leads to walking away from God.

The Tuesday Payoff You are driving home from a funeral for a friend who died way too young. The easy Christian platitudes people offered at the service ("God just needed another angel") actually made you angry. A cold wave of doubt hits you: *Is any of this actually true, or are we all just comforting ourselves with myths?* If you think doubt is a sin, you will shove that thought down and feel guilty. But if you know that God handles doubt with grace, you can cry in the car and yell at the windshield, knowing He is big enough to take the hit.

Lane 2 — Depth (30 minutes)

Define the Terms Doubt - An intellectual or emotional struggle to believe. It is asking questions. Unbelief - A hardened, willful refusal to believe or submit, despite the evidence. It is a **Close**d fist. Deconstruction - Taking apart your theological framework to examine the pieces. It can be healthy (removing cultural garbage) or destructive (abandoning orthodox truth).

Build the Doctrine (Scripture-forward)

God Welcomes the Questions If you read the Psalms, you will find some of the darkest, most aggressive questions ever asked of God. The writers accuse God of sleeping, of hiding, and of abandoning them. They didn't suppress their doubts; they canonized them.

Key texts: Psalm 13:1–2; Psalm 88

David cries out, "How long, Lord? Will you forget me forever? How long will you hide your face from me?" (Psalm 13). Psalm 88 ends with the cheerful phrase, "darkness is my **Close**st friend." The Bible does not require you to put a positive spin on your pain. Bringing your furious questions to God is not an act of rebellion; it is an act of profound faith. You don't yell at someone unless you believe they are in the room.

Doubt vs. Unbelief There is a massive difference between a doubting heart that is seeking the truth, and a hardened heart that has already decided to reject God.

Key texts: John 20:24–28

Thomas famously doubted the resurrection. He demanded physical proof. When Jesus appears a week later, He doesn't expel Thomas from the disciples. He offers him exactly the evidence he asked for: "Put your finger here; see my hands." Jesus is incredibly gentle with honest doubt. Unbelief, however—like the religious leaders who saw miracles and still plotted to kill Jesus—is met with severe judgment. Doubt says, "I want to believe, but I can't see it." Unbelief says, "Even if I see it, I won't bow."

The Danger of Cynicism While doubt can be a healthy engine for deeper faith, cynicism is toxic. Cynicism assumes the worst motives in everyone and positions itself as intellectually superior.

Key texts: Proverbs 18:1; Jude 22–23

"An unfriendly person pursues selfish ends and against all sound judgment starts quarrels" (Proverbs 18:1). When deconstruction turns into cynical isolation—where you spend all your time mocking the church on social media—you are no longer seeking truth; you are just nursing a wound. Jude commands the church to "be merciful to those who doubt." We need the community of believers to hold us up when our own faith is too weak to stand. Isolation is the enemy of a recovering faith.

BOX - What This Is NOT Saying We are NOT saying that staying in a permanent state of doubt is healthy; questions should lead to a pursuit of truth. We are NOT saying all "deconstruction" is good; dismantling core orthodox truth destroys faith. We are NOT saying the church's past failures invalidate the reality of Jesus.

BOX - Where Christians Differ The term "deconstruction" is highly polarizing right now. Some evangelicals use it purely as a negative term for apostasy (leaving the faith). Others use it positively, describing the necessary process of separating biblical Jesus from American cultural Christianity. The vital distinction is the destination: are you deconstructing to find the real Jesus, or are you deconstructing to justify living however you want?

Lane 3 — Deep Dive (Optional)

The Objection You're Already Thinking "But didn't Jesus say that if you have faith as small as a mustard seed you can move mountains? My doubts make me feel like I don't even have that much."

The Best Answer We often turn faith into a performance metric. We think faith is a substance we have to generate from within—like spiritual adrenaline. If we can just muster up enough certainty, God will answer us.

But biblical faith isn't about the *amount* of your certainty; it is entirely about the *object* of your certainty. A man with a massive, unshakeable faith who steps out onto one inch of thin ice will drown. A man with a terrifying, doubting, trembling faith who steps out onto three feet of solid ice will be perfectly safe. It is the ice that holds you, not the quality of your belief.

Jesus doesn't demand perfect, unwavering certainty. He demands that you place your fragile, doubting, mustard-seed-sized faith in Him. The strength of your Savior matters infinitely more than the strength of your faith.

Historical Lens Charles Spurgeon, one of the greatest preachers of the 19th century, famously battled severe, debilitating depression and doubt. He once preached, "Some of us know what it is to be too completely broken to believe." He didn't hide his darkness from his congregation. History is full of spiritual giants who wrestled with crushing doubt and were held securely by God anyway.

Real-Life Translation Many Gen Xers grew up in youth groups that relied heavily on emotional highs. If you felt it, it was real. Now, in midlife, the emotions are gone. You are tired. You've seen marriages fail, you've seen pastors fall, and you've been hurt by the institution of the church.

It is entirely normal that your faith needs a tear-down. You are taking the engine apart. The danger is leaving the pieces on the garage floor. Healthy deconstruction means systematically taking apart the youth-group hype, discarding the legalism and the culture-war politics, and putting the engine back together using only the historic, orthodox truth of Jesus Christ. The rebuilt engine won't be as flashy, but it will actually start in the cold.

Midlife Module - This Doctrine at 47 You are sitting in the back row of a church you've attended for ten years. The worship band is playing a triumphant song about victory, but you feel absolutely nothing. Your career is stalling, your marriage feels like a roommate situation, and you are exhausted. A quiet thought surfaces: *What if I'm just pretending? What if none of this is real?* Ten years ago, that thought would have sent you into a panic. You would have doubled down on volunteering to prove you were okay. But at 47, you are learning to breathe. You don't have to panic. You realize that God's grip on you is infinitely stronger than your grip on Him. You whisper the only prayer you can muster—"Help my unbelief"—and you trust that the solid ice will hold your trembling weight.

Practice + Prayer

This Week's Practice (3–7 minutes) The Honest Prayer. Identify the one area of your faith, theology, or life where you are harboring the most doubt or disappointment. Write it down in one brutal, honest sentence (e.g., "God, I don't understand why You let my mom get sick"). Pray that one sentence every day this week, out loud. Give God the messy truth, not the polished lie.

Prayer (100–160 words) God, You know every question in my mind before I even try to hide it. Thank You that Your love for me is not conditioned on my perfect theology or my unwavering certainty. Thank You for giving me Psalms that sound like my own frustration. When my faith feels fragile, remind me that Jesus is a solid rock. Protect me from the bitterness of cynicism and the arrogance of thinking I know better than You. Surround me with believers who will carry my mat when I am too spiritually paralyzed to walk. Hold on to me when I don't have the strength to hold on to You. Amen.

<u>**Reflection**</u>

Solo (3 prompts)

1. What was the culture around doubt like in the church or home where you grew up? Was it welcomed, or punished?

2. Looking back, can you identify a "crisis of faith" that actually resulted in a much deeper, healthier reliance on God?

3. What is the difference between asking a question because you want an answer, and asking a question because you want an excuse?

Small Group (3 prompts + 1 hard question)

1. Read Mark 9:22–24. Why is "I do believe; help my unbelief" such a powerful model for prayer?

2. Discuss the concept that faith is about the *object* (the ice) rather than the *amount* of certainty you have. How does this relieve pressure?

3. How can our small group create an environment where people feel safe bringing their doubts without fear of being judged?

Hard Question: Are you currently confusing "doubt" with a deliberate, stubborn refusal to obey what God has clearly commanded?

<u>**Close**</u>

One Sentence Recap: Honest doubt is a normal part of the Christian life, and God invites us to bring our questions directly to Him without fear.

If You Only Remember One Thing: It is the thickness of the ice that holds you, not the strength of your faith; put your fragile faith in a strong Savior.

Next Week Preview: This wraps up Part 1. Next week, we pivot to Part 2 and tackle the biggest topic of all: God—the One who actually exists.

Scripture References Used Psalm 13:1–2 Psalm 88 Proverbs 18:1 Mark 9:22–24 John 20:24–28 Jude 22–23

<u>**My Thoughts & Notes – What Did I Take From This?**</u>

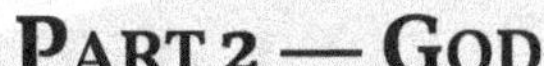

PART 2 — GOD

Growing up, most of us viewed God the way we viewed the principal's office, a place you only went when you were in deep trouble, run by a distant authority figure who was perpetually disappointed in you. As a result, we either lived in fear of Him or tried to ignore Him completely.

In Part 2, we are stripping away the cultural caricatures to look at the God who actually exists. We are going to tackle His terrifying holiness, the mind-bending reality of the Trinity, and how His absolute sovereignty applies to a random Tuesday when your life feels completely out of control. We are looking at the actual Boss.

WEEK 8 — GOD: THE ONE WHO ACTUALLY EXISTS

CORE QUESTION: Is GOD a reality that exists completely outside of us, or just a psychological crutch we invented to feel safe?

Why this matters: Because a God you invent can only echo your own thoughts; only a God who actually exists independently of you has the power to save you.

At a Glance (One Page)

Big Idea: God does not need us, He was not created by us, and He is not sustained by our belief in Him; He is the self-existent reality that everything else depends on.

Anchor Text: Exodus 3:14; Acts 17:24–28

We believe...: God is the self-existent, infinite, and personal Creator of the universe, depending on nothing outside Himself for His existence.

Key Words (3): Aseity - The theological term for God's self-existence. He depends on nothing; He just *is*. Theism - The belief in a personal God who created the universe and remains actively involved in it. Idolatry - Creating a god in our own image to serve our own preferences.

The One Mistake People Make: Acting like God is running a political campaign and needs our vote, our belief, or our defense to stay relevant.

Choose Your Lane: Lane 1 / Lane 2 / Lane 3

This Week's Practice: The Aseity Pause.

This Week's Prayer: Father, I spend so much of my life acting like everything depends on me. I manage my family, my career, and my image as if I am the center of my own universe. Forgive me for shrinking You down to the size of a life coach or a spiritual assistant. Remind me today that You existed before the world began and You will exist long after I am gone. Thank You that You do not need me, yet You still choose to love me. Anchor my frantic life to Your eternal, unshakeable existence. Amen.

Lane 1 — Clarity (10 minutes)

The Bottom Line We tend to treat God like a fragile celebrity whose relevance depends on how many followers He has. But the Bible introduces a God who possesses "aseity"—meaning He exists entirely from Himself. He doesn't need a universe, He doesn't need angels, and He doesn't need you. That sounds cold at first, but it is actually deeply comforting. A God who needs you cannot save you.

Scripture Snapshot Exodus 3:14: "God said to Moses, 'I am who I am. This is what you are to say to the Israelites: "I am has sent me to you."'"

Moses is standing at a burning bush, being told to go challenge the most powerful empire on earth (Egypt). He reasonably asks God, "Who should I say sent me?" God doesn't give a title, a rank, or a resume. He just says, "I AM." He is the uncaused cause. He is the only being in the universe who does not depend on anything else to exist.

Say It Out Loud (One Sentence) God does not depend on my belief to exist, but my existence depends entirely on Him.

Common Confusions Confusion #1: If people stop believing in God, He somehow loses power or relevance. Confusion #2: God created humanity because He was lonely and needed relationship.

The Tuesday Payoff It is Tuesday morning and the company layoffs were finally announced. Your name is on the list. The structure you built your identity on for the last decade just vanished with one HR email. If your God is just a concept—a vague "higher power" that gives you good vibes when things are going well—He will vanish with your job. But if God is the self-existent "I AM," your reality hasn't actually changed. The ground beneath you shifted, but the rock beneath the ground didn't move an inch.

Lane 2 — Depth (30 minutes)

Define the Terms Aseity - From the Latin *a se*, meaning "from himself." God's independent self-existence. Infinite - Not bound by the limits of time, space, or matter. Personal - Having intellect, emotion, and will; God is a "Who," not a "What."

Build the Doctrine (Scripture-forward)

He Doesn't Need Us One of the most radical claims of Christianity is that God did not create us out of deficiency. He wasn't bored, lonely, or lacking love before Genesis 1. Because God is a Trinity (which we cover in Week 11), He has existed eternally in perfect relationship.

Key texts: Acts 17:24–25

When Paul spoke to the philosophers in Athens, he dismantled their entire religious system in two sentences: "He is not served by human hands, as if he needed anything. Rather, he himself gives everyone life and breath and everything else." You cannot negotiate with a God who doesn't need anything from you. You can only worship Him.

He is Personal, Not a Force It is very trendy to talk about God as "the universe" or "an energy." But energy is impersonal. You cannot offend gravity, and electricity will never forgive you. The God of the Bible has a name, a will, and a heart.

Key texts: Psalm 103:13–14

"As a father has compassion on his children, so the Lord has compassion on those who fear him." Forces don't have compassion. Only a person can choose to love. God is infinitely massive, yet He intimately knows how we are wired.

He is Unchanging Because we are constantly changing—aging, learning, shifting opinions—we project that onto God. We assume God "grows" or adapts to modern times. But a perfect being cannot change, because any change would mean becoming less perfect or gaining a perfection He previously lacked.

Key texts: Malachi 3:6; James 1:17

"I the Lord do not change. So you, the descendants of Jacob, are not destroyed" (Malachi 3:6). His unchanging nature (immutability) is the basis of our survival. If God's character could change, His promises would be worthless.

BOX - What This Is NOT Saying We are NOT saying God is a cold, distant machine; He is deeply emotional and relational. We are NOT saying our actions don't matter to Him; He delights in us, He just doesn't *depend* on us. We are NOT saying we can fully comprehend His infinite nature.

BOX - Where Christians Differ Not a major point of disagreement this week. All historic branches of Christianity affirm that God is self-existent, unchanging in His essence, and the personal Creator of all things. Differences arise later in *how* He interacts with time and human will, but not in His independent existence.

Lane 3 — Deep Dive (Optional)

The Objection You're Already Thinking "Isn't the idea of God just a psychological crutch we invented to deal with our fear of death and the randomness of the universe?"

The Best Answer This is the classic argument made by Sigmund Freud: religion is just wish fulfillment. We are scared, so we invent a giant father figure in the sky to make us feel safe.

It's a smart objection, but it has a massive flaw. If humans invented a God purely for comfort, we did a terrible job. The God of the Bible is frequently terrifying. He demands total surrender, tells us to love our enemies, gives away our money, and frequently leads His followers into suffering and martyrdom. He explicitly says we are broken sinners who cannot save ourselves.

If you are going to invent a psychological crutch, you invent a cosmic life coach who promises you wealth and pats you on the back. You don't invent the holy, demanding, untamable God of the Bible. The fact that God constantly contradicts our preferences and challenges our comfort is strong evidence that He is a reality outside of our own minds.

Historical Lens In the early 20th century, many liberal theologians tried to redefine God simply as "the highest human ideals" (like love, justice, and progress). Then World War I and II happened, proving that human ideals lead to mustard gas and the Holocaust. Orthodox theologians like Karl Barth pushed back fiercely, insisting that God is "wholly other"—He is not just a better version of us; He is God.

Real-Life Translation We spend massive amounts of energy trying to prop up the things that give us security. We manage our retirement accounts, we obsess over our health metrics, and we curate our reputations. It is exhausting because everything we build is fundamentally fragile.

When you grasp the reality of God's aseity—that He just *is*—the pressure drops. You don't have to prop God up. You don't have to defend His honor on the internet. You don't have to worry that a bad week at church is going to put Him out of business. You can finally stop trying to hold your universe together and let the Uncreated One hold you.

Midlife Module - This Doctrine at 46 You are standing in the kitchen of the house you finally bought. It's late. You have the mortgage, the decent job, and the family you wanted when you were 25. And yet, there is a hollow ache in your chest that makes no sense. You achieved the goal, but the void is still there.

At 46, you realize that finite things—even good things like a house or a career—cannot satisfy an infinite soul. You have been treating temporary things as if they were ultimate things. You need something that exists independently of the economy, your health, and your accomplishments. The realization that God actually exists, outside of your spreadsheet and your suburban anxiety, isn't just a theological fact. It is the only cure for the midlife ache.

Practice + Prayer

This Week's Practice (3–7 minutes) The Aseity Pause. Sometime today, look at a massive inanimate object (a mountain, a large building, or a large tree). Think about the fact that it was there before you were born and will be there after you die. Then, recognize that God created it out of nothing, and He does not depend on it. Let His permanence make your current stress feel smaller.

Prayer (100–160 words) God, I am so easily consumed by my own small world. My problems feel massive, and my anxieties feel permanent. Forgive me for losing perspective. Thank You for being the Great I AM—the uncaused, unchanging, eternal reality. I am deeply relieved that You do not need me to keep the universe running. Help me to rest in Your self-existence. When I am tempted to rely on my own strength, remind me that my breath is a gift from You. Anchor my fleeting life to Your eternal presence. Amen.

Reflection

Solo (3 prompts)

1. In what ways do you functionally treat God like He needs your help to accomplish His goals?

2. Why is the idea of an "unchanging" God comforting when everything in our culture is constantly shifting?

3. Have you ever tried to treat God as an impersonal "force" because a personal God felt too demanding?

Small Group (3 prompts + 1 hard question)

1. Discuss the difference between a God who created us out of loneliness versus a God who created us out of an overflow of love.

2. Read Acts 17:24–25. How does this passage challenge the way modern people view religion and serving God?

3. How does knowing that God doesn't *need* us actually make His love for us more profound?

Hard Question: Are you treating God like a psychological crutch, only turning to Him when you are stressed but ignoring Him when you are comfortable?

<u>Close</u>

One Sentence Recap: God is the self-existent, infinite, and personal Creator who depends on nothing outside Himself.

If You Only Remember One Thing: A God who needs you cannot save you; rest in the God who simply is.

Next Week Preview: Next week we look at God's attributes—how He can be absolutely terrifying in His perfection, but totally approachable in His goodness.

Scripture References Used Exodus 3:14 Psalm 103:13–14 Malachi 3:6 Acts 17:24–28 James 1:17

<u>My Thoughts & Notes – What Did I Take From This?</u>

Week 9 — God's Attributes: Holy and Good

Core Question: How can God be absolutely terrifying in His moral perfection, but also gentle and approachable enough to forgive my worst mistakes?

Why this matters: Because if God is only holy, you will be crushed by guilt; if He is only good, you will become spiritually lazy and entitled.

At a Glance (One Page)

Big Idea: God is not a balancing act of different traits; He is infinitely holy and infinitely good at the exact same time, and both are necessary for our salvation.

Anchor Text: Isaiah 6:1–5; Psalm 103:8–12

We believe...: God is perfectly holy, just, and set apart from all sin, while simultaneously being perfectly loving, gracious, and merciful to broken people.

Key Words (3): Attributes - The characteristics or qualities that make God who He is. Holiness - God's absolute moral purity and infinite separation from anything sinful or broken. Grace - God's unmerited favor; giving us the goodness we do not deserve.

The One Mistake People Make: Creating a customized God by emphasizing His love while ignoring His justice, resulting in a harmless deity who never challenges them.

Choose Your Lane: Lane 1 / Lane 2 / Lane 3

This Week's Practice: The Tension Test.

This Week's Prayer: Father, I admit that I like to edit Your character. I love Your mercy, but Your holiness makes me uncomfortable. I want a God who forgives my sins, but I don't want a God who demands my total obedience. Forgive me for trying to tame You. Open my eyes to the terrifying beauty of Your absolute perfection. Let Your holiness lead me to deep repentance, and let Your goodness lead me to profound rest. Help me to worship You exactly as You are. Amen.

Lane 1 — Clarity (10 minutes)

The Bottom Line We tend to think of God's attributes like sliders on an audio mixing board—if He turns up the love, He has to turn down the justice. But God isn't made of parts. He doesn't just *have* love; He *is* love. He doesn't just act holy; He *is* holy. He is 100% holy and 100% merciful all the time. Learning to hold those two massive realities together is the secret to a resilient, mature faith.

Scripture Snapshot Isaiah 6:1–5: "I saw the Lord, high and exalted, seated on a throne... 'Woe to me!' I cried. 'I am ruined! For I am a man of unclean lips, and I live among a people of unclean lips, and my eyes have seen the King, the Lord Almighty.'"

Isaiah was a prophet, arguably the most moral guy in the nation. But when he gets a glimpse of the actual, unfiltered holiness of God, his immediate reaction is terror. He realizes he is ruined. Holiness isn't just "being good." It is a blazing, consuming purity that exposes everything dark in its presence. Before we can appreciate God's love, we have to stand in awe of His terrifying perfection.

Say It Out Loud (One Sentence) God is perfectly holy to judge my sin, and perfectly good to forgive it.

Common Confusions Confusion #1: The God of the Old Testament is angry and holy, while Jesus in the New Testament is just nice and loving. Confusion #2: God's love means He will eventually overlook or excuse my sin.

The Tuesday Payoff You are watching the news on Tuesday night. A corrupt executive who destroyed thousands of lives just avoided prison on a technicality. You feel a deep, visceral demand for justice. You want a holy, wrathful God who will balance the scales. But the next morning, you lose your temper and verbally shred your spouse. Suddenly, you don't want justice; you desperately want mercy and grace. A God who is only holy would destroy you. A God who is only loving would ignore the corrupt executive. You need a God who is both.

Lane 2 — Depth (30 minutes)

Define the Terms Incommunicable Attributes - Traits that belong only to God (like being eternal, all-knowing, and everywhere). Communicable Attributes - Traits God shares with us, though imperfectly (like love, justice, and mercy). Justice - God's commitment to do what is right and to punish what is wrong.

Build the Doctrine (Scripture-forward)

The Blazing Fire of Holiness Holiness is the only attribute of God repeated three times in a row in Scripture ("Holy, holy, holy" in Isaiah 6 and Revelation 4). It means He is entirely "other." He is free from all flaw, corruption, and compromise.

Key texts: 1 John 1:5; Habakkuk 1:13

John writes, "God is light; in him there is no darkness at all." God cannot tolerate sin. He cannot sweep it under the rug. Habakkuk says God's eyes "are too pure to look on evil." If God simply ignored sin, He would cease to be holy, just as a judge who lets murderers walk free ceases to be a good judge.

The Deep Well of Goodness While God's holiness demands judgment, His goodness drives Him to show mercy. Goodness isn't just a mood God is in; it is His fundamental posture toward His creation.

Key texts: Psalm 103:8–12; Exodus 34:6–7

When God reveals His glory to Moses in Exodus 34, He announces Himself: "The Lord, the Lord, the compassionate and gracious God, slow to anger, abounding in love and faithfulness." Even in the Old Testament, God leads with His mercy. Psalm 103 reminds us that "He does not treat us as our sins deserve." God's default setting toward broken people who repent is extreme compassion.

Where Holiness and Goodness Collide If God is holy and must punish sin, but He is good and wants to forgive sinners, how does He do both without compromising His character? This is the central problem of the entire Bible.

Key texts: Romans 3:25–26

The answer is the cross. Paul writes that God presented Christ as a sacrifice of atonement so that God could be "just and the one who justifies." At the cross, God's holiness was fully satisfied (sin was judged and punished in Jesus), and God's goodness was fully expressed (we are completely forgiven). The cross proves that God didn't lower His standard of holiness to show us love.

BOX - What This Is NOT Saying We are NOT saying God has a split personality; His justice and love are completely unified. We are NOT saying Jesus is the "good cop" and the Father is the "bad cop"; both are equally holy and good. We are NOT saying God's love is a sentimental feeling; it is an active, sacrificial commitment to our ultimate good.

BOX - Where Christians Differ Not a major point of disagreement. All orthodox believers affirm God's perfect holiness and infinite love. Some theological camps emphasize God's sovereignty and justice more heavily (Reformed traditions), while others emphasize His love and human free will (Arminian traditions), but all agree both attributes are fully true.

Lane 3 — Deep Dive (Optional)

The Objection You're Already Thinking "How can a 'good' God send people to hell? If He is really loving, shouldn't He just save everyone in the end?"

The Best Answer This is one of the hardest questions we face, and it demands honesty. We struggle with the idea of hell because we severely underestimate the horror of our own sin, and we fundamentally misunderstand what true love is.

Love cannot exist without justice. If a judge sees a man who has abused a child, and the judge says, "I am so loving that I forgive you; no penalty is required," we would not call that judge loving. We would call him corrupt. True love is fiercely opposed to anything that destroys what it loves. God's wrath is not a divine temper tantrum; it is His settled, holy opposition to the cancer of sin that is destroying His creation.

Furthermore, God does not lock the doors of hell from the outside. As C.S. Lewis famously noted, there are only two kinds of people: those who say to God, "Thy will be done," and those to whom God eventually says, "Thy will be done." Hell is the terrible trajectory of a human soul that demands to be entirely independent of its Creator.

Historical Lens In the second century, a man named Marcion became highly influential by claiming the God of the Old Testament was an evil, angry deity of justice, and the God of the New Testament was a completely different, loving deity of grace. The early church explicitly condemned Marcion as a heretic, recognizing that slicing God in half destroys the gospel entirely.

Real-Life Translation We have a habit of using God's attributes to justify our own bad behavior. When we want to judge someone else, we invoke God's holiness and justice. When we want to excuse our own sin, we invoke God's grace and love.

A healthy theology of God's attributes stops this hypocrisy. When you look at God's blinding holiness, it kills your pride because you realize how far short you fall. When you look at God's overwhelming goodness, it kills your despair because you realize you are fully loved anyway. You are too flawed to be arrogant, and too loved to be hopeless.

Midlife Module - This Doctrine at 51 You are 51, and the black-and-white certainty of your twenties has faded into a lot of gray. You've seen good people suffer and bad people succeed. You've made compromises you swore you never would. Sometimes, you wonder if God has just lowered His standards for you out of pity.

Understanding God's attributes corrects this. God hasn't lowered His standards; His holiness is still absolute. But His grace is deeper than your history of compromises. At midlife, you don't need a God who grades on a curve. You need a God whose holiness is strong enough to finally fix this broken world, and whose goodness is patient enough to walk with you while you stumble toward the finish line.

Practice + Prayer

This Week's Practice (3–7 minutes) The Tension Test. Read Psalm 103 (focusing on mercy) and Revelation 20:11-15 (focusing on the great white throne judgment). Sit in the tension of those two realities for three minutes without trying to explain one away. Acknowledge that the God you worship is both a fierce judge and a tender father.

Prayer (100–160 words) God, You are entirely too big for my mind to fully grasp. I stand in absolute awe of Your holiness. You are light, and there is no darkness or corruption in You at all. I confess that I often take Your grace for granted, treating Your forgiveness like an entitlement rather than a bloody sacrifice. Forgive me. Thank You for not compromising Your justice, and thank You for paying the price Yourself so that I could be spared. Keep me from pride by reminding me of Your holiness. Keep me from despair by reminding me of Your goodness. Amen.

<u>**Reflection**</u>

Solo (3 prompts)

1. Which attribute of God do you naturally prefer to focus on: His strict justice, or His patient love? Why?

2. Think about a time when you wanted God to be full of wrath toward someone else, but full of mercy toward you.

3. How does the cross of Jesus Christ perfectly combine God's justice and God's love?

Small Group (3 prompts + 1 hard question)

1. Read Isaiah 6:1–5. Why do you think a vision of God's absolute purity made Isaiah so immediately aware of his own sin?

2. We discussed how love requires justice. Can you think of real-world examples where an absence of justice actually proves a lack of love?

3. How does separating the "angry Old Testament God" from the "nice New Testament Jesus" actually destroy our understanding of the cross?

Hard Question: Are you currently minimizing a persistent sin in your life because you assume God is "too loving" to actually discipline you for it?

<u>**Close**</u>

One Sentence Recap: God is perfectly holy to judge our sin, and perfectly good to forgive it, proving both simultaneously at the cross.

If You Only Remember One Thing: You are too flawed to be arrogant, and too loved to be hopeless.

Next Week Preview: Next week we tackle the ultimate paradox: If God is completely sovereign and in control, do my choices actually matter?

Scripture References Used Exodus 34:6–7 Isaiah 6:1–5 Psalm 103:8–12 Habakkuk 1:13 Romans 3:25–26 1 John 1:5 Revelation 20:11–15

<u>My Thoughts & Notes – What Did I Take From This?</u>

Week 10 — Sovereignty and Human Responsibility

Core Question: If God is completely in control of the universe, do my choices actually matter, or are we all just following a script?

Why this matters: Because if God isn't in control, the world is terrifying; but if your choices don't matter, life is meaningless. You desperately need both to be true.

At a Glance (One Page)

Big Idea: The Bible unapologetically teaches two massive truths: God is sovereign over every detail of history, and human beings are completely responsible for their real, consequential choices.

Anchor Text: Ephesians 1:11; Philippians 2:12–13

We believe…: God is the sovereign King who orchestrates all things according to His will, yet He does so in a way that establishes, rather than eliminates, real human agency and moral responsibility.

Key Words (3): Sovereignty - God's absolute rule, control, and authority over all creation. Free Agency - The human ability to make real, willing choices based on our own desires, for which we are morally accountable. Paradox - Two statements that seem to contradict each other but are both simultaneously true.

The One Mistake People Make: Trying to solve the tension like a math equation by deleting one side—either making God weak so humans can be free, or making humans robots so God can be sovereign.

Choose Your Lane: Lane 1 / Lane 2 / Lane 3

This Week's Practice: The Release Valve.

This Week's Prayer: Father, I don't understand how Your control and my choices fit together. My mind wants to solve the puzzle, but You haven't given me all the pieces. I confess that sometimes I use Your sovereignty as an excuse to be lazy, and other times I rely on my own choices and become paralyzed by anxiety. Help me to rest in the massive reality that You are ruling the world, and give me the energy to take my daily obedience seriously. I trust that my life is in Your hands, and I pray for the wisdom to make good choices today. Amen.

Lane 1 — Clarity (10 minutes)

The Bottom Line The relationship between God's control and human free will is the most debated topic in church history. If you try to fully resolve it in your finite mind, you will get a headache. The Bible doesn't treat this as a problem to be solved; it treats it as a paradox to be trusted. God is 100% sovereign. You are 100% responsible. Both are true.

Scripture Snapshot Philippians 2:12–13: "Continue to work out your salvation with fear and trembling, for it is God who works in you to will and to act in order to fulfill his good purpose."

Paul smashes the two concepts together in one breath. First, he gives a command: *you* do the work. *You* make the choices. *You* sweat. Then, without pausing, he gives the reason: because *God* is the one actively working inside you, controlling the will and the action. Paul doesn't apologize for the tension. Our intense effort is required exactly because God's sovereign power is at work.

Say It Out Loud (One Sentence) God is completely in control, yet my choices matter deeply and carry real consequences.

Common Confusions Confusion #1: If God knows what I am going to do, I don't actually have a choice. Confusion #2: Believing in sovereignty means we shouldn't bother praying or evangelizing.

The Tuesday Payoff You are trying to sell your house, and the market is terrible. You are incredibly stressed. If you believe everything is entirely up to your own choices, you will lose your mind managing every detail, staging every room, and panicking over every showing. If you believe in hyper-sovereignty, you might not clean the house at all, assuming "God will sell it if He wants to." The biblical paradox demands that you scrub the floors, price it wisely, and negotiate sharply—while sleeping deeply at night because you know the closing date is ultimately in the sovereign hands of God.

Lane 2 — Depth (30 minutes)

Define the Terms Sovereignty - God's supreme authority to ordain and accomplish exactly what He wills. Providence - How God actively orchestrates circumstances, people, and nature to achieve His sovereign plan. Determinism (Fatalism) - The non-Christian idea that all events are locked in place by an impersonal fate, rendering choices meaningless.

Build the Doctrine (Scripture-forward)

God is Absolutely Sovereign The Bible does not picture God as a nervous spectator wringing His hands, waiting to see what humans will do so He can react. He is the author of the story, not just a character in it.

Key texts: Ephesians 1:11; Psalm 115:3

Paul writes that God "works out everything in conformity with the purpose of his will" (Ephesians 1:11). Everything. The psalmist is even more blunt: "Our God is in heaven; he does whatever pleases him" (Psalm 115:3). Nothing happens outside the boundary lines of God's sovereign permission and plan. Even random chance (like rolling dice) is under His jurisdiction (Proverbs 16:33).

Humans Make Real Choices God's sovereignty does not turn us into puppets. Puppets don't have desires, motives, or guilt. We do. The Bible constantly appeals to our will, commanding us to choose, to repent, and to act. When we sin, we do it because we want to, not because God forced us to.

Key texts: Joshua 24:15; Romans 14:12

Joshua stands before the nation and says, "Choose for yourselves this day whom you will serve." Paul warns that "each of us will give an account of ourselves to God" (Romans 14:12). If our choices were illusions, judgment would be unjust. God holds us accountable because our choices are real, willful, and consequential.

The Cross: The Ultimate Paradox The clearest example of sovereignty and responsibility colliding is the crucifixion of Jesus Christ.

Key texts: Acts 4:27–28

Listen to how the early church prayed about the crucifixion: "Herod and Pontius Pilate met together with the Gentiles and the people of Israel in this city to conspire against your holy servant Jesus... They did what your power and will had decided beforehand should happen."

Notice the tension. Herod and Pilate "conspired." They made wicked, arrogant, responsible choices, and they are guilty for them. But in doing so, they accomplished exactly what God's sovereign will "decided beforehand should happen." God sovereignly used their willing evil to accomplish our ultimate salvation.

BOX - What This Is NOT Saying We are NOT saying God is the author of sin or that He forces people to do evil. We are NOT saying human beings have absolute freedom (we are constrained by our nature and our limits). We are NOT saying our prayers don't matter; God ordains the means (prayer) as well as the ends.

BOX - Where Christians Differ This is the classic Calvinism vs. Arminianism debate. Broadly: Calvinists (Reformed) emphasize God's sovereignty, arguing that God predestines who will be saved because human wills are entirely enslaved to sin. Arminians emphasize human free agency, arguing that God provides grace to all, but humans have the decisive free will to accept or reject it. While the debate can get heated, both sides affirm that God is entirely in charge and humans are entirely accountable.

Lane 3 — Deep Dive (Optional)

The Objection You're Already Thinking "If God already knows what is going to happen, and is sovereign over it all, why should I even bother praying? It's not like I can change His mind."

The Best Answer If God is not sovereign, praying is useless, because He doesn't have the power to fix the situation anyway. We pray *because* He is sovereign.

The mistake is thinking that God only ordains the *ends* (the final outcome) without ordaining the *means* (how we get there). God doesn't just decree that your friend will be comforted; He decrees that your friend will be comforted *through your prayers*.

Think of it like a doctor prescribing medicine. The doctor guarantees that the medicine will cure the infection (the end). But you still have to swallow the pill (the means). Your action is essential to the outcome. God has wired the universe so that our prayers, our witness, and our actions are the actual mechanisms He uses to bring about His sovereign will. Your prayers don't change God's eternal plan; your prayers are a crucial part of God's eternal plan.

Historical Lens In the 18th century, a hyper-Calvinist told a young William Carey to sit down, saying, "If God wants to convert the heathen, He will do it without your help or mine." Carey ignored him, recognizing that God's sovereignty doesn't eliminate our mission. He went to India, sparked the modern missions movement, and proved that a high view of sovereignty produces bold action, not lazy fatalism.

Real-Life Translation When you face a massive trauma—a car accident, a violent crime, a sudden illness—the concept of free will offers you no comfort. If the universe is just a chaotic collision of random human choices, your suffering is utterly meaningless.

Sovereignty is the heavy blanket you need in the darkest night of your soul. It tells you that your pain is not an accident. It did not slip past God's notice. While He may not have actively caused the evil, He sovereignly permitted it, and He promises to bend it toward an ultimate good (Romans 8:28). Sovereignty means your suffering is not wasted.

Midlife Module - This Doctrine at 45 You are lying awake at 2:00 AM. Your 19-year-old child is making a series of catastrophic life choices. You did everything right: you took them to church, you modeled a good marriage, you prayed with them. Now, you are torturing yourself with guilt, replaying every parenting decision to figure out where you ruined them.

You desperately need the tension of sovereignty and responsibility. First, free agency reminds you that your child is making their own choices; you are not their savior, and you are not the ultimate cause of their sin. The guilt lifts. Second, sovereignty reminds you that your child's rebellion has not removed them from God's grip. God's arm is longer than their bad choices. You can go to sleep because you know that the Sovereign King loves your kid more than you do.

Practice + Prayer

This Week's Practice (3–7 minutes) The Release Valve. Take a blank piece of paper and draw a line down the middle. On the left side, write down the things you are stressing over that are entirely out of your control (the economy, someone else's opinion, medical test results). On the right side, write down what you can control today (your attitude, making a phone call, doing the laundry). Give the left side to God's sovereignty. Go get to work on the right side.

Prayer (100–160 words) God, my mind cannot fully grasp how Your absolute control and my daily choices exist together, but I choose to trust Your Word over my own understanding. Forgive me for the times I try to play God, trying to control circumstances and people that belong to You. Forgive me also for the times I am lazy, using Your sovereignty as an excuse to avoid hard work or difficult conversations. Give me the peace that comes from knowing You hold the universe together. Give me the urgency to obey You today. When I am paralyzed by fear of the future, remind me that You are already there. Amen.

<u>Reflection</u>

Solo (3 prompts)

1. Are you more prone to acting like everything depends on you (anxiety) or acting like nothing you do matters (fatalism)?

2. Think of a past failure. How does understanding human responsibility keep you from blaming God for it?

3. Think of a past success. How does understanding God's sovereignty keep you from taking all the credit for it?

Small Group (3 prompts + 1 hard question)

1. Discuss the story of Herod and Pilate in Acts 4:27–28. How does God use human evil without being blamed for the evil itself?

2. If someone asked you, "Why pray if God already knows what He's going to do?", how would you answer them using the "ends and means" concept?

3. How does resting in God's sovereignty actually make us bolder in our careers, parenting, and evangelism?

Hard Question: Are you using the excuse of "waiting on God to open a door" to hide your fear of making a hard, responsible decision?

<u>Close</u>

One Sentence Recap: God is the sovereign King who orchestrates all things, and He does so in a way that establishes real human agency and moral responsibility.

If You Only Remember One Thing: Pray like everything depends on God; work like everything depends on you.

Next Week Preview: Next week we look at the Trinity—why God being three persons in one actually changes everything about love and relationship.

Scripture References Used Joshua 24:15 Psalm 115:3 Proverbs 16:33 Acts 4:27–28 Romans 8:28 Romans 14:12 Ephesians 1:11 Philippians 2:12–13

<u>My Thoughts & Notes – What Did I Take From This?</u>

WEEK 11 — THE TRINITY: THREE PERSONS, ONE GOD

CORE QUESTION: DOES THE Trinity actually matter for everyday life, or is it just complicated theological math that we are supposed to blindly accept?

Why this matters: Because if God is not a Trinity, love is not eternal. If God was a solitary individual before creation, He would have needed to create us just so He wouldn't be lonely.

At a Glance (One Page)

Big Idea: The Trinity isn't a puzzle to be solved; it is the breathtaking reality that God is inherently relational, meaning love is woven into the very fabric of the universe.

Anchor Text: Matthew 28:19; 2 Corinthians 13:14

We believe...: There is only one living and true God, who eternally exists in three distinct persons: the Father, the Son, and the Holy Spirit, equal in power and glory.

Key Words (3): Trinity - The biblical teaching that God is one in essence and three in persons. Essence (or Nature) - *What* God is. There is only one divine essence. Person - *Who* God is. The Father, Son, and Holy Spirit are distinct persons within the one essence.

The One Mistake People Make: Trying to use physical analogies (like an egg, water, or a three-leaf clover) to explain the Trinity, which almost always ends up teaching a heresy.

Choose Your Lane: Lane 1 / Lane 2 / Lane 3

This Week's Practice: The Trinitarian Greeting.

This Week's Prayer: Father, Son, and Holy Spirit, I admit that I cannot fully wrap my mind around You. The math of the Trinity confounds me. Yet I know that a God I could perfectly understand would be too small to worship. Thank You that You did not create me out of loneliness, but out of the overflow of the perfect love You have shared eternally within Yourself. Draw me into that fellowship. Guard my mind from bad analogies and false ideas about who You are. I bow before the mystery and the majesty of the Triune God. Amen.

Lane 1 — Clarity (10 minutes)

The Bottom Line The word "Trinity" isn't in the Bible, but the reality of the Trinity is on almost every page. God is one "What" and three "Whos." The Father is God, the Son is God, and the Holy Spirit is God. But the Father is not the Son, the Son is not the Spirit, and the Spirit is not the Father. If your brain hurts a little bit, that is entirely normal. You are a finite creature trying to understand an infinite Creator.

Scripture Snapshot Matthew 28:19: "Therefore go and make disciples of all nations, baptizing them in the name of the Father and of the Son and of the Holy Spirit."

Notice the grammar Jesus uses in the Great Commission. He commands us to be baptized in the *name* (singular) of the Father, Son, and Holy Spirit. He doesn't say "names" (plural), which would imply three separate gods. He uses a singular name for three distinct persons. Jesus explicitly claims that the Father, the Son, and the Spirit share the exact same divine authority and identity.

Say It Out Loud (One Sentence) God is one in essence and three in persons, existing eternally in perfect love.

Common Confusions Confusion #1: The Trinity means Christians worship three different gods (polytheism). Confusion #2: The Trinity is just God putting on three different masks depending on the situation.

The Tuesday Payoff You are dealing with a deeply frustrating relationship conflict—maybe a tense standoff with a sibling or a massive breakdown in communication with your spouse. If God is just a solitary power in the sky, relationships are just a biological survival mechanism. But if God is a Trinity, relationship is the ultimate reality of the universe. When you do the hard work of forgiving, communicating, and sacrificing in a relationship, you aren't just surviving Tuesday. You are reflecting the eternal nature of the Triune God.

Lane 2 — Depth (30 minutes)

Define the Terms Monotheism - The belief that there is only one true God. Tritheism (Heresy) - The false belief that there are three separate gods. Modalism (Heresy) - The false belief that God is one person who just switches between three different roles or "modes" (sometimes acting as Father, sometimes as Son, sometimes as Spirit).

Build the Doctrine (Scripture-forward)

There Is Only One God Before we get to the "three," we have to fiercely defend the "one." Christianity is strictly monotheistic. The Bible completely rejects the idea of a pantheon of gods sharing power in heaven.

Key texts: Deuteronomy 6:4; Isaiah 45:5

The most famous prayer in Judaism, the Shema, begins: "Hear, O Israel: The Lord our God, the Lord is one." God declares in Isaiah, "I am the Lord, and there is no other; apart from me there is no God." Any understanding of the Trinity must begin and end with the unbreakable truth that there is only one divine essence.

The Father, Son, and Spirit Are All God While there is only one God, the Bible clearly assigns the title, attributes, and actions of God to three distinct persons.

Key texts: John 1:1; Acts 5:3–4

The Father is universally recognized as God. But John 1:1 explicitly states, "the Word [Jesus] was with God, and the Word was God." In Acts 5, when Peter confronts Ananias for lying to the Holy Spirit, he concludes by saying, "You have not lied just to human beings but to God." All three possess the full essence of deity.

The Three Persons Are Distinct The Father, Son, and Spirit are not just three titles for the same person. They interact with each other. They love each other. They speak to each other.

Key texts: Matthew 3:16–17

At the baptism of Jesus, we see all three persons simultaneously. Jesus (the Son) comes up out of the water. The Holy Spirit descends on Him like a dove. And the Father speaks from heaven: "This is my Son, whom I love." If God is just one person wearing different masks, this scene is an absurd theatrical illusion where God is essentially doing ventriloquism.

BOX - What This Is NOT Saying We are NOT saying 1 + 1 + 1 = 1. We are saying God is 1 in essence and 3 in persons. We are NOT saying the Son and Spirit were created by the Father later in time; all three are eternal. We are NOT saying we have three separate gods who just agree on everything.

BOX - Where Christians Differ Not a major point of disagreement. The doctrine of the Trinity is the defining boundary of historic Christian orthodoxy. If a group denies the Trinity (like Jehovah's Witnesses or Mormonism), they step outside the boundaries of historic, orthodox Christianity.

Lane 3 — Deep Dive (Optional)

The Objection You're Already Thinking "Why use analogies if they are all wrong? Isn't it easier to just say God is like water (ice, liquid, vapor) or like a man who is a father, son, and employee?"

The Best Answer We love analogies because we want to shrink God down to something we can hold in our hands. But almost every common analogy for the Trinity teaches a heresy.

The water analogy (ice, liquid, vapor) teaches Modalism—the heresy that God changes forms. Water cannot be ice and vapor at the exact same time in the same place. But the Father, Son, and Spirit exist simultaneously. The egg analogy (shell, white, yolk) teaches Partialism—the heresy that each person is only 1/3 of God. But the Father is 100% God, the Son is 100% God, and the Spirit is 100% God.

It is better to abandon the analogies and simply hold the tension of the biblical mystery. We shouldn't be surprised that the inner life of the Creator of the universe defies human comparison. If we could easily explain Him with a hard-boiled egg, He wouldn't be worthy of our worship.

Historical Lens The Council of Nicaea (325 AD) was convened specifically to deal with a man named Arius, who taught that Jesus was a created being, slightly lower than the Father. The early church realized that if Jesus isn't fully God, He cannot fully save us. They wrote the Nicene Creed to firmly establish that the Son is "of one substance with the Father," securing the doctrine of the Trinity for the rest of history.

Real-Life Translation If the Islamic or Unitarian view of God is true (a single, solitary person), then before God created the universe, He was entirely alone. He could not experience love, because love requires an object. In that view, God *had* to create us to have someone to love. We become necessary for God's emotional fulfillment.

But because God is a Trinity, the Father, Son, and Spirit have been perfectly loving each other for all eternity. God was not lonely. He did not create you because He needed you; He created you out of the overflowing joy and love that already existed within the Trinity. You are not a cosmic crutch for a lonely deity. You are the invited guest into an eternal fellowship.

Midlife Module - This Doctrine at 49 It is a Friday night. Your kids are out with friends, your spouse went to bed early, and your house is completely quiet. You suddenly feel a wave of profound, heavy isolation. At 49, you have a lot of acquaintances, but very few real friends.

The Trinity speaks directly into human isolation. You were created in the image of a Triune God. Your ache for relationship isn't a sign of weakness; it is a sign of your design. You are wired for deep, known, intimate connection because the God who made you exists in deep, known, intimate connection. The Trinity validates your midlife loneliness and invites you to find your ultimate relational rest in the fellowship of the Father, Son, and Holy Spirit.

Practice + Prayer

This Week's Practice (3–7 minutes) The Trinitarian Greeting. We end church services with "the grace of the Lord Jesus Christ, the love of God, and the fellowship of the Holy Spirit." This week, practice praying specifically to the different persons of the Trinity. Thank the Father for His sovereign plan. Thank the Son for His sacrifice. Ask the Holy Spirit for power and conviction today.

Prayer (100–160 words) Father, Son, and Holy Spirit, I worship You. My mind is too small to understand how You are three and yet one, but my heart rejoices in the truth of it. Father, thank You for Your perfect, orchestrating love. Jesus, thank You for stepping into our broken world to rescue us. Holy Spirit, thank You for living inside me and giving me the strength to obey. Keep me from reducing You to a simple formula. Let the mystery of Your nature lead me to awe. Teach me how to love others with the same selfless, unified love that You share within Yourself. Amen.

<u>**Reflection**</u>

Solo (3 prompts)

1. Which of the common Trinity analogies (water, egg, three-leaf clover) did you grow up hearing, and why are they actually unhelpful?

2. How does knowing that God has existed in perfect relationship for all eternity change how you view the concept of love?

3. Which person of the Trinity do you tend to ignore or forget about in your daily life?

Small Group (3 prompts + 1 hard question)

1. Read Matthew 3:16–17. Why is the baptism of Jesus such a critical moment for proving that God is not just one person wearing three different masks?

2. Discuss the difference between a God who created us because He was lonely, versus a Triune God who created us out of overflowing love.

3. How does the doctrine of the Trinity shape our understanding of human marriage, friendship, and church community?

Hard Question: Do you dismiss deep theological truths like the Trinity just because they are hard to understand, settling for a lazy, shallow faith?

<u>**Close**</u>

One Sentence Recap: God eternally exists in three distinct persons—Father, Son, and Holy Spirit—who share the exact same divine essence.

If You Only Remember One Thing: God didn't create you because He was lonely; He created you to invite you into the eternal love of the Trinity.

Next Week Preview: Next week we look at Providence—how God actively manages the ordinary, frustrating, and chaotic details of our daily lives.

Scripture References Used Deuteronomy 6:4 Isaiah 45:5 Matthew 3:16–17 Matthew 28:19 John 1:1 Acts 5:3–4 2 Corinthians 13:14

<u>My Thoughts & Notes – What Did I Take From This?</u>

Week 12 — Providence: God's Rule in Ordinary Life

Core Question: Is God actually managing the frustrating, ordinary details of my daily life, or is He just handling the big-picture stuff?

Why this matters: Because if God only cares about massive global events, you are entirely on your own when your car breaks down or your career stalls.

At a Glance (One Page)

Big Idea: God didn't just wind up the universe and walk away; He is actively, intimately involved in sustaining and directing every ordinary detail to fulfill His good purpose.

Anchor Text: Romans 8:28; Matthew 6:25–34

We believe…: God the Creator continuously upholds, directs, and governs all creatures, actions, and things, from the greatest to the smallest, by His completely wise and holy providence.

Key Words (3): Providence - God's continuous, active involvement in creation, providing for it and guiding it to its intended goal. Preservation - The reality that God actively holds the universe together moment by moment. Concurrence - God working through the ordinary actions of nature and humans to accomplish His will.

The One Mistake People Make: Thinking "God's will" is only found in dramatic, miraculous moments, while assuming the boring, frustrating parts of life are just random bad luck.

Choose Your Lane: Lane 1 / Lane 2 / Lane 3

This Week's Practice: The Coincidence Audit.

This Week's Prayer: Father, I confess that I usually act like a practical atheist. I trust You with my eternal salvation, but I panic when my daily plans fall apart, acting as if I am completely alone. Forgive my lack of trust. Open my eyes to Your providence. Help me to see that the frustrating delays, the sudden changes in direction, and the quiet, boring days are all being managed by Your steady hand. Give me the profound peace of knowing that absolutely nothing in my life is left to chance. Amen.

Lane 1 — Clarity (10 minutes)

The Bottom Line Sovereignty means God is the King who is absolutely in charge. Providence is *how* the King actually runs the kingdom. The doctrine of providence means there is no such thing as a completely random event. God isn't a watchmaker who wound the clock of the universe and retired. He is actively moving the hands of the clock. Every atom, every delayed flight, and every mundane Tuesday is being leveraged for His ultimate purpose.

Scripture Snapshot Matthew 6:25–34: "Look at the birds of the air; they do not sow or reap or store away in barns, and yet your heavenly Father feeds them. Are you not much more valuable than they?"

Jesus doesn't point to a blazing comet or a massive earthquake to prove God is in control. He points to a bird finding a worm. He points to grass growing. He uses the most ordinary, overlooked aspects of nature to prove a massive theological point: God micromanages the universe, and He does it with incredible care. If He is paying attention to the calorie intake of a sparrow, He is not ignoring the stress of your mortgage.

Say It Out Loud (One Sentence) God is actively managing every detail of the universe, which means my life is never at the mercy of random chance.

Common Confusions Confusion #1: Providence is just a religious word for fate or karma. Confusion #2: God only intervenes when we pray hard enough; otherwise, things run on their own.

The Tuesday Payoff You are stuck in brutal traffic on a Tuesday morning, making you ten minutes late for a crucial meeting. Your heart rate is spiking, and you are furious at the driver who caused the accident two miles ahead. If the universe is random, this is just terrible luck, and your anger is justified. But if providence is real, God allowed that traffic jam. Maybe He is protecting you from a different accident. Maybe He is simply teaching you patience. Providence doesn't make the traffic less annoying, but it removes the panic. It tells you that even the delays are part of the design.

Lane 2 — Depth (30 minutes)

Define the Terms Deism (Heresy) - The belief that God created the world but then stepped back to let it run entirely on natural laws without His involvement. Fate - An impersonal, blind, and meaningless force that locks events into place. Providence - A deeply personal, loving Father actively guiding events toward a purposeful, redemptive end.

Build the Doctrine (Scripture-forward)

He Holds the Glue God is not just the Creator; He is the Sustainer. If God stopped actively thinking about the universe for one second, it wouldn't just freeze; it would disintegrate into nothingness.

Key texts: Colossians 1:17; Hebrews 1:3

Paul writes about Jesus, "He is before all things, and in him all things hold together." The writer of Hebrews says the Son is "sustaining all things by his powerful word." Gravity isn't an independent force; gravity is just the regular, predictable way God chooses to hold the physical world together. You don't have to worry about the universe falling apart because God's grip never fails.

He Works Through Secondary Causes Providence doesn't mean God magically poofs things into existence every day. He usually works through "secondary causes"—the normal laws of nature and human choices. God is the primary cause (He ordains it), but He uses secondary causes (people, weather, physics) to execute it.

Key texts: Genesis 45:5–8

Joseph's brothers sold him into slavery out of jealousy (a secondary cause). They were guilty. But years later, Joseph looks at them and says, "It was not you who sent me here, but God" (the primary cause). God didn't bypass their human agency, but He providentially hijacked their evil action to position Joseph to save thousands of people from famine.

All Things For Good This is the hardest part of providence to trust. God is weaving millions of isolated, often painful events together to create a specific, beautiful outcome for His people.

Key texts: Romans 8:28

"And we know that in all things God works for the good of those who love him." Notice what Paul does not say. He does *not* say "all things are good." Cancer is not good. Betrayal is not good. Paul says God works *in* all things *for* the good. God is the master chef who takes raw, bitter ingredients (like flour and baking soda) and bakes them into something magnificent.

BOX - What This Is NOT Saying We are NOT saying that every bad thing that happens to you is a direct punishment from God. We are NOT saying you shouldn't make plans or work hard because "God will just provide anyway." We are NOT saying we will always understand *why* God allowed a specific event; providence is often invisible until looking backward.

BOX - Where Christians Differ Not a major point of disagreement on the core doctrine. All orthodox Christians believe God actively sustains and directs the world. The nuanced debate (again, Calvinism vs. Arminianism) centers on exactly *how*

God's providence interacts with human rebellion, but everyone agrees that God is actively driving history to its promised conclusion.

Lane 3 — Deep Dive (Optional)

The Objection You're Already Thinking "If God is micromanaging everything, why did He let my tire blow out on the highway today? Does He really care about parking spots and flat tires?"

The Best Answer We tend to divide the world into "spiritual things" (salvation, church, morality) and "secular things" (tires, weather, the stock market). We assume God cares deeply about the former and ignores the latter. But God does not recognize that division.

Every massive historical event pivots on tiny, seemingly insignificant details. A delayed flight prevents a businessman from being in a building that collapses. A flat tire causes a woman to meet a mechanic who eventually becomes her husband. If God is not in control of the flat tire, He is not in control of the marriage.

God is infinite. It does not exhaust His mental capacity to manage the spin of a galaxy and the air pressure in your front left tire at the same time. Believing that God manages the small things isn't arrogant; it is the logical requirement of having an infinite God.

Historical Lens The Heidelberg Catechism (written in 1563) gives one of the most beautiful definitions of providence in church history. It states that providence is God's power by which "leaf and blade, rain and drought, fruitful and lean years, food and drink, health and sickness, prosperity and poverty—all things, in fact, come to us not by chance but from his fatherly hand." The Reformers deeply understood that stripping "luck" out of our vocabulary is essential for finding peace.

Real-Life Translation We are exhausted because we are trying to play providence for our own lives. We aggressively manage our careers, obsess over our kids' schedules, and try to network with the right people to secure our future.

The doctrine of providence is an invitation to resign as the general manager of the universe. It doesn't mean you stop working hard—you still show up and use the talents God gave you. But it means you detach your identity from the outcome. You can work hard on a project, watch it fail due to circumstances entirely out of your control, and not have a mental breakdown. You know that if God **Close**d that door, He **Close**d it on purpose, and His purpose is better than your project.

Midlife Module - This Doctrine at 44 You are 44. The career trajectory you meticulously planned in your twenties didn't pan out. You were passed over for a promotion, or your industry fundamentally changed, and now you are working a job you never expected, living in a city you didn't choose. You feel a creeping sense of failure, assuming you must have taken a wrong turn ten years ago.

Providence rewrites this narrative. God is not pacing in heaven, frustrated that you ruined His plan by making a bad career choice at age 32. He factored in all your choices, your setbacks, and your limitations from the beginning. You are exactly where His providence has placed you. The pressure to "arrive" vanishes, replaced by the simple calling to be faithful right where you are.

Practice + Prayer

This Week's Practice (3–7 minutes) The Coincidence Audit. Look back at the last ten years of your life. Identify one major, positive relationship or event that only happened because of a completely random "coincidence" (e.g., you met your spouse because you accidentally went to the wrong coffee shop). Recognize that coincidence as the quiet providence of God, and thank Him for it.

Prayer (100–160 words) God, I confess that I want to be in control. I like predictable outcomes, and I get angry when my plans are interrupted. Thank You for being a Father who does not leave me to the mercy of blind fate or random chance. Thank You that You are actively involved in the mundane, frustrating details of my life. Forgive me for calling Your providence "bad luck." When I cannot see what You are doing, give me the faith to trust Your character. Help me to lay my head on the pillow tonight knowing that the universe is entirely secure in Your hands. Amen.

<u>Reflection</u>

Solo (3 prompts)

1. Do you function more like a Deist (God is distant) or a fatalist (nothing I do matters)? How does biblical providence correct both?

2. Why is the concept of "karma" (you get what you deserve) actually terrifying compared to the Christian concept of providence?

3. Think of a door that was **Close**d in your life that you were deeply angry about, but looking back, you are incredibly grateful it didn't open.

Small Group (3 prompts + 1 hard question)

1. Read Romans 8:28 carefully. Why is the distinction between "all things are good" and "God works in all things for good" so practically important for a suffering person?

2. Discuss the difference between a primary cause (God's will) and secondary causes (human choices, nature). How does the story of Joseph illustrate this?

3. We talked about resigning as the "general manager of the universe." What is one area of your life where you are still aggressively trying to play providence?

Hard Question: Are you using the phrase "God's will" as an excuse to passively avoid taking responsibility for your own bad decisions?

<u>Close</u>

One Sentence Recap: God is actively, intimately involved in sustaining and directing every ordinary detail to fulfill His good purpose.

If You Only Remember One Thing: God is not a watchmaker who wound the clock and walked away; He is actively moving the hands.

Next Week Preview: Next week we tackle miracles—if God usually works through the ordinary laws of nature, why does He occasionally break them?

Scripture References Used Genesis 45:5–8 Matthew 6:25–34 Romans 8:28 Colossians 1:17 Hebrews 1:3

<u>My Thoughts & Notes – What Did I Take From This?</u>

Week 13 — Miracles and the Supernatural

Core Question: Does God still break the rules of nature today, or are miracles just ancient myths we use to make a point?

Why this matters: Because if God cannot break into the natural world, our faith is entirely theoretical; but if we expect a miracle for every problem, our faith will become bitter when He says no.

At a Glance (One Page)

Big Idea: Miracles are not random parlor tricks; they are rare, deliberate signs where God temporarily interrupts the natural order to prove a point, validate His messengers, or give us a preview of His coming kingdom.

Anchor Text: John 20:30–31; Acts 2:22

We believe…: God, who established the natural laws of the universe, is entirely free to act outside of them to accomplish His redemptive purposes and validate His truth.

Key Words (3): Miracle - A less common kind of God's activity in which He arouses people's awe and wonder and bears witness to Himself. Naturalism - The philosophical belief that the physical, observable universe is all that exists, and the supernatural is impossible. Sign - The biblical word often used for miracles, indicating that the event is pointing to a larger truth.

The One Mistake People Make: Treating God like a cosmic vending machine, assuming that if they just have enough faith, they can force God to perform a miracle on command.

Choose Your Lane: Lane 1 / Lane 2 / Lane 3

This Week's Practice: The Kingdom Preview.

This Week's Prayer: Father, I live in a world that tells me only what I can see and measure is real. But I know that You are the Author of the laws of physics, and You are not bound by them. I confess that sometimes I doubt Your power to intervene, and other times I demand that You intervene on my terms. Give me the faith to pray boldly for healing and breakthrough. And give me the deeper faith to trust You entirely when Your answer is no. Remind me that the greatest miracle has already happened: a dead man walked out of a tomb. Amen.

Lane 1 — Clarity (10 minutes)

The Bottom Line A miracle is simply God doing something unusual. Since God invented the "normal" laws of nature (like gravity or cellular decay), He is perfectly free to hit pause on those laws whenever He wants. But the Bible shows that God doesn't do miracles just to show off. Miracles are signs. You don't stare at a street sign; you look at what it is pointing to. Miracles point to the reality of who Jesus is and give us a preview of what He is going to do to the whole world in the end.

Scripture Snapshot John 20:30–31: "Jesus performed many other signs in the presence of his disciples, which are not recorded in this book. But these are written that you may believe that Jesus is the Messiah, the Son of God, and that by believing you may have life in his name."

John doesn't call them "magic tricks." He calls them "signs." And he tells us exactly why he wrote them down: validation. Jesus healing a blind man wasn't just a random act of kindness; it was a deliberate, undeniable proof that He was exactly who He claimed to be. The miracle was the evidence; belief in the Messiah was the goal.

Say It Out Loud (One Sentence) God occasionally breaks the normal rules of nature to prove that He is the King who is coming to fix a broken world.

Common Confusions Confusion #1: If I just have enough faith, God is obligated to heal me or fix my problem. Confusion #2: Science has proven that miracles are impossible because the laws of nature cannot be broken.

The Tuesday Payoff You are sitting in a doctor's office on Tuesday afternoon, looking at a devastating MRI result. Your friends are telling you to "claim a miracle." If you believe miracles are guaranteed to those with enough faith, you will carry the crushing guilt of thinking your lack of faith is keeping you sick. If you don't believe in the supernatural at all, you have no hope. The biblical view offers a sturdy middle ground: you pray fiercely for a miracle because God *can* do it, but you rest in His providence if He chooses *not* to, knowing your final healing is guaranteed in the resurrection.

Lane 2 — Depth (30 minutes)

Define the Terms Miracle - God acting in the world without using the ordinary means of nature. Sign and Wonder - Biblical terms for miracles emphasizing their purpose (to point to truth) and their effect (to create awe). Cessationism vs. Continuationism - The debate over whether certain miraculous gifts (like speaking in tongues or physical healing) ceased after the apostles died, or continue today.

Build the Doctrine (Scripture-forward)

Science Doesn't Disprove Miracles The argument that "science proves miracles are impossible" is a logical fallacy. Science is the study of the regular, repeatable laws of nature. A miracle, by definition, is an unrepeatable exception to those laws caused by an outside force.

Key texts: Genesis 18:14; Jeremiah 32:17

"Is anything too hard for the Lord?" (Genesis 18:14). If you grant the very first verse of the Bible—that God created the entire universe out of nothing—then every other miracle is incredibly easy to believe. Making a blind eye see is child's play compared to inventing the concept of light. If God exists outside the box of the universe, He can absolutely reach His hand into the box.

Miracles Cluster in History If you read the Bible casually, it feels like miracles are happening every Tuesday. But if you map them out historically, you realize there are centuries of silence. Miracles actually cluster tightly around three major periods of new revelation:

1. Moses and Joshua (establishing the Law and the Nation).

2. Elijah and Elisha (saving the Nation from massive idolatry).

3. Jesus and the Apostles (establishing the New Covenant and the Church).

Key texts: Hebrews 2:3–4

"This salvation, which was first announced by the Lord, was confirmed to us by those who heard him. God also testified to it by signs, wonders and various miracles." Miracles were heavily concentrated during the first century to authenticate the apostles' message while the New Testament was being written. They are the signature on the document.

Previews of the Kingdom When Jesus healed the sick, cast out demons, and multiplied food, He wasn't just solving immediate problems. He was giving us a trailer for the movie.

Key texts: Matthew 11:2–5

When John the Baptist is in prison and starts to doubt, he sends a message to Jesus asking if He is really the Messiah. Jesus replies by pointing to the miracles: "The blind receive sight, the lame walk, those who have leprosy are cleansed, the deaf hear, the dead are raised." Jesus is saying, "Look at the signs." Every healing was a localized preview of the new creation, proving that Jesus has the power to ultimately reverse the curse of the Fall.

BOX - What This Is NOT Saying We are NOT saying God never does miracles today; He is sovereign and can act whenever He chooses. We are NOT saying a lack of healing means a lack of faith; the Apostle Paul prayed three times for healing and God said no (2 Cor. 12). We are NOT saying every unexplainable event is a miracle from God; demons and false teachers can also perform deceptive signs.

BOX - Where Christians Differ This is the Cessationist vs. Continuationist debate. Cessationists believe the dramatic miraculous gifts (healing on command, prophecy, tongues) were the "training wheels" for the early church and ceased once the Bible was completed. Continuationists (Pentecostals/Charismatics) believe all those gifts are still fully active today. Broad evangelicals typically land somewhere in the middle: God absolutely still heals and does miracles, but we shouldn't expect them to be the normal, daily experience of the church.

Lane 3 — Deep Dive (Optional)

The Objection You're Already Thinking "If God can heal people miraculously, why doesn't He do it for everyone? Why did He heal my friend's cancer but let my dad die?"

The Best Answer This is the most painful question regarding miracles. The hard truth is that in this current age, a miracle is a temporary delay of the inevitable. Every single person Jesus miraculously healed eventually died. Lazarus was raised from the dead, but he had to die again.

God's primary goal in this era is not to give us permanent physical comfort in a broken world; His primary goal is to secure our eternal souls and conform us to the image of Jesus. Sometimes a miraculous healing accomplishes that by creating awe and faith. But very often, God uses the agonizing reality of suffering, weakness, and physical death to accomplish that exact same goal.

We demand a miracle because we want the kingdom of heaven right now. God asks us to trust His timing. He will heal every disease, wipe away every tear, and raise every body. But the timeline is His, not ours.

Historical Lens During the Enlightenment (1700s), philosophers like David Hume argued heavily against miracles, stating that uniform human experience proves the laws of nature are absolute. Orthodox Christians pushed back, arguing that Hume was using circular reasoning: he assumed miracles don't happen, and therefore concluded that any report of a miracle must be a lie. History shows that eyewitness testimony to the resurrection was strong enough to build Western civilization.

Real-Life Translation We are often tempted by two extremes. The first is anti-supernaturalism, where we stop asking God for anything big because we just assume He won't do it. We only pray for safe travel and nice weather. The second extreme is hyper-supernaturalism, where we demand a miracle for every inconvenience and view normal medical care as a "lack of faith."

A mature faith embraces the tension. You go to the doctor, take your medicine, and do the hard work of physical therapy, thanking God for the providence of modern medicine. At the exact same time, you pray fiercely, laying hands on the sick, asking God to intervene and do what medicine cannot do. You ask boldly, and you submit humbly.

Midlife Module - This Doctrine at 53 You are 53, and you've been living with chronic pain for six years. In your twenties, you went to prayer services and confidently believed God was going to heal you instantly. Now, the pain is just a daily, exhausting reality.

You haven't lost your faith, but it has changed shape. You realize that a faith that only survives if God gives you a miracle is a very fragile faith. You have stopped demanding that God break the laws of nature for you, and you have started leaning heavily into the grace He provides to endure the pain. You still pray for healing, but you've discovered an even deeper miracle: the quiet, stubborn ability to worship a God who hasn't fixed your body yet.

Practice + Prayer

This Week's Practice (3–7 minutes) The Kingdom Preview. Read Mark 4:35–41 (Jesus calming the storm). Don't read it as a promise that Jesus will instantly calm every storm in your life. Read it as a preview of the day when Jesus will completely remove all chaos, natural disasters, and fear from the new earth. Let the miracle give you hope for the future.

Prayer (100–160 words) God, You are not bound by the limits of this physical world. You spoke the laws of physics into existence, and You hold them in Your hand. Forgive me for putting You in a box of my own understanding, assuming You can only do what makes sense to me. I ask boldly for Your intervention in the broken places of my life and my family right now. Please heal, restore, and provide. But Father, if Your answer requires me to wait, give me the grace to trust Your timeline. Protect me from the bitterness of an unanswered prayer. Anchor my hope in the ultimate miracle of the resurrection. Amen.

Reflection

Solo (3 prompts)

1. Have you ever experienced or witnessed something you could only explain as a miracle?

2. Why is the "name it and claim it" theology (where you demand a miracle based on your own faith) actually so destructive to people who are suffering?

3. How does knowing that miracles were "clustered" in history relieve the pressure of expecting one every day?

Small Group (3 prompts + 1 hard question)

1. Discuss the phrase "Miracles are signs." What happens when we become obsessed with the sign itself, rather than the Jesus it is pointing to?

2. Read John 20:30–31. According to John, what is the sole purpose of the miracles recorded in the Bible?

3. How can we balance a genuine belief that God still heals today with a realistic acceptance of medical science and human mortality?

Hard Question: Has your disappointment over a miracle God *didn't* do caused you to stop trusting Him entirely?

Close

One Sentence Recap: Miracles are rare, deliberate signs where God temporarily interrupts the natural order to validate His truth and preview His coming kingdom.

If You Only Remember One Thing: Pray fiercely for God to intervene, but rest peacefully if He chooses to use your weakness instead.

Next Week Preview: Next week we look into the unseen realm: angels, demons, and how to practice spiritual discernment without becoming weird or paranoid.

Scripture References Used Genesis 18:14 Jeremiah 32:17 Matthew 11:2–5 John 20:30–31 Acts 2:22 2 Corinthians 12 Hebrews 2:3–4

My Thoughts & Notes – What Did I Take From This?

WEEK 14 — ANGELS, DEMONS, AND DISCERNMENT

CORE QUESTION: IS THE spiritual realm actually real, and how do we engage with it without becoming weird, paranoid, or unhinged?

Why this matters: Because ignoring the spiritual realm makes you dangerously naive to the reality of evil, but obsessing over it makes you distracted from Jesus.

At a Glance (One Page)

Big Idea: The Bible presents a universe teeming with unseen spiritual realities, but it commands us to focus on the finished victory of Christ and stand firm in truth, rather than obsessing over demons.

Anchor Text: Ephesians 6:10–18; 1 Peter 5:8

We believe...: Angels are created spiritual beings who serve God, and demons are fallen angels who rebelled against God; Satan is a defeated enemy whose power is entirely restricted by God's sovereignty.

Key Words (3): Angels - Created, spiritual, moral beings with high intelligence and power, functioning as God's messengers and servants. Demons - Angels who rebelled alongside Satan, now actively opposing God and seeking to deceive humanity. Spiritual Warfare - The daily reality of resisting the lies of the enemy by trusting in the truth of the gospel.

The One Mistake People Make: Falling into one of two extremes: either acting like demons don't exist at all, or believing there is a demon behind every bush causing every flat tire and bad mood.

Choose Your Lane: Lane 1 / Lane 2 / Lane 3

This Week's Practice: The Armor Audit.

This Week's Prayer: Father, I admit that I am easily distracted. I tend to focus entirely on what I can see, touch, and measure, forgetting that there is a very real spiritual battle happening around me. Forgive me for my naivety. Yet, I also ask that You would keep me from fear and paranoia. Remind me that Satan is a defeated enemy on a leash. Give me the discernment to recognize the lies of the enemy in my own mind, and give me the courage to stand firm in the truth of the gospel. Amen.

Lane 1 — Clarity (10 minutes)

The Bottom Line C.S. Lewis famously said that humanity falls into two massive errors regarding devils: one is to disbelieve in their existence, and the other is to feel an unhealthy, obsessive interest in them. Satan is thrilled with either. The Bible is incredibly balanced. It treats the unseen realm as a basic, undeniable fact of reality. It tells us we have a real enemy. But it never tells us to go hunting for demons. It tells us to put on the armor of God, stand our ground, and keep our eyes entirely fixed on Jesus.

Scripture Snapshot Ephesians 6:11–12: "Put on the full armor of God, so that you can take your stand against the devil's schemes. For our struggle is not against flesh and blood, but against the rulers, against the authorities, against the powers of this dark world and against the spiritual forces of evil in the heavenly realms."

Paul tells the church in Ephesus a hard truth: the annoying person at work, the politician you hate, and your frustrating spouse are not your real enemies. They are flesh and blood. The real enemy is unseen. There is a coordinated, intelligent spiritual force actively scheming against your faith. But notice Paul's strategy. He doesn't say "go attack." He says "take your stand." The posture of a Christian is confident defense based on an already won war.

Say It Out Loud (One Sentence) I have a real spiritual enemy, but he is a defeated rebel whose only weapon is deception.

Common Confusions Confusion #1: People turn into angels when they die. (They don't; angels and humans are entirely different orders of creation). Confusion #2: Satan is God's equal opposite—a dark god fighting a light god. (He is not; Satan is a created being with severe limits).

The Tuesday Payoff You wake up on Tuesday morning with a heavy, irrational sense of despair and the recurring thought: *You are a fraud, and God has finally given up on you.* If you only view the world through a psychological lens, you might just assume you need more coffee or a new therapist. But if you understand spiritual warfare, you recognize that thought as an active, external lie from the enemy—a "flaming arrow." You don't have to spiral into panic. You simply hold up the shield of faith, remind yourself of what God's Word actually says about your justification, and go to work.

Lane 2 — Depth (30 minutes)

Define the Terms Satan - "The Adversary." The chief of the fallen angels. He is a creature, not a creator. He is not omniscient (all-knowing) or omnipresent (everywhere). Principalities and Powers - Biblical language for the organized, hierarchical structure of the demonic realm. Discernment - The Spirit-given ability to distinguish between truth and error, and between the voice of God and the deception of the enemy.

Build the Doctrine (Scripture-forward)

Angels Are Servants, Not Fluffy Mascots Culture has reduced angels to chubby babies with harps or beautiful women with bird wings. In the Bible, angels are terrifying warriors. Whenever an angel appears to a human, the first thing they have to say is, "Do not be afraid," because the human is usually curled up in a ball on the ground.

Key texts: Hebrews 1:14; Psalm 91:11

The writer of Hebrews asks, "Are not all angels ministering spirits sent to serve those who will inherit salvation?" God uses them to protect, deliver messages, and execute His judgments. They are powerful, but they are servants. We are strictly forbidden from worshiping them or praying to them (Revelation 22:8-9).

The Enemy is Real but Restricted Satan is real, and he hates you because you bear the image of the God he despises. But we must never engage in "dualism"—the idea that God and Satan are locked in a tight, 50/50 arm-wrestling match for the universe.

Key texts: Job 1:12; Colossians 2:15

In the book of Job, Satan cannot touch Job without God's explicit permission. Satan is a dog on a leash, entirely subject to God's sovereign boundaries. Furthermore, at the cross, Jesus completely disarmed the spiritual powers (Colossians 2:15). Satan is a defeated enemy who knows his time is short. He is dangerous, like a cornered animal, but the outcome of the war is not in question.

The Primary Weapon is the Lie We often expect spiritual warfare to look like a horror movie: spinning heads and flying furniture. But Jesus called Satan the "father of lies" (John 8:44). The enemy's primary strategy is not possession; it is deception.

Key texts: 2 Corinthians 11:14; 1 Peter 5:8

Satan "masquerades as an angel of light" (2 Corinthians 11:14). He twists the truth just enough to make disobedience look reasonable. He tells you that your sin isn't a big deal, or conversely, that your sin is too big for God to forgive. Peter warns us to be alert because the devil prowls like a roaring lion. Lions hunt the isolated, the weak, and the distracted. Spiritual warfare is largely a battle for what you believe in your mind.

BOX - What This Is NOT Saying We are NOT saying Christians can be demon-possessed; the Holy Spirit cannot share a residence with a demon. We are NOT saying every temptation is directly from a demon; our own fallen flesh generates plenty of sin on its own (James 1:14). We are NOT saying we should speak directly to the devil or taunt him; we submit to God and resist the devil.

BOX - Where Christians Differ Evangelicals agree on the reality of the spiritual realm. The difference is in emphasis. Some traditions (Pentecostal/Charismatic) emphasize active, vocal "deliverance ministries" and frequent binding of demons. Other traditions (Reformed/Mainline) emphasize that standard discipleship, preaching the Word, and normal church discipline are the primary means of spiritual warfare. Both agree that Christ has the ultimate victory.

Lane 3 — Deep Dive (Optional)

The Objection You're Already Thinking "I've lived my whole life without ever seeing an angel or a demon. Doesn't all this talk about the supernatural just sound like medieval superstition?"

The Best Answer It is completely understandable to feel skeptical if you've never experienced anything overtly supernatural. But remember the context you live in. You live in a post-Enlightenment, highly secularized, affluent Western culture.

If the enemy's primary goal is to keep people away from Jesus, his strategy will adapt to his environment. In parts of the world where animism and spirit-worship are common, the enemy uses overt, terrifying demonic displays to keep people in bondage through fear. But in the modern West, if the enemy manifested overtly, it would actually backfire—it would prove the spiritual realm is real and drive people to the church.

The smartest strategy for the enemy in our culture is to stay completely hidden and convince us he doesn't exist. He keeps us anesthetized with streaming services, political outrage, and career anxiety. Why use a dramatic demonic possession when an iPhone addiction accomplishes the exact same goal of keeping a soul distracted from its Creator?

Historical Lens In 1527, Martin Luther wrote the most famous hymn of the Reformation, *A Mighty Fortress Is Our God*. The third verse directly addresses spiritual warfare: "And though this world, with devils filled, should threaten to undo us, we will not fear, for God hath willed his truth to triumph through us." Luther famously threw an inkwell at the devil in his study. The early Protestants didn't ignore the spiritual realm; they simply believed the gospel was infinitely stronger than it.

Real-Life Translation Many Christians have a highly distorted view of spiritual warfare. They blame every inconvenience on demons—a flat tire, a bad cold, or a disagreement at church. This is dangerous because it removes personal responsibility and basic common sense.

True spiritual discernment is much quieter, and much harder. It is recognizing when a perfectly normal conversation subtly shifts into gossip. It is noticing when a legitimate desire for career success slowly morphs into an idol that destroys your family. It is catching the subtle lie that your worth is based on your performance. That is the real frontline of the spiritual war, and you fight it by soaking your mind so thoroughly in the truth of Scripture that a lie feels instantly out of place.

Midlife Module - This Doctrine at 48 You are 48, and you are cynical. You've seen the charismatic extremes of "spiritual warfare" in the 90s, where people were rebuking demons of gluttony and claiming everything was a curse. You reacted by swinging hard the other way, basically adopting a secular worldview with a Jesus bumper sticker.

But lately, the cynicism feels heavy. You are recognizing a darkness in the culture—and in your own heart—that psychology and sociology can't fully explain. At 48, it is time to reclaim a sober, biblical view of the unseen realm. You don't have to become weird or shout at the devil. You just have to wake up. You have an enemy who wants your marriage to fail and your kids to drift. The response isn't paranoia; the response is to quietly put on the armor of God every morning, pray fiercely for your family, and stop fighting flesh and blood.

Practice + Prayer

This Week's Practice (3–7 minutes) The Armor Audit. Read Ephesians 6:10–18. Notice that almost every piece of the armor is defensive, and almost every piece is tied to truth, righteousness, and the gospel. Pick the one piece of armor you feel you are currently missing (e.g., the belt of truth, because you are believing lies about yourself) and ask God to secure it on you today.

Prayer (100–160 words) God, open my eyes to the reality of the world I live in. Forgive me for ignoring the spiritual battle and fighting the wrong enemies. When I am tempted to attack the people who frustrate me, remind me that they are flesh and blood, and my real enemy is unseen. Thank You that Jesus Christ publicly defeated the powers of darkness on the cross. I do not have to live in fear. I ask for the protection of Your angels over my home, my mind, and my family. Expose the subtle lies the enemy is whispering to me today, and give me the strength to crush those lies with the truth of Your Word. Amen.

<u>Reflection</u>

Solo (3 prompts)

1. Which extreme do you naturally lean toward: treating demons like they don't exist, or blaming them for everything?

2. What is the most common, subtle lie you find yourself believing about God or yourself when you are tired?

3. How does knowing that Satan is a created, severely limited being (not an evil version of God) lower your anxiety?

Small Group (3 prompts + 1 hard question)

1. Read Ephesians 6:11–12. How would it change your approach to a difficult person if you genuinely viewed them as a captive of the enemy, rather than the enemy itself?

2. Discuss the C.S. Lewis quote about the two extremes (disbelief vs. unhealthy obsession). Where do you see these extremes in the church today?

3. Why is it significant that almost all the "armor of God" is defensive, and the only offensive weapon is the Word of God?

Hard Question: Are you currently blaming "the devil" for a sinful habit that you actually just refuse to give up?

<u>Close</u>

One Sentence Recap: The unseen spiritual realm is real, but we are commanded to stand firm in the victory of Christ rather than obsessing over the enemy.

If You Only Remember One Thing: The enemy's primary weapon isn't possession; it is subtle deception. Fight lies with the truth.

Next Week Preview: This brings us to the hardest question in theology. Next week, we look at Evil and Suffering—if God is good and in control, why does it hurt so much?

Scripture References Used Job 1:12 Psalm 91:11 John 8:44 Ephesians 6:10–18 Colossians 2:15 Hebrews 1:14 1 Peter 5:8 2 Corinthians 11:14 Revelation 22:8–9

<u>My Thoughts & Notes – What Did I Take From This?</u>

WEEK 15 — EVIL AND SUFFERING

CORE QUESTION: IF GOD is perfectly good and completely powerful, why is the world so full of horrific pain, and why doesn't He stop it?

Why this matters: Because shallow answers to this question will either turn you into a cynic who hates God, or a religious fake who suppresses their own grief.

At a Glance (One Page)

Big Idea: The Bible does not offer a neat philosophical equation to solve the problem of evil; instead, it offers a Savior who entered the agonizing depths of human suffering to defeat it from the inside.

Anchor Text: Genesis 50:20; Romans 8:18–28

We believe...: God is neither the author nor the approver of evil, but He sovereignly permits it in a fallen world, promising to ultimately defeat it and work through it for the eternal good of His people.

Key Words (3): Theodicy - The theological attempt to justify God's goodness and power in a world where evil exists. Moral Evil - Evil caused by the sinful choices of human beings (murder, betrayal, theft). Natural Evil - Suffering caused by the broken state of the physical world (hurricanes, cancer, earthquakes).

The One Mistake People Make: Trying to defend God by offering hollow, Christian platitudes to people who are in the middle of excruciating pain.

Choose Your Lane: Lane 1 / Lane 2 / Lane 3

This Week's Practice: The Ministry of Presence.

This Week's Prayer: Father, I do not understand why the world has to hurt this much. I do not understand why You allow certain tragedies. My mind demands an explanation, but I know an explanation wouldn't actually heal my heart anyway. When the pain is overwhelming, keep me from running away from You. Remind me that You are not a distant observer of human suffering; You are the God who wept at a tomb and bled on a cross. Help me to trust You in the dark, and give me the endurance to wait for the day when You make all things new. Amen.

Lane 1 — Clarity (10 minutes)

The Bottom Line The problem of evil is the single greatest intellectual and emotional obstacle to the Christian faith. If God is good, He would want to stop evil. If God is all-powerful, He could stop evil. But evil exists. Therefore, skeptics argue, God must be either weak or cruel. But the Bible offers a third option: God has a morally sufficient reason for permitting evil that our finite minds cannot fully grasp yet. More importantly, Christianity is the only worldview where God does not remain safe in heaven, but steps into the horror of our world to suffer alongside us.

Scripture Snapshot Genesis 50:20: "You intended to harm me, but God intended it for good to accomplish what is now being done, the saving of many lives."

Joseph is speaking to his brothers, who sold him into slavery, leading to decades of false imprisonment and suffering. Joseph doesn't excuse their evil. He says, "You intended to harm me." They are guilty. But he doesn't believe his suffering was random.

Overarching their evil intentions was God's redemptive intention. God didn't cause the brothers' sin, but He judo-flipped it to save an entire region from starvation.

Say It Out Loud (One Sentence) God is not the author of evil, but He is the master at bringing ultimate good out of unimaginable pain.

Common Confusions Confusion #1: God causes tragedies specifically to teach us a lesson. Confusion #2: If we suffer, it means we must have done something wrong to deserve it (the Karma myth).

The Tuesday Payoff You are sitting at a funeral for someone you loved deeply. People mean well, but their comments are infuriating: "Heaven gained another angel," or "God just needed them more." If your theology forces you to pretend everything is fine, you will bury your grief and it will destroy you from the inside out. But biblical theology gives you permission to be devastated. You can weep, be angry at death, and hate the brokenness of the world, while simultaneously holding onto the fierce hope that God will one day right every wrong.

Lane 2 — Depth (30 minutes)

Define the Terms Fallen World - The biblical reality that all of creation is corrupted and broken because of humanity's original rebellion against God. Free Will Defense - The theological argument that for love to be genuine, God had to give humans the real ability to choose, which opened the door to the possibility of evil. Lament - A passionate expression of grief or sorrow directed toward God.

Build the Doctrine (Scripture-forward)

God Did Not Create Evil God created a world that was "very good" (Genesis 1). Evil is not a substance that God manufactured. Evil is a parasite. It is a corruption of something good. Blindness is the lack of sight; cold is the absence of heat; evil is the distortion of God's good design.

Key texts: James 1:13–14

James is explicitly clear: "When tempted, no one should say, 'God is tempting me.' For God cannot be tempted by evil, nor does he tempt anyone." God is light. He does not engineer wickedness. The origin of moral evil lies in the rebellion of creatures (angels and humans) who chose themselves over their Creator.

The Cross is God's Answer When people ask, "Why doesn't God do something about the evil in the world?" the Christian points to a bloody hill in Jerusalem and says, "He did."

Key texts: Romans 8:32; 1 Peter 2:24

God did not sit in the bleachers while humanity bled on the field. He became a human. He experienced betrayal, injustice, physical torture, and execution. If you are suffering, you might doubt God's wisdom, but you can never doubt His empathy. The cross proves that whatever God's reason is for allowing suffering to continue for a time, it is not because He doesn't love us. He proved His love by absorbing the worst of the world's evil into Himself.

The Promise of the End The Christian answer to suffering is fundamentally forward-looking. God has promised to eradicate evil permanently, but He is being incredibly patient so that more people have time to repent before the final judgment.

Key texts: Romans 8:18; Revelation 21:4

Paul suffered shipwrecks, beatings, and starvation. Yet he writes, "I consider that our present sufferings are not worth comparing with the glory that will be revealed in us" (Romans 8:18). He isn't minimizing the pain; he is maximizing the future. The Bible ends with the absolute guarantee that God will wipe every tear from our eyes, and death, mourning, and pain will be destroyed forever (Revelation 21:4).

BOX - What This Is NOT Saying We are NOT saying you should easily understand or "be thankful for" a tragedy while you are bleeding. We are NOT saying evil is an illusion or a matter of perspective; it is real, objective, and horrific. We are NOT saying Job's friends were right; sometimes suffering has absolutely nothing to do with personal sin.

BOX - Where Christians Differ Philosophers and theologians have argued for centuries over *how* to defend God's goodness (Theodicy). Reformed theology leans heavily on God's sovereignty, arguing that even the worst evil is part of a secret, ultimate plan for God's glory. Arminian/Open theology leans heavily on human freedom, arguing that God takes huge risks to allow real love, resulting in real tragedy. The tension is unavoidable, but all agree that Jesus is the final answer.

Lane 3 — Deep Dive (Optional)

The Objection You're Already Thinking "But a lot of suffering isn't caused by human choices. What about tsunamis, childhood leukemia, and earthquakes? How is that anyone's fault?"

The Best Answer This is the distinction between *moral* evil (what we do to each other) and *natural* evil (what the planet does to us).

The biblical narrative is that humanity was given dominion over the earth as God's representatives. When humanity rebelled against the King in Genesis 3, the entire domain was fractured. The curse wasn't just spiritual; it was deeply physical. Paul says in Romans 8 that "creation was subjected to frustration" and is currently "groaning as in the pains of childbirth."

We live in a deeply unnatural, broken ecosystem. Disease and natural disasters are the physical symptoms of a cosmos that is out of alignment with its Creator. God permits this broken state to persist for a time to show the absolute horror of life separated from Him, but He promises to redeem not just our souls, but the physical earth itself.

Historical Lens After the Holocaust, Jewish and Christian theologians alike wrestled with how to speak about God. Elie Wiesel, a survivor, wrote of watching a young boy hang on a gallows in the camp. Someone behind him asked, "Where is God now?" Wiesel heard a voice within him answer, "Where is He? Here He is—He is hanging here on this gallows." The only theology that survives the camps is a theology of a God who suffers with us.

Real-Life Translation When someone you love is experiencing catastrophic pain, your natural instinct is to try and fix it with theology. You want to offer a Bible verse or a philosophical explanation to make it make sense.

Don't do it. When Job's life fell apart, his friends came and sat with him in silence for seven days. That was the best thing they did. The moment they opened their mouths to try and explain *why* God was doing it, they made it worse. Theology is what you build *before* the storm hits so your house doesn't collapse. But *during* the storm, people don't need a lecture on the sovereignty of God. They need you to sit in the ashes with them, hold their hand, and weep.

Midlife Module - This Doctrine at 50 You are 50. You just got the phone call that your mom passed away after a brutal, degrading decline with dementia. For three years, you watched a brilliant woman lose her mind, her dignity, and her memories. There is no neat, tidy bow to tie around this. It was just awful.

If you grew up with a shallow, "victorious" Christianity, this experience will shatter your faith because it doesn't fit the formula. But robust, historic theology holds you here. It gives you the Psalms of lament, giving you permission to scream at the sky. It reminds you that Jesus wept at the tomb of Lazarus, even knowing He was about to raise him. At midlife, you realize that faith isn't the absence of grief; faith is the grit to carry your grief directly to the Man of Sorrows.

Practice + Prayer

This Week's Practice (3–7 minutes) The Ministry of Presence. Think of someone in your circle who is currently going through a season of deep suffering or grief. Do not send them a Bible verse or a platitude. Send them a text that simply says: "I know things are incredibly heavy right now. You don't need to reply to this, but I want you to know I am thinking about you and I am so sorry."

Prayer (100–160 words) God, the pain in this world is often too heavy to carry. I look at the news, or I look at my own family, and I feel overwhelmed by the brokenness. I don't understand Your timing, and I don't understand Your ways. But I look at the cross, and I know that You are not indifferent. You did not stay safe in heaven. Thank You, Jesus, for taking the absolute worst of human evil upon Yourself. Give me the strength to endure the trials in my own life without becoming bitter. Make me a safe place for others who are grieving, keeping my mouth shut and my heart open. I am placing all my hope in the day when You finally make all things new. Amen.

Reflection

Solo (3 prompts)

1. What is the most unhelpful, cliché thing a Christian has ever said to you when you were hurting?

2. Why does the fact that Jesus suffered physical torture and betrayal make Him more trustworthy to you?

3. Have you ever experienced a time when a terrible event in your life was ultimately used by God to produce something beautiful?

Small Group (3 prompts + 1 hard question)

1. Read Romans 8:18–28. How does Paul balance the brutal reality of current suffering with the hope of future glory?

2. Discuss the difference between defending God philosophically and trusting God relationally. Which one is more important when you are actually in pain?

3. Why are Christians often so uncomfortable with unresolved grief, and why do we rush to "fix" people with platitudes?

Hard Question: Are you currently using a past tragedy as an excuse to hold onto a bitter, cynical heart toward God?

Close

One Sentence Recap: God sovereignly permits evil in a fallen world, but He entered into our suffering through Christ to ultimately defeat it and redeem it.

If You Only Remember One Thing: The cross proves that whatever God's reason is for allowing your pain, it isn't because He doesn't love you.

Next Week Preview: This completes Part 2. Next week, we start Part 3 by looking at Creation and Humanity—why did God make the world, and what exactly are you?

Scripture References Used Genesis 50:20 Job 38–42 Romans 8:18–28 Romans 8:32 James 1:13–14 1 Peter 2:24 Revelation 21:4

My Thoughts & Notes – What Did I Take From This?

When an old video game console stopped working, our entire generation shared the exact same diagnostic strategy: pull out the cartridge, blow the dust out of it, shove it back in, and hit the reset button. We didn't throw the game away; we knew the original hardware was basically good, it just got corrupted.

Part 3 is about God's original hardware. We are looking at why the physical world matters, what it actually means to be made in the Image of God, and why our souls often feel so glitchy. We will explore how to navigate the exhausting realities of our physical bodies, our daily work, and the digital noise that is constantly trying to rewrite our programming.

Week 16 — Creation and Why Origins Matter

Core Question: Does it really matter exactly how God created the world, as long as we believe He did it?

Why this matters: Because if the universe is just a cosmic accident, your life has no inherent purpose; but if you were intentionally created, you are deeply valued and accountable to the Creator.

At a Glance (One Page)

Big Idea: The biblical doctrine of creation isn't primarily a science textbook designed to win debates; it is the radical declaration that the universe has an Author, matter is good, and you are not an accident.

Anchor Text: Genesis 1:1–2; Colossians 1:16–17

We believe...: God created the entire universe out of nothing by the power of His word, and all He made was originally very good.

Key Words (3): Creation *Ex Nihilo* - Latin for "out of nothing." God did not rearrange pre-existing materials; He spoke reality into existence. Materialism - The philosophical belief that the physical world is all that exists, and there is no spiritual realm or Creator. Pantheism - The belief that God *is* the universe (like the "Force"), rather than the distinct Creator *of* the universe.

The One Mistake People Make: Getting so obsessed with debating the timeline of Genesis 1 that they completely miss the massive theological realities the chapter is actually teaching.

Choose Your Lane: Lane 1 / Lane 2 / Lane 3

This Week's Practice: The Material Gratitude.

This Week's Prayer: Father, I confess that I often take the physical world for granted. I live disconnected from the dirt, the trees, and the sky You formed. Thank You that the universe is not a cold, empty accident. Thank You for making it, and thank You for making me. Forgive me for treating my life as if it belongs to me. You are the Author; I am the creation. Help me to live today in a way that honors the One who spoke me into existence. Amen.

Lane 1 — Clarity (10 minutes)

The Bottom Line For decades, the church has treated Genesis 1 primarily as ammunition for a science debate. But the original audience wasn't asking questions about carbon dating or quantum physics; they were ancient Israelites asking, "Who is in charge of the world, and what is our place in it?" Genesis answers loudly: God is in charge. He didn't fight other gods to make the world. He didn't make the world out of His own body. He simply spoke, and reality obeyed.

Scripture Snapshot Colossians 1:16–17: "For in him all things were created: things in heaven and on earth, visible and invisible, whether thrones or powers or rulers or authorities; all things have been created through him and for him. He is before all things, and in him all things hold together."

Paul places Jesus squarely at the center of the creation event. Creation wasn't just the Father's project; it was entirely Trinitarian. Notice the profound shift in perspective Paul offers: you weren't just created *by* Him; you were created *for* Him.

The universe exists as a theater for the glory of Christ. You are not the main character of the universe, and ironically, realizing that is incredibly freeing.

Say It Out Loud (One Sentence) Because God created the universe out of nothing, everything I have is a gift, and I am ultimately accountable to Him.

Common Confusions Confusion #1: Faith and science are natural enemies that always contradict each other. Confusion #2: The physical world (dirt, bodies, food) is "unspiritual," and only our souls matter.

The Tuesday Payoff You are staring at a massive, complex spreadsheet at work on a Tuesday. The sheer volume of data is exhausting. If the physical world is just an accident of time and chance, your work organizing that data is ultimately meaningless. But if God is the Creator who ordered the cosmos—bringing structure out of chaos—then your attempt to bring order and structure to your corner of the world is actually a **<u>Reflection</u>** of His nature. Good theology turns boring Tuesday tasks into acts of worship.

Lane 2 — Depth (30 minutes)

Define the Terms Sovereignty of Creation - Because God made everything, He owns everything, and He alone has the right to set the rules for it. Goodness of Creation - Matter is not inherently evil. God looked at the physical dirt, water, and animals and called them "good." The Fall - The event (Genesis 3) where humanity rebelled, fracturing the originally good creation and bringing death into the world.

Build the Doctrine (Scripture-forward)

God the Independent Creator Every ancient pagan myth about creation involved gods fighting each other, or a god killing a monster and using its corpse to build the earth. The gods of the ancient world were part of the universe. The God of the Bible is entirely outside of it.

Key texts: Genesis 1:1; Psalm 33:6–9

"In the beginning God created the heavens and the earth" (Genesis 1:1). There is no struggle. There is no rival god. There is no raw material. "By the word of the Lord the heavens were made... For he spoke, and it came to be" (Psalm 33:6, 9). God's absolute power over creation establishes His absolute authority over our lives.

The Physical World is Good A heresy called Gnosticism has infected the church for centuries. It teaches that the spiritual world is "good" and the physical world (bodies, food, nature) is "bad." The Bible fiercely rejects this.

Key texts: Genesis 1:31; 1 Timothy 4:4

God looked at everything He had made—the dirt, the animals, the physical bodies of Adam and Eve—and declared it "very good." Paul later warns Timothy about false teachers who forbid people to eat certain foods, saying, "For everything God created is good, and nothing is to be rejected if it is received with thanksgiving." God loves the physical world. He invented it.

Creation Gives Us Our "Why" If we evolved purely through blind, unguided natural selection, there is no objective meaning to human life. We are just highly developed biological machines waiting to expire. You have to invent your own meaning.

Key texts: Revelation 4:11

The elders in heaven worship God with these words: "You are worthy, our Lord and God... for you created all things, and by your will they were created and have their being." The doctrine of creation provides the ultimate "why" for human existence. We exist by His will, and we exist for His glory. We don't have to carry the crushing burden of inventing our own purpose.

BOX - What This Is NOT Saying We are NOT saying science is evil; science is the glorious study of how God's creation actually works. We are NOT saying the physical world isn't currently broken by sin; it is groaning for redemption (Romans 8). We are NOT saying Christians must all agree on the exact age of the earth to be saved.

BOX - Where Christians Differ The exact timeline of Genesis 1 is highly debated.

1. Young Earth Creationists believe God created the universe in six literal 24-hour days, making the earth roughly 6,000 to 10,000 years old.

2. Old Earth Creationists believe the "days" of Genesis are long geological eras, aligning with the mainstream scientific consensus of an ancient universe.

3. Theistic Evolutionists (or Evolutionary Creationists) believe God used the mechanism of evolution to bring about life over billions of years. Broad evangelicalism includes orthodox, Bible-believing Christians in all three camps.

Lane 3 — Deep Dive (Optional)

The Objection You're Already Thinking "How can I take the Bible seriously if Genesis 1 sounds like a myth and contradicts modern scientific timelines?"

The Best Answer It is crucial to understand the genre of Genesis 1. It is not written like a modern, 21st-century science textbook. Moses wasn't writing for scientists; he was writing for a group of former slaves wandering in a desert who had just spent 400 years immersed in Egyptian mythology.

The Egyptians worshipped the sun, the moon, and the river. Genesis 1 is a brilliant, highly structured theological polemic against those false gods. Moses is essentially saying: *You know the sun god Ra? My God created the sun on day four to be a lamp. You know the sea monsters you fear? My God created them as pets.*

Genesis 1 is teaching us *who* created the world and *why* He did it. It is not primarily concerned with answering the modern, Western question of *how long* it took. You can hold to a high, infallible view of Scripture and still recognize that the text is using poetic, ancient Near Eastern structure to communicate absolute truth about the Creator.

Historical Lens In 1925, the Scopes "Monkey Trial" turned the creation/evolution debate into a massive cultural spectacle in America. It forced many Christians into a defensive, anti-intellectual posture that lasted for decades, treating scientists as the enemy. But historically, many of the greatest pioneers of modern science (Kepler, Newton, Boyle) were devout Christians who believed that because a rational God created the universe, the universe could be rationally studied.

Real-Life Translation Many Gen Xers grew up in an environment where questioning the age of the earth was treated as a denial of the gospel itself. It was a litmus test for whether you really loved Jesus. As a result, many people quietly walked away from the faith in college because they couldn't reconcile their biology textbook with their youth pastor's demands.

We need to lower the temperature on the timeline debate and raise the temperature on the theology of creation. Whether God took six literal days or six billion years, the breathtaking reality remains the same: the universe is not an accident. God made it, God sustains it, and God is coming back to redeem it.

Midlife Module - This Doctrine at 48 You are sitting on your back porch on a Saturday morning. You are 48. You have spent the last 25 years building a career, accumulating assets, and trying to carve out a legacy. But lately, you feel a lingering sense of futility. If you get hit by a bus tomorrow, your company replaces you in a week. Does any of this actually matter?

The doctrine of creation speaks directly to midlife futility. If materialism is true, your life is a brief, meaningless spark in a cold universe. But if creation is true, you are part of a deliberate story. Your value isn't based on your corporate utility or your bank account; it is rooted in the fact that the Author of the cosmos intentionally placed you here. You can exhale. You don't have to justify your existence.

Practice + Prayer

This Week's Practice (3–7 minutes) The Material Gratitude. This week, pick one completely ordinary physical thing you enjoy (a hot shower, the taste of coffee, the smell of a campfire). While you are experiencing it, pause and thank God specifically for inventing that physical sensation. Fight the Gnostic lie that only "spiritual" things please God.

Prayer (100–160 words) God, You are the Maker of heaven and earth. You spoke, and the galaxies were formed. I confess that I get easily distracted by the debates of this world and miss the breathtaking reality of Your power. Thank You for making a physical world that is good, beautiful, and complex. Forgive me for worshiping the created things instead of the Creator. When I feel insignificant, remind me that I am not an accident of nature, but a deliberate creation of Your mind. Help me to steward the physical body, the resources, and the world You have entrusted to me. Amen.

<u>**Reflection**</u>

Solo (3 prompts)

1. Did you grow up in a church culture that treated science as an enemy? How did that affect your faith?

2. Why is the idea of "Creation out of nothing" (no rival gods, no pre-existing struggle) so important for trusting God's absolute power?

3. Do you tend to view your physical body and physical pleasures as inherently "less holy" than spiritual activities like prayer?

Small Group (3 prompts + 1 hard question)

1. Read Colossians 1:16–17. What is the difference between believing you were created *by* God, and believing you were created *for* God?

2. Discuss the cultural impact of "materialism" (the belief that only the physical world exists). How does this belief change the way people view human value?

3. How can we maintain a firm belief in the biblical account of creation without turning the debate over the timeline into a toxic culture war?

Hard Question: Are you treating the earth and your physical body poorly, forgetting that God called the material world "very good"?

<u>**Close**</u>

One Sentence Recap: God created the entire universe out of nothing by the power of His word, meaning reality is deliberate, matter is good, and we belong to Him.

If You Only Remember One Thing: You are not a highly evolved accident; you are a deliberate creation living in a universe built for the glory of Christ.

Next Week Preview: Next week we zoom in on the pinnacle of creation—humanity. What does it actually mean to be made in the "image of God"?

Scripture References Used Genesis 1:1–2 Genesis 1:31 Psalm 33:6–9 Colossians 1:16–17 1 Timothy 4:4 Revelation 4:11

<u>**My Thoughts & Notes – What Did I Take From This?**</u>

WEEK 17 — IMAGE OF GOD: DIGNITY AND PERSONHOOD

CORE QUESTION: WHERE DOES human value actually come from in a world that only seems to value productivity, wealth, and youth?

Why this matters: Because if human value is based on what we can do, our worth will disappear when we fail or age; but if our value is based on the image of God, it is infinite and untouchable.

At a Glance (One Page)

Big Idea: Every single human being, from conception to final breath, possesses profound dignity and worth strictly because they are made in the image of the Creator, regardless of their utility or capacity.

Anchor Text: Genesis 1:26–27; Psalm 8:3–5

We believe...: Humanity is the pinnacle of God's creation, uniquely made in His image to reflect His character and represent His rule, granting all human life inherent and equal dignity.

Key Words (3): *Imago Dei* - Latin for "Image of God." The biblical truth that humans uniquely reflect the Creator. Inherent Dignity - Value that is built into your nature by God; it cannot be earned, and it cannot be erased. Utility - The cultural lie that a person's value is based on their usefulness, capacity, or contribution to society.

The **The One Mistake People Make:** Treating the people they disagree with politically or socially as less than human, forgetting that even their worst enemy bears the fingerprints of God.

Choose Your Lane: Lane 1 / Lane 2 / Lane 3

This Week's Practice: The Dignity Check.

This Week's Prayer: Father, I live in a culture that treats people like commodities. We judge each other by what we produce, how we look, and how much money we make. I confess I often judge myself by those exact same ruthless standards. Wash my mind with the truth of Genesis 1. Remind me that my value was settled the moment You created me in Your image. Give me the grace to treat every person I interact with today—even the ones who frustrate me—with the dignity that bears Your name. Amen.

Lane 1 — Clarity (10 minutes)

The Bottom Line In the ancient world, only the king was considered the "image" of the gods. Everyone else was just cheap labor. Genesis 1 dropped a philosophical nuclear bomb on that worldview. It declared that *every* human being—male and female, rich and poor, healthy and sick—carries the royal stamp of the Creator. Your value is not tied to your resume, your mental capacity, or your physical strength. Your value is tied to your design.

Scripture Snapshot Genesis 1:26–27: "Then God said, 'Let us make mankind in our image, in our likeness, so that they may rule over the fish in the sea and the birds in the sky...' So God created mankind in his own image, in the image of God he created them; male and female he created them."

God pauses before creating humanity. This isn't a casual addition to the animals; this is a deliberate, Trinitarian counsel ("Let *us* make"). He delegates royal authority to them. Notice that He explicitly includes both male and female as essential for reflecting His image. We are the mirrors meant to reflect God's character out into the world, and reflect the world's praises back to God.

Say It Out Loud (One Sentence) My worth is not determined by my productivity, but by the fact that I carry the image of my Creator.

Common Confusions Confusion #1: Being made in God's image means we look like God physically. (God is spirit; the image is about capacity and representation). Confusion #2: We lost the image of God completely when humanity sinned in the Fall.

The Tuesday Payoff You are at the grocery store on Tuesday evening. The cashier is painfully slow, entirely apathetic, and makes a mistake that costs you ten minutes. Your natural, culturally conditioned response is to view them as an obstacle, an annoyance, or a machine that isn't working right. But the *Imago Dei* hits the brakes on your frustration. That cashier is not a machine. They are an eternal soul, stamped with the image of the Sovereign God of the universe. Good theology forces you to treat annoying people with terrifying respect.

Lane 2 — Depth (30 minutes)

Define the Terms Representation - Like an ancient statue of a king placed in a distant territory, humans are placed on earth to represent God's rule and presence. Sanctity of Life - The belief that human life is sacred and untouchable because to destroy a human is to attack the image of God Himself. Depravity - The reality that while the image of God remains in us, it has been severely distorted and broken by sin.

Build the Doctrine (Scripture-forward)

Value Without Utility If human value comes from evolution, then the weak, the old, and the sick are a drain on the species. Only the strong survive. But the Bible flips the script. Value comes from the Creator, not the creature's capacity.

Key texts: Psalm 8:3–5; Proverbs 14:31

David looks at the massive universe and asks God, "What is mankind that you are mindful of them?" His answer: "You have made them a little lower than the angels and crowned them with glory and honor." A newborn baby with severe disabilities, an elderly man with advanced dementia, and a high-powered CEO all possess the exact same amount of glory and honor. "Whoever oppresses the poor shows contempt for their Maker" (Proverbs 14:31).

The Image is Broken, Not Erased When Adam and Eve sinned (the Fall), humanity did not stop being human. We didn't lose the image of God, but it was shattered, like a mirror dropped on a concrete floor. It still reflects light, but the **<u>Reflection</u>** is jagged and distorted.

Key texts: Genesis 9:6; James 3:9

Thousands of years after the Fall, God tells Noah that murder is punishable "for in the image of God has God made mankind" (Gen 9:6). In the New Testament, James writes about the tongue: "With it we praise our Lord and Father, and with it we curse human beings, who have been made in God's likeness" (James 3:9). You cannot worship God while verbally destroying a person who bears His broken image.

Jesus is the Perfect Image If we are broken mirrors, how do we know what the image of God is supposed to look like? We look at Jesus.

Key texts: Colossians 1:15; Romans 8:29

Paul calls Jesus "the image of the invisible God" (Colossians 1:15). Jesus is what humanity was always supposed to be. Salvation isn't just about escaping hell; it is the process of God sweeping up the broken pieces of our mirror and putting them back together. God's ultimate goal is to "conform us to the image of his Son" (Romans 8:29).

BOX - What This Is NOT Saying We are NOT saying humans are divine or "little gods." We are reflectors, not the source of light. We are NOT saying humanity is basically good; the image is deeply corrupted by sin. We are NOT saying animals don't matter (we are called to steward them), but they do not bear the image of God.

BOX - Where Christians Differ Not a major point of theological disagreement. All orthodox Christians affirm the *Imago Dei*. Where Christians sometimes differ is in the political and social application of this doctrine—debating exactly how the church should address systemic poverty, criminal justice, and human rights—but the foundation of human dignity is universally agreed upon.

Lane 3 — Deep Dive (Optional)

The Objection You're Already Thinking "If Christians believe every human has the image of God, why has the church been complicit in so many human rights abuses, racism, and slavery throughout history?"

The Best Answer This is a devastating critique, and the only honest response is repentance. Throughout history, Christians have frequently failed to live up to the massive demands of the *Imago Dei*. When we have engaged in racism, slavery, or abuse, we have operated in direct contradiction to our own Scriptures. We adopted the culture of the world instead of the theology of the Bible.

However, we must also recognize that the very concept of "human rights" is a uniquely Christian invention. In ancient Rome or Greece, there was no concept of universal human dignity. The strong crushed the weak, and it was considered a virtue. It was the explosive, biblical idea of the *Imago Dei* that eventually dismantled the Roman caste system, built the first hospitals, outlawed child sacrifice, and provided the moral foundation for the abolition of slavery. The church has often failed its own standard, but the Bible provided the only standard strong enough to save the world from itself.

Historical Lens In the 4th century, the Roman Empire regularly practiced "exposure"—abandoning unwanted infants (especially girls or the disabled) in the woods to die. The early Christians shocked the Roman world by going into the woods, rescuing the abandoned babies, and raising them as their own. They didn't do this because it was economically beneficial; they did it because their theology demanded that those babies were stamped with the image of the King.

Real-Life Translation We have an incredibly hard time separating who we *are* from what we *do*. If you ask a Gen Xer, "Who are you?", they will almost always answer with their job title. "I am a manager," "I am a nurse," "I am a stay-at-home mom."

The problem with defining yourself by your utility is that you will eventually lose your utility. You will retire. You will get sick. Your kids will move out. If your identity is tied to your production, your identity will collapse. The doctrine of the *Imago Dei* is the ultimate psychological safety net. It tells you that your worth was locked in stone by God before you ever answered an email or changed a diaper.

Midlife Module - This Doctrine at 52 You are 52, and you are sitting in a nursing home next to your father. He used to be a brilliant, capable man who could fix any engine and solve any problem. Now, vascular dementia has stolen his mind. He doesn't know your name. He cannot contribute to society. According to modern, secular logic, his life has lost its value.

But as you hold his frail hand, your theology catches you. You look at him and realize that his value has not dropped a single percentage point. His mind is broken, but his dignity is untouched. He is still the image of God. This doctrine gives you the strength to care for him with fierce honor, not because of what he can do, but because of who he is.

Practice + Prayer

This Week's Practice (3–7 minutes) The Dignity Check. Scroll through your social media feed or watch a political news segment. Find a person you profoundly disagree with—someone whose opinions make you angry. Pause and say out loud, "God created that person in His image, and Jesus Christ died for them." Notice how it kills the venom in your heart without requiring you to agree with their politics.

Prayer (100–160 words) God, thank You for the stunning reality that You created humanity to reflect Your glory. I confess that I often buy into the world's lie that my value is tied to my bank account, my appearance, or my success. Free me from the exhausting treadmill of trying to prove my worth. Forgive me for the times I have treated other people as obstacles, categories, or enemies, forgetting that they bear Your image. Give me the eyes of Christ to see the profound dignity in the poor, the weak, the unborn, and the elderly. When the mirror of my own life feels broken by sin, please conform me more and more into the image of Jesus. Amen.

<u>**Reflection**</u>

Solo (3 prompts)

1. If you suddenly lost your ability to work or produce tomorrow, what would happen to your sense of self-worth?

2. Which group of people in our society do you think is most often stripped of their *Imago Dei* and treated as less than human?

3. How does the truth that the image of God includes *both* male and female change how we view gender?

Small Group (3 prompts + 1 hard question)

1. Read Genesis 1:26–27. Why do you think God gave humanity "rule" over the earth immediately after declaring they were made in His image?

2. Discuss the difference between a culture that values "utility" (what you can do) versus a culture that values "dignity" (who you are).

3. How does James 3:9 challenge the way we speak about politicians, celebrities, or people on the internet?

Hard Question: Are you currently justifying treating someone terribly in your life because you believe their bad behavior removed their right to be treated with dignity?

<u>**Close**</u>

One Sentence Recap: Humanity is the pinnacle of God's creation, uniquely made in His image, granting all human life inherent, untouchable dignity.

If You Only Remember One Thing: Your value was settled the moment God created you; you do not have to exhaust yourself trying to earn it.

Next Week Preview: Next week we look at the tension between your body and your soul. You are not a ghost driving a meat machine.

Scripture References Used Genesis 1:26–27 Genesis 9:6 Psalm 8:3–5 Proverbs 14:31 Romans 8:29 Colossians 1:15 James 3:9

<u>**My Thoughts & Notes – What Did I Take From This?**</u>

Week 18 — Body and Soul: You Are Not a Machine

Core Question: Am I just a highly evolved biological computer, or is there a soul that survives the death of my body?

Why this matters: Because if you are only a body, your existence ends at the grave; but if you are only a soul, your physical health, your habits, and the material world don't actually matter.

At a Glance (One Page)

Big Idea: You are a deeply unified composite of a physical body and an eternal soul; God designed both, He cares about both, and He plans to resurrect both.

Anchor Text: Matthew 10:28; 1 Corinthians 6:19–20

We believe...: Human beings are created as a profound unity of material body and immaterial soul/spirit. The soul survives physical death, awaiting the final bodily resurrection.

Key Words (3): Soul (or Spirit) - The immaterial, eternal part of a human being that relates to God and survives physical death. Dualism (Heresy) - The false idea that the body is an evil prison and the soul is the "real," pure you trying to escape. Resurrection - The future promise that God will raise and glorify our physical bodies, not just leave us as floating spirits in heaven.

The One Mistake People Make: Thinking that the ultimate goal of Christianity is to "escape this physical world and go to heaven as a spirit," rather than the biblical promise of a new physical body on a new physical earth.

Choose Your Lane: Lane 1 / Lane 2 / Lane 3

This Week's Practice: The Sleep Audit.

This Week's Prayer: Father, I admit that I rarely think about how You designed me. I either ignore my body entirely, pushing it past its limits to get work done, or I obsess over it, making my physical appearance an idol. Forgive my imbalance. Thank You for crafting my physical body, and thank You for breathing an eternal soul into me. Help me to honor You with both today. Give me the wisdom to care for the temple You gave me, and the faith to trust You with the soul that will live forever. Amen.

Lane 1 — Clarity (10 minutes)

The Bottom Line Culture gives you two bad options for who you are. The secular world says you are just meat and chemicals; your thoughts are just electrical misfires in your brain, and when you die, you rot. The new-age world says you are pure spiritual energy temporarily trapped in a meat suit. The Bible rejects both. You are an integrated whole. You don't *have* a body; you *are* a body. You don't *have* a soul; you *are* a soul. God designed both to exist together.

Scripture Snapshot 1 Corinthians 6:19–20: "Do you not know that your bodies are temples of the Holy Spirit, who is in you, whom you have received from God? You are not your own; you were bought at a price. Therefore honor God with your bodies."

The Corinthian church thought that because their souls were saved, they could do whatever they wanted with their bodies (specifically regarding sexual immorality). Paul fiercely corrects them. God doesn't just buy your soul; He buys the whole package. The physical body is so sacred that the Holy Spirit chooses to use it as His actual temple on earth. What you do with your physical hands, eyes, and stomach is an inherently spiritual issue.

Say It Out Loud (One Sentence) God created me as a unified body and soul, meaning my physical habits and my spiritual health are deeply connected.

Common Confusions Confusion #1: When we die, we become angels. (We do not; human souls remain human souls). Confusion #2: Christianity is just about saving souls for eternity. (It is about redeeming the whole person—body and soul).

The Tuesday Payoff It's Tuesday morning. You are exhausted, highly irritable, and feeling completely disconnected from God. You feel guilty, assuming you must be experiencing a deep spiritual crisis. You try to pray, but you can't focus. But the reality is: you aren't in a spiritual crisis. You just slept three hours last night and drank four cups of coffee instead of eating breakfast. Because your body and soul are connected, physical exhaustion masquerades as spiritual depression. Sometimes the most spiritual thing you can do on a Tuesday isn't to read your Bible; it is to take a nap and honor the body God gave you.

Lane 2 — Depth (30 minutes)

Define the Terms Materialism - The secular belief that only the physical body exists. Gnosticism (Heresy) - The ancient belief that the material world (body) is evil and the spiritual world (soul) is good. Intermediate State - The period between your physical death (where your soul is with the Lord) and the future bodily resurrection.

Build the Doctrine (Scripture-forward)

The Breath and the Dirt We see the unity of body and soul right in the creation account. God doesn't just speak humans into existence from a distance. He gets His hands dirty.

Key texts: Genesis 2:7

"Then the Lord God formed a man from the dust of the ground and breathed into his nostrils the breath of life, and the man became a living being." Notice the two ingredients: dirt and divine breath. Material and immaterial. The man didn't become a living being until both were united. To be fully human requires both.

The Soul Survives Death While body and soul are designed to be together, death temporarily tears them apart. This is why death feels so unnatural and horrific—it is literally ripping apart what God joined together. Yet, the Bible is clear that the soul does not cease to exist when the heart stops beating.

Key texts: Matthew 10:28; Luke 23:43

Jesus tells His disciples, "Do not be afraid of those who kill the body but cannot kill the soul" (Matthew 10:28). The soul survives the violence of the world. On the cross, Jesus tells the thief next to Him, "Truly I tell you, today you will be with me in paradise" (Luke 23:43). The thief's body was thrown in a grave that evening, but his conscious soul was immediately in the presence of Christ.

The Final Goal is a New Body This is the most misunderstood doctrine in modern Christianity. The ultimate goal of the gospel is not to float in the clouds playing harps as disembodied spirits forever. Heaven is a temporary waiting room. The final goal is the bodily resurrection.

Key texts: Romans 8:23; Philippians 3:20–21

Paul writes that we "groan inwardly as we wait eagerly for our adoption to sonship, the redemption of our bodies" (Romans 8:23). God is going to raise your physical body from the grave, remove the curse of sin and disease from it, and place you on a newly restored, physical earth. God doesn't throw the body in the trash; He recycles and glorifies it.

BOX - What This Is NOT Saying We are NOT saying you have to have a perfect diet or a gym membership to be holy. We are NOT saying cremation is a sin; God has zero problem resurrecting a body that has turned to ashes. We are NOT saying mental health issues are always just spiritual problems; they are often deeply physical/chemical and require doctors.

BOX - Where Christians Differ There is an academic debate between "Dichotomy" (humans are two parts: body and soul/spirit) and "Trichotomy" (humans are three parts: body, soul, and spirit). Most broad evangelicals hold to Dichotomy, seeing "soul" and "spirit" as interchangeable words in Scripture for our immaterial nature. However, both sides agree that the immaterial part of us survives death.

Lane 3 — Deep Dive (Optional)

The Objection You're Already Thinking "If neuroscience can prove that my personality, memories, and emotions are just chemical reactions in my brain, doesn't that prove the 'soul' doesn't exist?"

The Best Answer Neuroscience has brilliantly mapped how the brain correlates to our thoughts and feelings. When you feel joy, a specific part of your brain lights up on a scan. But correlation is not causation.

Think of a musician playing a piano. The piano is the physical brain; the musician is the soul. If the piano gets damaged (like a brain injury or dementia), the music sounds terrible. The musician is trying to play the song, but the instrument is broken. A materialist looks at the broken piano and concludes, "See? The musician doesn't exist; it was just the piano all along." A Christian looks at it and says, "The instrument is currently broken, but the musician is still there."

Science can measure the physical hardware (the brain), but it cannot measure the software of consciousness, morality, and spiritual awareness (the soul). You are more than your chemistry.

Historical Lens In the early centuries of the church, many Greek philosophers mocked Christianity. To the Greeks, the physical body was a prison, and salvation meant your spirit finally escaping it. The idea that God would become a physical human (the Incarnation), and that He would resurrect physical bodies from the dead, was considered disgusting. Christianity completely revolutionized the Western world by declaring that the physical body matters deeply to God.

Real-Life Translation We tend to punish our bodies in the name of productivity. We brag about our lack of sleep. We fuel ourselves with caffeine and adrenaline to meet deadlines, treating our bodies like rental cars we are trying to run into the ground before returning them.

Then, when we inevitably burn out, experience severe anxiety, or face a moral failure, we wonder why God feels so distant. We forgot that we are a unified body and soul. You cannot abuse the physical temple of the Holy Spirit for a decade and expect your spiritual life to remain thriving. Honoring God with your body means resting. It means honoring your physical limits. It means recognizing that you are a finite creature, not an infinite machine.

Midlife Module - This Doctrine at 46 You are 46. You just tweaked your lower back by bending over to pick up a dropped pen. You look in the mirror and notice the gray hair and the changing shape of a body that doesn't bounce back like it did at 25. There is a quiet grief in watching your physical capacity decline.

If you believe you are just a body, aging is a tragedy because your expiration date is approaching. But biblical theology gives you incredible hope. This current body is just a tent (2 Corinthians 5:1). It is wearing out. That is frustrating, but it isn't final. You don't have to obsessively fight aging with surgeries or toxic diets. You can age with grace, knowing that this declining body is eventually going to be traded in for a resurrected, glorified one that will never experience pain again.

Practice + Prayer

This Week's Practice (3–7 minutes) The Sleep Audit. The most profoundly theological thing you can do for your body and soul this week is to acknowledge you are not God, and go to sleep. Pick one night this week to turn off all screens at 9:00 PM and get a full 8 hours of sleep. Recognize your physical limits as a gift, not a curse.

Prayer (100–160 words) God, thank You for the intricate, brilliant design of my physical body. And thank You for breathing a soul into me that will live forever. I confess that I frequently mistreat the body You gave me, either through neglect, stress, or idolatry. Forgive me for acting like a machine that never needs to stop. Remind me that Jesus took on a physical body, got tired, and slept on boats. Give me the wisdom to care for my physical and mental health. When my body breaks down, aches, or ages, keep me from despair. Fix my hope entirely on the promise of the resurrection, when You will make all things—including me—completely new. Amen.

<u>**Reflection**</u>

Solo (3 prompts)

1. Do you tend to lean towards Materialism (ignoring your soul) or Gnosticism (ignoring your body)?

2. Have you ever experienced a time when physical exhaustion directly caused you to struggle with your faith or morality?

3. How does knowing that your final destination is a *physical* resurrected body on a new earth change the way you think about "heaven"?

Small Group (3 prompts + 1 hard question)

1. Read 1 Corinthians 6:19–20. How does viewing your body as a "temple of the Holy Spirit" change the way you think about your daily physical habits?

2. Discuss the analogy of the "musician and the piano" regarding the soul and the brain. How does this help explain things like Alzheimer's or brain injuries?

3. Why do you think modern church culture often focuses only on saving souls, while completely ignoring the biblical promise of bodily resurrection?

Hard Question: Are you currently neglecting your physical health in a way that is actively damaging your ability to serve your family and honor God?

<u>**Close**</u>

One Sentence Recap: You are a deeply unified composite of a physical body and an eternal soul; God designed both, cares about both, and plans to resurrect both.

If You Only Remember One Thing: Sometimes the most spiritual thing you can do on a Tuesday is take a nap and honor the physical limits God gave you.

Next Week Preview: Next week we wade into one of the most explosive topics in our culture: identity, sex, and gender. How do we hold the line with truth and massive compassion?

Scripture References Used Genesis 2:7 Matthew 10:28 Luke 23:43 Romans 8:23 1 Corinthians 6:19–20 2 Corinthians 5:1 Philippians 3:20–21

<u>My Thoughts & Notes – What Did I Take From This?</u>

Week 19 — Identity, Sex, and Gender: Truth and Compassion

Core Question: How do we hold to the Bible's teaching on sex and gender without becoming the angry, culture-war Christians we grew up with?

Why this matters: Because abandoning God's design leaves people to the chaotic exhaustion of inventing their own identity, while weaponizing God's design drives broken people away from Jesus.

At a Glance (One Page)

Big Idea: God created sex and gender as deliberate, beautiful gifts to be expressed within His boundaries for our flourishing; our role is to fiercely trust His design while offering massive, Christ-like compassion to a confused world.

Anchor Text: Genesis 1:27; 1 Corinthians 6:9–11

We believe...: God intentionally created humanity as male and female, and He designed sexual intimacy to be expressed exclusively within the covenant of marriage between one man and one woman.

Key Words (3): Design - The biblical belief that our bodies and gender are not accidental or malleable, but intentionally crafted by God for a purpose. Identity - The core truth of who you are, which the Bible roots primarily in your relationship to God, not your sexual desires. Compassion - "To suffer with." The requirement to love and walk alongside broken people without compromising the truth of Scripture.

The One Mistake People Make: Thinking they have to choose between being perfectly loving (by affirming everything) or perfectly truthful (by being combative and mean). Jesus demands we be both.

Choose Your Lane: Lane 1 / Lane 2 / Lane 3

This Week's Practice: The Log-Removal Strategy.

This Week's Prayer: Father, I admit that I am tired of the culture war. It is exhausting, polarizing, and often lacks any resemblance to Jesus. Give me the courage to stand firmly on the truth of Your Word regarding how You designed men and women. Keep me from bowing to cultural pressure. But Father, simultaneously break my heart for the people around me. Strip away my self-righteousness. Remind me that I am a broken sinner saved entirely by grace. Give me the wisdom to speak truth with a tone of overwhelming love. Amen.

Lane 1 — Clarity (10 minutes)

The Bottom Line We are living through a cultural earthquake regarding sex and gender. The modern secular rule is: *Your deepest desires are your true identity, and you must alter your body and your life to fit those desires.* The biblical rule is the exact opposite: *Your body is a purposeful gift from God, and you must submit your desires to His design.* We cannot compromise what the Bible clearly teaches about male, female, and marriage. But if we deliver that truth with anger, mockery, or political tribalism, we have fundamentally failed the gospel.

Scripture Snapshot 1 Corinthians 6:9–11: "Or do you not know that wrongdoers will not inherit the kingdom of God? Do not be deceived: Neither the sexually immoral nor idolaters nor adulterers nor men who have sex with men... And that is what some of you were. But you were washed, you were sanctified, you were justified in the name of the Lord Jesus Christ."

Paul doesn't pull his punches on truth. He clearly lists sexual immorality—including homosexuality and adultery—as outside the kingdom of God. But look at verse 11: "And that is what some of you *were.*" The Corinthian church was full of people who had been saved out of those exact lifestyles. They weren't the enemy outside the church; they were the brothers and sisters inside the church. The gospel didn't cancel them; it washed them.

Say It Out Loud (One Sentence) God's design for sex and gender is good, and it requires us to hold the line of truth with a heart of deep compassion.

Common Confusions Confusion #1: Jesus never talked about homosexuality or gender, so He must not have cared. (He clearly affirmed the Genesis definition of male, female, and marriage in Matt. 19). Confusion #2: If you don't affirm someone's sexual choices, you must hate them.

The Tuesday Payoff You are at a neighborhood block party, and a couple you genuinely like introduces you to their teenager, who has recently transitioned. Inside, you feel the tension. The culture demands you applaud the transition. Your old religious background demands you start an argument. But Jesus offers a third way. You don't have to wave a flag, and you don't have to preach a sermon by the grill. You smile, introduce yourself, treat them with profound dignity, and begin the long, patient work of building a relationship where the gospel might eventually be heard. You can hold your convictions quietly and love your neighbor loudly.

Lane 2 — Depth (30 minutes)

Define the Terms Orthodox Sexuality - The historic Christian belief that sexual intimacy is reserved for a covenant marriage between one man and one woman. Expressive Individualism - The modern cultural philosophy that the highest good in life is discovering your authentic inner desires and expressing them without constraint. Sanctification - The slow, often painful process of God bringing our broken desires (of all kinds) into alignment with His will.

Build the Doctrine (Scripture-forward)

The Goodness of the Binary The Bible does not view the physical body as a blank canvas for us to paint our own identity on. The body is revelation. When God created humanity, He did so with deliberate, binary categories.

Key texts: Genesis 1:27; Matthew 19:4–5

"Male and female he created them" (Gen 1:27). This isn't just an Old Testament relic. When Jesus was asked about marriage, He anchored His entire argument in the original creation: "Haven't you read that at the beginning the Creator 'made them male and female'...?" (Matt 19:4). The binary of male and female is not a social construct or an oppressive patriarchy; it is the brilliant, complementary design of a good Creator.

The Boundaries of Sex God invented sex. He is not a prudish deity trying to ruin our fun. Because He designed it, He knows exactly where it belongs in order to produce human flourishing and protect human hearts.

Key texts: Hebrews 13:4; 1 Thessalonians 4:3–4

"Marriage should be honored by all, and the marriage bed kept pure" (Hebrews 13:4). The biblical boundary for sexual intimacy is a covenant marriage between a man and a woman. Any sexual activity outside of that boundary—whether it is premarital sex, adultery, pornography, or homosexual behavior—is a distortion of God's design. The Bible treats all of these as serious sins that require repentance.

Identity is Received, Not Achieved The heaviest burden our culture places on people is the demand that they must define themselves. If your identity is rooted in your sexual desires, you will be exhausted, because desires shift.

Key texts: Ephesians 1:4–5; Galatians 2:20

The gospel removes the burden of self-creation. Your core identity is not "gay" or "straight." If you are in Christ, your core identity is "chosen," "adopted," and "beloved." Paul says, "I have been crucified with Christ and I no longer live, but Christ lives in me" (Galatians 2:20). We do not have to curate our identity. We receive our identity as a gift from the Creator.

BOX - What This Is NOT Saying We are NOT saying same-sex attraction is the "unforgivable sin"; it is a temptation to be resisted, just like any other temptation. We are NOT saying Christians who experience gender dysphoria or same-sex attraction aren't real Christians. We are NOT saying the church has historically handled this well; we have often been cruel and hypocritical.

BOX - Where Christians Differ Historically, the global church (Protestant, Catholic, and Orthodox) has universally affirmed the traditional, biblical definition of marriage and gender. In recent decades, some mainline Protestant denominations have revised this theology to affirm same-sex marriage and transgender identities. However, broad evangelicalism firmly maintains that we cannot rewrite God's clear, biblical design to accommodate modern cultural shifts, even as we seek to be more compassionate in our pastoral care.

Lane 3 — Deep Dive (Optional)

The Objection You're Already Thinking "But if someone is born with same-sex attraction or gender dysphoria, how can a loving God demand they deny who they really are?"

The Best Answer This objection relies entirely on the cultural assumption that "who you really are" is defined by your strongest internal feelings. But Christianity fundamentally disagrees with that premise.

The Bible teaches that every single human being is born with a fallen, broken nature. We are all born with desires that contradict God's design. Some are born with a deep propensity toward anger. Some toward greed. Some toward heterosexual lust, and some toward homosexual lust. The presence of a desire does not make it holy, and it does not make it your core identity.

God does not ask anyone to deny *who they are*; He asks everyone to deny *what they naturally want* in order to follow Him. Jesus said, "Whoever wants to be my disciple must deny themselves and take up their cross and follow me" (Matthew 16:24). The demand for sexual purity and self-denial is not a special burden placed only on the LGBTQ community; it is the universal requirement of following Jesus for every single Christian, married or single.

Historical Lens In the first century, the Roman Empire was completely saturated with sexual fluidity, exploitation, and same-sex behavior. The Christian sexual ethic (chastity before marriage, absolute fidelity within it) was considered bizarre and intensely restrictive. Yet, it was this exact ethic that ultimately protected women and children from exploitation and drew millions of people into the church. The biblical sexual ethic wasn't oppressive; it was the ultimate protection against an abusive culture.

Real-Life Translation Many Christians approach the topic of sexuality as a culture-war battle to be won. We post angry articles, boycott companies, and talk about the LGBTQ community as if they are the primary threat to the church.

This approach completely forgets the gospel. The primary threat to the church is our own pride. When we turn people into political enemies, we lose the ability to evangelize them. You cannot genuinely love someone you are actively mocking. Truth without grace is just a club. We have to be a people who hold the unbending truth of Genesis 1, while having the radically welcoming, table-fellowship posture of Jesus in the Gospels. We hold the line, but we keep the door wide open.

Midlife Module - This Doctrine at 47 You are 47. You are sitting at the kitchen table having a difficult conversation with your teenager. They live in a digital world where gender fluidity is the absolute norm, and they are accusing you of being hateful and bigoted because you hold to a biblical view of marriage.

It is terrifying because you feel like you might lose the relationship. The temptation is to either scream at them and enforce compliance, or completely abandon your theology to keep the peace. You must do neither. You look at your kid, stay entirely calm, and say, "I love you with my whole life. My convictions about what the Bible teaches are strong, but my love for you is stronger. I'm not changing my mind on the Bible, and I'm never walking away from you." You hold the tension. You stay in the room.

Practice + Prayer

This Week's Practice (3–7 minutes) The Log-Removal Strategy. Before you spend any time this week worrying about the sexual sins of the culture, spend five minutes dealing with your own. Read Matthew 5:27–28. Confess your own lust, your own consumption of media that degrades the body, or your own pride. You cannot minister to a broken world if you are blind to your own brokenness.

Prayer (100–160 words) God, You are the Author of life, the Creator of our bodies, and the Designer of marriage. I trust that Your design is good, even when the culture tells me it is oppressive. Give me the courage to stand firm on the truth of Your Word without apologizing for it. But God, break my heart for people who are confused, hurting, and lost. Strip away my political anger and my self-righteousness. Forgive me for the times I have weaponized Your truth. Give me the grace to love my neighbors radically, to listen patiently, and to reflect the compassion of Jesus to a world that desperately needs Him. Amen.

Reflection

Solo (3 prompts)

1. Do you tend to lean more toward compromising truth to keep the peace, or weaponizing truth and being unkind?

2. Why is it exhausting to believe that your core identity is based on your shifting internal feelings?

3. How does viewing the body as a "good gift from God" change the way we view the modern concept of transitioning?

Small Group (3 prompts + 1 hard question)

1. Read 1 Corinthians 6:9–11. Why is the phrase "and that is what some of you *were*" so incredibly hopeful for the church?

2. Discuss the cultural idea of "Expressive Individualism" (your desires equal your identity). How does the gospel completely dismantle this idea?

3. How can our church practically become a place that does not compromise on biblical marriage, but is also a genuinely safe and loving place for someone struggling with same-sex attraction?

Hard Question: Are you using your outrage over the culture's sexual sins as a smokescreen to hide the private sexual sins in your own life (like pornography or emotional affairs)?

Close

One Sentence Recap: God created sex and gender as deliberate, beautiful gifts for our flourishing, and we must fiercely trust His design while offering Christ-like compassion to a confused world.

If You Only Remember One Thing: The demand for self-denial is not a special burden placed on a few; it is the universal requirement of following Jesus for everyone.

Next Week Preview: Next week we tackle something you spend most of your waking hours doing: Work. Is it just a curse to pay the bills, or is there a deeper calling?

Scripture References Used Genesis 1:27 Matthew 5:27–28 Matthew 16:24 Matthew 19:4–5 1 Corinthians 6:9–11 Galatians 2:20 Ephesians 1:4–5 1 Thessalonians 4:3–4 Hebrews 13:4

My Thoughts & Notes – What Did I Take From This?

Week 20 — Work and Calling: More Than a Paycheck

Core Question: Is MY job just a curse to pay the bills, or does my daily grind actually matter to God?

Why this matters: Because if work is just a necessary evil, you will resent it; but if work is your ultimate identity, you will inevitably burn out.

At a Glance (One Page)

Big Idea: Work is not a punishment for sin; it is a holy assignment given to humanity before the Fall to bring order out of chaos, meaning all honest labor matters to God.

Anchor Text: Genesis 2:15; Colossians 3:23–24

We believe…: God created humans to work as an act of worship and stewardship, and while the Fall made work difficult and frustrating, it remains a primary way we reflect the image of our Creator.

Key Words (3): Vocation - From the Latin *vocare* (to call). The understanding that God calls us to specific roles in the world, not just in the church. Dominion - The God-given responsibility to actively steward, cultivate, and bring order to creation. Idolatry of Work - The cultural lie that your career determines your value and identity.

The One Mistake People Make: Creating a false divide between "sacred" work (being a pastor or missionary) and "secular" work (plumbing, accounting, or changing diapers).

Choose Your Lane: Lane 1 / Lane 2 / Lane 3

This Week's Practice: The Friday Hand-Off.

This Week's Prayer: Father, I spend most of my waking hours working, and if I am honest, most of it feels incredibly ordinary. Sometimes it just feels like a frustrating treadmill. Forgive me for treating my job as either my ultimate savior or an ultimate curse. Thank You for the dignity of labor. Help me to see my daily tasks—the emails, the meetings, the manual labor, the laundry—as an act of worship. Give me the grit to work with excellence, and the wisdom to know when to turn off my laptop and rest. Amen.

Lane 1 — Clarity (10 minutes)

The Bottom Line The modern world tells you to find your identity in your career. When your career goes well, you feel like a god; when you get laid off, you feel completely worthless. The Bible offers a much healthier view. Work was God's idea, established before sin ever entered the world. God is a worker (He created the universe), and because you are made in His image, you are designed to work. Your job is how you love your neighbor and bring order to the world.

Scripture Snapshot Colossians 3:23–24: "Whatever you do, work at it with all your heart, as working for the Lord, not for human masters, since you know that you will receive an inheritance from the Lord as a reward. It is the Lord Christ you are serving."

Paul is writing to people living in the Roman Empire, many of whom were actual slaves doing grueling, unappreciated manual labor. He doesn't tell them their work is meaningless. He tells them it has cosmic significance. The boss who signs the paycheck is just middle management. The actual CEO you report to is Jesus Christ. That changes the dignity of the task entirely.

Say It Out Loud (One Sentence) All honest work—whether swinging a hammer or writing code—is a holy calling if it is done for the glory of God.

Common Confusions Confusion #1: Work is a curse from the Fall. (The *frustration* of work is the curse; the *act* of work is a gift). Confusion #2: God only cares about my job if I use it to evangelize my coworkers.

The Tuesday Payoff It is Tuesday afternoon, and you are fixing a massive, tedious error in a spreadsheet that someone else caused. Nobody is going to thank you for it. If your work is just a secular transaction, you will do it with deep, simmering resentment. But if you view your work through the lens of Colossians 3, bringing order to that spreadsheet is an act of dominion. You are bringing order out of chaos, loving the coworkers who rely on that data, and serving Jesus in the quiet anonymity of your cubicle.

Lane 2 — Depth (30 minutes)

Define the Terms Sacred/Secular Divide - The false belief that religious activities please God, while ordinary jobs are just neutral tasks to survive. Stewardship - Managing resources, skills, and opportunities that ultimately belong to God, not to you. Rest (Sabbath) - The deliberate, commanded cessation of work to remember that God is God and we are not.

Build the Doctrine (Scripture-forward)

Work Existed Before the Fall We often assume Adam and Eve just laid in hammocks eating grapes until they sinned, and then God punished them by making them get jobs. That is entirely unbiblical.

Key texts: Genesis 2:15

"The Lord God took the man and put him in the Garden of Eden to work it and take care of it." Work was commanded in Paradise. God made a wild, untamed garden, and He gave humanity the job of cultivating it, organizing it, and making it flourish. Work isn't a penalty; it is part of the original, perfect design of human existence.

The Fall Made Work Frustrating If work is a good gift, why does it often feel soul-crushing? Because of Genesis 3. When humanity rebelled, the ground was cursed.

Key texts: Genesis 3:17–19

God tells Adam, "Through painful toil you will eat food from it all the days of your life. It will produce thorns and thistles for you." Work isn't the curse; the *thorns* are the curse. This perfectly explains the modern workplace. You will experience friction, corrupt bosses, layoffs, and tasks that feel meaningless. The doctrine of the Fall gives you realistic expectations so you aren't surprised when your job is hard.

All Honest Work is Holy The church has a bad habit of elevating pastors and missionaries to the "first tier" of Christianity, while treating mechanics, accountants, and teachers as the "second tier" who just fund the first tier.

Key texts: 1 Corinthians 10:31

"So whether you eat or drink or whatever you do, do it all for the glory of God." Fixing a transmission with integrity glorifies God. Balancing a ledger with honesty glorifies God. Changing a diaper with patience glorifies God. God cares about the structural integrity of the bridge you are building just as much as He cares about the sermon your pastor is preaching.

BOX - What This Is NOT Saying We are NOT saying you have to love your job every day; thorns are real, and frustration is normal. We are NOT saying you can't quit a toxic job; stewardship sometimes means finding a better place to use your gifts. We are NOT saying your worth is tied to your productivity; your identity is secure in Christ, whether you are a CEO or unemployed.

BOX - Where Christians Differ Not a major point of theological disagreement. During the Middle Ages, the Catholic Church elevated the monastic life (monks/nuns) as a higher spiritual calling than ordinary labor. The Protestant Reformation explicitly rejected this, re-establishing the "priesthood of all believers" and declaring that a farmer plowing a field was doing work just as sacred as a priest leading a mass. Broad evangelicalism fully embraces this Protestant view of vocation.

Lane 3 — Deep Dive (Optional)

The Objection You're Already Thinking "This sounds great if you have a fulfilling career, but my job is incredibly boring, repetitive, and completely disconnected from anything spiritual."

The Best Answer We have bought into the cultural myth that a job only matters if it "changes the world" or fulfills our deepest passions. But the biblical purpose of work is much simpler: love your neighbor and provide for your family.

If you drive a garbage truck, your work is profoundly loving your neighbor by preventing disease from overrunning the city. If you scan groceries, you are facilitating the feeding of a community. If your boring, repetitive job simply puts food on the table for your children so they don't starve, you are doing holy, immensely valuable work (1 Timothy 5:8). You do not need a glamorous job to please God; you only need to do an ordinary job with extraordinary faithfulness.

Historical Lens Martin Luther heavily emphasized the theology of vocation. He famously taught that God milks the cows through the vocation of the milkmaid. When we pray, "Give us this day our daily bread," God answers that prayer not by dropping bread from the sky, but through the farmer, the miller, the truck driver, and the baker. Our ordinary jobs are the actual masks God wears to care for the human race.

Real-Life Translation Many Gen Xers entered the workforce in the late 90s or early 2000s, driven by a hyper-competitive hustle culture. You were told to climb the ladder, define yourself by your title, and outwork everyone else.

But over time, work makes a terrible god. If you worship your career, it will eventually demand your marriage, your health, and your peace of mind as a sacrifice. The biblical theology of work is deeply freeing. It demotes your job from "ultimate identity" down to "useful assignment." You can log off at 5:00 PM without guilt, because you know you are a steward, not the savior of the company.

Midlife Module - This Doctrine at 48 You are 48, and you have officially hit the ceiling of your career. You look at your boss, realize you don't actually want their job, and you look at your 401k, realizing you can't retire for another 17 years. The midlife career crisis hits hard because the upward momentum has stopped.

The gospel offers a radical pivot here. You don't have to panic, buy a sports car, or burn down your career to find meaning. You simply shift your focus from *advancement* to *faithfulness*. You realize your job isn't about proving your worth anymore; it is just the place God has stationed you to mentor younger employees, provide for your family, and practice integrity. Hitting the ceiling isn't a failure; it is the freedom to stop climbing and start serving.

Practice + Prayer

This Week's Practice (3–7 minutes) The Friday Hand-Off. At the end of your work week, before you **Close** your laptop or leave the site, literally hold your hands out and pray: "God, I did what I could this week. I leave the unfinished tasks, the stressful projects, and the outcomes in Your hands. I am stepping out of the role of worker, and into the role of child. I trust You."

Prayer (100–160 words) God, thank You for the dignity of work. You did not create me to be idle, but to partner with You in bringing order and beauty to the world. I confess that I often complain about the thorns and thistles of my job, forgetting what a privilege it is to have strength and opportunity. Forgive me for finding my ultimate identity in my resume, and forgive me for the times I have been lazy or cut corners when no one was watching. Give me a vision for how my ordinary, boring tasks are actually loving my neighbor. Help me to work hard for Your glory, and help me to rest deeply in Your grace. Amen.

<u>**Reflection**</u>

Solo (3 prompts)

1. Have you ever fallen into the trap of thinking a pastor's work is inherently more "pleasing to God" than your own work?

2. What are the specific "thorns and thistles" (frustrations) in your current job, and how does knowing they are a result of the Fall change your expectations?

3. How much of your self-worth is currently tied to your job title or your income?

Small Group (3 prompts + 1 hard question)

1. Read Colossians 3:23–24. How does viewing Jesus as your actual boss change the way you respond to an unfair or difficult earthly boss?

2. Discuss Martin Luther's concept that God provides daily bread through the farmer and the baker. How does this elevate the dignity of blue-collar jobs?

3. We talked about shifting from "advancement" to "faithfulness" in midlife. What does that practically look like in your specific industry?

Hard Question: Are you currently overworking and neglecting your family because you are secretly addicted to the validation your career gives you?

<u>**Close**</u>

One Sentence Recap: Work is a holy assignment given by God to reflect His image, meaning all honest labor matters deeply to Him.

If You Only Remember One Thing: Your job is not your identity; it is just the current station where God has asked you to love your neighbor.

Next Week Preview: Next week we look at the hardest job of all: the family. How do we raise kids and stay sane when the culture is pulling us in a thousand directions?

Scripture References Used Genesis 2:15 Genesis 3:17–19 1 Corinthians 10:31 Colossians 3:23–24 1 Timothy 5:8

<u>**My Thoughts & Notes – What Did I Take From This?**</u>

Week 21 — Family and Formation: Legacy and Limits

Core Question: How do I raise decent kids and maintain a sane family when the culture is pulling us in a thousand different directions?

Why this matters: Because the family is God's primary engine for spiritual formation, but if you make your family your ultimate idol, the pressure will crush them.

At a Glance (One Page)

Big Idea: The family was designed by God to be the primary training ground for faith and character, requiring intentional discipleship while firmly recognizing the limits of our control over our kids' choices.

Anchor Text: Deuteronomy 6:4–9; Ephesians 6:4

We believe...: The family is the foundational institution of human society ordained by God, designed to reflect His covenant love, care for the vulnerable, and formally train the next generation in the truth of Scripture.

Key Words (3): Formation - The slow, daily process of shaping a person's loves, habits, and beliefs. Discipleship - Teaching someone to follow Jesus; in the home, this happens through both formal instruction and daily modeling. Idolatry of Family - Elevating the family from a good gift to an ultimate god, expecting your spouse or kids to provide the perfect happiness only God can give.

The One Mistake People Make: Outsourcing their kids' spiritual formation entirely to the church youth group, assuming a one-hour Sunday program can counteract 40 hours of secular screen time.

Choose Your Lane: Lane 1 / Lane 2 / Lane 3

This Week's Practice: The Driveway Liturgy.

This Week's Prayer: Father, I feel the immense weight of leading a family. The culture is loud, the schedules are exhausting, and I often feel entirely inadequate for the task. I confess that I sometimes care more about my children's athletic success or academic resume than their spiritual formation. Forgive me. Give me the grace to model what repentance looks like in my own home. Help me to fiercely love my family without turning them into an idol. I dedicate my home to You; let it be a place where Your name is honored and Your grace is obvious. Amen.

Lane 1 — Clarity (10 minutes)

The Bottom Line God created the family before He created the church or the government. It is the bedrock of civilization. The biblical view of the family is deeply intentional: it is a purposeful unit designed to show the world what God's covenant love looks like, and to pass the faith to the next generation. But we have to hold a hard tension. We are commanded to aggressively disciple our children, but we are also commanded to release them, knowing we cannot ultimately control their souls.

Scripture Snapshot Deuteronomy 6:6–7: "These commandments that I give you today are to be on your hearts. Impress them on your children. Talk about them when you sit at home and when you walk along the road, when you lie down and when you get up."

Moses is preparing the Israelites to enter a culture that worships false gods. His strategy for their survival isn't building a massive school or a political action committee. His strategy is the kitchen table. He tells parents that spiritual formation isn't a weekly event; it is the constant, organic background noise of daily life—in the car, at dinner, and at bedtime.

Say It Out Loud (One Sentence) God designed the family to be the primary engine for passing the faith to the next generation, but He is the only one who can save them.

Common Confusions Confusion #1: If I just parent perfectly and follow all the biblical rules, my kids are guaranteed to be Christians. Confusion #2: Being single or childless means you are missing out on God's best. (Jesus and Paul were both single; the church is the ultimate eternal family).

The Tuesday Payoff It's Tuesday night. You are driving your kids home from practice, everyone is hungry, and an argument breaks out in the backseat. The secular view says your goal right now is just behavior modification—get them to be quiet so you can have peace. The biblical view says this stressful car ride is a prime discipleship moment. How you handle the conflict, how you ask for forgiveness when you lose your temper, and how you speak to them is forming their theology of God's grace in real-time. The car ride is the classroom.

Lane 2 — Depth (30 minutes)

Define the Terms Nuclear Family - A father, mother, and their children. While the modern West highly isolates the nuclear family, the Bible views it embedded within a larger, supportive community. Covenant - A binding, sacrificial promise. Marriage is a covenant, not a consumer contract you can break when you are no longer satisfied. Provocation - Unjustly using your authority to frustrate or embitter your children through harshness or inconsistency.

Build the Doctrine (Scripture-forward)

The First Institution Before there were priests, kings, or presidents, there was a husband and a wife. God wired the family into the absolute fabric of creation.

Key texts: Genesis 2:24

"That is why a man leaves his father and mother and is united to his wife, and they become one flesh." The family is not a cultural construct that evolved for biological survival; it was explicitly ordained by God to provide deep intimacy, multiply image-bearers, and serve as the foundational building block of human society. When the family breaks down, the society breaks down.

Parents Are the Primary Pastors You cannot outsource your child's spiritual formation. The church is a vital, necessary partner, but God explicitly gives the primary responsibility to parents.

Key texts: Ephesians 6:4

Paul writes, "Fathers, do not exasperate your children; instead, bring them up in the training and instruction of the Lord." Notice the negative command first: do not provoke them to anger. Hypocrisy, arbitrary rules, and a lack of grace in the home will harden a child's heart to the gospel faster than anything else. Formation requires both solid instruction and a gracious environment.

The Limits of Your Control This is where Christian parenting literature has often failed terribly. We were sold formulas: "Do X, Y, and Z, and your child will be a guaranteed success." That is a lie. Proverbs are general principles of wisdom, not mechanical guarantees.

Key texts: Ezekiel 18:20

"The one who sins is the one who will die. The child will not share the guilt of the parent, nor will the parent share the guilt of the child." God gives every human being free agency. You can build the perfect greenhouse, but you cannot force the seed to grow. God holds you accountable for your faithfulness as a parent; He does not hold you accountable for the ultimate free choices of your adult children.

BOX - What This Is NOT Saying We are NOT saying a broken or blended family is a failure; God's grace thrives in messy, imperfect households. We are NOT saying single parents are inadequate; God promises to be a "father to the fatherless" (Psalm 68:5). We are NOT saying the nuclear family is your ultimate allegiance; your highest allegiance is to Christ and His church.

BOX - Where Christians Differ Broad evangelicalism is completely united on the biblical definition of marriage and the necessity of discipling children. Differences arise in how the church formally incorporates children. Traditions that practice infant baptism (Presbyterian, Anglican) emphasize the covenant community, viewing children of believers as part of the visible church. Traditions that practice believer's baptism (Baptist, non-denominational) emphasize individual conversion, viewing children as needing personal faith before entering the visible church. Both fiercely emphasize family discipleship.

Lane 3 — Deep Dive (Optional)

The Objection You're Already Thinking "I grew up in an incredibly toxic, broken family. The idea of 'family as God's design' just sounds like a reminder of everything I didn't have. How does this apply to me?"

The Best Answer The Bible is brutally realistic about family trauma. If you read Genesis, you will read about horrific family dysfunction: deceit, favoritism, betrayal, and brothers selling each other into slavery. God does not sanitize the reality of broken families.

If your family of origin was a place of pain rather than protection, you need to know two things. First, the dysfunction you experienced was a violation of God's design, and He grieves that with you. Second, the gospel offers you a completely new family of origin.

When you place your faith in Christ, you are adopted into the family of God (Romans 8:15). The church is meant to be the place where the fatherless find fathers, the lonely find siblings, and the broken find a table. Furthermore, the cycle of generational trauma stops at the cross. By the power of the Holy Spirit, you can build a new family legacy that looks entirely different from the one you inherited.

Historical Lens In the Roman Empire, the father (the *paterfamilias*) had absolute legal power of life and death over his wife and children. He could legally abandon an infant or kill a disobedient child. The Apostle Paul's command in Ephesians for husbands to lay down their lives sacrificially for their wives, and for fathers to not provoke their children, was a radical, society-altering challenge to absolute patriarchal tyranny. Christianity invented the concept of servant-leadership in the home.

Real-Life Translation Many Gen Xers were raised by the "latchkey" generation model, where parents were heavily focused on careers and kids were left to figure things out on their own. In response, many Gen Xers have swung to the opposite extreme: hyper-parenting. We obsess over our kids' schedules, track their locations, and try to engineer perfect, pain-free lives for them.

This hyper-parenting is often driven by an idol. We need our kids to be successful to validate our own worth. But making your children the center of the universe is a terrible burden for them to carry. Biblical theology demotes the child from "center of the universe" to "fellow image-bearer." It allows you to love them fiercely, discipline them fairly, and entrust them fully to a God who loves them more than you do.

Midlife Module - This Doctrine at 45 You are in the classic midlife squeeze: the Sandwich Generation. You have a teenager who is pulling away, testing boundaries, and stressing you out. At the exact same time, you are managing the medical care of an aging parent who is losing their independence. You are exhausted by the sheer volume of caretaking.

The culture tells you to prioritize yourself and cut ties with anything that drains you. But biblical theology tells you that this exhausting, unglamorous caretaking is profound, holy work. Caring for vulnerable teenagers and vulnerable parents is the exact arena where sanctification happens. You are being forced to rely on God's strength because your own strength ran out three years ago. You are right where you are supposed to be.

Practice + Prayer

This Week's Practice (3–7 minutes) The Driveway Liturgy. Before you walk into your house after work, pause in the driveway for 60 seconds. Take a deep breath and pray: "God, I am leaving my work behind. I am entering my primary ministry. Give me the energy to be present, the patience to be kind, and the grace to forgive quickly." Then walk through the door.

Prayer (100–160 words) God, thank You for the gift of family, in all of its messy, loud, and complicated reality. I confess that I often fail to lead my home well. I am prone to frustration, selfishness, and letting the culture disciple my kids while I sit back. Forgive me. Give me the intentionality to talk about Your Word when we sit at home and when we drive down the road. Protect my marriage from the drift of busyness. Help me to break any generational cycles of anger or neglect. When I feel overwhelmed by the needs of my family, remind me that You are the ultimate Father, and I can entrust the people I love into Your sovereign hands. Amen.

Reflection

Solo (3 prompts)

1. What was the unspoken "idol" in the family you grew up in (e.g., academic success, appearing perfect to outsiders, financial security)?

2. How do you handle the tension of taking responsibility for your child's discipleship without trying to force or control their salvation?

3. Where are you most tempted to outsource your family's spiritual formation to someone else?

Small Group (3 prompts + 1 hard question)

1. Read Deuteronomy 6:6–7. What are some practical, non-awkward ways to actually talk about faith during the normal rhythms of the day?

2. Discuss the shift from "latchkey" parenting to "hyper-parenting." How does the idol of our kids' success ultimately damage them?

3. How can our church do a better job of functioning as a true family for those who are single, divorced, or estranged from their biological relatives?

Hard Question: Does your family only get the exhausted, irritable leftovers of your energy after you've given your absolute best to your career?

Close

One Sentence Recap: The family is God's primary training ground for faith and character, requiring intentional discipleship and a deep trust in God's grace for the outcomes.

If You Only Remember One Thing: You cannot outsource the spiritual formation of your home; the car ride and the kitchen table are your primary classrooms.

Next Week Preview: This brings us to the final chapter of Part 3. Next week, we look at the device in your pocket. Is technology a neutral tool, or is it actively changing your soul?

Scripture References Used Genesis 2:24 Deuteronomy 6:4–9 Psalm 68:5 Ezekiel 18:20 Romans 8:15 Ephesians 6:4

My Thoughts & Notes – What Did I Take From This?

Week 22 — Technology and Formation: Attention and Anxiety

Core Question: Is my phone just a neutral tool, or is it actively changing the way I think, feel, and relate to God?

Why this matters: Because if you don't intentionally manage your attention, technology will hijack it, leaving you chronically anxious, constantly outraged, and spiritually numb.

At a Glance (One Page)

Big Idea: Technology is not morally neutral; it actively forms our desires and fragments our attention, requiring deliberate limits and regular silence to hear the voice of God.

Anchor Text: Romans 12:2; Psalm 46:10

We believe…: While human innovation is a **Reflection** of the Creator's image, unhindered consumption of digital technology distorts our view of reality, isolates us from true community, and creates noise that drowns out the Holy Spirit.

Key Words (3): Formation - The reality that your habits, including your digital habits, are actively rewiring your brain and shaping your soul. Attention Economy - The business model of modern technology that profits off keeping you distracted, outraged, and scrolling. Sabbath - The intentional, commanded practice of stopping our productivity and our consumption to rest in God's presence.

The One Mistake People Make: Believing they are smart enough to passively consume four hours of social media and news a day without it completely destroying their baseline peace.

Choose Your Lane: Lane 1 / Lane 2 / Lane 3

This Week's Practice: The Analog Hour.

This Week's Prayer: Father, my mind is full of noise. I am connected to thousands of people online, but I often feel deeply lonely. I know what is happening in the news cycle, but I have forgotten what is happening in Your Word. I confess that I reach for my phone for comfort, distraction, and validation instead of reaching for You. Give me the discipline to set boundaries. Help me to reclaim my attention. Teach me how to be quiet again, so that I can actually hear Your voice. Amen.

Lane 1 — Clarity (10 minutes)

The Bottom Line Gen X remembers life before the internet. We remember video rental stores, dial-up tones, and looking out the window during a car ride. But we are just as addicted to the modern digital world as our teenagers. The danger of a smartphone isn't primarily that you will look at bad things; the danger is that it will train you to never look up. We are drowning in a sea of information but starving for wisdom. To follow Jesus in the modern world, you have to ruthlessly protect your attention.

Scripture Snapshot Romans 12:2: "Do not conform to the pattern of this world, but be transformed by the renewing of your mind. Then you will be able to test and approve what God's will is—his good, pleasing and perfect will."

Paul warns that the "world" has a pattern—a gravity that naturally pulls you into its way of thinking. You don't have to try to be conformed; you just have to drift. In our era, the pattern of the world is algorithmic outrage, comparison, and constant distraction. Transformation requires aggressive resistance. You have to actively renew your mind with truth, or the algorithm will renew your mind with anxiety.

Say It Out Loud (One Sentence) What I give my attention to is what will ultimately shape my soul.

Common Confusions Confusion #1: Technology is completely neutral; it just depends on how you use it. (It is not neutral; algorithms are designed to hijack your dopamine). Confusion #2: Fasting is only about food. (In the modern world, fasting from screens is often the most urgent spiritual discipline).

The Tuesday Payoff You have a rare twenty minutes of downtime on a Tuesday evening between dinner and putting the kids to bed. Your brain is tired. Your immediate reflex is to pull out your phone and doomscroll the news or social media. By the time the twenty minutes are up, your heart rate is elevated, you are annoyed at a politician, and you feel envious of a friend's vacation photos. You didn't rest; you just consumed anxiety. Recognizing how technology forms you allows you to put the phone in a drawer, sit on the porch in silence, and actually let your soul catch its breath.

Lane 2 — Depth (30 minutes)

Define the Terms Discarnate - Without a body. Technology creates a "discarnate" world where we interact with pixels and profiles rather than flesh-and-blood humans. Omnipresence - The illusion that technology allows us to be everywhere and know everything at once—attributes that belong only to God. Solitude - The intentional choice to be alone with God, free from human interaction and digital inputs.

Build the Doctrine (Scripture-forward)

We Are What We Behold You become like what you worship, and you worship what you give your attention to. If you stare at something long enough, it changes your character.

Key texts: Psalm 115:8; 2 Corinthians 3:18

Speaking of people who worship idols, the Psalmist writes: "Those who make them will be like them, and so will all who trust in them." The law of human nature is that we absorb the image of whatever dominates our vision. If your vision is dominated by a screen engineered to make you angry and comparative, you will become angry and competitive. If your vision is fixed on Christ, you are "transformed into his image with ever-increasing glory" (2 Cor 3:18).

The Loss of Silence God does not usually shout. He speaks in a still, small voice. If your life is packed with a continuous stream of podcasts, music, and notifications from the moment you wake up to the moment you sleep, you leave no margin for the Holy Spirit to convict, comfort, or guide you.

Key texts: Psalm 46:10; 1 Kings 19:11–12

"Be still, and know that I am God" (Psalm 46:10). The command to "be still" isn't a suggestion for relaxation; it is a theological requirement for knowing God. When Elijah met God on the mountain, God wasn't in the wind, the earthquake, or the fire. He was in the "gentle whisper" (1 Kings 19). You cannot hear a whisper if you have AirPods in 24/7.

The Limits of the Body The internet tells you a lie: that you are a limitless god. You can instantly know about a tragedy in India, an election in Europe, and a scandal in Hollywood, all while sitting in your living room in Ohio. But God did not design your physical brain to carry the emotional weight of the entire globe.

Key texts: Psalm 131:1

David writes, "My heart is not proud, Lord, my eyes are not haughty; I do not concern myself with great matters or things too wonderful for me." There is a deep, holy humility in accepting your limits. You are not omniscient. It is okay to turn off the news. You are only responsible to love the actual, physical neighbors God placed directly in front of you.

BOX - What This Is NOT Saying We are NOT saying you need to throw your phone in a river and live off the grid. We are NOT saying technology hasn't provided massive benefits (medical advancements, global gospel reach). We are NOT saying all entertainment is a sin; relaxing with a good movie is a gift.

BOX - Where Christians Differ Not a point of theological disagreement, but a massive spectrum of practical application. Some Christians lean toward the "Benedict Option," creating highly insulated communities with very strict limits on technology to protect their families. Others advocate for being heavily present in digital spaces to act as "salt and light." Wisdom requires finding the balance between engaging the culture and protecting your soul from its toxicity.

Lane 3 — Deep Dive (Optional)

The Objection You're Already Thinking "But my job requires me to be online, and my family group text is how we stay connected. I can't just opt out of the digital world without abandoning my responsibilities."

The Best Answer The goal is not isolation; the goal is intentionality. You cannot opt out of the modern world, but you absolutely must build fences within it.

Think of technology like water. If water stays within the banks of a river, it is incredibly useful—it generates power and irrigates crops. But if the river floods its banks, it destroys everything in its path. Right now, for most of us, the digital river has flooded the house. It is in our beds, at our dinner tables, and in our bathrooms.

You don't have to drain the river, but you have to rebuild the banks. You need clear, unbending boundaries where technology is not allowed. No phones at the dinner table. No phones in the bedroom. You dictate when the tool is used; you do not let the tool dictate when you are available.

Historical Lens When the printing press was invented, it fundamentally rewired human history. It democratized information, fueled the Reformation, and allowed people to read the Bible for themselves. But it also required society to adapt to a massive influx of ideas. The smartphone is the printing press on steroids, but instead of just giving us information, it tracks us and manipulates our psychology for profit. We have adopted this world-altering technology faster than any society in history, and we are only now realizing we didn't build a theology robust enough to handle it.

Real-Life Translation You know the feeling. You open an app just to check a message, and 45 minutes later you are deep in a comment section reading arguments between strangers about a political issue you barely understand. You **Close** the app feeling a heavy, low-grade exhaustion.

This isn't an accident. Billions of dollars have been spent by the brightest engineers in the world to hijack your psychological reward system. Your attention is the product they are selling to advertisers.

To survive this, you have to realize that managing your screen time isn't just a "life hack" for productivity; it is a profound matter of spiritual warfare. The enemy doesn't need to tempt you with a massive moral failure if he can just keep you perpetually distracted until you die. Reclaiming your attention is the first step to reclaiming your soul.

Midlife Module - This Doctrine at 49 You are 49. You frequently lecture your teenager about the dangers of TikTok and how much time they spend staring at a screen. But late one night, you check your own "Screen Time" report on your phone, and the number makes your stomach drop. Between email, news apps, and endless scrolling, you are spending four hours a day looking at your phone.

The hypocrisy hits you hard. You realize that your inability to be present isn't just a "kids these days" problem; it is your problem. At midlife, the realization dawns that you have fewer days ahead of you than behind you. You do not want to spend the rest of your limited, precious life staring at a glowing rectangle. The urgency of midlife demands that you look up, make eye contact with your spouse, and actually live the life God gave you.

Practice + Prayer

This Week's Practice (3–7 minutes) The Analog Hour. Pick one hour this week—maybe Saturday morning or Sunday afternoon—and turn your phone completely off (not just on silent). Put it in a drawer in another room. Spend that hour doing something entirely physical: read a paper book, go for a walk, or prep a meal. Notice how uncomfortable the first ten minutes feel, and how peaceful the last ten minutes feel.

Prayer (100–160 words) God, I confess that my attention is fractured. I am addicted to the constant drip of information, validation, and distraction. I reach for my phone before I reach for You in the morning, and I look at a screen right before I go to sleep. Forgive my idolatry. Break the hold that technology has on my mind. Give me the courage to embrace silence, even when it feels uncomfortable, because I know that is where I will hear Your voice. Help me to accept my limits and stop trying to carry the anxieties of the entire world. Give me the grace to be fully present with the people sitting right in front of me today. Amen.

Reflection

Solo (3 prompts)

1. Be honest: what is the specific emotional trigger (boredom, anxiety, loneliness) that usually causes you to mindlessly pick up your phone?

2. How does the constant stream of terrible global news affect your ability to trust God's sovereignty?

3. When was the last time you sat in complete silence for more than five minutes without any input (no music, no podcast, no screen)?

Small Group (3 prompts + 1 hard question)

1. Read Romans 12:2. What are the specific "patterns of this world" that social media actively trains us to conform to?

2. Discuss the concept of human limits. Why is it actually a relief to admit that you aren't supposed to know everything happening in the world?

3. What are some practical "banks" (boundaries) your family has tried to build to keep the digital river from flooding your home?

Hard Question: If God spoke to you in a "gentle whisper" right now, would your life be quiet enough for you to actually hear it?

Close

One Sentence Recap: Technology is not morally neutral; it actively forms our desires and fragments our attention, requiring deliberate limits to protect our souls.

If You Only Remember One Thing: The enemy doesn't need to tempt you with a massive moral failure if he can just keep you perpetually distracted until you die.

Next Week Preview: This completes Part 3. Next week we move into Part 4, tackling the darkest and most necessary topic: Sin and Grace. What is actually wrong with us, and how does God fix it?

Scripture References Used 1 Kings 19:11–12 Psalm 46:10 Psalm 115:8 Psalm 131:1 Romans 12:2 2 Corinthians 3:18

My Thoughts & Notes – What Did I Take From This?

PART 4 — SIN & GRACE

Every Gen Xer has, at some point, driven a car with the "check engine" light glowing ominously on the dashboard. Instead of taking it to a mechanic, we just put a piece of black tape over the light, turned the radio up louder, and hoped the problem would fix itself. It never does.

Part 4 looks under the hood at the total engine failure of the human heart. We are going to drop the polite, modern therapeutic language ("mistakes" and "blind spots") and look honestly at the absolute wreckage of human sin. Then, we will look at the scandalous, unfair, massive reality of God's grace that pays a repair bill we could never afford.

<h1 style="text-align: center;">WEEK 23 — SIN: NOT JUST MISTAKES</h1>

CORE QUESTION: WHAT IS actually wrong with us, and why can't we just fix it with more education or therapy?

Why this matters: Because if you misdiagnose the disease as just a "mistake," the cure of the cross will seem like a massive, unnecessary overreaction.

At a Glance (One Page)

Big Idea: Sin is not just breaking a rule or making a mistake; it is a fundamental, treasonous rebellion against the Creator that infects our entire nature and separates us from God.

Anchor Text: Romans 3:23; Jeremiah 17:9

We believe...: Sin is any failure to conform to the moral law of God in act, attitude, or nature, leaving us entirely guilty, corrupted, and spiritually dead before a holy God.

Key Words (3): Sin - To miss the mark. But more accurately in Scripture, to actively rebel against God's authority. Total Depravity - The reality that sin has corrupted every part of human nature (mind, will, and emotions), leaving us incapable of saving ourselves. Idolatry - The root of all sin; replacing God with a created thing to find our ultimate meaning and security.

The One Mistake People Make: Using therapeutic language to excuse bad behavior—calling a sin a "mistake," a "lapse in judgment," or a "struggle"—to avoid dealing with the reality of guilt.

Choose Your Lane: Lane 1 / Lane 2 / Lane 3

This Week's Practice: The Confession Audit.

This Week's Prayer: Father, I live in a culture that tells me I am basically a good person who just makes occasional mistakes. But when I am honest in the quiet of my own mind, I know that isn't true. I know how selfish, angry, and proud my heart actually is. Forgive me for trying to rename my sin to make it sound less offensive. Give me the courage to look at the darkness inside me without flinching, because I know that Your grace is deeper than my depravity. Strip away my self-righteousness. Amen.

Lane 1 — Clarity (10 minutes)

The Bottom Line We want to believe that human beings are fundamentally good, and that if we just get the right education, the right government, or the right therapy, we can fix the world. History proves this is a lie. The Bible calls the disease "sin." It isn't just doing bad things; it is the natural, hardwired desire to be our own gods. Until we admit that our primary problem is not external circumstances, but internal rebellion, we will never understand our need for a Savior.

Scripture Snapshot Romans 3:23: "For all have sinned and fall short of the glory of God."

Paul doesn't say we fall short of our own potential. He doesn't say we fall short of the guy next door. He says we fall short of the *glory of God*. We tend to grade on a curve—as long as we aren't committing murder, we assume we are doing fine. Paul shatters the curve. The standard is the absolute, blazing perfection of God's character. Compared to that, the serial killer and the suburban accountant are in the exact same boat: completely disqualified.

Say It Out Loud (One Sentence) Sin is not just a behavior problem to be managed; it is a heart condition that must be resurrected.

Common Confusions Confusion #1: If I didn't intend to hurt anyone, it wasn't really a sin. (Sin includes thoughts, attitudes, and omitting the good we should have done). Confusion #2: My environment and my trauma are responsible for my bad choices. (Trauma is real and terrible, but we are still morally responsible for how we respond).

The Tuesday Payoff You send a passive-aggressive email to a coworker on Tuesday morning. When you review it later, you justify it: "I was just tired, and they were being completely unreasonable." The therapeutic culture tells you to give yourself grace. The biblical culture demands you tell the truth. It wasn't just fatigue; it was pride. It was a desire to punish someone. Calling it a sin removes your excuses, but ironically, it is the only way to actually be free. You cannot repent of a "lapse in judgment." You can only repent of a sin.

Lane 2 — Depth (30 minutes)

Define the Terms Treason - A helpful modern equivalent for sin. It is active rebellion against the rightful King of the universe. Original Sin - The doctrine that we are not born neutral; we are born with a sinful nature inherited from Adam. Sins of Omission - Failing to do the good things God commands us to do (like failing to love our neighbor).

Build the Doctrine (Scripture-forward)

Sin is Against God First When we hurt another person, we assume our sin is only against them. But the Bible views all sin—even a sin against a neighbor—as an ultimate offense against the Creator.

Key texts: Psalm 51:4

David slept with another man's wife and then had the man murdered. Yet, when he prays in Psalm 51, he says to God, "Against you, you only, have I sinned and done what is evil in your sight." David isn't minimizing his crime against Uriah; he is recognizing that breaking the law is ultimately an act of treason against the Lawgiver.

The Heart is the Factory We often view sin like a virus we caught from the outside world. We think if we just isolate ourselves from bad influences, we will be pure. Jesus entirely rejected this.

Key texts: Mark 7:21–23; Jeremiah 17:9

Jesus said, "For it is from within, out of a person's heart, that evil thoughts come—sexual immorality, theft, murder, adultery, greed, malice... All these evils come from inside and defile a person" (Mark 7). Jeremiah warns that "The heart is deceitful above all things and beyond cure." The problem isn't the environment. The problem is the engine. Our hearts are idol-factories, constantly producing new ways to avoid relying on God.

The Gravity of the Penalty We struggle to understand hell or God's wrath because we evaluate our sin based on how it affects *us*. But justice is measured by the dignity of the one offended.

Key texts: Romans 6:23

"For the wages of sin is death." If you punch a wall, you break your hand. If you punch a police officer, you go to jail. If you punch a king, you are executed. The act is the same, but the penalty increases based on the authority of the one offended. Because God is infinitely holy, even the smallest rebellion against Him carries an infinite penalty. Death—both physical and spiritual—is the just wage for treason.

Total Inability This is the most offensive part of the doctrine of sin to the modern mind: you cannot save yourself. You cannot just "try harder."

Key texts: Ephesians 2:1–3

Paul writes, "As for you, you were dead in your transgressions and sins." He doesn't say you were sick, drowning, or injured. He says you were dead. A dead body cannot ask for help, take medicine, or throw a rope. Total depravity means that sin has so completely infected our will that, left to ourselves, we will never naturally choose God. We don't need a life coach; we need a resurrection.

BOX - What This Is NOT Saying We are NOT saying humans are as completely evil as they could possibly be; God's common grace restrains a lot of evil. We are NOT saying people who don't know Jesus can't do good things (like give to charity); they can, but those actions cannot earn salvation. We are NOT saying therapy or psychology is useless; it is a profound gift, but it cannot cure spiritual death.

BOX - Where Christians Differ The main debate is over *Total Inability*. Reformed (Calvinist) theology teaches that because we are spiritually dead, God must entirely regenerate our hearts before we can even have the faith to believe. Arminian theology teaches that while we are totally corrupted by sin, God gives "prevenient grace" to all people, restoring their free will enough so they can choose whether to accept or reject salvation. Both agree, however, that the human heart is radically broken and cannot be saved without divine intervention.

Lane 3 — Deep Dive (Optional)

The Objection You're Already Thinking "I am basically a good person. I pay my taxes, I love my kids, and I don't break the law. Why does the Bible insist on calling me depraved?"

The Best Answer The claim that you are "basically a good person" is true if you use society as your standard. If the goal is keeping a clean criminal record and being a decent neighbor, millions of people achieve that without God.

But Jesus exposed the flaw in this standard during the Sermon on the Mount. He said, "You have heard that it was said to the people long ago, 'You shall not murder'… But I tell you that anyone who is angry with a brother or sister will be subject to judgment" (Matthew 5:21-22).

Jesus moves the standard from external compliance to internal purity. You may have never murdered anyone, but have you ever wished someone was dead? You may have never committed adultery, but have you consumed pornography? You may pay your taxes, but do you secretly view the poor with contempt? When the standard is absolute moral perfection in thought, word, and deed, the illusion of the "basically good person" completely collapses.

Historical Lens In the 5th century, a British monk named Pelagius taught that humans are born basically good and can choose to live a sinless life by their own sheer willpower. Augustine fiercely combated this, arguing from Scripture that humanity is entirely corrupted by the Fall and relies 100% on God's grace for salvation. The church condemned Pelagius as a heretic. Today, most of secular America is functionally Pelagian—believing we can fix ourselves if we just try harder.

Real-Life Translation We spend a massive amount of psychological energy trying to convince ourselves and others that we are right. When a marriage conflict happens, we build a legal defense in our heads. We minimize our faults and maximize our spouse's faults.

The doctrine of total depravity is actually the greatest relief for a marriage. If you already know and admit that you are a deeply flawed, selfish sinner at your core, you don't have to defend your ego so aggressively when your spouse points out a failure. You can simply say, "You are right. I was arrogant, and I was wrong." A robust doctrine of sin destroys the need to perform, ending the exhaustion of self-justification.

Midlife Module - This Doctrine at 46 You are 46. You are watching a destructive pattern repeat itself in your life for the third time—maybe it's a fractured friendship, a financial mistake, or a specific kind of anger you swore you wouldn't pass down to your kids. In your twenties, you blamed your parents. In your thirties, you blamed your boss or your spouse.

Now, at midlife, you are running out of people to blame. The chilling realization sets in: *I am the common denominator in all my failures.* This is the exact moment the doctrine of sin becomes useful. It gives you a diagnosis for the disease you have been trying to ignore. It stops the exhausting cycle of blame and forces you to your knees, which is the only place grace can actually find you.

Practice + Prayer

This Week's Practice (3–7 minutes) The Confession Audit. Tonight, before you sleep, think of one specific thing you did wrong today. Do not use the words "mistake," "slip-up," or "I was just tired." Say it out loud to God using biblical language: "God, I was impatient with my child today, and that was a sin. It was an act of pride." Call it what it is, and then thank Him that the cross covers it entirely.

Prayer (100–160 words) God, my natural instinct is to hide my darkness from You. I want to look like a good person. I want to believe that my sins are just minor flaws. But Your Word tells the truth about my heart. I am deeply broken, frequently selfish, and entirely incapable of saving myself. Thank You for not leaving me to my own devices. Thank You for diagnosing my disease accurately so that I can understand the magnitude of Your cure. Give me a deep hatred for my own sin, and a deep love for Your mercy. Teach me to run to the cross quickly, without making excuses. Amen.

Reflection

Solo (3 prompts)

1. What is your favorite therapeutic word for "sin" (e.g., struggle, issue, mistake, blind spot)?

2. Why does evaluating your sin by comparing yourself to worse people keep you spiritually stagnant?

3. How does admitting your own "total depravity" actually make you more patient with the annoying people in your life?

Small Group (3 prompts + 1 hard question)

1. Read Mark 7:21–23. Why is it terrifying to realize that the source of our sin is inside our own hearts, rather than outside in the culture?

2. Discuss the difference between treating a behavior as a "mistake" versus treating it as "treason." How does the vocabulary change our response?

3. We talked about how a robust doctrine of sin is a relief for marriage. Have you seen this play out in your own relationships?

Hard Question: Are you currently hiding a habitual sin by calling it a "struggle," rather than actively putting it to death through repentance?

Close

One Sentence Recap: Sin is not just a mistake; it is a treasonous rebellion against the Creator that infects our entire nature and leaves us guilty before God.

If You Only Remember One Thing: You cannot repent of a "lapse in judgment"—you can only repent of a sin. Call it what it is.

Next Week Preview: Next week we trace the origin story of our brokenness. Why does the world feel so bent, and how did it get this way?

Scripture References Used Jeremiah 17:9 Psalm 51:4 Matthew 5:21–22 Mark 7:21–23 Romans 3:23 Romans 6:23 Ephesians 2:1–3

My Thoughts & Notes – What Did I Take From This?

Week 24 — The Fall: Why the World Feels Bent

Core Question: If God created a perfect world, why does everything from our bodies to our politics feel fundamentally broken?

Why this matters: Because understanding the Fall gives you permission to stop expecting heaven on earth, drastically lowering your frustration with a chronically broken world.

At a Glance (One Page)

Big Idea: The original sin of humanity fractured our relationship with God, with each other, and with creation itself, introducing death and decay into the very fabric of the universe.

Anchor Text: Genesis 3:4–7; Romans 5:12

We believe...: Through the historical disobedience of Adam, sin and death entered the world, causing all of humanity to inherit a corrupted nature and subjecting creation to a curse.

Key Words (3): The Fall - The historic event in Genesis 3 where Adam and Eve rebelled against God, plunging the world into sin. Original Sin - The theological truth that we are born with a sinful nature inherited from Adam; we are not born morally neutral. Federal Headship - The concept that Adam acted as the legal representative for all of humanity; when he fell, we fell with him.

The One Mistake People Make: Believing the secular myth of "progress"—the idea that humanity is naturally getting better through technology and education, ignoring the persistent reality of human evil.

Choose Your Lane: Lane 1 / Lane 2 / Lane 3

This Week's Practice: The Blame Fast.

This Week's Prayer: Father, I am so easily frustrated when things break down. I get angry at my failing body, I get furious at corrupt politicians, and I despair over the state of the world. Remind me today that this is not the world You originally designed. This is a fallen world, groaning under the weight of sin. Forgive me for expecting perfection in a place under a curse. Help me to grieve the brokenness without losing my hope in the One who came to reverse the curse. Amen.

Lane 1 — Clarity (10 minutes)

The Bottom Line If you buy a brand-new car and the engine immediately explodes, you blame the manufacturer. People do this with God. They look at cancer, war, and greed and say, "God must be a terrible engineer." The doctrine of the Fall is the biblical defense of the Engineer. God made a perfect car. Humanity, given the keys, drove it off a cliff. We are now living in the wreckage. The world feels bent because it actually *is* bent.

Scripture Snapshot Genesis 3:4–5: "'You will not certainly die,' the serpent said to the woman. 'For God knows that when you eat from it your eyes will be opened, and you will be like God, knowing good and evil.'"

The first temptation wasn't about an apple. The fruit was just the mechanism. The actual temptation was autonomy. Satan looked at Eve and offered her the ultimate human delusion: *You don't need God to tell you what is right and wrong. You can be your own god.* That same lie is the engine driving every single sin you commit today. Every time we sin, we are recreating Genesis 3, deciding we know better than the Creator.

Say It Out Loud (One Sentence) The world is broken because humanity chose independence from God, and independence from the Source of Life results in death.

Common Confusions Confusion #1: The story of Adam and Eve is just a metaphor to explain why bad things happen. (Paul treats Adam as a literal, historical figure necessary for the gospel to work). Confusion #2: Adam's sin only hurt himself. (Adam's sin functioned like a virus, infecting the entire human race).

The Tuesday Payoff You are trying to fix a leaking pipe under your sink on a Tuesday night. Your back hurts, the wrench slips, and you cut your knuckles. You are furious. If you don't understand the Fall, you will constantly feel like you are the victim of terrible luck, assuming life is supposed to be easy. The doctrine of the Fall manages your expectations. It reminds you that you are living in Genesis 3. Thorns, thistles, leaking pipes, and failing joints are the norm. The Fall gives you the theology to survive Tuesday without losing your mind.

Lane 2 — Depth (30 minutes)

Define the Terms Autonomy - "Self-law." The desire to govern oneself independently of God's authority. The Curse - God's holy judgment on creation following the Fall, subjecting the physical world to decay and frustration. Pelagianism (Heresy) - The false belief that we are born entirely innocent and only become sinners when we individually choose to sin.

Build the Doctrine (Scripture-forward)

The Immediate Consequence: Shame and Hiding Before the Fall, Adam and Eve were "naked, and they felt no shame" (Gen 2:25). They had absolute, unhindered intimacy with God and each other. The moment they sinned, the entire psychological framework of humanity broke.

Key texts: Genesis 3:7–8

"Then the eyes of both of them were opened, and they realized they were naked; so they sewed fig leaves together... and they hid from the Lord God among the trees." The first consequence of sin was the invention of hiding. We have been sewing fig leaves ever since—using our careers, our humor, and our self-righteousness to cover our shame and hide from a holy God.

The Destruction of Relationships Sin immediately turned humans against each other. When God confronts Adam, the very first human marriage instantly descends into blame-shifting.

Key texts: Genesis 3:12

"The man said, 'The woman you put here with me—she gave me some fruit from the tree, and I ate it.'" Adam throws his wife under the bus, and implicitly blames God for giving her to him. The Fall fractured human relationships, introducing defensiveness, abuse, and the refusal to take responsibility.

The Physical Curse The Fall wasn't just a spiritual event; it was an ecological disaster. The physical earth itself was caught in the crossfire of human rebellion.

Key texts: Genesis 3:17–19; Romans 8:20–22

God tells Adam, "Cursed is the ground because of you... By the sweat of your brow you will eat your food until you return to the ground." Paul echoes this in Romans 8, stating that creation was "subjected to frustration" and is "groaning as in the pains of childbirth." Hurricanes, tsunamis, cancer cells, and arthritis are the physical symptoms of the Curse. The earth is broken because its stewards rebelled.

Adam's Virus We did not just learn to sin by watching other people; we inherited a sinful nature directly from our first father.

Key texts: Romans 5:12

"Therefore, just as sin entered the world through one man, and death through sin, and in this way death came to all people, because all sinned." Adam acted as the legal representative (the federal head) of the human race. When he signed the declaration of independence from God, he signed it for all of us. We are born into the world with the virus already running in our blood.

BOX - What This Is NOT Saying We are NOT saying physical intimacy or the human body is evil; they were created good, but damaged by the Fall. We are NOT saying women are more to blame than men because Eve ate first; Adam was standing right there and failed to protect her. We are NOT saying God was surprised by the Fall; He had the plan of redemption in place before the foundation of the world (Eph 1:4).

BOX - Where Christians Differ Not a major point of disagreement on the core issue. All orthodox Christians believe that humanity fell in Eden and that we all inherit a sinful nature. The exact mechanics of *how* that guilt is transmitted (Federal Headship vs. Natural Headship) is debated in seminaries, but the street-level reality is agreed upon: we are all born broken.

Lane 3 — Deep Dive (Optional)

The Objection You're Already Thinking "It is completely unfair that I am punished and born a sinner just because of what one guy did thousands of years ago in a garden. I didn't vote for Adam to represent me."

The Best Answer This is a very Western, individualistic objection. We hate the idea of someone else representing us. But you have to remember two things.

First, if you had been in the Garden, you would have done the exact same thing. You know this is true because you do the exact same thing every day. Every time you lie, cheat, or lash out in anger, you are confirming Adam's choice. You are ratifying his vote. You aren't suffering for a choice you wouldn't have made yourself.

Second, and far more importantly, the entire gospel depends on this concept of representation. If you demand to stand entirely on your own record and reject the idea that one man can represent you, then you cannot be saved. Romans 5:19 says, "For just as through the disobedience of the one man [Adam] the many were made sinners, so also through the obedience of the one man [Jesus] the many will be made righteous."

If you reject Adam's representation, you must also reject Christ's representation. You cannot have the Second Adam save you if you deny that the First Adam sank you.

Historical Lens The doctrine of Original Sin was heavily formalized by Augustine in the 400s AD. He argued that humanity is a *massa damnata* (a ruined mass). This doctrine fundamentally shaped Western civilization, directly influencing the American Founding Fathers. Because they believed humans were inherently sinful and prone to corruption, they designed a government with heavy checks and balances. They knew you could not trust human nature with absolute power.

Real-Life Translation We are exhausted by utopian politics. Every four years, a politician stands at a podium and promises that if we just pass their policies, we will eradicate poverty, end crime, and usher in a golden era. And every four years, we are disappointed.

The doctrine of the Fall cures political idolatry. It tells you that no human system, no matter how brilliant, can fix a fundamentally bent human heart. We should absolutely work for justice, vote wisely, and care for the poor. But we do it without the crushing, naive expectation that we can build heaven on earth. The Fall frees you to be a joyful realist.

Midlife Module - This Doctrine at 50 You are 50, and you are sitting in a doctor's office waiting for the results of a biopsy. Your joints ache in the morning. Your eyesight is fading. You exercise, you eat well, but the unavoidable reality is setting in: your body is quietly, slowly decaying.

The culture tells you to fight aging as if it were a moral failure. The beauty industry demands you hide it. But biblical theology gives you a different lens. Your physical decline is the outworking of Genesis 3: "For dust you are and to dust you will return." It is completely normal. Grieve the loss of your youth, but do not be surprised by it. Let the breakdown of your current body make you desperately hungry for the resurrected body Jesus promised to give you.

Practice + Prayer

This Week's Practice (3–7 minutes) The Blame Fast. Pick 24 hours this week where you refuse to blame anyone else for your own bad mood, failure, or frustration. When you snap at your spouse or make a mistake at work, stop sewing fig leaves. Own the failure entirely, apologize without caveats, and break the curse of Genesis 3:12.

Prayer (100–160 words) God, I look at the news, and I look at my own heart, and I see the devastating effects of the Fall. Nothing works the way it was designed to. I confess that I am just like Adam and Eve. I want to be my own god. I want to define my own morality. And when I fail, my immediate instinct is to hide from You and blame someone else. Forgive me for my autonomy. Thank You for not abandoning humanity in the Garden. Thank You for sending the Second Adam, Jesus Christ, to succeed where the first Adam failed. Give me the endurance to live faithfully in this broken world while I wait for You to make all things new. Amen.

Reflection

Solo (3 prompts)

1. In what specific area of your life are you currently "sewing fig leaves" to hide your shame or failure from others?

2. How does the belief in "human progress" (that we are getting better over time) contradict the history of the 20th century?

3. How does understanding the concept of Federal Headship make the cross of Jesus Christ so much more powerful?

Small Group (3 prompts + 1 hard question)

1. Read Genesis 3:4–5. Why is the desire for autonomy (being your own god) the root of all other sins?

2. Discuss the physical curse of the Fall (thorns, disease, death). How does knowing that the world is *supposed* to be hard right now actually lower your daily anxiety?

3. We talked about how the Founding Fathers used the doctrine of Original Sin to build checks and balances. Where else do we see the reality of human depravity shaping society?

Hard Question: Are you currently blaming your spouse, your boss, or your childhood for a sin that you are actively choosing to commit?

Close

One Sentence Recap: The original sin fractured our relationship with God and creation, introducing death into the world and leaving us with a corrupted nature.

If You Only Remember One Thing: If you reject the idea that Adam's sin could condemn you, you must also reject the idea that Christ's righteousness can save you.

Next Week Preview: Next week we look at the Law. If we are completely broken, why did God give us the Ten Commandments? Is it just a ladder we are supposed to climb?

Scripture References Used Genesis 2:25 Genesis 3:4–8 Genesis 3:12 Genesis 3:17–19 Romans 5:12 Romans 5:19 Romans 8:20–22 Ephesians 1:4

My Thoughts & Notes – What Did I Take From This?

Week 25 — Law, Conscience, and Moral Confusion

Core Question: How do we actually know what is right and wrong without just relying on what is culturally acceptable right now?

Why this matters: Because if morality is just a cultural agreement, you have no grounds to condemn injustice; but if God's law is real, you have a massive standard you cannot meet on your own.

At a Glance (One Page)

Big Idea: God has written His moral law on the human heart and revealed it clearly in Scripture, not to give us a ladder to climb to heaven, but to show us our desperate need for a Savior.

Anchor Text: Romans 2:14–15; Romans 3:20

We believe…: God's moral law is binding on all people, perfectly reflecting His holy character, and while it cannot save us, it restrains evil, exposes our sin, and drives us to Christ.

Key Words (3): Moral Law - The unchanging standard of right and wrong, reflecting God's character, summarized in the Ten Commandments. Conscience - The internal, God-given alarm system that registers guilt when we violate the moral law. Legalism - The toxic, false belief that we can earn God's love and secure our salvation by keeping the rules.

The One Mistake People Make: Viewing the Ten Commandments as an entrance exam for heaven, rather than an MRI machine designed to expose the cancer of our sin.

Choose Your Lane: Lane 1 / Lane 2 / Lane 3

This Week's Practice: The MRI Check.

This Week's Prayer: Father, I live in a world that insists I can define my own morality. I confess that I often prefer my own rules to Yours because Yours are too demanding. Thank You for not leaving humanity to guess what is right and wrong. Thank You for the gift of a guilty conscience that warns me when I am drifting. But God, when I look at Your perfect law, I am crushed by how often I fail. Protect me from the pride of legalism. Let Your law do its heavy work: crush my self-reliance and drive me straight into the arms of Jesus. Amen.

Lane 1 — Clarity (10 minutes)

The Bottom Line Our culture claims that morality is relative—what is true for you isn't true for me. But nobody actually lives that way. When someone steals your wallet or lies about you at work, you don't say, "Well, they are just living their truth." You demand justice. Why? Because the Creator hardwired an unbending moral law into the human hard drive. The Bible reveals this law clearly. But here is the catch: God didn't give us the law so we could prove how good we are. He gave us the law to prove exactly how broken we are.

Scripture Snapshot Romans 2:14–15: "Indeed, when Gentiles, who do not have the law, do by nature things required by the law... they show that the requirements of the law are written on their hearts, their consciences also bearing witness, and their thoughts sometimes accusing them and at other times even defending them."

Paul is answering a common objection: *What about people who have never read the Bible? How can God judge them?* Paul says they have a Bible written on their chest. Even cultures that have never seen the Ten Commandments have laws against murder and theft. They have a conscience. The internal smoke alarm of guilt proves that humanity is accountable to an objective, external Lawgiver.

Say It Out Loud (One Sentence) The law of God cannot save me; its job is to diagnose my sin and drive me to the only One who can.

Common Confusions Confusion #1: The Old Testament law doesn't matter anymore because we are under grace. (The ceremonial laws are fulfilled, but the moral law—like not murdering—is eternal). Confusion #2: A guilty conscience means God hates you. (A guilty conscience is a gift; a silent conscience means you are spiritually numb).

The Tuesday Payoff You are filling out an expense report at work on a Tuesday. It would be incredibly easy to pad the numbers and get an extra $200. No one will ever know. The culture of your industry says "everyone does it." But as your finger hovers over the keyboard, your chest tightens. That isn't just anxiety; that is the *Imago Dei* sounding the alarm. Your conscience is testifying to the moral law. Ignoring it sears your soul. Submitting to it honors the God who wrote the code.

Lane 2 — Depth (30 minutes)

Define the Terms Ceremonial Law - Old Testament laws regarding animal sacrifices and temple worship, which were fulfilled and ended by Jesus. Civil Law - Laws governing the ancient political nation of Israel, which do not directly apply to modern governments. Moral Law - The eternal, unchanging rules of human behavior based on God's character (e.g., the Ten Commandments).

Build the Doctrine (Scripture-forward)

The Law Reflects the Lawgiver The Ten Commandments are not an arbitrary list of rules God came up with to ruin our fun. They are a transcript of His actual character.

Key texts: Leviticus 19:2; 1 Peter 1:16

God says, "Be holy because I, the Lord your God, am holy." We are commanded not to lie because God is truth. We are commanded not to murder because God is life. We are commanded to be faithful in marriage because God is a covenant-keeping God. If you break the moral law, you aren't just breaking a rule; you are acting in direct contradiction to the nature of the universe.

The Mirror, Not the Ladder The deadliest heresy in the church is the belief that if you try really hard to keep the Ten Commandments, God will let you into heaven. The law was never designed to save you.

Key texts: Romans 3:20; Galatians 3:24

Paul writes, "Therefore no one will be declared righteous in God's sight by the works of the law; rather, through the law we become conscious of our sin." The law is an MRI machine. If you go to the hospital with a broken arm, the MRI takes a picture and says, "Your bone is shattered." But the MRI cannot set the bone. The law takes a picture of your soul, exposes the cancer of your sin, and drives you to the surgeon (Christ).

The Conscience Can Be Damaged While everyone has a conscience, it is not an infallible guide. "Let your conscience be your guide" is terrible advice if your conscience has been damaged by repeated sin.

Key texts: 1 Timothy 4:2; Titus 1:15

Paul warns about hypocritical liars "whose consciences have been seared as with a hot iron" (1 Tim 4:2). If you ignore your smoke alarm enough times, you eventually take the batteries out. Every time you sin and ignore the conviction of the Holy Spirit, your conscience develops scar tissue. Over time, you can become completely numb to massive moral failures.

BOX - What This Is NOT Saying We are NOT saying Christians shouldn't care about obedience; we obey out of gratitude for salvation, not to earn it. We are NOT saying the Old Testament is useless; it is a masterclass in understanding the absolute holiness of God. We are NOT saying a struggling conscience means you aren't saved; conviction of sin is proof the Holy Spirit is working.

BOX - Where Christians Differ There are minor debates regarding the "Civil Law" of the Old Testament. Some smaller fringe groups (Christian Reconstructionists/Theonomists) believe modern nations should adopt the strict civil laws and penalties of ancient Israel. Broad evangelicalism rejects this, holding that the specific civil structure of Israel ended when the New Covenant began, though the underlying moral principles of justice still inform how we should vote and live today.

Lane 3 — Deep Dive (Optional)

The Objection You're Already Thinking "Morality is just a biological evolutionary trait we developed to keep the tribe surviving. There is no absolute 'right' and 'wrong'."

The Best Answer If morality is purely an evolutionary survival mechanism, then there is no objective difference between a mother feeding her baby and a dictator murdering millions of people. Both are just biological organisms acting on chemical impulses.

If morality is relative, you lose the right to be outraged by injustice. If a culture decides that slavery is good, on what basis do you tell them they are wrong? You can't. You can only say, "I personally don't like it."

But the fact that you *do* feel moral outrage when you see a child abused proves that you know there is a standard above human culture. You inherently know that some things are objectively evil, regardless of what the culture votes on. An objective moral law requires an objective Moral Lawgiver. Your outrage at injustice is one of the strongest proofs that God exists.

Historical Lens In 1515, a monk named Martin Luther was driving himself insane trying to keep the Law of God perfectly. He would spend hours in confession, beating himself up over the smallest infractions, terrified of God's wrath. He viewed the Law as a ladder he had to climb. When he finally read Romans and realized that the Law was meant to crush his self-reliance so he would trust entirely in the grace of Jesus, it launched the Protestant Reformation. The shift from "I must achieve" to "Christ has achieved" changed world history.

Real-Life Translation Many Gen X Christians grew up in the purity culture and legalism of the 1990s. The message was clear: read your Bible, don't drink, don't curse, wait until marriage, and God will bless your life.

The problem with legalism is that it produces two kinds of people: the arrogant and the crushed. If you successfully keep the rules, you become an arrogant Pharisee who looks down on everyone else. If you fail to keep the rules, you become crushed by guilt and eventually walk away from the church, assuming God hates you.

The gospel destroys both. It tells the arrogant rule-keeper, "Your rule-keeping can't save you." It tells the crushed rule-breaker, "Your rule-breaking can't separate you from the grace of Christ."

Midlife Module - This Doctrine at 48 You are 48, and you are exhausted by the pressure of being a "good person." You've kept the big rules—you haven't robbed a bank, you haven't murdered anyone. But as you get older, you are increasingly aware of the internal rot. You see the deep pride, the quiet coveting of your neighbor's house, and the persistent resentment you hold toward your spouse.

If you view the law as a behavior checklist, you can fake it at midlife. But if you view the law as Jesus did in the Sermon on the Mount—judging the invisible motives of the heart—you are ruined. This midlife realization of your own hypocrisy isn't a crisis; it is a breakthrough. It is the Law finally doing its job. It shatters the illusion of your own goodness so you can finally lean your full, heavy weight on Jesus.

Practice + Prayer

This Week's Practice (3–7 minutes) The MRI Check. Read Matthew 5:21–28. This is Jesus taking the MRI to the human heart, equating anger with murder and lust with adultery. Read it not to beat yourself up, but to completely destroy any lingering idea that you can earn your way to heaven by being a "good person." Let it make you grateful for the cross.

Prayer (100–160 words) God, You are perfectly holy, and Your law is perfectly good. I confess that my heart rebels against Your authority. I try to lower Your standards to make myself look better, and I judge others to make myself feel superior. Thank You for the gift of the Law, which exposes the depth of my sin. Thank You for the gift of a conscience, which warns me when I stray. But above all, thank You for Jesus Christ, who perfectly obeyed the Law on my behalf and took the penalty for my law-breaking on the cross. Soften my seared conscience. Keep me from the exhaustion of legalism, and let me live a life of joyful obedience fueled entirely by Your grace. Amen.

<u>**Reflection**</u>

Solo (3 prompts)

1. Do you naturally tend to be an arrogant rule-keeper (judging others) or a crushed rule-breaker (hiding in shame)?

2. Think of a time when your conscience screamed at you to stop doing something. Did you listen, or did you sear it?

3. How does viewing the Ten Commandments as an "MRI machine" change the way you read the Old Testament?

Small Group (3 prompts + 1 hard question)

1. Read Romans 2:14–15. How does the reality of the human conscience give us common ground when talking to non-Christians?

2. Discuss the moral argument for God (that objective evil requires an objective standard). How does this answer the cultural claim of "my truth"?

3. We talked about how legalism creates either arrogance or despair. Where do you see legalism creeping into modern church culture?

Hard Question: Are you currently ignoring a persistent, quiet sense of guilt from your conscience because confronting the sin would be too inconvenient?

<u>**Close**</u>

One Sentence Recap: God's moral law cannot save us; it restrains evil, exposes our deep sin, and drives us to the grace of Christ.

If You Only Remember One Thing: The Law is an MRI machine—it can perfectly diagnose the cancer of your sin, but only Jesus can cure it.

Next Week Preview: Next week we look at the word "Covenant." How do all the random stories and laws in the Bible actually fit into one unbroken plot?

Scripture References Used Leviticus 19:2 Matthew 5:21–28 Romans 2:14–15 Romans 3:20 Galatians 3:24 1 Timothy 4:2 Titus 1:15 1 Peter 1:16

<u>**My Thoughts & Notes – What Did I Take From This?**</u>

Week 26 — Covenant: The Bible's Big Story in One Frame

Core Question: How do all the random stories, laws, and letters in the Bible actually fit together into one coherent plot?

Why this matters: Because if you read the Bible as a collection of disconnected fables, you will miss the massive, unbroken promise of God to rescue His people.

At a Glance (One Page)

Big Idea: The Bible is not an encyclopedia; it is a unified legal and relational drama built on covenants—God's binding, sacrificial promises to redeem humanity through the work of Jesus Christ.

Anchor Text: Genesis 12:1–3; Luke 22:20

We believe...: God relates to humanity through covenants, culminating in the New Covenant sealed by the blood of Christ, which fulfills all the promises and demands of the Old Testament.

Key Words (3): Covenant - A binding, solemn agreement between two parties, usually sealed with blood, establishing a deep relational bond. Old Covenant - The conditional agreement God made with Israel through Moses, demanding perfect obedience to the Law. New Covenant - The unconditional promise fulfilled by Jesus, where God forgives our sins and writes His law directly on our hearts.

The One Mistake People Make: Treating the Bible like a rulebook or an ancient history textbook, failing to see the single red thread of God's covenant promises running from Genesis to Revelation.

Choose Your Lane: Lane 1 / Lane 2 / Lane 3

This Week's Practice: The Covenant Communion.

This Week's Prayer: Father, I confess that I often find the Bible confusing. The ancient names, the strange laws, and the complex history overwhelm me. Help me to step back and see the massive, beautiful framework holding it all together. Thank You for being a God who makes promises and binds Himself to broken people. When I fail to keep my end of the bargain, thank You that my salvation rests entirely on the blood of the New Covenant, secured by Jesus. Give me the peace of knowing Your promises cannot be broken. Amen.

Lane 1 — Clarity (10 minutes)

The Bottom Line If you pick up a novel and read a random page in chapter 4, then a paragraph in chapter 12, it makes no sense. Many Christians do this with the Bible. They pull a comforting verse out of Psalms, a moral rule out of Leviticus, and a parable out of Luke, and they wonder why it feels disconnected. The doctrine of "Covenant" is the spine of the book. It is the structure holding the 66 books together. God doesn't do casual relationships; He does covenants. Every story in the Bible is either establishing a covenant, showing humans breaking a covenant, or pointing to Jesus fulfilling the ultimate covenant.

Scripture Snapshot Luke 22:20: "In the same way, after the supper he took the cup, saying, 'This cup is the new covenant in my blood, which is poured out for you.'"

Jesus is sitting with His disciples at the Last Supper, celebrating Passover (an Old Covenant meal commemorating Israel's rescue from Egypt). But Jesus fundamentally rewrites the script. He takes the cup and uses the exact language of Jeremiah

31—the promise of a "new covenant." He is announcing that the centuries of animal sacrifices, complex laws, and temple rituals are coming to an end tonight. He is about to bleed to seal the final, unbreakable promise.

Say It Out Loud (One Sentence) The entire Bible is one unified story of God making and keeping His covenant promise to rescue humanity through Jesus Christ.

Common Confusions Confusion #1: A covenant is just an ancient word for a legal contract. (A contract protects your assets; a covenant binds your actual life to someone). Confusion #2: The Old Testament God of law is different from the New Testament God of grace. (It is the exact same God executing a single, unfolding rescue plan).

The Tuesday Payoff You receive a terrifying medical diagnosis on Tuesday afternoon. If your relationship with God is built on a "contract" mentality, you will panic. You will wonder if God is punishing you for not reading your Bible enough last week. Contracts are canceled when performance drops. But if your relationship with God is a "covenant," secured entirely by the blood of Jesus, your performance isn't the glue holding it together. The diagnosis is terrifying, but your status with God is immovable. Covenants don't break when you get sick.

Lane 2 — Depth (30 minutes)

Define the Terms Contract - An agreement based on mutual exchange (you do X, I do Y). If you fail, I am released. Covenant - An agreement based on sacrificial commitment (I am with you, regardless of the cost). Progressive Revelation - The reality that God reveals His plan slowly over time; the Old Testament is the shadow, the New Testament is the reality.

Build the Doctrine (Scripture-forward)

God Initiates the Promise Immediately after humanity rebels and ruins the world, God goes to work. He doesn't wait for humans to fix themselves. He approaches a pagan named Abram and initiates a massive, unconditional promise.

Key texts: Genesis 12:1–3

God tells Abram, "I will make you into a great nation... and all peoples on earth will be blessed through you." This is the Abrahamic Covenant. God promises land, descendants, and a global blessing. Abram did nothing to earn this. God initiated it purely out of sovereign grace. The rest of the Bible is the story of God keeping this specific promise, culminating in Jesus (the ultimate descendant who blesses the globe).

God Walks Through the Blood In the ancient world, to seal a covenant, you cut an animal in half and both parties walked between the pieces, essentially saying, "If I break this promise, may I be torn apart like this animal."

Key texts: Genesis 15:12–18

God tells Abram to prepare the animals. But then God puts Abram into a deep sleep. Abram doesn't walk through the blood. Only God (represented by a smoking firepot) passes through the pieces. God is making a unilateral promise: *I will keep my end of the covenant, and when you fail to keep your end, I will take the curse of the torn animal upon myself.* Thousands of years later, Jesus is torn apart on the cross to fulfill this exact moment.

The Old Covenant (Law) Shows the Need Hundreds of years after Abraham, God makes a different kind of covenant with Israel through Moses at Mount Sinai. This one is conditional.

Key texts: Exodus 19:5–6; Jeremiah 31:32

God says, "Now if you obey me fully and keep my covenant, then out of all nations you will be my treasured possession." This is the Mosaic Covenant (The Law). It was designed to govern the nation, but it had a fatal flaw: human depravity. The people continually broke it. God tells Jeremiah, "They broke my covenant, though I was a husband to them." The Old Covenant proved that even with clear rules, humans cannot fix their own hearts.

The New Covenant Finishes the Work Because the Law couldn't save us, God enacted the final phase of the plan: the New Covenant.

Key texts: Hebrews 8:6; Hebrews 9:15

"But in fact the ministry Jesus has received is as superior to theirs as the covenant of which he is mediator is superior to the old one." Jesus perfectly obeyed the Law (fulfilling the Mosaic Covenant), and He took the curse of our disobedience on the cross (fulfilling the Abrahamic Covenant). In the New Covenant, the Holy Spirit is given to change us from the inside out. The heavy lifting is finished.

BOX - What This Is NOT Saying We are NOT saying the Old Testament is bad and the New is good; they are perfectly unified chapters in one book. We are NOT saying Israel was saved by keeping the law; anyone saved in the Old Testament was saved by faith in God's future promise. We are NOT saying modern Christians have to keep the civil and dietary laws of ancient Israel.

BOX - Where Christians Differ The major debate here is between Covenant Theology (Reformed) and Dispensationalism. Covenant Theology emphasizes the absolute unity of the Bible, viewing Israel and the Church as one continuous people of God saved by one overarching Covenant of Grace. Dispensationalism chops the Bible into distinct eras ("dispensations"), maintaining a sharp distinction between God's plan for physical Israel and God's plan for the Church. Broad evangelicalism includes both, though the unifying nature of God's redemptive covenants is affirmed by all.

Lane 3 — Deep Dive (Optional)

The Objection You're Already Thinking "I usually just read the Psalms and the Gospels. Why do I need to understand all this heavy, ancient covenant theology? Isn't it enough to just love Jesus?"

The Best Answer You can absolutely be saved simply by trusting Jesus, without ever understanding the mechanics of covenant theology. But staying ignorant of the Bible's overarching plot leaves your faith incredibly vulnerable to doubt.

If you only read the New Testament, Jesus looks like a sudden, impromptu rescue mission God came up with because His first plan (the Old Testament) failed. If you view God as reacting to emergencies, you will assume He is reacting to the emergencies in your life, too.

But when you understand covenant theology, you see that Jesus was not Plan B. He was Plan A from before the foundation of the world. Every strange law in Leviticus, every bloody sacrifice, and every prophecy was meticulously laying the groundwork for the cross. Understanding the covenants proves that God is a master architect who executes a flawlessly detailed plan over thousands of years. It anchors your faith in the massive, sovereign competence of God.

Historical Lens In the 16th and 17th centuries, the Reformers and Puritans heavily developed "Covenant Theology" to combat the fear and legalism of the medieval church. By showing that salvation was rooted in an eternal "Covenant of Redemption" made between the Father and the Son before time began, they proved that a believer's salvation is anchored in the unshakeable agreement of the Trinity, not the fragile performance of the human.

Real-Life Translation We are a culture built entirely on consumer contracts. You hire a contractor to fix your roof. If it leaks, you sue them and terminate the contract. You pay for Netflix. If the shows get bad, you cancel the subscription.

Tragically, we have imported this consumer contract mentality into the two places where it is most destructive: marriage and our relationship with God. When marriage gets hard, or our spouse fails us, we look for the exit clause. When God doesn't answer our prayers the way we want, we threaten to walk away from the faith.

The doctrine of covenant destroys the consumer mindset. A covenant says, "I am stepping into the fire with you, and I am not leaving when it gets expensive." Understanding God's covenant with us is the only thing that gives us the power to keep our covenants with each other.

Midlife Module - This Doctrine at 45 You are 45, and you have been married for 18 years. The romance of your twenties is a distant memory. You are currently navigating a season of brutal, grinding friction with your spouse. The culture is telling you to prioritize your own happiness and find an exit strategy. You are treating the marriage like a failed contract.

The theology of covenant changes the oxygen in the room. A contract protects your rights; a covenant requires your death. You remember that God did not abandon you when you rebelled against Him. He walked through the torn pieces. He bled to keep His promise. At midlife, the realization hits: you do not stay married because your spouse is perfect. You stay married because your covenant reflects the ironclad, unbreakable faithfulness of God to a broken people. You stay in the room.

Practice + Prayer

This Week's Practice (3–7 minutes) The Covenant Communion. The next time you take communion at church, do not treat it as a funeral dirge where you just feel guilty about your sins. Treat it as a covenant renewal ceremony. When you hold the cup, remember Jesus saying, "This is the new covenant in my blood." Drink it as a celebration that the contract is paid in full.

Prayer (100–160 words) God, thank You for the stunning, unified story of Your Word. Thank You that You did not leave humanity to die in the Garden, but immediately initiated a plan of rescue. I confess that I often treat my relationship with You like a consumer contract—expecting Your blessing only when I perform well, and doubting Your love when life gets hard. Forgive my shallow faith. Thank You that my salvation rests securely on the New Covenant, sealed by the blood of Jesus Christ. Give me the strength to be a covenant-keeper in my own life. Help me to be fiercely loyal to my spouse, my children, and my church, reflecting Your unbreakable love to the world. Amen.

Reflection

Solo (3 prompts)

1. Do you naturally read the Bible as one unified story, or as a random collection of inspiring quotes and moral rules?

2. How does the story of God putting Abram to sleep and walking through the animal pieces Himself (Gen 15) change your view of grace?

3. In what relationships do you operate with a "consumer contract" mentality rather than a "covenant" mentality?

Small Group (3 prompts + 1 hard question)

1. Read Luke 22:20. Why is it so significant that Jesus instituted the New Covenant during the Passover meal?

2. Discuss the difference between a contract (exchange of goods) and a covenant (exchange of persons). How does this apply to modern marriage?

3. We talked about how Jesus is not "Plan B." How does seeing the massive, thousand-year architecture of the Bible increase your confidence in God's control today?

Hard Question: Are you currently looking for a loophole to exit a commitment you made, simply because it has become too difficult or expensive to keep?

Close

One Sentence Recap: The Bible is a unified drama built on covenants—God's binding, sacrificial promises to redeem humanity through Jesus Christ.

If You Only Remember One Thing: Contracts are canceled when performance drops; covenants hold firm when you fail.

Next Week Preview: Next week we tackle the most beautiful and scandalous word in the Christian dictionary: Grace. What happens when God gives you what you absolutely do not deserve?

Scripture References Used Genesis 12:1–3 Genesis 15:12–18 Exodus 19:5–6 Jeremiah 31:32 Luke 22:20 Hebrews 8:6 Hebrews 9:15

My Thoughts & Notes – What Did I Take From This?

Week 27 — Grace: What God Gives That You Can't Earn

Core Question: What happens when God gives you what you absolutely do not deserve, and why is that so hard for us to accept?

Why this matters: Because if you think you have to earn God's love, you will be exhausted and arrogant; grace is the only thing that actually frees you to be honest about your failures.

At a Glance (One Page)

Big Idea: Grace is not a discount on the price of salvation or a reward for trying hard; it is the scandalous, one-way love of God rescuing people who are actively rebelling against Him.

Anchor Text: Ephesians 2:8–10; Titus 3:4–7

We believe…: Salvation is an entirely free gift from God, given by grace alone, received through faith alone, and cannot be earned by any human effort or moral performance.

Key Words (3): Grace - God's unmerited, unearned, and undeserved favor. Giving us the ultimate good when we deserve the ultimate bad. Mercy - God withholding the punishment that we actually deserve. Merit - Anything we do to try and earn or maintain our standing with God (which the gospel entirely rejects).

The One Mistake People Make: Treating grace like a coupon that covers the rest of the bill after we've paid what we can, rather than a complete bailout for someone who is completely bankrupt.

Choose Your Lane: Lane 1 / Lane 2 / Lane 3

This Week's Practice: The Anti-Hustle Pause.

This Week's Prayer: Father, I live in an economy where I only get what I pay for. I am wired to hustle, perform, and earn my keep. I confess that I bring that exact same exhausting mindset into my relationship with You. I secretly believe You love me more on the days I read my Bible and love me less on the days I lose my temper. Forgive my arrogant self-reliance. Thank You for the scandalous, offensive, and breathtaking reality of grace. Give me the humility to stop trying to pay You back, and the freedom to simply receive what Jesus bought for me. Amen.

Lane 1 — Clarity (10 minutes)

The Bottom Line The human brain is wired for karma: do good things, get good things. Every other religion in the world operates on this premise. Christianity is the only system that completely short-circuits it. Grace means that God looked at a humanity that was actively rebelling against Him, and instead of wiping them out, He absorbed the cost of their rebellion Himself. You cannot earn it, you cannot buy it, and you cannot maintain it by trying harder. It is profoundly offensive to our pride, and it is the only thing that can save us.

Scripture Snapshot Ephesians 2:8–10: "For it is by grace you have been saved, through faith—and this is not from yourselves, it is the gift of God—not by works, so that no one can boast. For we are God's handiwork, created in Christ Jesus to do good works, which God prepared in advance for us to do."

Paul locks all the doors to human pride in this passage. How are you saved? By grace. But what if I have really strong faith? Even the faith isn't from you; it is a gift. But what if I do good works? Not by works, so you can't brag. Paul completely separates our performance from our salvation. He places "good works" in verse 10, not as the *cause* of our salvation, but as the *result* of it. You don't work to get saved; you work because you already are.

Say It Out Loud (One Sentence) Grace means my worst days cannot make God love me less, and my best days cannot make God love me more.

Common Confusions Confusion #1: Grace means God doesn't care if I sin. (Grace forgives sin, but it also provides the power to destroy sin). Confusion #2: Grace is just for the beginning of the Christian life, and then I have to maintain it by keeping the rules.

The Tuesday Payoff You blow a massive deadline at work on a Tuesday, and then you come home and lose your temper with your kids. As you lie in bed, the shame is suffocating. If you live under a performance-based religion, you are terrified. You assume God is disgusted with you and you have to spend the next two weeks "doing better" to get back in His good graces. But if you understand grace, you don't hide. You confess the failure immediately, knowing that your standing with God was secured by Jesus' performance on the cross, not your performance on Tuesday. Grace lets you sleep.

Lane 2 — Depth (30 minutes)

Define the Terms Justification - God's legal declaration that we are completely righteous, based entirely on the record of Jesus Christ credited to us. Sanctification - The ongoing, lifelong process of becoming holy (which is fueled by grace, not legalism). Antinomianism (Heresy) - "Anti-law." The false belief that because we are saved by grace, we can sin as much as we want without consequence.

Build the Doctrine (Scripture-forward)

Grace is Not a Wage If you work a 40-hour week, your paycheck is not a gift. Your boss owes it to you. You earned it. Grace operates in the exact opposite economy.

Key texts: Romans 4:4–5

Paul writes, "Now to the one who works, wages are not credited as a gift but as an obligation. However, to the one who does not work but trusts God who justifies the ungodly, their faith is credited as righteousness." If you try to earn your way into heaven by being a good person, God owes you justice (which means hell, because you aren't perfect). But if you stop working, admit you are bankrupt, and trust Jesus, God gives you righteousness as a free gift.

Grace Appears When We Are Enemies We love the idea of grace for people who are trying hard but just need a little help. We hate the idea of grace for people who are actively hostile to us. God's grace targets the hostile.

Key texts: Romans 5:8–10; Titus 3:4–5

"But God demonstrates his own love for us in this: While we were still sinners, Christ died for us." Paul goes on in verse 10 to say that we were "God's enemies" when we were reconciled to Him. God did not wait for us to clean ourselves up, apologize, and start going to church before He extended grace. He rescued us while we were actively fighting Him.

Grace Trains Us to Be Holy The biggest fear religious people have is that if you tell people salvation is entirely free, they will just go live like the devil. But biblical grace does the exact opposite.

Key texts: Titus 2:11–12

"For the grace of God has appeared that offers salvation to all people. It teaches us to say 'No' to ungodliness and worldly passions, and to live self-controlled, upright and godly lives in this present age." The law can tell you what to do, but it cannot give you the desire to do it. Grace melts the heart. When you realize the staggering cost of what Jesus did for you, it doesn't make you want to sin; it makes you want to honor Him.

BOX - What This Is NOT Saying We are NOT saying grace gives you a free pass to continue in habitual, unrepentant sin without discipline. We are NOT saying your obedience doesn't matter; it matters deeply as a response to God's love. We are NOT saying grace makes life easy; following Jesus will often cost you everything.

BOX - Where Christians Differ The major debate here is Calvinism vs. Arminianism regarding "Irresistible Grace." Calvinists believe that human hearts are so dead in sin that God's saving grace must be irresistible—if God elects to save you, His grace will effectively overcome your resistance. Arminians believe that God's grace is offered to all, but can be freely resisted and rejected by human free will. However, both groups adamantly agree that salvation is impossible without the unmerited grace of God initiating the rescue.

Lane 3 — Deep Dive (Optional)

The Objection You're Already Thinking "If God just freely forgives everything by grace, doesn't that make Him unjust? If a judge lets a criminal walk free just to be 'gracious,' we call that judge corrupt."

The Best Answer This is a brilliant objection, and it hits at the very core of the gospel. You are exactly right: a judge who simply dismisses a murder charge with a wave of his hand and says "I forgive you" is a corrupt judge. Justice demands a penalty.

The scandal of Christian grace is not that God ignores the law or sweeps our sin under the rug. The scandal is that the Judge stepped down from the bench, took off His robes, and paid the penalty Himself.

At the cross, every single ounce of justice was served. Sin was punished with absolute, terrifying precision. Jesus drank the cup of God's wrath down to the dregs. Grace is free to us, but it was not cheap. It cost the life of the Son of God. God can be incredibly gracious to you precisely because He was incredibly just at the cross.

Historical Lens Martin Luther (1483–1546) was a brilliant monk who nearly drove himself to physical collapse trying to earn God's favor through fasting, prayer, and penance. He hated the phrase "the righteousness of God" because he viewed it as a standard he could never meet. When he finally realized that the "righteousness of God" is not a standard we must achieve, but a gift God freely gives to those who believe, the Reformation was born. The shift from "I achieve" to "I receive" changed the world.

Real-Life Translation From the moment you are born, you are trained to perform. You perform for your parents to get praise. You perform in school to get grades. You perform at work to get a promotion. You perform on social media to get likes. The treadmill never stops.

When you bring that mindset into the church, you view God as just another boss you have to impress. If you have a good week, you feel spiritually confident. If you have a bad week, you hide.

Grace is the only thing that unplugs the treadmill. It tells you that the ultimate verdict on your life has already been secured by someone else. You are loved, accepted, and adopted, and there is nothing you can do tomorrow to ruin it. It is the most terrifying and liberating truth in the universe.

Midlife Module - This Doctrine at 51 You are 51, and you've hit a massive wall. Maybe it is a moral failure you thought you were too mature to commit. Maybe it is a brutal divorce, or a financial collapse that was entirely your fault. The self-reliance that carried you through your twenties and thirties is shattered. You look in the mirror and realize you are just as broken as you were at 20.

At midlife, the illusion of your own competence finally dies. And that is the exact place where grace does its best work. Grace doesn't meet you on the mountaintop of your success; it meets you in the crater of your failure. At 51, you finally stop trying to prove to God that you are a good investment, and you simply let Him love you as a broken child.

Practice + Prayer

This Week's Practice (3–7 minutes) The Anti-Hustle Pause. Pick one day this week. When you wake up, before your feet hit the floor, say out loud: "There is nothing I can do today to make God love me more, and there is nothing I can do today to make God love me less." Then, get up and go to work out of gratitude, rather than hustle.

Prayer (100–160 words) God, my pride hates the concept of grace. I want to earn my own way. I want to be able to point to my good behavior and justify why You should bless me. Forgive me for treating the cross of Jesus Christ as if it wasn't enough. Thank You for loving me when I was actively ignoring You. Thank You for paying the massive debt I owed. Wash away my exhaustion from trying to perform for You. Let the reality of Your unmerited favor absolutely crush my self-righteousness, and replace it with a deep, unshakeable joy. Teach me to give this exact same grace to the people who offend me today. Amen.

<u>Reflection</u>

Solo (3 prompts)

1. Have you ever viewed grace as a "coupon" (God covers the rest after you do your best) rather than a complete bailout?

2. Why is the concept of a free gift so offensive to highly capable, successful people?

3. What is one area of your life where you are currently trying to "earn" God's approval through your performance?

Small Group (3 prompts + 1 hard question)

1. Read Ephesians 2:8–10. Why is it so crucial that Paul completely separates our "works" from our salvation in this passage?

2. Discuss **The Objection** that grace makes God an "unjust judge." How does the cross completely solve this problem?

3. How does fully resting in God's grace actually make you work harder and love people better than living in fear of His judgment?

Hard Question: Are you currently withholding grace from someone who hurt you, secretly demanding they "earn" your forgiveness, while expecting God to freely forgive you?

<u>Close</u>

One Sentence Recap: Salvation is an entirely free gift from God, given by grace alone and received through faith alone, totally apart from our performance.

If You Only Remember One Thing: Grace means God doesn't love a future, fixed-up version of you; He loves the current, broken version of you.

Next Week Preview: If grace is completely free, does that mean we just sit back and do nothing? Next week we tackle Repentance and Faith—the required response to grace.

Scripture References Used Romans 4:4–5 Romans 5:8–10 Ephesians 2:8–10 Titus 2:11–12 Titus 3:4–5

<u>My Thoughts & Notes – What Did I Take From This?</u>

Week 28 — Repentance and Faith: Turning and Trusting

Core Question: What is our actual required response to God's grace, and is feeling guilty the same thing as repenting?

Why this matters: Because feeling guilty about your sin will just make you miserable, but actually repenting of your sin will make you free.

At a Glance (One Page)

Big Idea: The only biblical response to the gospel is "conversion"—a two-sided coin where we radically turn away from our sin (repentance) and cast our entire weight upon Jesus Christ (faith).

Anchor Text: Mark 1:15; Acts 20:21

We believe...: Salvation requires a genuine turning from sin in repentance and a complete reliance on Jesus Christ in faith, which are both gifts of God's grace.

Key Words (3): Conversion - The decisive turning of a human heart away from sin and toward God. Repentance - A change of mind that leads to a change of direction; grieving the sin and actively turning away from it. Faith - Not just intellectual agreement, but a profound, personal trust in the person and work of Jesus Christ.

The One Mistake People Make: Thinking that repentance is just feeling bad and promising to "do better next time," while keeping the sin safely hidden in the background.

Choose Your Lane: Lane 1 / Lane 2 / Lane 3

This Week's Practice: The 180-Degree Apology.

This Week's Prayer: Father, I confess that I am an expert at feeling guilty without actually changing. I am sorry for the consequences of my sin, but I often don't hate the sin itself. And I confess that my faith is often just intellectual agreement—I believe facts about You, but I struggle to actually trust You with my life. Give me the gift of true repentance. Break my heart for what breaks Yours, and give me the power to turn around. Give me a faith that stops trying to save itself and simply rests its entire weight on the finished work of Jesus. Amen.

Lane 1 — Clarity (10 minutes)

The Bottom Line When Jesus started preaching, He didn't say, "Clean up your life and try harder." He gave two massive, urgent commands: Repent and Believe. These are the two pedals on the bicycle of conversion. You cannot have one without the other. You cannot turn toward God without turning away from your idols. And you cannot truly turn away from your sin unless you have something infinitely better (Jesus) to turn toward. Repentance is not self-hatred, and faith is not a blind leap in the dark. They are the sane, logical responses of a person who has finally realized their house is on fire and the rescue ladder is right outside the window.

Scripture Snapshot Mark 1:15: "'The time has come,' he said. 'The kingdom of God has come near. Repent and believe the good news!'"

These are the very first recorded words of Jesus' public ministry in the Gospel of Mark. He announces a massive shift in human history (the Kingdom is here). And He demands an immediate response. He does not offer a gentle suggestion to incorporate some spirituality into your busy life. He demands a complete reorientation of your existence. You drop your rebellion (repent) and you trust the King (believe).

Say It Out Loud (One Sentence) True conversion requires me to hate my sin enough to turn away from it, and love Jesus enough to trust Him completely.

Common Confusions Confusion #1: Faith means ignoring logic and believing something without evidence. (Biblical faith is trusting a proven, reliable God based on historical evidence). Confusion #2: Repentance means you have to be perfectly sinless before God accepts you. (Repentance is a change of direction, not instant perfection).

The Tuesday Payoff You get caught in a lie at work on Tuesday. Your boss calls you out. Your natural instinct is damage control—you make excuses, blame a miscommunication, and feel terrible because your reputation took a hit. That is worldly sorrow. True repentance looks entirely different. You look at your boss and say, "I lied. There is no excuse. It was a failure of integrity, and I am deeply sorry." Repentance removes the exhausting burden of managing your PR. It hurts the ego, but it cleans the soul.

Lane 2 — Depth (30 minutes)

Define the Terms Contrition - Genuine, God-honoring sorrow over the fact that your sin offended a holy God. Attrition - Worldly sorrow. Feeling bad only because you got caught or have to face the consequences. Assent - Intellectually agreeing that certain facts are true (even demons have assent). Trust - The core of biblical faith; resting your weight entirely on those facts.

Build the Doctrine (Scripture-forward)

Worldly Sorrow vs. Godly Sorrow There is a massive difference between feeling bad about your sin and actually repenting of it. Judas felt terrible about betraying Jesus—he felt so guilty he killed himself—but he never repented. Peter betrayed Jesus, wept bitterly, and returned to the Lord.

Key texts: 2 Corinthians 7:10

Paul writes, "Godly sorrow brings repentance that leads to salvation and leaves no regret, but worldly sorrow brings death." Worldly sorrow is entirely focused on yourself ("I can't believe I messed up; I look terrible"). Godly sorrow is focused on God ("I have offended the God who loves me; I must return to Him"). One leads to a PR campaign; the other leads to the cross.

Repentance is a U-Turn The Greek word for repentance is *metanoia*, which literally means "a change of mind." But in the biblical worldview, your mind drives your feet. If you genuinely change your mind about your sin—realizing it is toxic rather than satisfying—you will change your direction.

Key texts: Acts 26:20

Paul describes his ministry message: "I preached that they should repent and turn to God and demonstrate their repentance by their deeds." A verbal apology without a change in behavior is manipulation. True repentance always leaves a trail of changed actions. If you claim to repent of greed but keep hoarding your money, you haven't repented.

Faith is Resting Your Weight We often treat faith as a feeling we have to generate. But biblical faith isn't a substance; it is an action. It is the act of transferring your trust from yourself to Christ.

Key texts: Hebrews 11:1; Ephesians 2:8

The classic illustration is a chair. You can look at a chair, study its engineering, and intellectually agree that it can hold a human being (Assent). But you do not have *faith* in the chair until you actually sit down and pick your feet off the floor (Trust). Faith is looking at the finished work of Jesus Christ on the cross and finally picking your feet off the floor.

BOX - What This Is NOT Saying We are NOT saying you only repent once; repentance is the daily posture of the Christian life. We are NOT saying your faith has to be perfectly strong; a weak faith in a strong Savior still saves you. We are NOT saying repentance earns your forgiveness; only the blood of Christ earns forgiveness.

BOX - Where Christians Differ A major debate in the late 20th century was the "Lordship Salvation" controversy. Some argued that you could accept Jesus as "Savior" (justification by faith) without immediately submitting to Him as "Lord" (repentance and obedience). Broad evangelicalism, led by theologians like J.I. Packer and John MacArthur, rejected this. They affirmed that while we are saved by faith alone, true saving faith is never alone—it always includes a posture of repentance and submission to Christ's lordship. You cannot divide Jesus in half.

Lane 3 — Deep Dive (Optional)

The Objection You're Already Thinking "I want to trust God, but I just feel like I don't have enough faith. My doubts are too strong. Will God still accept me if my faith is weak?"

The Best Answer We are obsessed with measuring the *amount* of our faith. We think of faith like spiritual currency—if we can just scrape together enough of it, God will hear us.

But it is never the *amount* of your faith that saves you; it is the *object* of your faith. A man stepping onto an airplane might be absolutely terrified, shaking, and filled with doubt that the plane will fly. A second man steps onto the same airplane with absolute, unshakeable confidence. When the plane takes off, both men fly. The first man's weak faith didn't crash the plane, and the second man's strong faith didn't keep it in the air. The engineering of the plane did the work.

Jesus is the airplane. If your faith is tiny, frail, and plagued by questions, but you place that tiny faith in Jesus Christ, you are entirely safe. He does the saving.

Historical Lens The first of Martin Luther's famous 95 Theses, which sparked the Reformation in 1517, stated: "When our Lord and Master Jesus Christ said, 'Repent,' he willed the entire life of believers to be one of repentance." The medieval church had reduced repentance to a mechanical sacrament of penance (paying a priest to absolve a specific sin). Luther reclaimed the biblical truth that repentance isn't a transactional fine you pay; it is the permanent, joyful posture of a heart returning to its Creator.

Real-Life Translation We have an incredibly hard time apologizing. Whether it is in our marriages, our friendships, or our workplaces, when we are caught in a failure, our ego builds a wall. We offer the classic non-apology: "I'm sorry if you were offended," or "I'm sorry, but you have to understand how stressed I am."

That is worldly sorrow. It defends the ego. Biblical repentance requires the ego to die. It requires you to look at your spouse and say, "I was harsh. It was entirely my fault. I was wrong, and I ask for your forgiveness." It feels like a small death in the moment, but it is the only thing that actually brings a relationship back to life. Repentance isn't just for salvation; it is the oxygen of a healthy marriage.

Midlife Module - This Doctrine at 46 You are 46, and you've been a Christian for twenty years. But if you are honest, you are stuck in a comfortable, cynical rut. You've learned how to manage your sins so they don't look too bad to the outside world. The idea of radical, weeping repentance feels like a young person's game—something for youth retreats, not middle-aged suburbanites.

But the Holy Spirit does not grade on a curve for age. Managing a sin is not the same thing as killing it. At midlife, repentance is exactly what keeps your heart from turning to stone. It means you stop making excuses for the lingering resentment, the quiet alcohol habit, or the emotional detachment in your home. You turn the ship around. Repentance at 46 isn't as loud as it was at 16, but it is infinitely deeper.

Practice + Prayer

This Week's Practice (3–7 minutes) The 180-Degree Apology. The next time you have a conflict at home or at work where you are even partially at fault, apologize without using the word "but." State exactly what you did wrong, own the failure entirely, and stop talking. Experience the terrifying freedom of not defending yourself.

Prayer (100–160 words) God, I am a master at making excuses. I know how to justify my actions, minimize my failures, and feel sorry for myself without actually changing. I am tired of playing games with You. Give me the gift of Godly sorrow. Show me the ugliness of my sin so that I can see the breathtaking beauty of Your grace. I repent of my pride, my autonomy, and my idolatry. I turn away from the things that are destroying my soul, and I turn entirely toward You. I bring no good works to bargain with. I simply place my weak, frail faith in the finished work of Jesus Christ. Hold me fast. Amen.

Reflection

Solo (3 prompts)

1. What is the difference between feeling guilty that you got caught, and feeling grieved that you offended God?

2. Why is "I'm sorry, but..." the exact opposite of biblical repentance?

3. Have you been treating faith as an intellectual agreement (assent) or are you actually resting your weight on Jesus (trust)?

Small Group (3 prompts + 1 hard question)

1. Read Mark 1:15. Why do you think Jesus commanded repentance *before* He commanded belief?

2. Discuss the airplane analogy from Lane 3. How does this relieve the crushing pressure of feeling like you "don't have enough faith"?

3. We discussed Martin Luther's statement that the "entire life of believers should be one of repentance." What does daily repentance look like in a healthy marriage or workplace?

Hard Question: Are you demanding that someone else repent and change their behavior before you will forgive them, while you stubbornly refuse to change your own behavior before God?

Close

One Sentence Recap: Salvation requires a genuine turning from sin in repentance and a complete reliance on Jesus Christ in faith, both of which are gifts of grace.

If You Only Remember One Thing: A weak faith in a strong Savior is infinitely better than a strong faith in yourself.

Next Week Preview: This wraps up Part 4. Next week we begin Part 5, diving into the most central figure of human history. Who exactly is Jesus?

Scripture References Used Mark 1:15 Acts 20:21 Acts 26:20 2 Corinthians 7:10 Ephesians 2:8 Hebrews 11:1

My Thoughts & Notes – What Did I Take From This?

PART 5 — CHRIST

If you ever worked retail or food service in your teens, you knew the exact moment things had gone hopelessly wrong: the manager had to step out of the back office, roll up their sleeves, and get behind the register. Things were too broken for the employees to fix on their own.

In Part 5, we arrive at the bloody center of human history, where the Creator of the universe stepped out of heaven and into the dirt. We are looking at Jesus... fully God and fully man. We will explore how His death actually works like a legal transaction, why the empty tomb is an undeniable historical fact, and exactly what He is doing right now while the world feels like it's burning.

Week 29 — Jesus: Fully God and Fully Man

Core Question: Was Jesus just a great moral teacher who got misunderstood, or is He actually the Creator of the universe in a human body?

Why this matters: Because if Jesus was just a man, His death cannot save you; but if He was just God wearing a human costume, He cannot represent you. You desperately need Him to be both.

At a Glance (One Page)

Big Idea: Jesus Christ is one person with two distinct but undivided natures—He is 100% God and 100% human—making Him the only qualified bridge between heaven and earth.

Anchor Text: John 1:1–14; Colossians 2:9

We believe...: Jesus Christ is the eternal Son of God who became man, without ceasing to be God, being conceived by the Holy Spirit and born of the virgin Mary, in order to reveal God and redeem sinful humanity.

Key Words (3): Hypostatic Union - The theological term for how Jesus' two natures (divine and human) are perfectly united in one person. Christology - The specific study of the person, nature, and role of Jesus Christ. Heresy - A teaching that severely distorts or destroys the core truth of who Jesus is, effectively creating a false savior.

The One Mistake People Make: Viewing Jesus primarily as a good example of how to live a moral life, rather than the sovereign Lord to whom we owe our absolute allegiance.

Choose Your Lane: Lane 1 / Lane 2 / Lane 3

This Week's Practice: The "Good Teacher" Fast.

This Week's Prayer: Father, I confess that I often try to shrink Jesus down to a manageable size. I am comfortable with Jesus the teacher, Jesus the healer, and Jesus the friend. I am far less comfortable with Jesus the Sovereign Creator of the universe. Forgive me for treating Him like a mascot for my own lifestyle. Give me the profound awe that comes from realizing the infinite God took on flesh and bones to rescue me. Help me to bow before Him as my Lord, and trust Him entirely as my Savior. Amen.

Lane 1 — Clarity (10 minutes)

The Bottom Line Everyone likes Jesus. Even other religions and secular historians usually admit He was a brilliant teacher who cared for the poor. But the Bible doesn't give us the option of just calling Him a "good guy." C.S. Lewis famously pointed out that a man who claims to forgive sins and claims to be God is not just a great moral teacher. He is either a lunatic, a liar, or exactly who He says He is. The core of Christianity is the explosive claim that the carpenter from Nazareth was the eternal God walking around in sandals.

Scripture Snapshot John 1:1, 14: "In the beginning was the Word, and the Word was with God, and the Word was God... The Word became flesh and made his dwelling among us. We have seen his glory, the glory of the one and only Son, who came from the Father, full of grace and truth."

John starts his Gospel by rewriting Genesis 1. The "Word" existed before time began. The Word wasn't just *with* God; the Word *was* God. Then, in verse 14, John drops the hammer: the eternal, uncreated God wrapped Himself in physical flesh and pitched His tent in our neighborhood. He didn't just send a memo; He moved in.

Say It Out Loud (One Sentence) Jesus is fully God to have the power to save me, and fully man to have the right to represent me.

Common Confusions Confusion #1: Jesus is 50% God and 50% man. (He is 100% God and 100% man; the math of the Hypostatic Union isn't a fraction). Confusion #2: Jesus didn't exist until He was born in Bethlehem. (The Son of God is eternal; He simply took on a human body at the incarnation).

The Tuesday Payoff You are dealing with a brutal, unfair situation at work on a Tuesday. You feel completely misunderstood and targeted. If your God is a distant power in the sky, you might pray, but you assume He has no idea what your Tuesday actually feels like. But if Jesus is fully human, the game changes. Your God actually knows what it feels like to be exhausted, betrayed by friends, and treated unfairly by corrupt management. He isn't offering you generic advice from an ivory tower; He is leading you through the dirt He has already walked.

Lane 2 — Depth (30 minutes)

Define the Terms Incarnation - The act of the eternal Son of God taking on a human nature. Virgin Birth - The miracle by which Jesus was conceived by the Holy Spirit without a human father, ensuring He was fully human but without inherited original sin. Mediator - Someone who stands between two hostile parties (God and humanity) to bring them together; requiring them to relate perfectly to both sides.

Build the Doctrine (Scripture-forward)

He Is Fully God The Bible does not hide the deity of Jesus. It is screaming it on every page. He accepted worship, He forgave sins (which only God can do), and He claimed eternal existence.

Key texts: Colossians 2:9; John 8:58

Paul writes, "For in Christ all the fullness of the Deity lives in bodily form." Not a piece of God. Not a spark of the divine. The *fullness*. When the religious leaders challenged Jesus' age, He replied, "Before Abraham was born, I am!" (John 8:58). He claimed the exact divine title God used at the burning bush. The leaders immediately tried to stone Him because they knew exactly what He was claiming: absolute equality with God.

He Is Fully Human Jesus didn't just look like a man; He was a man. He had a human mind, a human will, and a human body that was subject to the exact same physical limits we experience.

Key texts: Luke 2:52; John 4:6

Luke records that "Jesus grew in wisdom and stature." His human brain had to learn how to read. He experienced severe thirst, hunger, and physical exhaustion. John records that Jesus was "tired from the journey" and sat down by a well. If Jesus was just God in a human costume, pretending to be tired, the Gospel is a theatrical lie. He was truly, fully human.

Why We Need Both If Jesus was not fully man, He could not have died in our place. A spirit cannot bleed. Humanity sinned, so a human had to pay the price. But if Jesus was not fully God, His death would have only been enough to pay for His own life.

Key texts: 1 Timothy 2:5

"For there is one God and one mediator between God and mankind, the man Christ Jesus." A mediator must have a foot in both camps. Because He is man, He can grab humanity by the hand. Because He is God, He can grab the Father by the hand. He is the only bridge strong enough to span the infinite gap caused by our sin.

BOX - What This Is NOT Saying We are NOT saying Jesus had a human body but a divine mind; He had both a fully human mind and a fully divine mind. We are NOT saying the Father died on the cross; only the Son took on flesh and suffered. We are NOT saying Jesus stopped being human after the resurrection; He retains His glorified human body forever.

BOX - Where Christians Differ Not a point of disagreement. The doctrine of the Hypostatic Union (fully God, fully man) was permanently settled at the Council of Chalcedon in 451 AD. It is the absolute bedrock of Christian orthodoxy. If a church or group denies either the deity of Christ (like Jehovah's Witnesses) or the humanity of Christ (ancient Gnosticism), they are operating completely outside the bounds of historical Christianity.

Lane 3 — Deep Dive (Optional)

The Objection You're Already Thinking "How can one person be two completely different things at the same time? It violates logic to be infinite and finite simultaneously."

The Best Answer It violates *human* logic, but it does not violate reality. We struggle with this because we only have our own nature to compare it to. You only have one nature (human). But God is not bound by our limits.

Think of an author writing a book. The author is entirely outside the story, possessing a nature completely different from the characters on the page. But if the author chooses to write himself into the story as a character, he now has a dual reality. He is the infinite creator of the world, and he is simultaneously a finite character operating within the rules of the world he created.

The incarnation is God writing Himself into the human story. He didn't subtract His deity to become human; He *added* humanity to His deity.

Historical Lens In the 4th century, a highly popular teacher named Arius claimed that Jesus was the first and greatest creation of God, but not eternally God Himself. A bishop named Athanasius fiercely opposed him, realizing that a created savior cannot save creation. Athanasius was exiled five times for holding the line, but his stubborn defense of Christ's deity led to the Nicene Creed, permanently cementing the truth that Jesus is "begotten, not made, of one being with the Father."

Real-Life Translation We are a culture addicted to self-improvement. We look for life hacks, gurus, and podcasts to optimize our lives. We desperately want Jesus to just be the ultimate life-coach—someone who gives us great advice on how to love our enemies and manage our anxiety.

But if Jesus is the Creator of the universe in human flesh, you cannot just take His advice. You must surrender to His authority. You can ignore a life-coach if you don't like their methods. You cannot ignore the King. The deity of Christ destroys the casual, buffet-style Christianity where we only obey the parts of the Bible we agree with. It demands our absolute, terrifying, and joyful submission.

Midlife Module - This Doctrine at 48 You are 48. Over the last two decades, you have watched a lot of your heroes fall. Politicians you trusted turned out to be corrupt. Pastors you admired had massive moral failures. Even your own parents have proven to be deeply flawed. The midlife realization is heavy: every human role model eventually breaks your heart.

This is why you need a Savior who is more than just a good man. If Jesus is just the best guy who ever lived, it is only a matter of time before you find a flaw. But Jesus is fully God. He is the only anchor that will never rot, bend, or fail you. The utter perfection of His divine nature guarantees that your trust in Him will never, ever be disappointed.

Practice + Prayer

This Week's Practice (3–7 minutes) The "Good Teacher" Fast. Notice how often the culture (or even your own mind) refers to Jesus simply as a good teacher, a revolutionary, or a moral example. Every time you hear it this week, mentally correct it by adding the title Thomas used when he saw the resurrected Jesus: "My Lord and my God."

Prayer (100–160 words) God, my mind cannot fully comprehend the mystery of the incarnation. I cannot understand how the One who holds the galaxies together allowed Himself to be held in the arms of a human mother. Forgive me for trying to reduce Jesus to a safe, comfortable teacher who just agrees with my politics and lifestyle. I confess that He is the Sovereign

King. Thank You that He was fully human, meaning He intimately understands my weakness, my pain, and my temptations. And thank You that He is fully God, meaning He actually has the power to save me from them. I bow my knee to Jesus Christ today. Amen.

Reflection

Solo (3 prompts)

1. Do you naturally lean toward treating Jesus just as a "buddy" (ignoring His deity) or as a distant, intimidating force (ignoring His humanity)?

2. Why does the fact that Jesus had to learn to read and got physically exhausted make Him more trustworthy to you?

3. How does viewing Jesus as the "Author who wrote Himself into the story" help you understand His two natures?

Small Group (3 prompts + 1 hard question)

1. Read Colossians 2:9. Why is it dangerous to claim that Jesus only had a "spark" of the divine, rather than the "fullness" of God?

2. Discuss the C.S. Lewis "Liar, Lunatic, or Lord" argument. Why doesn't the Bible give us the option to just call Jesus a good moral teacher?

3. We talked about how every human role model eventually fails. How does the deity of Christ provide the ultimate psychological security?

Hard Question: Are you treating Jesus like a life-coach—only taking His advice when it's convenient—rather than obeying Him as your sovereign God?

Close

One Sentence Recap: Jesus is 100% God and 100% human, making Him the only qualified bridge between heaven and earth.

If You Only Remember One Thing: You can take advice from a good teacher, but you must surrender your entire life to the King.

Next Week Preview: Next week we look **Close**r at the Incarnation itself. Why did the infinite God choose to experience the brutal limits of a human body?

Scripture References Used John 1:1–14 John 4:6 John 8:58 Luke 2:52 Colossians 2:9 1 Timothy 2:5

My Thoughts & Notes – What Did I Take From This?

Week 30 — Incarnation: God Came Close

Core Question: Why did the infinite God have to become a crying, bleeding, limited human being?

Why this matters: Because a God who stays comfortably in heaven cannot relate to the brutal reality of your human suffering; you need a God who actually felt the nails.

At a Glance (One Page)

Big Idea: The Incarnation means God did not shout instructions from heaven; He voluntarily laid aside His glory to enter the dirt, pain, and limits of human existence to rescue us from the inside.

Anchor Text: Hebrews 2:14–18; Philippians 2:5–8

We believe...: The eternal Son of God voluntarily emptied Himself of His visible glory, took on human flesh, and lived a perfect life of submission to the Father to become our merciful High Priest.

Key Words (3): Incarnation - From Latin meaning "in flesh." The event of God becoming a human being. Kenosis - The "emptying" of Christ; laying aside the independent use of His divine privileges to live fully as a man dependent on the Spirit. Sympathy - The ability to understand and share the feelings of another; secured perfectly by Christ's human experience.

The One Mistake People Make: Thinking that Jesus used His "God powers" to cheat His way through human suffering, completely missing the fact that He endured pain, temptation, and grief as a real man.

Choose Your Lane: Lane 1 / Lane 2 / Lane 3

This Week's Practice: The Empathy Shift.

This Week's Prayer: Father, I confess that when life hurts, my first instinct is to assume You are distant and indifferent. I look at my pain and assume You don't care. Forgive me. The manger and the cross prove that You are not a distant spectator. Thank You for Jesus. Thank You that He did not hold onto His comfort, but stepped into the cold, brutal reality of this world. When I feel misunderstood or isolated, remind me that I have a Savior who knows exactly what it feels like to be broken. Amen.

Lane 1 — Clarity (10 minutes)

The Bottom Line Every other religion features humans trying to climb a ladder to reach God. They meditate, sacrifice, or obey rules, desperately trying to get God's attention in the sky. Christianity is the only worldview where God climbs down the ladder to us. The Incarnation means God didn't just send a lifeboat; He jumped into the freezing water. He didn't just understand our pain in theory; He learned it in practice by feeling the betrayal of a friend, the grief of a funeral, and the physical agony of a Roman cross.

Scripture Snapshot Philippians 2:5–7: "In your relationships with one another, have the same mindset as Christ Jesus: Who, being in very nature God, did not consider equality with God something to be used to his own advantage; rather, he made himself nothing by taking the very nature of a servant, being made in human likeness."

Paul is telling the church to stop being selfish. To prove his point, he points to the ultimate example of unselfishness. Jesus had it all. He had the constant, unhindered worship of angels. But He didn't use His status for His own advantage. He "made himself nothing" (the Greek word is *kenosis*, meaning to empty). He didn't empty Himself of His deity; He emptied Himself of His glory. He traded a crown for a towel.

Say It Out Loud (One Sentence) God did not stay safe in heaven; He took on human flesh so He could suffer with us and save us.

Common Confusions Confusion #1: Jesus stopped being God when He became a baby. (He remained fully God; He simply veiled His glory). Confusion #2: Because Jesus was God, the temptations He faced weren't actually hard. (They were actually harder, because He never gave in to relieve the pressure).

The Tuesday Payoff It's Tuesday, and you are feeling completely isolated. Maybe your spouse doesn't understand your stress, or your boss is demanding the impossible. You feel the specific ache of being utterly alone in your burden. The doctrine of the Incarnation is the antidote to that isolation. When you pray, you aren't talking to a pristine, untouched deity who has never had a bad day. You are talking to a Savior who was mocked, misunderstood, abandoned by His **Close**st friends, and falsely accused. He doesn't just pity you; He sympathizes with you.

Lane 2 — Depth (30 minutes)

Define the Terms Immanuel - A biblical name for Jesus meaning "God with us." Condescension - Not the modern meaning of being arrogant, but the theological meaning of a superior willingly lowering themselves to interact with an inferior. High Priest - The Old Testament role of representing the people before God, perfectly fulfilled by Jesus.

Build the Doctrine (Scripture-forward)

He Shared Our Flesh and Blood In order to break the curse of death, the Savior had to actually be capable of dying. You cannot execute a spirit.

Key texts: Hebrews 2:14–15

"Since the children have flesh and blood, he too shared in their humanity so that by his death he might break the power of him who holds the power of death... and free those who all their lives were held in slavery by their fear of death." The incarnation was a tactical military maneuver. Jesus took on a physical body specifically so He could use it as a weapon to destroy the power of death from the inside out.

He Experienced Real Temptation If Jesus used a "divine forcefield" to easily deflect temptation, His victory wouldn't help us. He had to fight our battles using the same human limits and reliance on the Holy Spirit that we have.

Key texts: Hebrews 4:15

"For we do not have a high priest who is unable to empathize with our weaknesses, but we have one who has been tempted in every way, just as we are—yet he did not sin." Jesus knows the brutal, grinding weight of temptation. C.S. Lewis noted that a man who gives in to temptation after five minutes never knows the full force of it. Only the man who resists to the very end feels the absolute maximum pressure of the enemy. Jesus felt the maximum pressure.

He Learned Obedience Through Suffering This is one of the most stunning concepts in Scripture. As God, Jesus knew everything. But as a human, He had to actually experience the process of trusting the Father in the dark.

Key texts: Hebrews 5:8

"Son though he was, he learned obedience from what he suffered." He didn't learn obedience because He was previously disobedient. He "learned" it in the sense of physically experiencing it. It is one thing to know *in theory* what a marathon feels like; it is another to actually run it. Jesus ran the agonizing marathon of human suffering so He could be a perfectly qualified, sympathetic Savior.

BOX - What This Is NOT Saying We are NOT saying Jesus ever sinned; He remained completely morally perfect. We are NOT saying the incarnation was a temporary state; the Son of God is united to human flesh forever. We are NOT saying God the Father suffered on the cross; only the Son became incarnate.

BOX - Where Christians Differ Not a major point of disagreement in broad evangelicalism. The exact mechanics of *Kenosis* (what precisely Jesus laid aside in Philippians 2) is a subject of deep academic debate. Some argue He laid aside His divine attributes completely (a heresy known as Kenotic Theology), while orthodox evangelicals maintain He simply laid aside the *independent use* of those attributes, choosing to live in complete reliance on the Holy Spirit to model human obedience.

Lane 3 — Deep Dive (Optional)

The Objection You're Already Thinking "If God loves us so much, why didn't He just snap His fingers and fix the world from heaven? Why go through the messy, humiliating process of being born as a human?"

The Best Answer God absolutely has the power to snap His fingers and eradicate all evil and suffering instantly. But if He did that, He would have to eradicate *you*. We are part of the evil and rebellion of the world. A simple display of raw, sovereign power from heaven would destroy the human race in a fraction of a second.

God's goal wasn't just to destroy evil; His goal was to save His people while destroying the evil inside them. You cannot do that with a lightning bolt. You can only do that with a substitute.

If a judge just snaps his fingers and declares a guilty criminal innocent, the law is mocked. The penalty had to be paid by someone who actually belonged to the human race, but who owed no debt of their own. The Incarnation was necessary because God's justice demanded a human payment, and God's love demanded He make the payment Himself.

Historical Lens In the 2nd century, the Gnostics taught that matter was evil, so God would never touch it. They claimed Jesus only *appeared* to have a physical body, like a ghost or a hologram. The early church fathers, specifically Irenaeus, fought this violently. They understood that "what is not assumed is not healed." If Jesus didn't take on a real human mind, He can't save our minds. If He didn't take on real human flesh, He can't resurrect our flesh. The gritty, physical reality of the manger is essential to salvation.

Real-Life Translation We spend our entire lives trying to climb upward. We want to move from the mailroom to the corner office, from a small apartment to a big house, from being a nobody to being a somebody. The direction of human pride is always *up*.

The Incarnation is the ultimate reversal of human pride. The direction of God is *down*. He moved from the throne room to a feeding trough. He moved from absolute power to absolute vulnerability.

If you are a follower of the Incarnate Christ, your life cannot be entirely about upward mobility, avoiding discomfort, and isolating yourself from the pain of others. The Incarnation calls us to move *downward* toward the broken, the poor, and the hurting. We do not stay safe in our Christian bubbles. We move into the mess, just like He did.

Midlife Module - This Doctrine at 47 You are 47, and your physical limits are no longer theoretical. You can't function on four hours of sleep anymore. You have a lingering injury that won't heal. You find yourself forgetting names. The humiliating reality of human frailty is becoming your daily companion.

The Incarnation changes how you view this decline. You aren't experiencing something foreign to God. Jesus knows what a migraine feels like. He knows the sharp pain of a pulled muscle and the exhaustion of a sleepless night. He voluntarily subjected Himself to the exact same biological fragility you are currently experiencing. Your physical limits are not a sign that God has abandoned you; they are the exact places where the sympathy of Christ meets you most profoundly.

Practice + Prayer

This Week's Practice (3–7 minutes) The Empathy Shift. When someone tells you about a problem this week, stop yourself from offering a quick fix, a Bible verse, or a piece of advice. Do what Jesus did in the incarnation: just sit in the discomfort with them. Say, "That sounds incredibly heavy, and I am so sorry." Practice descending into their mess rather than shouting instructions from above.

Prayer (100–160 words) God, my pride naturally seeks comfort, power, and safety. I am stunned by the humility of Jesus. Thank You for not remaining a distant, unapproachable God. Thank You for Immanuel—God with us. Thank You that Jesus laid aside His glory, took on the fragility of a human body, and learned obedience through the things He suffered. When I am tempted, remind me that Jesus faced the exact same pressure and won. When I am exhausted, remind me that Jesus wept and slept. Give me the profound comfort of knowing I have a High Priest who actually understands my weakness. And give me the courage to step into the mess of other people's lives with that exact same incarnational love. Amen.

<u>**Reflection**</u>

Solo (3 prompts)

1. Do you function as if God is standing above you judging your pain, or sitting beside you understanding it?

2. Why is it important that Jesus faced temptation as a dependent human, rather than using His "God powers" to easily deflect it?

3. In what area of your life are you obsessively trying to climb "upward" (status, comfort), while Jesus is calling you to move "downward" (sacrifice, service)?

Small Group (3 prompts + 1 hard question)

1. Read Philippians 2:5–7. What does the "mindset of Christ" practically look like in a marriage or a workplace?

2. Discuss the quote: "What is not assumed is not healed." Why did Jesus have to take on a real, physical body to save us?

3. We talked about how Jesus didn't just snap His fingers from heaven to fix the world. How does this reality change the way we pray for God to fix our own problems?

Hard Question: Are you currently avoiding a messy, difficult relationship in your church or family simply because you prefer the safety and comfort of your own bubble?

<u>**Close**</u>

One Sentence Recap: God laid aside His glory to enter the dirt, pain, and limits of human existence so He could rescue us from the inside.

If You Only Remember One Thing: You are not praying to an untouchable deity who pities you; you are praying to a High Priest who sympathizes with you.

Next Week Preview: Next week we arrive at the bloody center of human history: The Atonement. How exactly does a man dying on a cross forgive your sins?

Scripture References Used Philippians 2:5–8 Hebrews 2:14–15 Hebrews 4:15 Hebrews 5:8

<u>**My Thoughts & Notes – What Did I Take From This?**</u>

WEEK 31 — ATONEMENT: WHAT THE CROSS ACCOMPLISHED

CORE QUESTION: HOW DOES an innocent man dying on a Roman cross two thousand years ago actually forgive my sins today?

Why this matters: Because if you don't understand the mechanics of the cross, you will spend your entire life exhausting yourself trying to pay off a debt that has already been canceled.

At a Glance (One Page)

Big Idea: On the cross, Jesus acted as our substitute, absorbing the holy wrath of God that we deserved, and crediting His perfect righteousness to our account.

Anchor Text: Isaiah 53:4–6; 2 Corinthians 5:21

We believe…: Jesus Christ died on the cross as a substitutionary sacrifice, completely satisfying the justice of God, averting His wrath, and securing the reconciliation of all who believe.

Key Words (3): Atonement - The work Christ did on the cross to mend the broken relationship between God and humanity by paying the penalty for sin. Penal Substitution - The specific biblical truth that Jesus took our penalty (penal) by standing in our place (substitution). Imputation - A financial term meaning to credit to someone's account. Our sin was imputed to Christ; His righteousness is imputed to us.

The One Mistake People Make: Viewing the cross merely as a tragic example of how much God loves us, completely missing the fact that it was a brutal, legal transaction required to satisfy God's justice.

Choose Your Lane: Lane 1 / Lane 2 / Lane 3

This Week's Practice: The Debt Cancellation.

This Week's Prayer: Father, my pride wants to earn my own salvation. I want to pay my own way. But when I look at the cross, I am forced to admit that my debt was completely unpayable. Thank You for not lowering Your standard of justice. And thank You for not leaving me to face it alone. I am stunned that You would offer Your own Son to take the blow that I deserved. Stop me from trying to add my own good works to the finished work of Jesus. Let the reality of His sacrifice crush my pride and fill me with absolute peace. Amen.

Lane 1 — Clarity (10 minutes)

The Bottom Line Many people view the cross like a man jumping off a bridge to prove to his wife how much he loves her. That isn't love; that is crazy. The cross only makes sense if the wife is drowning in the river, and the man jumps in to push her to safety, drowning in her place. The cross was not just a symbol of love. It was a rescue mission built on a legal exchange. We owed a massive debt of treason to a holy God. Jesus stepped into the courtroom, pushed us out of the defendant's chair, and took the lethal injection we earned.

Scripture Snapshot 2 Corinthians 5:21: "God made him who had no sin to be sin for us, so that in him we might become the righteousness of God."

This is the greatest exchange in human history, often called "The Great Exchange." Think of it as two bank accounts. You have billions in debt (sin). Jesus has billions in wealth (perfect righteousness). At the cross, the accounts are swapped. God treats Jesus on the cross as if He committed every sin you ever committed, and God treats you right now as if you lived the perfect life Jesus lived.

Say It Out Loud (One Sentence) Jesus took the punishment I deserved so I could receive the perfect record I could never earn.

Common Confusions Confusion #1: The cross was "cosmic child abuse" where an angry Father punished an unwilling Son. (The Trinity was perfectly unified in love; the Son willingly laid down His life). Confusion #2: Jesus paid the devil a ransom to get us back. (We did not owe the devil anything; the debt of justice was owed entirely to God).

The Tuesday Payoff You are lying awake at 3:00 AM on a Tuesday, overwhelmed by guilt over a past failure. Your brain is replaying the tape of what you did. You feel the desperate need to "make it up" to God by volunteering more or reading your Bible harder. The doctrine of the Atonement stops this exhausting cycle. It tells your 3:00 AM brain: *The debt is paid. The wrath is satisfied. The check cleared.* You don't have to punish yourself, because Jesus was already punished for it. You can finally go to sleep.

Lane 2 — Depth (30 minutes)

Define the Terms Propitiation - A sacrifice that turns away the righteous wrath of God by satisfying the demands of His justice. Expiation - The removal or wiping away of our guilt and sin. Reconciliation - The restoration of a fractured relationship; moving from enemies to adopted children.

Build the Doctrine (Scripture-forward)

The Problem of Forgiveness We think forgiveness is easy. If someone breaks your lamp, you just say, "Don't worry about it." But forgiveness is never free; it just transfers the cost. If you forgive the broken lamp, *you* absorb the cost of buying a new one.

Key texts: Hebrews 9:22

"And without the shedding of blood there is no forgiveness." God cannot just wave His hand and ignore our treason. A good judge cannot let a murderer walk free without destroying justice. For God to forgive our massive debt, He had to absorb the infinite cost of it Himself. The cross is God absorbing the cost of our rebellion.

The Innocent Substitute Seven hundred years before Jesus was born, the prophet Isaiah perfectly described the mechanics of Penal Substitution.

Key texts: Isaiah 53:4–6

"But he was pierced for our transgressions, he was crushed for our iniquities; the punishment that brought us peace was on him, and by his wounds we are healed... and the Lord has laid on him the iniquity of us all." The language is unavoidable. Jesus wasn't just murdered by the Romans; He was crushed by the Father's justice. He took the penalty (pierced for our transgressions) by standing in our place (laid on him the iniquity of us all).

The Cry of Abandonment The physical torture of the Roman crucifixion was horrific, but it was not the worst part of the cross. Thousands of people were crucified in history. What made Jesus' death unique was the spiritual agony.

Key texts: Matthew 27:46

"About three in the afternoon Jesus cried out in a loud voice... 'My God, my God, why have you forsaken me?'" For all of eternity past, the Father and the Son had existed in perfect, unbroken intimacy. But on the cross, as Jesus absorbed the sin of the world, the Father turned His face away. Jesus experienced the absolute terror of hell—total separation from the presence of God—so that we would never have to.

BOX - What This Is NOT Saying We are NOT saying the cross is the only important thing Jesus did; His perfect life and resurrection are equally vital. We are NOT saying God is a bloodthirsty tyrant; the cross was the ultimate expression of God's love (John 3:16). We are NOT saying the cross saves people who refuse to believe; the atonement must be received by faith.

BOX - Where Christians Differ There are several historical "theories" of the atonement. The *Christus Victor* view emphasizes that the cross defeated Satan and the powers of evil. The *Moral Influence* view emphasizes that the cross demonstrates God's love to melt our hard hearts. Broad evangelicalism affirms both of those are true, but insists that *Penal Substitutionary Atonement* (Jesus paying our legal penalty to satisfy God's wrath) is the foundational anchor. Without the legal payment, the other theories collapse.

Lane 3 — Deep Dive (Optional)

The Objection You're Already Thinking "The idea of a blood sacrifice sounds barbaric and primitive. Why couldn't an advanced, loving God just forgive us without all the blood and violence?"

The Best Answer We recoil at the blood of the cross because we live in incredibly insulated, sanitized cultures. We hide our slaughterhouses and our dying people. But the ancient world understood visceral reality: life is in the blood. When you violate the Source of Life (God), the result is death.

The violence of the cross was not arbitrary. It was a mirror reflecting exactly how horrific and violent our sin actually is. We treat our pride, our gossip, and our lust as minor character flaws. God treats them as a violent tearing apart of His good creation.

If God just quietly forgave us without the cross, we would never understand the gravity of our rebellion. The brutal, bloody violence of the cross forces us to look at the true cost of our sin. It kills our casual approach to evil. It is shocking, offensive, and barbaric because our sin is shocking, offensive, and barbaric.

Historical Lens On the Day of Atonement (Yom Kippur) in the Old Testament, the High Priest would take two goats. The first goat was slaughtered, and its blood was sprinkled on the altar to pay for the sins of the people (propitiation). The priest would then lay his hands on the second goat (the scapegoat), confessing the sins of the nation over it, and send it away into the wilderness, symbolically carrying their sins away (expiation). Jesus explicitly fulfilled both. He is the blood that pays the penalty, and He is the scapegoat who carries our sins completely out of sight.

Real-Life Translation We have a massive cultural problem with "cancel culture." If you make a mistake, say the wrong thing, or fail publicly, the culture demands you be canceled, fired, and ruined. There is no mechanism for forgiveness. We are a society screaming for justice but totally devoid of grace.

The cross is the only answer to a cancel culture. If you belong to Jesus, the ultimate "canceling" already happened to Him on your behalf. You do not have to live in terror of the court of public opinion. You do not have to exhaust yourself trying to defend your reputation. The only Court that actually matters has already banged the gavel and declared you "Not Guilty" based on the blood of the Substitute.

Midlife Module - This Doctrine at 49 You are 49. You are looking at a mortgage that won't be paid off for twenty years, credit card debt from a bad year, and the impending cost of your kids' college. The financial pressure is a constant, heavy weight on your chest. You feel like you will be paying off debts until the day you die.

The financial pressure is real, but it is temporary. The doctrine of the Atonement speaks directly to the deeper, eternal debt you owed. You owed a moral debt of perfection to God that you could not pay off in a million lifetimes. At the cross, Jesus didn't just refinance your debt; He stamped it "Paid in Full." You may have to work hard to pay off the bank, but you never have to work a single day to pay off God. You are entirely clear.

Practice + Prayer

This Week's Practice (3–7 minutes) The Debt Cancellation. Take a physical bill you have recently paid (a utility bill or a credit card statement). Take a red pen and write "Paid in Full by Christ" across it. Keep it on your desk this week. Every time your mind tries to bring up a past failure or a lingering guilt, look at the paper and remind yourself that the spiritual debt is already canceled.

Prayer (100–160 words) God, I do not understand a love this deep. My instinct is to defend myself, to make excuses, and to try and pay You back for my sins by being a better person. Forgive my arrogant self-reliance. When I look at the cross, I see the absolute horror of my sin, and the breathtaking depth of Your grace. Thank You, Jesus, for willingly walking into the courtroom, taking my seat, and absorbing the holy wrath of the Father that I deserved. Thank You for the Great Exchange. I lay down my heavy burden of guilt today. I accept Your perfect record as my own. Help me to live the rest of my life in joyful, staggered gratitude for the debt You canceled. Amen.

Reflection

Solo (3 prompts)

1. Do you secretly believe that you still have to "make it up to God" when you sin, even though Jesus already died for it?

2. How does the "Great Exchange" (our sin for His righteousness) destroy the idea that good people go to heaven and bad people go to hell?

3. Why is it important to remember that the Father and the Son were perfectly unified in the decision to go to the cross?

Small Group (3 prompts + 1 hard question)

1. Read 2 Corinthians 5:21. What happens to our daily anxiety when we realize God currently views us through the perfect track record of Jesus?

2. Discuss the difference between a "Propitiation" (satisfying wrath) and just a general "forgiveness." Why did a penalty have to be paid?

3. We talked about how the cross is the antidote to "cancel culture." How should the reality of the atonement change the way Christians treat people who fail publicly?

Hard Question: Are you continuing to wallow in guilt and self-hatred over a past sin, essentially telling God that the blood of Jesus wasn't quite enough to cover it?

Close

One Sentence Recap: On the cross, Jesus acted as our substitute, absorbing the holy wrath of God we deserved, and crediting His perfect righteousness to our account.

If You Only Remember One Thing: You cannot pay off a debt that has already been canceled; rest in the finished work of the cross.

Next Week Preview: A dead savior is completely useless. Next week we look at the Resurrection. Did it actually happen, and why does it change absolutely everything?

Scripture References Used Isaiah 53:4–6 Matthew 27:46 2 Corinthians 5:21 Hebrews 9:22

My Thoughts & Notes – What Did I Take From This?

Week 32 — Resurrection: History and Hope

Core Question: Did Jesus actually rise from the dead physically, or is the resurrection just an inspiring metaphor for new beginnings?

Why this matters: Because if the tomb wasn't empty, Christianity is a pathetic scam; but if Jesus actually walked out of the grave, death is completely defeated.

At a Glance (One Page)

Big Idea: The physical, historical resurrection of Jesus Christ is the absolute bedrock of the Christian faith, proving He is the Son of God, validating His sacrifice, and guaranteeing our future resurrection.

Anchor Text: 1 Corinthians 15:3–4, 14–17; Luke 24:36–43

We believe...: On the third day, Jesus Christ bodily rose from the grave, conquering sin and death, and ensuring the future physical resurrection of all who are united to Him by faith.

Key Words (3): Resurrection - God raising a dead person back to life in a transformed, physical body that can never die again. Falsifiability - The reality that Christianity rests on a historical claim that could be proven false if the physical body of Jesus was ever found. Firstfruits - An agricultural term Paul uses to describe Jesus' resurrection as the first guarantee of the massive harvest of resurrections to come.

The One Mistake People Make: Treating the resurrection like a spiritual fairy tale meant to inspire us, rather than a brutal, verifiable historical event that demands our absolute allegiance.

Choose Your Lane: Lane 1 / Lane 2 / Lane 3

This Week's Practice: The Friday/Sunday Perspective.

This Week's Prayer: Father, I live in a world that is terrified of death. We spend billions of dollars trying to delay it, hide it, and ignore it. I confess that I often live as if the grave is the final word. Remind me today that the tomb in Jerusalem is empty. Thank You that Christianity is not just a philosophy, but a faith built on the historical reality of a resurrected King. Give me the unshakeable confidence that because Jesus lives, my future is entirely secure. Amen.

Lane 1 — Clarity (10 minutes)

The Bottom Line Most religions are based on the teachings of their founder. If you could prove that the Buddha or Muhammad never actually lived, their moral philosophies might still be helpful. Christianity is completely different. It does not rest on the teachings of Jesus; it rests entirely on the event of His resurrection. If Jesus stayed dead, His teachings on loving your enemies are useless because He lied about being God. The Apostle Paul was brutally honest: if the resurrection is a myth, Christians are the most pathetic people on earth. But if it is history, it is the hinge upon which the entire universe turns.

Scripture Snapshot 1 Corinthians 15:14, 17: "And if Christ has not been raised, our preaching is useless and so is your faith... And if Christ has not been raised, your faith is futile; you are still in your sins."

Paul doesn't offer a backup plan. He stakes the entire Christian religion on one historical, physical event. He says that if the bones of Jesus are still in a grave somewhere in the Middle East, you should **Close** your Bible, walk away from the church, and go live however you want. The resurrection is not a secondary issue you can respectfully disagree on. It is the entire foundation of the house.

Say It Out Loud (One Sentence) Because the tomb is empty, the cross was successful, and my future is secure.

Common Confusions Confusion #1: Jesus just rose "spiritually" in the hearts of His disciples. (He rose physically, eating fish and showing them His scars). Confusion #2: The resurrection is just a metaphor for the cycle of nature (like spring following winter).

The Tuesday Payoff You are standing in a cemetery on a rainy Tuesday afternoon, burying someone you love. The finality of the casket is crushing. The secular world offers you nothing but generic platitudes: "They live on in our memories." But memories fade. You need something stronger than sentimentality. The historical, physical resurrection of Jesus Christ is the only thing that holds your weight at a grave. It tells you that the casket is not a permanent vault; it is a temporary waiting room. Jesus picked the lock on the grave from the inside, ensuring that death does not get the final word.

Lane 2 — Depth (30 minutes)

Define the Terms Bodily Resurrection - Jesus did not come back as a ghost or a pure spirit; He came back with a physical, recognizable, glorified human body. Resuscitation - Bringing someone back to life only for them to eventually die again (like Lazarus). Resurrection is coming back to a life that can never end. Glorification - The final step of our salvation where we receive perfect, sinless, physical bodies identical to Christ's resurrected body.

Build the Doctrine (Scripture-forward)

It Was a Physical Body The early church lived in a Greek culture that hated the physical body. If the disciples were going to invent a myth to start a religion, a "spiritual" resurrection would have been much easier to sell. But they insisted it was physical.

Key texts: Luke 24:38–43

When Jesus appears to the terrified disciples, He immediately addresses their assumption that He is a ghost. "Look at my hands and my feet. It is I myself! Touch me and see; a ghost does not have flesh and bones, as you see I have." Then, to prove the point, He asks for a piece of broiled fish and eats it in front of them. Ghosts don't digest fish. The resurrection was a gritty, biological, material reality.

It Validates the Cross How do we know that Jesus' death on Friday actually paid the penalty for our sins? How do we know God accepted the payment?

Key texts: Romans 4:25

"He was delivered over to death for our sins and was raised to life for our justification." Think of the cross as Jesus writing a massive check to pay off our debt to God's justice. The resurrection is the cleared check coming back from the bank. If Jesus stayed dead, it means the wages of sin were too heavy for Him. His resurrection is the Father's public declaration that the debt is fully paid and the sacrifice is accepted.

The Guarantee of Our Future Jesus' resurrection wasn't just an isolated miracle to prove He was God. It was the prototype for what is going to happen to every believer.

Key texts: 1 Corinthians 15:20–22

Paul calls Christ the "firstfruits of those who have fallen asleep." In farming, the firstfruits are the first crops that ripen, guaranteeing that a massive harvest is right behind them. When Jesus walked out of the tomb, He broke the structural integrity of death. Because you are united to Him by faith, what happened to Him must eventually happen to you. Your body will be raised.

BOX - What This Is NOT Saying We are NOT saying everyone goes to heaven when they die; the Bible speaks of a resurrection to life and a resurrection to judgment (John 5:29). We are NOT saying we become angels when we resurrect; we will have physical, human bodies on a physical, new earth. We are NOT saying believing in the resurrection is anti-intellectual; it is grounded in historical eyewitness testimony.

BOX - Where Christians Differ Not a point of disagreement. The physical, bodily resurrection of Jesus Christ on the third day is the absolute center of the Christian faith, affirmed by the Apostles' Creed and every major orthodox tradition. If a theologian or pastor claims the resurrection was merely "spiritual" or a "metaphor," they have abandoned historic Christianity entirely.

Lane 3 — Deep Dive (Optional)

The Objection You're Already Thinking "How can an educated person in the 21st century believe that a dead body came back to life? Isn't it more likely the disciples just stole the body or hallucinated?"

The Best Answer Skeptics have tried to explain away the empty tomb for 2,000 years. The "stolen body" theory falls apart immediately because men do not allow themselves to be tortured and executed for a lie they invented. If the disciples stole the body, they knew it was a scam. Yet almost all of them were violently martyred for claiming they saw Him alive. People die for lies they *believe* are true; they don't die for lies they *know* they invented.

The "hallucination" theory fails because hallucinations are individual, internal experiences. Five hundred people do not have the exact same hallucination at the exact same time (1 Cor 15:6). Furthermore, hallucinations don't eat fish.

The easiest way for the Roman or Jewish authorities to crush Christianity would have been to simply produce the rotting corpse of Jesus and parade it through the streets of Jerusalem. They didn't do it, because the tomb was empty. The most historically logical explanation for the explosive birth of the church in the exact city where Jesus was executed is that He actually walked out of the grave.

Historical Lens In the first century, the idea of a single person resurrecting in the middle of history was completely foreign to both Jewish and Greek thought. Jews believed in a general resurrection at the very end of time. Greeks believed the soul escaped the body at death and never returned. The disciples did not invent the concept of Jesus' resurrection because it didn't fit their theological framework. It took the physical, shocking reality of the empty tomb to change their minds.

Real-Life Translation We are a society obsessed with avoiding aging and death. We inject Botox, take supplements, and curate our lives to maintain the illusion of youth. Underneath it all is a deep, paralyzing fear that the clock is running out.

The resurrection destroys the fear of missing out (FOMO). If this life is all there is, you have to frantically cram every experience, every vacation, and every success into your brief 80 years. But if the resurrection is true, this life is just the prologue. You are going to live forever in a glorified physical body on a restored physical earth. You don't have to panic about missing out on a few experiences now, because you have an eternity of joy ahead of you. The resurrection allows you to age gracefully and live peacefully.

Midlife Module - This Doctrine at 49 You are 49, and the math of your life is shifting. You are starting to attend more funerals than weddings. The people who anchored your childhood are passing away. The reality of death is no longer an abstract concept; it is an intruder in your immediate circle.

Without the resurrection, midlife becomes an exercise in grim endurance, just waiting for the inevitable end. But the empty tomb changes the trajectory. It tells you that the best part of your life is not behind you in your twenties. The best part of your life is in front of you. Because Jesus lives, every funeral you attend for a believer is an interruption, not an ending. The resurrection gives you the steel in your spine required to face the second half of your life with unshakeable hope.

Practice + Prayer

This Week's Practice (3–7 minutes) The Friday/Sunday Perspective. Pick a problem in your life that currently feels dead, hopeless, or unfixable (a fractured relationship, a career dead-end, a chronic struggle). View it through the lens of Saturday.

The disciples thought Saturday was the permanent end of the story. Remind yourself that God does His best work in the dark, and Sunday is coming.

Prayer (100–160 words) God, I praise You for the empty tomb. Thank You that Christianity is not just a philosophy to help me live a better life, but a historical rescue mission that defeated my greatest enemy. When I look at the aging of my own body, and when I stand at the graves of the people I love, protect me from despair. Remind me that Jesus holds the keys to death and hell. Give me the profound peace of knowing that because He lives, I will also live. Help me to stop living in fear of the future. Anchor my heart in the absolute guarantee of the resurrection, and let that hope change the way I live today. A men.

Reflection

Solo (3 prompts)

1. If an archaeologist definitively found the bones of Jesus tomorrow, how would it change your faith?

2. Why is the physical, bodily nature of the resurrection (eating fish, scars) so important to the Christian faith?

3. How does the promise of a future resurrection free you from the frantic pressure to experience "everything" in this current life?

Small Group (3 prompts + 1 hard question)

1. Read 1 Corinthians 15:14–17. Why is Paul so willing to admit that if the resurrection is fake, our faith is entirely useless?

2. Discuss the "stolen body" and "hallucination" theories. Why do these secular explanations for the empty tomb ultimately fail?

3. We talked about how the resurrection changes the way we age. How can our church better support people who are dealing with the fear of death and physical decline?

Hard Question: Are you living your daily life as a functional atheist—terrified of aging, obsessed with your legacy, and acting as if this life is all there is?

Close

One Sentence Recap: The physical resurrection of Jesus Christ is the absolute bedrock of the faith, validating His sacrifice and guaranteeing our future resurrection.

If You Only Remember One Thing: The casket is not a permanent vault; because Jesus picked the lock from the inside, it is only a temporary waiting room.

Next Week Preview: This completes Part 5. Next week we look at the Ascension. Jesus didn't just rise from the dead; He went somewhere, and He is doing something right now.

Scripture References Used Luke 24:36–43 John 5:29 Romans 4:25 1 Corinthians 15:3–4 1 Corinthians 15:14–17 1 Corinthians 15:20–22

My Thoughts & Notes – What Did I Take From This?

Week 33 — Ascension and Reign: Jesus Is Not Past Tense

Core Question: Where is Jesus right now, and what is He actually doing while the world feels like it is falling apart?

Why this matters: Because if Jesus just vanished into the clouds after the resurrection, we are orphaned; but if He ascended to a throne, He is actively running the universe today.

At a Glance (One Page)

Big Idea: The Ascension was not a disappearing act; it was a coronation. Jesus physically ascended to heaven to sit at the right hand of the Father, where He currently rules the cosmos and advocates for us.

Anchor Text: Acts 1:9–11; Ephesians 1:20–23

We believe...: Forty days after His resurrection, Jesus Christ bodily ascended into heaven, where He sits at the right hand of God the Father, ruling over all things and interceding for His people.

Key Words (3): Ascension - The historical event where the resurrected Jesus physically departed earth and returned to the presence of the Father. Session - The theological term for Jesus "sitting down" at the right hand of God, indicating that His atoning work is finished and His ruling authority is absolute. Intercession - Jesus actively intervening, praying, and advocating for us before the Father.

The One Mistake People Make: Thinking about Jesus entirely in the past tense (what He did on the cross) or the future tense (when He comes back), completely forgetting what He is doing right now.

Choose Your Lane: Lane 1 / Lane 2 / Lane 3

This Week's Practice: The News Fast.

This Week's Prayer: Father, I confess that I act like an orphan. I look at the chaos in the world, the corruption in politics, and the stress in my own home, and I assume no one is in charge. Forgive my functional atheism. Remind me today that Jesus did not just rise from the dead; He ascended to a throne. Give me the profound peace of knowing that there is a human being sitting at the control center of the universe. Help me to trust His invisible reign when all I can see is the visible chaos. Amen.

Lane 1 — Clarity (10 minutes)

The Bottom Line We celebrate Christmas (the Incarnation) and Easter (the Resurrection) with massive church services, but we almost entirely ignore the Ascension. We treat it like a footnote—the moment Jesus finally left to go take a nap in the clouds. But in the Bible, the Ascension is the climax of the story. It is the moment the victorious warrior returns home to receive the crown. Jesus is not retired. He is actively ruling history, guiding His church, and speaking to the Father on your behalf.

Scripture Snapshot Ephesians 1:20–22: "...he raised Christ from the dead and seated him at his right hand in the heavenly realms, far above all rule and authority, power and dominion... And God placed all things under his feet and appointed him to be head over everything for the church."

Paul wants the Ephesians to understand the current zip code of Jesus. He isn't just "in our hearts." He is seated in the position of ultimate cosmic authority (the right hand). Paul explicitly says Jesus is currently outranking every single political ruler, spiritual power, and human authority in existence. The government may be passing laws, but Jesus is running the board.

Say It Out Loud (One Sentence) Jesus is not a past-tense historical figure; He is the present-tense King ruling the universe right now.

Common Confusions Confusion #1: Jesus left His human body behind when He went back to heaven. (He ascended bodily; there is a physical human being in heaven right now). Confusion #2: The Ascension means God is farther away from us. (It actually allowed the Holy Spirit to be sent so God could be **_Closer_** to us).

The Tuesday Payoff You are watching the evening news on Tuesday, and a wave of deep anxiety hits you. The economy is shaking, global conflicts are escalating, and the political rhetoric is toxic. If Jesus is just a past-tense Savior who died for your sins but has no power today, you have every right to panic. But the Ascension tells your nervous system to stand down. The anchor of the universe holds. The man who bled for you is currently managing the geopolitical timeline of the world. You can turn off the news and go to sleep.

Lane 2 — Depth (30 minutes)

Define the Terms The Right Hand of God - A biblical metaphor for the position of highest honor, power, and executive authority. Advocate - A defense attorney; someone who pleads your case before a judge. Omnipresence - While Jesus' _human body_ is located in one place (heaven), His _divine nature_ remains present everywhere.

Build the Doctrine (Scripture-forward)

He Sat Down (The Work is Finished) In the Old Testament, the priests in the temple never sat down. There were no chairs in the tabernacle because their work of sacrificing animals was never finished.

Key texts: Hebrews 10:11–12

"Day after day every priest stands and performs his religious duties; again and again he offers the same sacrifices, which can never take away sins. But when this priest [Jesus] had offered for all time one sacrifice for sins, he sat down at the right hand of God." Jesus sitting down is a massive theological statement. The debt is paid. The atonement is complete. You do not have to keep sacrificing yourself to earn God's favor.

He Intercedes (The Work Continues) While the work of atonement is finished, the work of applying that grace to your daily life is ongoing. Jesus is actively praying for you right now.

Key texts: Romans 8:34; Hebrews 7:25

"Christ Jesus who died—more than that, who was raised to life—is at the right hand of God and is also interceding for us" (Romans 8:34). When you fail, when you are discouraged, or when you are under spiritual attack, Jesus is serving as your defense attorney before the Father. He doesn't defend you by claiming you are innocent; He defends you by pointing to His own scars and saying, "I already paid for that."

He Rules (The King is Active) The Ascension means the kingdom of God has a reigning King. History is not a random collision of events; it is being steered toward a specific, triumphant conclusion.

Key texts: Psalm 110:1; 1 Corinthians 15:25

Psalm 110 is the most quoted Old Testament passage in the New Testament: "The Lord says to my lord: 'Sit at my right hand until I make your enemies a footstool for your feet.'" Jesus is currently ruling in the midst of His enemies. He is allowing history to play out, slowly putting every enemy (including death) under His feet, until the day He returns to finish the job.

BOX - What This Is NOT Saying We are NOT saying the world is perfect right now; we live in the "already, but not yet" phase of the Kingdom. We are NOT saying Jesus is physically walking the earth; He is bodily in heaven, but spiritually present through the Holy Spirit. We are NOT saying we have to literally look up at the clouds to pray to Him.

BOX - Where Christians Differ Not a major point of theological disagreement. The bodily Ascension and current Session of Christ at the right hand of the Father are affirmed by all historic Christian traditions. Differences usually only arise in discussions about the Lord's Supper (whether Christ's physical body can be present in the bread if He is bodily in heaven), but the reality of His heavenly reign is undisputed.

Lane 3 — Deep Dive (Optional)

The Objection You're Already Thinking "If Jesus is ruling the universe right now, why is everything such a mess? If He is really in charge, why doesn't He stop the suffering, the wars, and the corruption immediately?"

The Best Answer This is the tension of living between D-Day and V-E Day. In World War II, the successful invasion of Normandy on D-Day guaranteed the Allies would win the war. The enemy's back was broken. But the war didn't end that afternoon. There were still months of brutal fighting, casualties, and suffering before Victory in Europe (V-E) Day was finally declared.

The cross and the resurrection were D-Day. The decisive battle has been won. Sin, death, and Satan have been dealt a fatal blow. Jesus ascended to the throne, guaranteeing the final outcome. But we are currently living in the messy, painful overlap of the ages—the time between His ascension and His final return.

Jesus is delaying the final, crushing conclusion of the war (V-E Day) for a specific reason: grace. Peter writes, "He is patient with you, not wanting anyone to perish, but everyone to come to repentance" (2 Peter 3:9). He is ruling with restraint, allowing the timeline to stay open so that more people can be saved before the doors finally **Close**.

Historical Lens The Heidelberg Catechism (1563) asks a beautiful question about the Ascension: "How does Christ's ascension into heaven benefit us?" One of the answers is profound: "We have our own flesh in heaven as a sure pledge that Christ our head will also take us, his members, up to himself." The early Protestants realized the immense comfort of having a human representative who understands our weakness permanently stationed in the throne room of God.

Real-Life Translation We spend a massive amount of psychological energy trying to secure our own future. We obsess over our investments, our health, and our children's choices. We want to be in the control room of our own lives.

The Ascension is God's gentle reminder that the control room is already occupied, and you are not qualified to sit there. If you believe Jesus is at the right hand of the Father, it frees you to be a finite, limited human being. You can work hard at your job, love your family deeply, and then go to sleep at night knowing that the ultimate outcomes of history are resting on the shoulders of the King, not on you.

Midlife Module - This Doctrine at 47 You are 47, and you are dealing with a lingering, quiet sense of failure. You thought you would be further along by now—spiritually, financially, or relationally. You feel like God has moved on to younger, more useful people. You feel forgotten.

The doctrine of Christ's Intercession speaks directly into this midlife ache. Jesus is currently at the right hand of the Father, and He is explicitly praying for you. He hasn't forgotten your name, and He isn't frustrated by your slow progress. The King of the universe is actively advocating for your endurance, your joy, and your faith today. You are fiercely, constantly defended.

Practice + Prayer

This Week's Practice (3–7 minutes) The News Fast. The 24-hour news cycle is designed to convince you that the world is completely out of control. This week, take a 48-hour total fast from all political news and commentary. Use the time you would have spent doomscrolling to read Ephesians 1. Re-anchor your mind in the reality of who is actually in charge.

Prayer (100–160 words) God, my eyes deceive me. When I look at the world, I see chaos, injustice, and pain. I confess that I often doubt Your control. Thank You for the undeniable truth of the Ascension. Thank You that Jesus did not abandon us, but took His rightful place on the throne. I am deeply comforted knowing that a man who has experienced physical pain, rejection, and exhaustion is currently running the universe. Thank You, Jesus, for praying for me when I am too weak to pray for myself. Give me the faith to trust Your invisible reign. Help me to live today not as an anxious orphan, but as a confident citizen of an unshakeable Kingdom. Amen.

<u>**Reflection**</u>

Solo (3 prompts)

1. Do you naturally tend to view Jesus as a past historical figure or a present, active King?

2. Why is it significant that there is a physical human body in heaven right now representing us?

3. How does knowing that Jesus "sat down" (meaning the work of earning salvation is over) relieve your daily religious anxiety?

Small Group (3 prompts + 1 hard question)

1. Read Hebrews 10:11–12. Discuss the difference between the Old Testament priests who never sat down and Jesus who did.

2. We discussed the D-Day vs. V-E Day analogy. How does this help explain why we still experience intense suffering even though Jesus is King?

3. How does the reality of Christ's current intercession (praying for us) change the way we view our own failures?

Hard Question: Are you currently losing your mind over politics because you secretly believe the government has more power over your future than the ascended Christ?

<u>**Close**</u>

One Sentence Recap: Jesus physically ascended to heaven to sit at the right hand of the Father, where He currently rules the cosmos and advocates for us.

If You Only Remember One Thing: The government may be passing laws, but Jesus is running the board.

Next Week Preview: We know Jesus is King, but what else does He do? Next week we look at His three specific jobs: Prophet, Priest, and King.

Scripture References Used Psalm 110:1 Romans 8:34 1 Corinthians 15:25 Ephesians 1:20–23 Hebrews 7:25 Hebrews 10:11–12 2 Peter 3:9

<u>My Thoughts & Notes – What Did I Take From This?</u>

Week 34 — Prophet, Priest, King: What Jesus Does for You

Core Question: What exactly does Jesus do for me on a daily basis, other than just saving me from hell when I die?

Why this matters: Because if you don't understand how Jesus practically functions in your life today, your faith will be a stale, abstract concept rather than a living relationship.

At a Glance (One Page)

Big Idea: To completely rescue us, Jesus fulfills the three great offices of the Old Testament: He is the Prophet who speaks God's truth to us, the Priest who connects us to God, and the King who rules and protects us.

Anchor Text: Hebrews 4:14–16; Revelation 19:16

We believe...: Jesus Christ is the sole Mediator between God and humanity, perfectly executing the offices of Prophet (revealing God), Priest (reconciling us to God), and King (ruling over us and defending us).

Key Words (3): Prophet - Someone who speaks on behalf of God to the people, revealing truth and calling out sin. Priest - Someone who represents the people before God, offering sacrifices to atone for sin and interceding on their behalf. King - Someone who has supreme authority to rule, protect, and guide His subjects.

The One Mistake People Make: Taking one piece of Jesus and ignoring the rest—wanting His priestly forgiveness when they mess up, but rejecting His kingly authority when He tells them how to live.

Choose Your Lane: Lane 1 / Lane 2 / Lane 3

This Week's Practice: The Office Audit.

This Week's Prayer: Father, I confess that I want a customized Savior. I want the Priest to forgive me when I fail, but I don't want the Prophet to convict me of my sin, and I certainly don't want the King telling me what to do with my money or my time. Forgive me for trying to slice Jesus into pieces. Thank You that He is exactly what I need. Open my ears to hear His truth, open my heart to receive His grace, and bend my knees to submit to His rule. Amen.

Lane 1 — Clarity (10 minutes)

The Bottom Line In the Old Testament, God appointed three specific roles to manage the nation of Israel: prophets, priests, and kings. The problem was that the humans in these roles constantly failed. The prophets were ignored, the priests were corrupt, and the kings were tyrants. The entire Old Testament is a massive flashing sign pointing to the need for someone better. Jesus arrives and assumes all three offices perfectly. He doesn't just hold the titles; He executes the jobs on your behalf every single day.

Scripture Snapshot Hebrews 4:14–16: "Therefore, since we have a great high priest who has ascended into heaven, Jesus the Son of God, let us hold firmly to the faith we profess... Let us then approach God's throne of grace with confidence, so that we may receive mercy and find grace to help us in our time of need."

The writer of Hebrews is laser-focused on the daily, functional reality of Jesus as our Priest. Because Jesus has ascended and is currently holding the office, you do not have to cower in fear when you fail. You do not have to clean yourself up before you pray. You can walk straight into the throne room of the universe—with confidence—because the Priest standing next to the throne is your brother, and He has already paid your entry fee.

Say It Out Loud (One Sentence) Jesus speaks truth to me as a Prophet, forgives my sin as a Priest, and defends my life as a King.

Common Confusions Confusion #1: Jesus only acted as a Prophet and Priest on earth; He won't be a King until He returns. (He is ruling as King right now over His church and the cosmos). Confusion #2: We need other human mediators (like saints or earthly priests) to get to God. (Jesus is the sole, sufficient mediator between God and man).

The Tuesday Payoff You are making a complex ethical decision at work on a Tuesday. The culture tells you to do whatever maximizes profit. But you need guidance. You need the **Prophet** to give you the truth of God's Word through the Spirit. You make the hard choice, and it causes friction. You feel anxious and attacked. You need the **King** to protect your heart and remind you who actually rules your future. Later, you lose your temper and snap at a coworker out of stress. You need the **Priest** to apply grace and secure your forgiveness. You need all three offices just to survive Tuesday.

Lane 2 — Depth (30 minutes)

Define the Terms Mediator - A go-between who resolves a conflict between two parties. Jesus is the only mediator between God and man (1 Tim 2:5). Atonement - The work of a priest offering a sacrifice to pay for sin. Sovereignty - The absolute right of a king to govern his domain.

Build the Doctrine (Scripture-forward)

The Perfect Prophet A prophet's job is to reveal God to humanity. In the Old Testament, prophets spoke *for* God ("Thus says the Lord"). But Jesus is entirely different. He doesn't just speak for God; He *is* God speaking.

Key texts: Hebrews 1:1–2; John 14:9

"In the past God spoke to our ancestors through the prophets... but in these last days he has spoken to us by his Son" (Heb 1:1-2). Jesus said, "Anyone who has seen me has seen the Father" (John 14:9). As our Prophet today, Jesus illuminates our minds through the Holy Spirit and the Word, exposing our blind spots and revealing the exact character of God.

The Perfect Priest A priest's job is to represent humanity before God by offering sacrifices for sin. Earthly priests had to keep offering animals every day because the blood of a goat can't actually clear a human conscience.

Key texts: Hebrews 9:24–26; 1 John 2:1

Jesus didn't offer a goat; He offered Himself. He was both the Priest and the Sacrifice. And because He rose from the dead, He remains our Priest forever. "But if anybody does sin, we have an advocate with the Father—Jesus Christ, the Righteous One" (1 John 2:1). When you sin today, you don't need to sacrifice an animal or punish yourself; your Priest is already standing in the gap.

The Perfect King A king's job is to rule, protect, and provide for his people. But Jesus is not a politician taking polls. He is an absolute monarch whose kingdom operates on entirely different rules than the empires of the world.

Key texts: Revelation 19:16; John 18:36

When Jesus stood before Pilate, He said, "My kingdom is not of this world" (John 18:36). He rules not by military force, but by the transforming power of the gospel. He subdues our rebellious hearts, protects us from the ultimate power of the enemy, and will one day return as the "King of kings and Lord of lords" (Rev 19:16) to completely eradicate evil.

BOX - What This Is NOT Saying We are NOT saying Jesus changes hats and performs these roles separately; He is always simultaneously Prophet, Priest, and King. We are NOT saying earthly pastors are our priests; in the New Covenant, all believers are part of a "royal priesthood" with direct access to God. We are NOT saying Jesus' kingdom is a political party; His rule transcends all human politics.

BOX - Where Christians Differ Not a major point of theological disagreement. The "Threefold Office" (Munus Triplex) of Christ was heavily popularized by John Calvin during the Reformation, but it is firmly rooted in the early church and is taught across broad evangelicalism, Reformed, and mainline traditions. It is simply the most robust, biblical way to categorize the work of Christ.

Lane 3 — Deep Dive (Optional)

The Objection You're Already Thinking "The idea of a 'King' sounds like a tyrant who demands blind submission. Why would I want to surrender my freedom to an absolute monarch?"

The Best Answer Our hesitation with the word "King" is completely justified because almost every human king in history has been a tyrant. Human kings use their subjects to protect themselves. They send the peasants to die on the front lines so the king can stay safe in the castle.

But Jesus reverses the flow of power. He is the Servant King. Instead of sending His subjects to die for Him, He leaves the castle, goes to the front lines, and dies for His subjects. He uses His absolute power not to oppress us, but to serve us and wash our feet.

True freedom is not the absence of authority; it is submitting to the *right* authority. If you don't submit to the King of Kings, you will submit to something else—your career, your addictions, or public opinion—and those masters are incredibly cruel. Surrendering your freedom to a King who bleeds for you is the only way to actually be free.

Historical Lens During the Reformation, the church fought heavily against the medieval Catholic system that placed human priests, saints, and the Pope as necessary mediators between the believer and God. By aggressively reclaiming the biblical teaching that Jesus is our *only* High Priest (1 Timothy 2:5), the Reformers demolished the religious hierarchy. They gave everyday plumbers, farmers, and mothers the astonishing theological right to walk directly into the presence of God without needing an earthly middleman.

Real-Life Translation We all have a tendency to treat Jesus like a buffet, taking the parts of His job description we like and leaving the rest.

When you feel guilty, you love Jesus the **Priest**. You want forgiveness. But when Jesus the **Prophet** tells you that your financial habits are greedy, you get defensive and ignore Him. When Jesus the **King** commands you to forgive the person who ruined your reputation, you refuse to submit.

You cannot divide Jesus. If you want the comfort of His priesthood, you must submit to the authority of His kingship and the conviction of His prophetic Word. A healthy, mature Christian life is a life lived in submission to all three offices simultaneously.

Midlife Module - This Doctrine at 51 You are 51. You are the boss at work, you are the leader in your home, and people are constantly looking to you for answers. The sheer weight of having to make the decisions, protect the family, and fix the problems is exhausting. You are tired of being in charge.

The threefold office of Christ is a massive relief for the exhausted leader. It reminds you that you are not the ultimate Prophet, Priest, or King of your family or your company. You don't have to know the future (He is the Prophet). You don't have to fix the spiritual failures of your kids (He is the Priest). You don't have to control the chaotic outcomes of the economy (He is the King). You can step down from the throne you were never meant to occupy and let Him carry the weight.

Practice + Prayer

This Week's Practice (3–7 minutes) The Office Audit. Identify which of the three offices you currently resist the most. Do you ignore the Prophet (avoiding the Bible because it convicts you)? Do you doubt the Priest (refusing to believe you are truly forgiven)? Or do you resist the King (refusing to obey a clear command)? Confess that specific resistance to Him today.

Prayer (100–160 words) God, thank You for sending Jesus to be everything I desperately need. I confess that I want the benefits of Your grace without the demands of Your rule. Forgive my rebellion. Jesus, thank You for being the perfect Prophet who speaks truth into my confusion. Thank You for being the merciful High Priest who stands in the gap for my sin, ensuring that I am always welcomed by the Father. And thank You for being the Sovereign King who defends me from the enemy and rules over the chaos of my life. Help me to stop trying to be the king of my own small kingdom. Give me the joy of total surrender to Your perfect leadership. Amen.

Reflection

Solo (3 prompts)

1. Which of the three offices of Christ (Prophet, Priest, King) brings you the most comfort right now, and why?

2. How does viewing Jesus as the "Servant King" change your perspective on submitting to His authority?

3. Have you been relying on any "human mediators" (a pastor, a podcaster, a spouse) to connect you to God, rather than going directly to Jesus?

Small Group (3 prompts + 1 hard question)

1. Read Hebrews 4:14–16. How does the reality that our High Priest can "empathize with our weaknesses" change the way we pray when we are ashamed?

2. Discuss the concept of the "buffet Jesus" from Lane 3. Why is it so tempting to accept His forgiveness but ignore His commands?

3. We talked about how earthly kings use their subjects, while Jesus died for His. How should this model change the way Christians lead in the workplace or the home?

Hard Question: Are you currently ignoring a clear, prophetic conviction from the Holy Spirit regarding a specific sin in your life?

Close

One Sentence Recap: Jesus perfectly executes the offices of Prophet (revealing God), Priest (reconciling us to God), and King (ruling over us and defending us).

If You Only Remember One Thing: You cannot divide Jesus; you cannot have the comfort of His priesthood without submitting to the authority of His kingship.

Next Week Preview: Now that we know who the King is, what exactly is His mission? Next week we look at the Kingdom of God and why we are still here.

Scripture References Used John 14:9 John 18:36 1 Timothy 2:5 Hebrews 1:1–2 Hebrews 4:14–16 Hebrews 9:24–26 1 John 2:1 Revelation 19:16

My Thoughts & Notes – What Did I Take From This?

WEEK 35 — KINGDOM AND MISSION: WHY WE'RE HERE

CORE QUESTION: IF JESUS already saved us, why did He leave us in this broken world instead of just taking us straight to heaven?

Why this matters: Because if you don't understand your mission, you will treat Christianity as a waiting room for heaven, completely wasting your life on earth.

At a Glance (One Page)

Big Idea: Jesus inaugurated the Kingdom of God on earth and left the church here as His authorized ambassadors, commanded to make disciples and demonstrate His reign until He returns.

Anchor Text: Matthew 28:18–20; Acts 1:8

We believe...: The Kingdom of God is currently present in the world through the Spirit-empowered church, which is commissioned to proclaim the gospel, make disciples of all nations, and push back the darkness of a fallen world.

Key Words (3): Kingdom of God - The dynamic reign and rule of God, breaking into human history through Jesus, though not yet fully consummated. Great Commission - The final, binding command of Jesus for His followers to go into all the world and make disciples. Witness - Someone who publicly testifies to what they have seen and heard regarding the reality of Jesus Christ.

The One Mistake People Make: Viewing "missions" as a specialized activity reserved only for radical people who move to foreign countries, rather than the basic job description of every ordinary Christian.

Choose Your Lane: Lane 1 / Lane 2 / Lane 3

This Week's Practice: The Neighborhood Walk.

This Week's Prayer: Father, I confess that I often live as a tourist in Your kingdom rather than an ambassador. I treat the church like a consumer product designed to meet my needs, and I treat the lost world like an annoyance to be avoided. Forgive my selfishness. Remind me that I was saved for a purpose. Open my eyes to the people right in front of me who are desperate for hope. Give me the courage to speak the truth of the gospel, and the grace to live a life that actually backs up my words. Use my ordinary life for Your eternal mission. Amen.

Lane 1 — Clarity (10 minutes)

The Bottom Line The Christian life is not a cruise ship where you sit on the deck drinking iced tea while waiting to dock in heaven. It is a battleship. The moment you are saved, you are drafted. Jesus brought the Kingdom of God to earth, dealt a fatal blow to the enemy at the cross, and then handed the keys to His followers. He didn't leave us here to be comfortable; He left us here to be witnesses. Whether you are a software engineer, a stay-at-home parent, or a mechanic, your primary identity is an ambassador of the reigning King, stationed behind enemy lines to rescue people.

Scripture Snapshot Matthew 28:18–20: "Then Jesus came to them and said, 'All authority in heaven and on earth has been given to me. Therefore go and make disciples of all nations, baptizing them in the name of the Father and of the Son and of the Holy Spirit, and teaching them to obey everything I have commanded you.'"

Notice the foundation of the Great Commission. Jesus doesn't start by telling us to try hard. He starts by establishing His absolute authority. Because He owns the universe, we have the right to go anywhere in it and declare His name. The command is not to "get decisions" or "increase church attendance." The command is to make disciples—teaching people how to submit their entire lives to the King.

Say It Out Loud (One Sentence) I am not just waiting for heaven; I am an ambassador stationed on earth to advance the Kingdom of Jesus.

Common Confusions Confusion #1: Expanding the Kingdom means taking over the government and passing Christian laws. (The Kingdom expands through changed hearts, not political coercion). Confusion #2: Evangelism means awkwardly manipulating people into praying a prayer. (Evangelism is simply telling the truth about Jesus and leaving the results to God).

The Tuesday Payoff You are walking into a tense, toxic workplace on Tuesday morning. People are gossiping, cutting corners, and stressing out. If your only goal is to pay the bills, you will just put your head down and survive. But if you understand the mission, the office is an outpost. You are the Kingdom representative in that room. When you refuse to gossip, when you show bizarre grace to an annoying coworker, and when you do excellent work without demanding credit, you are demonstrating the reality of the invisible King. Your boring job is frontline mission work.

Lane 2 — Depth (30 minutes)

Define the Terms Inaugurated Eschatology - The "Already, but Not Yet" nature of the Kingdom. The Kingdom is already here, but not yet fully realized. Ambassador - An official representative sent to live in a foreign country, authorized to speak on behalf of their home ruler (2 Cor 5:20). Evangelism - The joyful announcement of the "Good News" that Jesus is Lord and Savior.

Build the Doctrine (Scripture-forward)

The Kingdom is Already Here Many Christians believe the Kingdom of God is just a synonym for "heaven after you die." But Jesus consistently preached that the Kingdom had invaded the present timeline.

Key texts: Mark 1:15; Luke 17:20–21

"The kingdom of God has come near," Jesus announced (Mark 1:15). When the Pharisees asked when it was coming, He replied, "The coming of the kingdom of God is not something that can be observed... because the kingdom of God is in your midst" (Luke 17). Wherever the King is obeyed, the Kingdom is present. It is currently operating like yeast in dough—quietly, subversively expanding across the globe through the local church.

The Mission is Holistic We often divide mission into two competing camps: preaching the gospel (evangelism) vs. doing good deeds (justice/mercy). The biblical mission demands both. We declare the truth with our mouths and demonstrate the truth with our hands.

Key texts: Matthew 5:16; 1 Peter 3:15

Jesus says, "Let your light shine before others, that they may see your good deeds and glorify your Father in heaven." Our radical generosity, care for the poor, and ethical integrity make the gospel visible. But good deeds alone don't save souls. Peter tells us to "Always be prepared to give an answer to everyone who asks you to give the reason for the hope that you have." We must use words to explain *why* we live differently.

The Power is the Spirit The Great Commission is a terrifyingly massive assignment. Changing human hearts is impossible. Jesus knew we would panic, so He attached a massive promise to the command.

Key texts: Acts 1:8

"But you will receive power when the Holy Spirit comes on you; and you will be my witnesses in Jerusalem, and in all Judea and Samaria, and to the ends of the earth." We are not asked to accomplish the mission in our own strength, with our own clever marketing, or our own apologetic arguments. The Holy Spirit does the heavy lifting of conviction and regeneration. We are simply asked to open our mouths and be faithful witnesses to what we have seen.

BOX - What This Is NOT Saying We are NOT saying Christians will successfully fix the entire world before Jesus returns; full restoration requires His second coming. We are NOT saying you need a theology degree to share the gospel; a witness simply testifies to what Jesus did for them. We are NOT saying you should force your faith on people; we persuade with gentleness and respect (1 Peter 3).

BOX - Where Christians Differ There are differing views on how the Kingdom relates to culture. Some traditions (Transformationalist/Neo-Calvinist) emphasize active involvement in politics, arts, and business to "redeem the culture" for Christ. Other traditions (Two Kingdoms) emphasize a sharper distinction, focusing the church's mission strictly on preaching the gospel and administering the sacraments, while leaving cultural improvement to individual citizens. Both agree, however, that the Great Commission to make disciples is non-negotiable.

Lane 3 — Deep Dive (Optional)

The Objection You're Already Thinking "I hate the idea of evangelism. It feels like I'm a slick salesperson trying to manipulate my friends into joining a club, and it usually just ruins the relationship."

The Best Answer Many Gen X Christians grew up in the 1990s era of highly aggressive, formulaic evangelism. We were trained to pass out tracts, corner people on airplanes, and force a scripted presentation on them. It felt manipulative because it was.

But biblical evangelism is not sales. A salesperson's job depends on closing the deal. A witness's job is entirely different. In a courtroom, a witness is not responsible for the verdict. The judge and the jury decide the verdict. The witness is only responsible to sit in the chair and tell the truth about what they saw.

You are not responsible for saving your friends. You cannot argue anyone into the kingdom of God. Your only job is to live a radically authentic life of love, and when they ask you why you have hope, you introduce them to Jesus. It takes the exhausting pressure of "closing the deal" off your shoulders and puts it back on the Holy Spirit where it belongs.

Historical Lens In the early centuries of the church, Christianity was an illegal, heavily persecuted minority religion. They didn't have massive conferences, political power, or radio stations. So how did they conquer the Roman Empire within 300 years? They practiced radical hospitality. When plagues hit a city, the wealthy pagans fled, but the Christians stayed to nurse the sick. They adopted abandoned babies. They loved their enemies. Their visible love made their invisible message utterly undeniable.

Real-Life Translation We spend the first half of our lives obsessed with building our own tiny kingdoms. We want the house, the title, the comfortable bank account, and the perfectly curated family. But by midlife, you realize that your tiny kingdom is incredibly fragile. It can be wiped out by a single diagnosis or a market crash. And even when it succeeds, it isn't big enough to satisfy your soul.

The mission of Jesus invites you to abandon the exhausting project of building your own kingdom, and integrate your life into a Kingdom that will never end. It means your money, your home, and your career are no longer ends in themselves; they are resources you leverage to bless your neighbors and advance the gospel. You trade a fragile, temporary kingdom for an unshakeable, eternal one.

Midlife Module - This Doctrine at 46 You are 46, and your kids are starting to leave the house. For twenty years, your entire mission was keeping them alive, fed, and educated. Now, the house is getting quieter, and you are staring at a massive, terrifying question: *What is my purpose now?*

This is the beauty of the Great Commission. Your primary mission wasn't just raising kids; your primary mission is making disciples. The empty nest isn't a retirement from purpose; it is a redeployment. You now have the time, the financial stability, and the hard-earned wisdom to mentor younger couples, open your home for hospitality, and serve the church in ways you couldn't when you were drowning in diapers. Your mission is just entering its most effective phase.

Practice + Prayer

This Week's Practice (3–7 minutes) The Neighborhood Walk. Go for a walk around your block or your office building without your headphones. Pray specifically for the physical houses or desks you walk past. Ask God to show you one person in your immediate proximity who needs a ridiculous, unearned act of grace this week, and then do it.

Prayer (100–160 words) God, thank You for the profound privilege of being invited into Your mission. You don't need my help to save the world, but in Your grace, You allow me to be a part of the rescue operation. I confess that I am often cowardly. I care more about what my neighbors think of me than I care about their eternal souls. Forgive me for building my own comfortable kingdom while ignoring Yours. Fill me with the Holy Spirit. Give me a genuine, weeping love for the lost. Help me to view my home, my money, and my career as weapons to be used for the gospel. Make my life a clear, undeniable witness to the goodness of the King. Amen.

Reflection

Solo (3 prompts)

1. Do you view your daily job as a secular distraction from your faith, or as an active outpost for the Kingdom of God?

2. Why is it a relief to remember that you are a "witness" (telling the truth) rather than a "salesperson" (closing the deal) when sharing the gospel?

3. What is one specific way your life would have to change if you actually treated your home as a tool for hospitality and mission, rather than just a private retreat?

Small Group (3 prompts + 1 hard question)

1. Read Matthew 5:16 and 1 Peter 3:15. Why does biblical mission require *both* visible good deeds and verbal explanation? What happens if we only do one?

2. Discuss the difference between building your own tiny kingdom (career, status) and advancing God's Kingdom. Where do those two things usually collide?

3. We talked about how the early church grew through radical hospitality during plagues. What is the modern equivalent of that kind of undeniable, sacrificial love?

Hard Question: Are you staying silent about Jesus out of "respect for other people's beliefs," or are you actually just staying silent because you are embarrassed and want to be liked?

Close

One Sentence Recap: The Kingdom of God is currently present through the church, which is commissioned to make disciples and demonstrate God's reign until Jesus returns.

If You Only Remember One Thing: You are not a salesperson responsible for saving your friends; you are simply a witness called to tell the truth about what Jesus has done.

Next Week Preview: If we are called to be witnesses, what do we say to people of other faiths? Next week we tackle exclusivity—is Jesus really the only way?

Scripture References Used Matthew 5:16 Matthew 28:18–20 Mark 1:15 Luke 17:20–21 Acts 1:8 1 Peter 3:15

My Thoughts & Notes – What Did I Take From This?

Week 36 — Jesus and Other Religions: Truth Without Arrogance

Core Question: Is Jesus really the *only* way to God, and isn't it incredibly arrogant to claim that every other religion is wrong?

Why this matters: Because if all roads lead to God, the brutal death of Jesus was a tragic, unnecessary mistake; but if He is the only way, we must share Him with profound urgency and humility.

At a Glance (One Page)

Big Idea: The claim that Jesus is the only way to salvation is not a statement of Christian arrogance; it is the logical reality that only Jesus actually solved the massive problem of human sin.

Anchor Text: John 14:6; Acts 4:12

We believe…: Jesus Christ is the absolute, exclusive, and only Savior of humanity; salvation is found in no one else, and no other religion or philosophy can reconcile a sinful human to a holy God.

Key Words (3): Exclusivism - The biblical belief that conscious faith in Jesus Christ is the only way to be saved. Pluralism - The cultural belief that all major religions are equally valid paths to the same God. Universalism (Heresy) - The false belief that all people will eventually be saved and go to heaven, regardless of what they believe.

The One Mistake People Make: Confusing "tolerance" (treating people with different beliefs with massive respect and dignity) with "pluralism" (pretending all beliefs are equally true).

Choose Your Lane: Lane 1 / Lane 2 / Lane 3

This Week's Practice: The Humble Listening.

This Week's Prayer: Father, I live in a culture that hates absolute truth. It is so much easier to just agree that everyone is right and avoid the conflict. Forgive my cowardice. I know that You did not crush Your own Son on the cross if there was some other way for us to be saved. Give me the unbending conviction that Jesus is the only way, the truth, and the life. But Father, please strip away any arrogance or superiority in my heart. Let me speak this exclusive truth with the overwhelming tears and compassion of a beggar who simply found bread. Amen.

Lane 1 — Clarity (10 minutes)

The Bottom Line The modern world loves the metaphor of the mountain: God is at the peak, and all the different religions are just taking different paths up the same mountain. It sounds beautiful and tolerant. But it is fundamentally flawed. The major religions do not teach the same thing. They make completely contradictory claims about who God is, what the human problem is, and how to fix it. If Islam is right that Jesus did not die on a cross, then Christianity is a lie. They cannot both be true. Claiming Jesus is the only way isn't bigotry; it is taking His own words seriously.

Scripture Snapshot John 14:6: "Jesus answered, 'I am the way and the truth and the life. No one comes to the Father except through me.'"

Jesus did not leave the door open for pluralism. He did not say He was *a* way, or a *better* way, or the *Western* way. He made an absolute, exclusive claim to be the only access point to God. If Jesus was wrong about this, He was a delusional narcissist, and you shouldn't follow Him at all. If He was right, then following any other path is spiritually lethal.

Say It Out Loud (One Sentence) Jesus is the only way to God because He is the only one who actually died to pay the penalty for our sins.

Common Confusions Confusion #1: Saying Jesus is the only way means Christians think they are better than everyone else. (It means Christians admit they are too broken to save themselves). Confusion #2: All religions basically teach the Golden Rule. (Morality is common in many religions, but Christianity is the only one that offers grace instead of requiring you to earn salvation).

The Tuesday Payoff You are grabbing coffee with a coworker who practices a different religion, or no religion at all. The topic of faith comes up. The pressure is massive to just smile and say, "Well, we all believe in the same God anyway." But true friendship requires honesty. If you love them, you don't lie to them to keep things comfortable. You tell them the truth about Jesus. You don't have to win an argument or be a jerk. You simply say, "I am a complete mess, and Jesus is the only one who was willing to save me." You offer them the exclusive truth wrapped in radical humility.

Lane 2 — Depth (30 minutes)

Define the Terms General Revelation - The knowledge of God available to everyone through creation (which makes us accountable, but cannot save us). Special Revelation - The specific knowledge of God given through the Bible and Jesus (which provides the mechanism of salvation). Syncretism - The dangerous blending of Christian beliefs with the practices or beliefs of other religions.

Build the Doctrine (Scripture-forward)

The Apostles Were Exclusive The early church was born into the Roman Empire, which was incredibly pluralistic. Rome didn't care if you worshiped Jesus, as long as you added Him to the shelf with all the other gods. The apostles refused.

Key texts: Acts 4:12; 1 Timothy 2:5

Peter, standing before the hostile religious leaders who just executed Jesus, says clearly: "Salvation is found in no one else, for there is no other name under heaven given to mankind by which we must be saved" (Acts 4:12). Paul reiterates this to Timothy: "For there is one God and one mediator between God and mankind, the man Christ Jesus" (1 Tim 2:5). The early church was persecuted entirely because of their exclusivity.

Only Jesus Solved the Problem The reason Jesus is the only way is not because Christians are inherently superior. The reason is mechanical. Every other religion requires you to climb the mountain to reach God through your own moral performance (karma, the Five Pillars, the Eightfold Path).

Key texts: Galatians 2:21

Paul writes, "I do not set aside the grace of God, for if righteousness could be gained through the law, Christ died for nothing!" If humanity could reach God through Buddhism, Islam, or just being a good person, the cross was a horrific, unnecessary mistake. Jesus is the only way because He is the only one who stepped down the mountain to pay the debt we owed. We don't have another Savior to choose from.

Arrogance is Anti-Gospel If you believe that you are saved because you are smarter, more moral, or more spiritual than your Muslim or secular neighbor, you do not understand the gospel.

Key texts: Ephesians 2:8–9

Because we are saved by grace through faith—and "not by works, so that no one can boast"—exclusivity must kill arrogance. A Christian claiming Jesus is the only way is not a billionaire bragging about his wealth; it is a starving beggar telling another starving beggar where he found free bread. Exclusivity without humility is toxic.

BOX - What This Is NOT Saying We are NOT saying there is no truth or beauty in other religions; God's common grace allows other cultures to discover genuine moral truths. We are NOT saying you should treat people of other faiths with disrespect; they are made in the image of God and deserve absolute dignity. We are NOT saying Christians perfectly understand God; we see dimly, but we trust the clear revelation of Jesus.

BOX - Where Christians Differ The major debate is the destiny of the "Unevangelized"—those who live and die without ever hearing the name of Jesus.

1. Exclusivism (Broad Evangelical view): Conscious faith in Christ is necessary for salvation; those who never hear are judged justly based on their rejection of general revelation (Romans 1).

2. Inclusivism (Some mainline/Catholic views): Jesus is the only Savior, but God might apply His saving grace to people who faithfully follow the light they have in other religions, even if they don't know Jesus' name. Evangelicals reject Inclusivism because it fundamentally undermines the urgent, biblical command for global missions (Romans 10:14).

Lane 3 — Deep Dive (Optional)

The Objection You're Already Thinking "But what about the person living on an isolated island who never gets the chance to hear about Jesus? Is it fair for God to send them to hell just because a missionary never showed up?"

The Best Answer This is the most emotionally difficult question in all of theology, and we must approach it with massive reverence. First, we must ground ourselves in the absolute, unshakeable justice of God. Abraham asks in Genesis 18:25, "Will not the Judge of all the earth do right?" God will not make a single unjust decision on judgment day. Nobody will go to hell who did not actively choose rebellion.

Second, the Bible teaches in Romans 1 that no one is truly "innocent." General revelation (creation and conscience) provides enough evidence of God's power that all humans are "without excuse" for suppressing the truth and worshiping idols. People are not condemned simply because they haven't heard of Jesus; they are condemned because they are sinners who rebelled against the light they *did* have.

Finally, we must admit what we do not know. The Bible does not give us exhaustive details on how God handles every hypothetical scenario. What the Bible *does* give us is a command. We are told that Jesus is the only name that saves, and we are commanded to go tell the world. The "isolated islander" shouldn't make us angry at God's justice; it should make us angry at the church's apathy in not getting a missionary to that island faster.

Historical Lens In the early 20th century, a movement called Theological Liberalism swept through Western seminaries. They sought to strip Christianity of its exclusive claims and miracles, reducing it to a generic moral philosophy of "the fatherhood of God and the brotherhood of man" so it would be more palatable to modern culture. The result was catastrophic. The mainline denominations that abandoned the exclusivity of Christ have been hemorrhaging members for decades, because a religion that claims to be "just one of many equally valid paths" gives nobody a compelling reason to get out of bed on Sunday morning.

Real-Life Translation We are terrified of being labeled intolerant. In our culture, the ultimate sin is claiming that someone else's deeply held belief is wrong. So, to keep the peace, we soften our theology.

But true love requires warning people of danger. If you know that a bridge is out on a dark highway, it is not "intolerant" to stand in the road and wave a flashlight, telling cars they must take a different route. It would actually be the height of hatred to smile, wave them through, and say, "All roads lead home," knowing they are about to drive off a cliff.

Holding to the exclusivity of Christ is the most profoundly loving thing you can do for your neighbor, provided you do it with tears in your eyes and genuine respect in your voice.

Midlife Module - This Doctrine at 50 You are 50, and your circle of friends looks very different than it did at 20. You have coworkers, neighbors, and extended family members who practice different religions or passionately embrace atheism. You care about these people deeply. You don't want to view them as a "project," and you are exhausted by the thought of arguing with them.

You don't have to argue. At midlife, you realize that nobody was ever debated into the kingdom of heaven. You lean into the quiet confidence of exclusivity. You treat your Muslim, Hindu, or secular friends with breathtaking generosity. You invite them to your dinner table. You listen to their stories. And when the door opens, you simply and calmly tell them about the Jesus who rescued you. You leave the heavy lifting of conviction to the Holy Spirit.

Practice + Prayer

This Week's Practice (3–7 minutes) The Humble Listening. This week, ask a coworker or friend who does not follow Jesus a simple question about their worldview: "I'd love to understand what you actually believe about what happens after we die/how the world gets fixed." *Do not correct them.* Do not argue. Just listen, say "Thank you for sharing that," and quietly pray for them.

Prayer (100–160 words) God, I confess that I often shrink back from the exclusive claims of Jesus because I want to be liked by the culture. Forgive my fear of man. Give me the unshakeable conviction that Jesus Christ is the only way, the truth, and the life. But Father, please guard my heart against spiritual pride. Remind me that I am not saved because I am smarter or better than anyone else; I am saved entirely by Your unmerited grace. Break my heart for the billions of people who do not know Your name. Give me the courage to speak the truth, the humility to listen well, and the love to treat every single person I meet with absolute dignity. Use my life to point a confused world to the only Savior. Amen.

Reflection

Solo (3 prompts)

1. Why is the cultural idea that "all religions teach the same thing" actually incredibly disrespectful to the distinct beliefs of those religions?

2. How does remembering your own depravity and need for grace keep you from being arrogant when discussing faith with an unbeliever?

3. What is your biggest fear when it comes to sharing the exclusive claims of Jesus with a friend?

Small Group (3 prompts + 1 hard question)

1. Read Acts 4:12. Why do you think the early church was willing to be executed rather than just adding Jesus to the Roman pantheon of acceptable gods?

2. Discuss the mountain metaphor (all paths lead to the top) vs. the gospel reality (God came down the mountain). How does this practically change the conversation?

3. We talked about the difference between tolerance (respecting the person) and pluralism (agreeing with their belief). How can we practice true tolerance without compromising truth?

Hard Question: If you truly believe Jesus is the only way to be saved from eternal judgment, does your actual prayer life and evangelism reflect that urgency, or do you act like it doesn't really matter?

Close: One Sentence Recap: Jesus Christ is the absolute, exclusive, and only Savior of humanity because He alone solved the problem of human sin.

If You Only Remember One Thing: Claiming Jesus is the only way isn't bragging about your religion; it is a starving beggar telling another starving beggar where he found free bread.

Scripture References Used Genesis 18:25 John 14:6 Acts 4:12 Romans 10:14 Galatians 2:21 Ephesians 2:8–9 1 Timothy 2:5

My Thoughts & Notes – What Did I Take From This?

PART 6 — SALVATION

You know the sinking feeling of realizing a home renovation project is vastly bigger than you thought. You planned to just put up some new drywall and fresh paint, but when you opened the wall, you found black mold and rotten studs. You can't just paint over it; you have to strip the house down to the foundation.

In Part 6, we explore exactly how God saves us. He doesn't just give us a fresh coat of moral paint; He tears out our heart of stone and gives us a new one. We'll look at the unshakeable roadmap of salvation, how we are legally justified in God's courtroom, and why the agonizingly slow process of actually becoming a better person takes a lifetime.

WEEK 37 — THE SALVATION ROADMAP

CORE QUESTION: How DOES God actually apply salvation to my life, from start to finish?

Why this matters: Because if you think your salvation depends entirely on your ability to hold onto God, you will live in constant anxiety; but if it is anchored in God's eternal plan, you can finally rest.

At a Glance (One Page)

Big Idea: Salvation isn't just a panicked, last-minute prayer; it is a massive, unbreakable chain of events orchestrated by God from eternity past to eternity future.

Anchor Text: Romans 8:29–30; Ephesians 1:3–14

We believe...: Salvation is entirely the work of God, who foreknew, predestined, called, justified, and will ultimately glorify all those who are united to Christ.

Key Words (3): *Ordo Salutis* - Latin for "the order of salvation." The logical sequence of how God applies grace to a human life. Predestination - The biblical teaching that God sovereignly chose to save a people for Himself before the foundation of the world. Glorification - The final, future step of salvation where believers are given perfect, sinless, resurrected bodies.

The One Mistake People Make: Viewing salvation as a fragile, 50/50 partnership where God did His part on the cross, and now we have to desperately maintain our part to avoid losing it.

Choose Your Lane: Lane 1 / Lane 2 / Lane 3

This Week's Practice: The Golden Chain Review.

This Week's Prayer: Father, I confess that I often view my salvation as fragile. I base my security on my current emotional state and my daily performance, assuming You are constantly evaluating whether to keep me or drop me. Thank You for the staggering truth of Romans 8. Thank You that my salvation started in Your mind before the universe was formed, and it will end with me glorified in Your presence. Give me the profound peace of knowing that You finish what You start. Anchor my anxious heart in Your unbreakable chain. Amen.

Lane 1 — Clarity (10 minutes)

The Bottom Line We often reduce salvation to a single moment: the day you walked an aisle, raised a hand, or prayed a prayer. That moment matters, but it is just one visible link in a massive, invisible chain. The Bible presents salvation as a comprehensive roadmap engineered entirely by God. He thought of you before time began, He called you when you were dead in sin, He declared you righteous when you trusted Jesus, and He guarantees He will bring you safely home. Understanding this roadmap destroys religious anxiety.

Scripture Snapshot Romans 8:29–30: "For those God foreknew he also predestined to be conformed to the image of his Son... And those he predestined, he also called; those he called, he also justified; those he justified, he also glorified."

Theologians call this passage the "Golden Chain of Salvation." Notice the subject of every single verb: *God* foreknew, *God* predestined, *God* called, *God* justified, *God* glorified. You are not the primary actor in this sentence; God is. Also, notice the tense. Paul writes "glorified" in the past tense, even though it is a future event. In the mind of God, your ultimate arrival in heaven is so absolutely certain that Paul talks about it as if it has already happened.

Say It Out Loud (One Sentence) My salvation is an unbreakable chain forged by God, from His choice in eternity past to my glorification in eternity future.

Common Confusions Confusion #1: Predestination means humans don't have a real choice. (God's sovereignty and human responsibility are both 100% true, even if our minds can't fully reconcile them). Confusion #2: Knowing you are secure makes you lazy. (Knowing you are deeply loved actually makes you work harder out of gratitude).

The Tuesday Payoff You wake up on Tuesday morning with a deep sense of spiritual apathy. You haven't prayed in days, you snapped at your family, and you feel incredibly distant from God. If your salvation depends on your daily grip on God, you are in serious trouble this morning. But if your salvation depends on the Golden Chain, you can breathe. Your bad Tuesday did not break the chain. God's grip on you is infinitely stronger than your grip on Him. You can repent and move forward with absolute security.

Lane 2 — Depth (30 minutes)

Define the Terms Foreknowledge - Not just God looking into the future to see facts, but God setting His covenant love and affection on specific people beforehand. Calling - The act of the Holy Spirit effectively opening a spiritually dead person's eyes to see the beauty of the gospel. Adoption - The act of God making justified sinners His legal children, securing their inheritance.

Build the Doctrine (Scripture-forward)

Chosen Before Time Before you had done a single good or bad thing, God made a decision about you. Your salvation did not start the day you believed; it started before Genesis 1.

Key texts: Ephesians 1:4–5

Paul writes, "For he chose us in him before the creation of the world to be holy and blameless in his sight. In love he predestined us for adoption to sonship through Jesus Christ." This doctrine is not meant to start arguments; Paul writes it to cause worship. If God chose you before the world was created, He didn't choose you because of your impressive resume. He chose you purely out of grace.

The Call and the Verdict When the time comes in history for a person to be saved, the Holy Spirit issues a call. This is more than just hearing a sermon; it is the Spirit regenerating the heart so that the person freely and joyfully chooses to believe. Once they believe, God issues a legal verdict.

Key texts: 1 Corinthians 1:9; Romans 3:24

"God is faithful, who has called you into fellowship with his Son" (1 Cor 1:9). Following the call, we are "justified freely by his grace through the redemption that came by Christ Jesus" (Rom 3:24). Justification is the judge banging the gavel and declaring you "Not Guilty." The chain moves from the eternal mind of God straight into the courtroom of your life.

The Final Destination The chain doesn't end with you just barely scraping into heaven. The final goal of God's roadmap is your glorification—a complete transformation of your body and soul.

Key texts: Philippians 3:20–21; 1 John 3:2

Jesus "will transform our lowly bodies so that they will be like his glorious body" (Phil 3:21). John adds, "We know that when Christ appears, we shall be like him, for we shall see him as he is." Glorification is the absolute removal of all sin, disease, and brokenness. The God who started the work of salvation guarantees He will finish the job.

BOX - What This Is NOT Saying We are NOT saying you don't have to believe or repent; God ordains the end (salvation) and the means (our faith). We are NOT saying God forces people to go to hell against their will; people who reject God are acting on their own desires. We are NOT saying we can fully understand the mystery of election; the Bible commands us to trust it, not solve it.

BOX - Where Christians Differ The doctrine of Predestination is one of the most hotly debated topics in church history.

1. Calvinists believe God unconditionally elects specific individuals to salvation based entirely on His sovereign pleasure, and His grace ensures they will believe.

2. Arminians believe God elects based on His "foreknowledge"—meaning He looked down the corridor of time, saw who would freely choose Him, and elected them based on their future choice. While the mechanics are debated, both sides agree that Romans 8 offers profound comfort: God has a specific, loving plan to bring His people home.

Lane 3 — Deep Dive (Optional)

The Objection You're Already Thinking "If God predestines who is going to be saved, then why should we even bother preaching the gospel or going to church? Won't God just save them anyway?"

The Best Answer This objection relies on a massive misunderstanding of how God's sovereignty works. God does not just ordain the final destination; He also completely ordains the road to get there.

If a doctor tells you, "You are absolutely guaranteed to be cured of this infection," he means you are guaranteed to be cured *if you take the antibiotics.* The guarantee of the outcome requires the participation in the means.

God has sovereignly guaranteed that a massive multitude of people will be saved (Revelation 7:9). But He has also sovereignly ordained that the primary mechanism He will use to save them is the preaching of the gospel by ordinary Christians (Romans 10:14). If you know God has people in your city who belong to Him, it doesn't make you lazy; it makes you incredibly bold in sharing your faith, because you know your witness will actually be successful.

Historical Lens During the Reformation, John Calvin heavily emphasized the doctrine of predestination, not as a cold philosophical theory, but as a deeply pastoral comfort. In an era where the Catholic Church sold "indulgences" and kept peasants in constant terror regarding their salvation, Calvin pointed to the unshakeable sovereignty of God. He argued that if your salvation depends on your performance, you will never have peace; but if it depends entirely on God's eternal choice, your soul is completely secure.

Real-Life Translation We spend our entire lives trying to secure our own future. We build portfolios, we buy insurance, and we obsess over our health. But at a fundamental level, we know we are deeply fragile. A single phone call can destroy the life we built.

The Golden Chain of Romans 8 is the ultimate insurance policy. It tells you that the deepest, most vital core of your identity—your soul and your standing with the Creator of the universe—is entirely outside the reach of the economy, cancer, or divorce. It is locked in a vault in heaven. God started the process before you were born, and He will finish the process when He gives you a resurrected body. Your life is not a random series of accidents; it is a meticulously planned rescue operation.

Midlife Module - This Doctrine at 52 You are 52. You look back at your life and see a messy string of decisions. You changed careers, you moved cities, you suffered a major failure, and you endured a deep loss. From your perspective on the ground, your life looks chaotic and disjointed. You wonder if you ruined the plan.

The *Ordo Salutis* (Order of Salvation) pulls you up to a 30,000-foot view. It shows you that underneath the apparent chaos of your choices, there is a massive, unbreakable steel cable holding your life together. God did not drop the cable when you failed. He didn't let go when you doubted. At 52, you don't need a theology of human potential; you need a theology of divine grip.

Practice + Prayer

This Week's Practice (3–7 minutes) The Golden Chain Review. Read Romans 8:29–30 slowly. Circle or underline the five verbs: foreknew, predestined, called, justified, glorified. Notice that "you" are not the subject of any of those verbs. Spend three minutes simply thanking God that He does the heavy lifting of your salvation.

Prayer (100–160 words) God, my mind is too small to understand the depths of eternity past. But I am overwhelmed by the truth that You thought of me, chose me, and loved me before You ever spoke the world into existence. I confess that I often try to steal the credit for my own salvation, acting as if I was smart enough to figure it out on my own. Forgive my pride. Thank You for the unbreakable chain of grace. Thank You that the One who called me will also be the One to glorify me. When I am battered by the chaos of this world, anchor my mind to this unshakeable roadmap. Give me the profound rest of knowing that my future is entirely secure in Your hands. Amen.

Reflection

Solo (3 prompts)

1. Do you naturally tend to view your salvation as something God achieved, or something you achieved?

2. Why is it a massive relief to know that your ultimate glorification is so certain that Paul talks about it in the past tense?

3. How does knowing God has a definitive "roadmap" for salvation change the way you read the Bible?

Small Group (3 prompts + 1 hard question)

1. Read Ephesians 1:3–5. What does it mean to be chosen "in love" rather than just chosen for a task?

2. Discuss the Golden Chain in Romans 8:29–30. Why is it impossible for a person to be "justified" but fail to reach "glorification"?

3. We talked about how God's sovereignty should make us bolder in evangelism, not lazier. How does that practically work?

Hard Question: Are you terrified of losing your salvation because you secretly know you are relying on your own good behavior instead of the finished work of Jesus?

Close

One Sentence Recap: Salvation is entirely the work of God, who foreknew, predestined, called, justified, and will ultimately glorify all those who trust in Christ.

If You Only Remember One Thing: Your bad Tuesday did not break the chain; God's grip on you is infinitely stronger than your grip on Him.

Next Week Preview: How exactly do we move from being spiritually dead to being alive? Next week we look at Calling and Conversion.

Scripture References Used Romans 3:24 Romans 8:29–30 Romans 10:14 1 Corinthians 1:9 Ephesians 1:3–5 Philippians 3:20–21 1 John 3:2 Revelation 7:9

My Thoughts & Notes – What Did I Take From This?

WEEK 38 — CALLING AND CONVERSION: HOW CHANGE HAPPENS

CORE QUESTION: How DOES a stubborn, broken person actually change their mind about God?

Why this matters: Because if you think you just stumbled into faith by being smart, you will be arrogant; but if you know God had to specifically call your name, you will be deeply grateful.

At a Glance (One Page)

Big Idea: You didn't just stumble into faith or figure it out on your own; God the Holy Spirit specifically called you, opening your spiritually blind eyes to see the undeniable beauty of Jesus.

Anchor Text: John 6:44; Acts 16:14

We believe...: Conversion is the result of the Holy Spirit's inward, effective call, which gives us the ability and the desire to willingly turn from sin and trust in Christ.

Key Words (3): General Call - The outward preaching of the gospel to all people, which can be rejected (e.g., a sermon or a tract). Effectual Call - The inward work of the Holy Spirit perfectly opening a specific heart to receive the gospel. Illumination - The Holy Spirit removing our spiritual blindness so we can understand and believe the Bible.

The One Mistake People Make: Taking credit for their own salvation by assuming they were just a little more spiritual or intelligent than their neighbor who rejected the exact same message.

Choose Your Lane: Lane 1 / Lane 2 / Lane 3

This Week's Practice: The Origin Story Check.

This Week's Prayer: Father, I confess that I like to take the credit. I like to think that I chose You because I was wise enough to see the truth. Strip away my arrogance. I know that my heart was hard, blind, and deeply rebellious. Thank You for not leaving me in the dark. Thank You for the Holy Spirit, who broke through my defenses, opened my eyes, and made Jesus look more beautiful than my sin. I owe my entire conversion to Your relentless grace. Amen.

Lane 1 — Clarity (10 minutes)

The Bottom Line Two people sit in the exact same church, listening to the exact same sermon. One person is bored and checks their phone. The other person is weeping, deeply convicted of their sin, and trusts Jesus. Why the difference? It isn't because the second person is smarter, better educated, or has a superior moral compass. The difference is the Holy Spirit. The Bible calls this the "effectual call." God doesn't just broadcast the gospel into the universe and hope someone is smart enough to tune in. He specifically dials into dead hearts, opens blind eyes, and grants us the ability to believe.

Scripture Snapshot Acts 16:14: "One of those listening was a woman from the city of Thyatira named Lydia, a dealer in purple cloth. She was a worshiper of God. The Lord opened her heart to respond to Paul's message."

Paul is preaching by a river in Philippi. Lydia is a successful businesswoman listening to the message. But notice the mechanics of her conversion. Paul preached the words, but Paul couldn't open her heart. Only God can do that. The text says, "The Lord opened her heart." Lydia absolutely made a real, willing choice to respond to the gospel, but she was only able to make that choice because God went first and unlocked the door from the inside.

Say It Out Loud (One Sentence) I am a Christian today because the Holy Spirit opened my blind eyes and gave me the desire to trust Jesus.

Common Confusions Confusion #1: Conversion is just agreeing with a new set of intellectual facts. (It is a radical reorientation of the heart's affections). Confusion #2: God dragged me into the kingdom against my will. (God doesn't force you; He changes your heart so that you *willingly* and joyfully run to Him).

The Tuesday Payoff You have a family member or a friend who is deeply hostile to the faith. You have argued with them, given them books, and presented perfect logic on a Tuesday night, but they still refuse to believe. You are exhausted and frustrated. Understanding the doctrine of the "Call" takes the burden entirely off your shoulders. You cannot argue a blind person into seeing color. You cannot debate a dead heart into beating. You speak the truth in love, but you rely entirely on the Holy Spirit to open their heart. You stop arguing, and you start praying.

Lane 2 — Depth (30 minutes)

Define the Terms Conversion - Our willing response to the gospel, consisting of repentance and faith. Regeneration - The secret act of God imparting new spiritual life to us. Monergism - The theological truth that God alone does the work of changing our spiritual nature (we do not cooperate to bring ourselves back to life).

Build the Doctrine (Scripture-forward)

We Are Born Blind and Deaf Before the Holy Spirit issues the call, the human heart isn't just neutral or slightly confused. It is entirely hostile to God and completely blind to spiritual truth.

Key texts: 1 Corinthians 2:14; Romans 8:7

Paul writes, "The person without the Spirit does not accept the things that come from the Spirit of God but considers them foolishness, and cannot understand them because they are discerned only through the Spirit" (1 Cor 2:14). To an uncalled heart, the cross looks like a stupid, weak fairy tale. You cannot simply educate someone out of spiritual blindness.

The Outward vs. Inward Call Jesus used parables to explain the difference between the general invitation everyone hears and the specific call that actually saves.

Key texts: Matthew 22:14; John 6:44

Jesus said, "For many are invited, but few are chosen" (Matt 22:14). The outward call of the gospel goes to everyone. But the inward, effective call is highly specific. Jesus makes this absolute claim: "No one can come to me unless the Father who sent me draws them" (John 6:44). The Greek word for "draw" implies a powerful, magnetic pull. Unless God initiates the rescue, no one ever comes.

God Gives the Light When conversion happens, it is described as a massive, sovereign act of creation happening inside the human mind.

Key texts: 2 Corinthians 4:6

Paul connects your conversion to the first day of creation: "For God, who said, 'Let light shine out of darkness,' made his light shine in our hearts to give us the light of the knowledge of God's glory displayed in the face of Christ." When you finally understood the gospel, it wasn't because you figured out a puzzle. It was because the Creator commanded light to flood your dark mind.

BOX - What This Is NOT Saying We are NOT saying you don't actually make a choice to trust Jesus; your choice is entirely real, but it is enabled by grace. We are NOT saying evangelism is useless; the outward preaching of the Word is the exact tool the Spirit uses to issue the inward call. We are NOT saying you will always know the exact date and time of your conversion.

BOX - Where Christians Differ The major debate is over whether the inward call of the Holy Spirit can be successfully resisted by human free will. Calvinists refer to this as "Irresistible Grace" (or Effectual Calling), arguing that when God the

Spirit truly calls a specific heart, He overcomes all resistance and guarantees conversion. Arminians believe the Spirit strongly woos and enables, but humans retain the final, decisive free will to resist and reject the call.

Lane 3 — Deep Dive (Optional)

The Objection You're Already Thinking "If God has to open my heart for me to believe, doesn't that make me a robot? Where is my free will?"

The Best Answer The idea of being a robot implies that God is dragging you into heaven kicking and screaming against your own desires. That is not how grace works.

Think of a person whose taste buds are severely damaged. They hate the taste of honey and think it is poison. If you put honey in front of them, they will freely and willingly reject it every single time, because their nature is broken.

Now, imagine a doctor perfectly heals their taste buds. Suddenly, they taste the honey and realize it is incredibly sweet. They freely and willingly choose to eat it.

God doesn't bypass your free will. He heals your broken spiritual "taste buds." He removes the blindness so you can see that Jesus is actually beautiful, satisfying, and true. Once your eyes are opened, you don't choose Jesus because you are forced to; you choose Jesus because He is suddenly the most desirable thing in the universe. Your will was healed, not hijacked.

Historical Lens The great preacher George Whitefield (1714–1770) was a leading figure in the Great Awakening. He preached to crowds of thousands in open fields. But he deeply understood the limits of his own persuasion. He famously said that he could preach the gospel to the ear, but only God could preach it to the heart. This theology fueled massive revivals, because the preachers relied entirely on the Holy Spirit to do the actual converting, rather than relying on emotional manipulation or perfectly crafted arguments.

Real-Life Translation We put immense pressure on ourselves when it comes to the people we love who don't know Jesus. We think if we just find the perfect book, or invite them to the perfect church service, or win the political argument at Thanksgiving, they will finally surrender.

When they reject us, we feel like we failed. But if conversion is the sovereign work of the Holy Spirit, you are relieved of the savior complex. Your job is to simply be a faithful witness (tell the truth and love them well). God's job is to open the heart. You can sleep peacefully at night knowing that the salvation of your children, your spouse, or your friends is resting in hands far more capable than your own.

Midlife Module - This Doctrine at 54 You are 54, and you are exhausted by trying to fix people. You have spent twenty years trying to change your spouse's habits, trying to steer your adult children's choices, or trying to manage your aging parents. The midlife crisis of control is realizing that you cannot actually change anyone.

The doctrine of the Effectual Call is the only theology that offers peace here. It reminds you that human hearts are locked from the inside. You do not have the key. You can influence, you can love, and you can set boundaries, but only the Holy Spirit can reach into the control room of a human soul and re-wire the desires. You can finally resign from the exhausting job of trying to play the Holy Spirit in other people's lives.

Practice + Prayer

This Week's Practice (3–7 minutes) The Origin Story Check. Think back to how you became a Christian. Did someone share the gospel with you? Did you read a book? Recognize the human instrument, but spend two minutes praising the Divine cause. Say out loud, "Thank You, Holy Spirit, for opening my eyes when I was blind."

Prayer (100–160 words) God, I look back at my life and I see Your relentless pursuit of my soul. I know exactly how stubborn and arrogant I was. If You had left me to my own free will, I would have run away from You forever. Thank You for not leaving me alone. Thank You for issuing the call that broke through my defenses. Thank You for commanding light to shine in my dark mind. I ask You to do that exact same miracle for the people in my life who are currently hostile to You. I cannot argue them into the Kingdom. Please send Your Holy Spirit to heal their spiritual blindness, soften their hearts, and make Jesus irresistible to them. I trust Your perfect timing. Amen.

<u>**Reflection**</u>

Solo (3 prompts)

1. Have you ever secretly looked down on an unbeliever, assuming you were saved because you made a smarter choice than they did?

2. How does the story of Lydia (Acts 16:14) change the way you view the results of evangelism?

3. Why is it actually a massive relief to admit that you cannot change the hearts of the people you love?

Small Group (3 prompts + 1 hard question)

1. Read 1 Corinthians 2:14. Why is it pointless to get into angry debates with people who do not have the Holy Spirit?

2. Discuss the analogy of the "broken taste buds" from Lane 3. How does this explain the concept of free will and God's sovereign grace?

3. We discussed how George Whitefield relied on the Spirit rather than manipulation. What does emotional manipulation look like in modern evangelism?

Hard Question: Are you currently deeply anxious about a family member's salvation because you believe their eternal destiny rests entirely on your ability to say the right thing?

<u>**Close**</u>

One Sentence Recap: Conversion is the result of the Holy Spirit's inward call, which gives us the ability and the desire to willingly turn from sin and trust Christ.

If You Only Remember One Thing: You cannot argue a blind person into seeing color; you must rely on the Holy Spirit to open their eyes.

Next Week Preview: Once your eyes are opened, what actually happens inside you? Next week we look at the New Birth. Can you just turn over a new leaf, or do you need a new heart?

Scripture References Used Matthew 22:14 John 6:44 Acts 16:14 Romans 8:7 1 Corinthians 2:14 2 Corinthians 4:6

<u>**My Thoughts & Notes — What Did I Take From This?**</u>

WEEK 39 — NEW BIRTH: REGENERATION AND THE HEART

CORE QUESTION: Is BECOMING a Christian just deciding to turn over a new leaf, or do I actually need a completely new heart?

Why this matters: Because if Christianity is just behavior modification, you will eventually burn out trying to be good; but if it is a new birth, you have a completely new power source.

At a Glance (One Page)

Big Idea: Salvation is not a self-improvement project; it is a spiritual resurrection where the Holy Spirit removes your heart of stone and gives you a new nature capable of loving God.

Anchor Text: John 3:1–8; Ezekiel 36:26

We believe...: Regeneration (the new birth) is the secret, sovereign work of the Holy Spirit that imparts new spiritual life to a dead sinner, resulting in a radical change of desires and actions.

Key Words (3): Regeneration - The theological term for the "new birth." God's act of giving us a new, living spiritual nature. Flesh - In the New Testament, this often refers not just to the physical body, but to our fallen, rebellious human nature. Heart - The biblical control center of a human being; the seat of your desires, will, and intellect.

The One Mistake People Make: Trying to live the Christian life using their old, unregenerate willpower, which is like trying to run an electric car with a gas engine.

Choose Your Lane: Lane 1 / Lane 2 / Lane 3

This Week's Practice: The White-Knuckle Audit.

This Week's Prayer: Father, I am exhausted by self-improvement. I have tried so many times to clean up my act, manage my habits, and simply "do better." But my willpower always eventually runs out. I realize I do not just need a new strategy; I need a new nature. Thank You for the miracle of regeneration. Thank You for taking my heart of stone and replacing it with a heart of flesh. Give me the wisdom to stop relying on my own strength, and the humility to rely entirely on the new life You have placed inside me. Amen.

Lane 1 — Clarity (10 minutes)

The Bottom Line The culture tells you that if you want to change your life, you need a new routine, a new diet, or a new mindset. It treats humans like software that just needs an update. But the Bible gives a much more drastic diagnosis. Jesus looked at one of the most moral, educated men of His day and told him that his good behavior was completely useless. He didn't need an upgrade; he needed to be born all over again. Christianity is not God giving you a list of rules to follow. Christianity is God giving you a brand new heart that actually wants to follow the rules.

Scripture Snapshot John 3:3: "Jesus replied, 'Very truly I tell you, no one can see the kingdom of God unless they are born again.'"

Nicodemus was a Pharisee—the ancient equivalent of a theological scholar and a supreme court justice. He came to Jesus looking for an intellectual conversation between two teachers. Jesus completely bypasses his intellect and strikes at his nature.

Jesus tells this highly successful, religious man that his current life is disqualified. Being "born again" (or born from above) means you must experience a complete, fundamental restart of your spiritual existence. You can't earn it any more than a baby can earn its physical birth.

Say It Out Loud (One Sentence) God does not just demand new behavior from me; He provides a new heart to produce it.

Common Confusions Confusion #1: Being "born again" is just a label for intense, emotional Christians. (It is the absolute requirement for every single person who enters heaven). Confusion #2: Once I get a new heart, I will never sin again. (The new heart battles the lingering habits of the old flesh until we die).

The Tuesday Payoff You are trying to break a deeply ingrained, destructive habit on a Tuesday—maybe anger, drinking, or cynicism. You've been "white-knuckling" it for three days, using pure willpower. By 4:00 PM, your willpower is gone, and you fail again. If salvation is just behavior modification, you are a complete failure. But if you have experienced the new birth, you know that the power to change doesn't come from your clenched fists; it comes from the Holy Spirit living inside you. You stop trying to muscle through it, and you start asking the Spirit to change what you actually desire.

Lane 2 — Depth (30 minutes)

Define the Terms New Creation - Paul's description of a regenerated person: "The old has gone, the new is here!" (2 Cor 5:17). Monergism - The belief that regeneration is the work of God alone, without our cooperation, just as physical birth is the work of the parents, not the baby. Willpower - The human capacity to control behavior, which is entirely insufficient to cure a sinful heart.

Build the Doctrine (Scripture-forward)

The Heart Transplant The Old Testament promised a day when God would stop dealing with humanity through external laws carved on stone, and do something entirely new on the inside.

Key texts: Ezekiel 36:26–27

"I will give you a new heart and put a new spirit in you; I will remove from you your heart of stone and give you a heart of flesh. And I will put my Spirit in you and move you to follow my decrees." A heart of stone is dead, cold, and unresponsive. You can shout at a rock, but it won't move. God says He will perform a radical, spiritual heart transplant. He gives us a heart of flesh—living, beating, and capable of actually loving Him.

It is the Work of the Spirit Jesus uses a specific metaphor to explain how this new birth happens. It is not something you can control, schedule, or manufacture.

Key texts: John 3:8; Titus 3:5

Jesus says, "The wind blows wherever it pleases... So it is with everyone born of the Spirit." You cannot tame the wind. You cannot force the Holy Spirit to regenerate someone. Paul echoes this in Titus, saying God saved us "not because of righteous things we had done, but because of his mercy. He saved us through the washing of rebirth and renewal by the Holy Spirit." Regeneration is a sovereign, unilateral miracle of God.

The Proof is the Fruit If regeneration is invisible and internal, how do you know it actually happened? You look for the pulse. A new heart produces a new kind of life.

Key texts: 1 John 3:9; Matthew 7:16

John writes a controversial verse: "No one who is born of God will continue to sin, because God's seed remains in them." John isn't saying Christians never commit a sin (he denies that earlier in the same letter). He is saying that a person with a new heart cannot live in unbroken, habitual, unrepentant rebellion. If you plant an apple seed, you eventually get apples. If God plants His Spirit in you, you eventually get holiness.

BOX - What This Is NOT Saying We are NOT saying the "old flesh" is completely eradicated; we will struggle with our old, sinful habits until we die (Romans 7). We are NOT saying regeneration happens through water baptism; baptism is a physical symbol of the spiritual reality of the new birth. We are NOT saying you will instantly feel perfect; regeneration is immediate, but growth (sanctification) is slow.

BOX - Where Christians Differ Again, the Calvinist and Arminian debate surfaces here regarding the *order* of events. Calvinists believe that Regeneration *precedes* Faith—God must first give you a new, living heart before you have the ability to believe the gospel. Arminians believe that Faith *precedes* Regeneration—God gives you enough grace to choose Him, and when you believe, He regenerates you. Both agree absolutely that without the miracle of the new birth, no one will see the kingdom of heaven.

Lane 3 — Deep Dive (Optional)

The Objection You're Already Thinking "I know people who claimed to be 'born again,' but then a few years later they completely walked away from the faith. How is that possible if God gave them a new heart?"

The Best Answer This is a devastating reality in the modern church, often called "deconversion." The biblical answer is difficult but clarifying.

Jesus addressed this exactly in the Parable of the Sower (Matthew 13). Some seed falls on rocky ground. It springs up quickly with intense joy and emotion. To everyone watching, it looks like a living plant. But it has no root. When the sun comes out (hardship or persecution), it immediately withers and dies.

Emotional experiences, youth group highs, and cultural conformity can look exactly like regeneration for a short period of time. People can turn over a new leaf, learn the vocabulary, and genuinely enjoy the community of the church without ever actually receiving a new heart. When they inevitably walk away, the Apostle John explains the reality: "They went out from us, but they did not really belong to us. For if they had belonged to us, they would have remained with us" (1 John 2:19). A true new birth is permanent.

Historical Lens In the 18th century, the Church of England was highly formal, rigid, and filled with people who attended services out of cultural duty but had no real spiritual life. Preachers like John Wesley and George Whitefield began preaching outdoors, hammering on the absolute necessity of the "New Birth." The religious establishment hated it, calling them "enthusiasts" (fanatics). But the message that you must be fundamentally changed by the Holy Spirit sparked the Great Awakening, waking up thousands of nominal Christians to real faith.

Real-Life Translation Most of our frustration with ourselves comes from relying on willpower. You decide you are going to stop yelling at your kids, or stop looking at pornography, or start being more generous. You make a spreadsheet. You try really hard for two weeks, and then you fail. The cycle of self-improvement is crushing.

Willpower is trying to hold a beachball underwater. You can do it for a while, but eventually, your arms get tired, and the ball blasts to the surface.

The doctrine of regeneration tells you to stop trying to hold the ball underwater. Your problem is not a lack of discipline; your problem is what you actually *love*. You need God to reach in and change your desires. When you ask the Holy Spirit to kill your affection for the sin and increase your affection for Jesus, the fight changes. You aren't just resisting bad behavior; you are being propelled by a new, living heart.

Midlife Module - This Doctrine at 48 You are 48. You have tried a dozen different self-help programs over the last twenty years. You've read the books on how to optimize your habits, fix your marriage, and find your purpose. And while some of them helped briefly, the fundamental, restless anxiety in your chest is still there.

At midlife, the myth of self-optimization is finally exposed. You realize you cannot fix yourself. This is the exact moment the New Birth becomes beautiful. You don't need another program. You need a resurrection. The pressure to reinvent yourself at 48 vanishes, replaced by the profound relief of knowing the Creator has already done the heavy lifting of making you a new creation.

Practice + Prayer

This Week's Practice (3–7 minutes) The White-Knuckle Audit. Identify the one sin or bad habit you are currently trying to fix entirely through your own willpower. Stop trying to muscle through it. This week, every time the temptation hits, pray a two-second prayer: "Holy Spirit, I cannot change my desires, but You can. Give me a new affection for Christ right now."

Prayer (100–160 words) God, I am so prone to treating Christianity like a self-improvement project. I focus entirely on my outward behavior, while ignoring the coldness of my heart. Forgive me for trying to impress You with my willpower. Thank You for the breathtaking promise of Ezekiel—that You actually remove our hearts of stone and replace them with hearts of flesh. Thank You for the miracle of the new birth. I ask that the Holy Spirit would take complete control of my desires, my affections, and my will today. When I am tempted to rely on my own strength, remind me that I am a new creation. Breathe Your life into the dead areas of my faith. Amen.

Reflection

Solo (3 prompts)

1. Have you been treating Christianity as a set of rules to follow, or as a fundamentally new life to experience?

2. What is the difference between an emotional religious experience and actual regeneration?

3. Why does relying on pure willpower to fight sin usually end in exhaustion and failure?

Small Group (3 prompts + 1 hard question)

1. Read John 3:1–8. Why do you think Jesus used the analogy of the wind to describe the work of the Holy Spirit in salvation?

2. Discuss Ezekiel 36:26. What does a "heart of stone" look like practically in modern life? What does a "heart of flesh" look like?

3. We talked about "deconversion" in Lane 3. How does the Parable of the Sower help us understand people who appear to be Christians but walk away?

Hard Question: Are you terrified that you might not actually be "born again" because you know your religious life is entirely a performance for other people?

Close

One Sentence Recap: Regeneration is the sovereign work of the Holy Spirit that imparts new spiritual life to a dead sinner, resulting in a radical change of desires.

If You Only Remember One Thing: Willpower is like holding a beachball underwater; you don't need more discipline, you need a completely new heart.

Next Week Preview: If we get a new heart, how do we get a new legal record? Next week we look at Justification—the most important word in the Protestant Reformation.

Scripture References Used Ezekiel 36:26–27 Matthew 13:1–23 Matthew 7:16 John 3:1–8 John 3:8 Romans 7 2 Corinthians 5:17 Titus 3:5 1 John 2:19 1 John 3:9

My Thoughts & Notes – What Did I Take From This?

Week 40 — Justification: Declared Righteous

Core Question: How CAN a perfectly holy God look at my messy, flawed life and declare me completely innocent?

Why this matters: Because if you don't understand justification, you will spend your entire life trying to prove your worth to God, your boss, and your family, and you will die exhausted.

At a Glance (One Page)

Big Idea: God does not make you perfectly good in order to accept you; He legally declares you righteous in His courtroom based entirely on the perfect record of Jesus Christ credited to your account.

Anchor Text: Romans 3:21–26; Galatians 2:16

We believe...: Justification is an instantaneous legal act of God in which He thinks of our sins as forgiven and Christ's righteousness as belonging to us, completely apart from our own works.

Key Words (3): Justification - A legal, courtroom term where a judge declares a defendant "Not Guilty" and righteous in the eyes of the law. Imputation - The act of transferring or crediting something to someone else's account (Christ's righteousness credited to us). Faith Alone (*Sola Fide*) - The truth that we receive justification solely by trusting in Christ, not by adding any of our own good works.

The One Mistake People Make: Confusing justification (the instant, legal declaration that you are right with God) with sanctification (the slow, messy process of actually becoming a better person).

Choose Your Lane: Lane 1 / Lane 2 / Lane 3

This Week's Practice: The Courtroom Dismissal.

This Week's Prayer: Father, I confess that I live my life as if I am constantly on trial. I am always trying to build a resume of good works to prove that I am a decent person. I am terrified of being exposed as a fraud. Thank You for the staggering truth of justification. Thank You that You did not demand I clean myself up before You accepted me. Thank You for slamming the gavel and declaring me righteous based entirely on the blood of Jesus. Silence the prosecuting attorney in my mind today, and let me rest in Your perfect verdict. Amen.

Lane 1 — Clarity (10 minutes)

The Bottom Line The human heart is addicted to a legalistic math equation: *If I am good, God will accept me. If I am bad, God will reject me.* But the Bible destroys that equation. If God waits for you to be perfectly good before He accepts you, you will go to hell. Justification is the explosive truth that God accepts you while you are still a complete mess. He doesn't wait for you to become righteous. He brings you into His courtroom, looks at the perfect life and death of Jesus, credits it to your account, and bangs the gavel. "Not Guilty." You don't earn the verdict; you just receive it by faith.

Scripture Snapshot Romans 3:23–24: "For all have sinned and fall short of the glory of God, and all are justified freely by his grace through the redemption that came by Christ Jesus."

Paul writes the most important paragraph in the history of theology. He establishes the bad news first: absolutely everyone is disqualified. No one can clear the bar. Then he delivers the atomic bomb of grace: we are justified *freely*. The Greek word literally means "as a gift, without a cause." There was no cause in you that forced God to declare you righteous. The only cause was the redemption purchased by the blood of Jesus.

Say It Out Loud (One Sentence) I am declared perfectly righteous by God right now, not because of what I have done, but because of what Jesus did for me.

Common Confusions Confusion #1: God ignores our sin because He is loving. (God punished every single sin perfectly on the cross; His justice was completely satisfied). Confusion #2: Faith is a "good work" that earns my justification. (Faith is just the empty hand that reaches out to accept the free gift).

The Tuesday Payoff You receive a highly critical performance review at work on a Tuesday. Your boss outlines your failures in detail. If your ultimate identity is tied to your performance, this review will crush you. You will either become deeply defensive or spiral into depression, because you feel like your worth is on trial. But if you understand justification, the stakes are dramatically lowered. Your boss can judge your spreadsheet, but they cannot judge your soul. The Supreme Judge of the universe has already reviewed your ultimate file, stamped it with the righteousness of Christ, and cleared you. You can take the feedback without taking the devastation.

Lane 2 — Depth (30 minutes)

Define the Terms Verdict - The official decision of a judge in a courtroom. Justification is a verdict, not a process. Grace Alone (*Sola Gratia*) - The truth that salvation is entirely a gift, unprompted by anything good in us. Christ Alone (*Solus Christus*) - The truth that Jesus is the only Savior; we do not need to add the merits of saints, Mary, or our own works.

Build the Doctrine (Scripture-forward)

The Courtroom, Not the Hospital We often view salvation like a hospital: we are sick, and God gives us medicine (grace) so we can slowly get better. That is the doctrine of sanctification. Justification is entirely different. It is a courtroom.

Key texts: Romans 8:33–34

"Who will bring any charge against those whom God has chosen? It is God who justifies. Who then is the one who condemns?" You are the defendant. Satan is the prosecuting attorney, bringing a massive list of legitimate charges against you. But God the Judge dismisses the case. He doesn't say you are innocent; He says your penalty has already been fully served by your Substitute. The case is permanently **Close**d.

Imputation: The Great Exchange How can a holy judge declare a guilty criminal righteous? If he just lets the criminal go, the judge is corrupt. The answer is imputation.

Key texts: 2 Corinthians 5:21; Philippians 3:9

Paul writes that he wants to be found in Christ, "not having a righteousness of my own that comes from the law, but that which is through faith in Christ" (Phil 3:9). God takes your massive debt of sin and imputes (credits) it to Christ on the cross. Then, God takes the perfect, flawless, obedient life of Jesus and imputes it to your account. When God looks at you, He does not see your failures; He sees the perfect resume of His Son.

Faith is Just the Instrument If works don't save us, does our faith save us? No. Jesus saves us. Faith is simply the instrument we use to connect to Jesus.

Key texts: Galatians 2:16

"Know that a person is not justified by the works of the law, but by faith in Jesus Christ." Think of a man trapped in a burning building. A firefighter extends a ladder. The man grabs the ladder and is pulled to safety. The man's grip didn't save him; the firefighter saved him. The grip was just the connection point. Your faith doesn't impress God into saving you; your faith is just the empty hand grabbing the ladder of Christ.

BOX - What This Is NOT Saying We are NOT saying a justified person will never sin again; we remain flawed in practice while being perfect in legal status. We are NOT saying justification is a process; it happens completely and fully the exact millisecond you trust Christ. We are NOT saying good works are optional; true faith *always* produces a changed life (James 2).

BOX - Where Christians Differ This doctrine is the exact fault line of the Protestant Reformation. The Roman Catholic Church teaches that justification is a *process*. They believe God infuses grace into you through the sacraments, making you actually righteous over time, and if you become good enough, you are finally justified. The Protestant Reformers (Luther, Calvin) fiercely argued from Scripture that justification is an *instantaneous legal declaration* based entirely on Christ's imputed righteousness, not our internal goodness. Broad evangelicalism firmly holds the Protestant view: we are justified by faith alone, instantly.

Lane 3 — Deep Dive (Optional)

The Objection You're Already Thinking "But the book of James says, 'A person is considered righteous by what they do and not by faith alone' (James 2:24). Doesn't that directly contradict Paul?"

The Best Answer For centuries, people have tried to pit Paul against James. Martin Luther even wanted to remove James from the Bible because he thought it contradicted grace! But there is no contradiction if you understand the different problems they were addressing.

Paul was fighting *legalism* (people who thought they could earn salvation by doing good works). So Paul hammers the truth: works cannot save you; only faith in Christ saves you.

James was fighting *antinomianism* (people who claimed to have faith, but lived completely wicked lives, treating grace like a cheap get-out-of-jail-free card). James hammers the truth: if your "faith" doesn't produce any change in your behavior, it is a dead, fake faith.

Paul is talking about the *root* of salvation (faith). James is talking about the *fruit* of salvation (works). John Calvin summarized it perfectly: "We are justified by faith alone, but the faith that justifies is never alone." True faith always brings a changed life with it.

Historical Lens In 1521, Martin Luther was summoned before the Holy Roman Emperor at the Diet of Worms and commanded to recant his writings on Justification by Faith Alone. He knew that refusing would likely mean being burned at the stake. He famously replied, "My conscience is captive to the Word of God. I cannot and will not recant anything... Here I stand, I can do no other." The doctrine of justification was not a dry academic debate; it was a truth so liberating that men and women joyfully bled to defend it.

Real-Life Translation We are all desperately trying to justify our existence. We want to prove that our lives matter. We use our careers, our physical appearance, the success of our children, or our political outrage to build a resume. We present this resume to the world, begging the culture to declare us "worthy" and "righteous."

It is utterly exhausting. The culture is a cruel judge. The moment you fail, the culture tears up your resume and cancels you.

The doctrine of Justification by Faith is the only thing that unplugs you from the matrix of human approval. You no longer have to wake up every morning and build a resume to prove you have a right to exist. The Creator of the universe has already handed down the ultimate, unappealable verdict: you are completely accepted in Christ. The trial is over. You are free to simply live.

Midlife Module - This Doctrine at 52 You are 52, and you are taking inventory of your life. The resume is written. You see the places where you succeeded, and the glaring, painful places where you failed. You realize you are not going to achieve the massive, world-changing dreams you had at 25. A heavy, lingering sense of mediocrity threatens to settle over you.

Justification dismantles midlife despair. It reminds you that your ultimate worth was never tied to your career achievements or your parenting successes in the first place. You do not have to arrive at the end of your life clutching a pathetic list of your own good deeds to show God. You will arrive with empty hands, wrapped entirely in the flawless, breathtaking robe of Christ's righteousness. Your resume doesn't matter; His does.

Practice + Prayer

This Week's Practice (3–7 minutes) The Courtroom Dismissal. The next time you experience an attack of anxiety, shame, or the feeling of "not being enough," visualize a courtroom. Picture Satan presenting the evidence of your failure. Then picture Jesus stepping in front of you, pointing to His scars, and the Judge dismissing the case. Say out loud: "There is therefore now no condemnation for those who are in Christ Jesus" (Romans 8:1).

Prayer (100–160 words) God, You are the perfectly just Judge of the universe. I have broken Your law, and if I stand before You on my own merit, I will be condemned. I confess that I spend most of my life trying to prove my own worth and justify my own existence. Stop my frantic striving. Thank You for the stunning, scandalous truth of the gospel. Thank You for taking my massive debt and nailing it to the cross of Jesus. And thank You for taking His perfect, flawless record and wrapping it around my shoulders. When the enemy whispers accusations against me, give me the courage to point him to the cross. Let me rest in the permanent verdict of grace today. Amen.

Reflection

Solo (3 prompts)

1. In what specific ways do you try to "justify your existence" to other people (e.g., bragging, overworking, curating social media)?

2. Why is the Catholic idea that justification is a "slow process of becoming good" actually terrifying for a person with a guilty conscience?

3. What is the difference between a fake, dead faith and a true, justifying faith?

Small Group (3 prompts + 1 hard question)

1. Read Romans 3:23–24. How does realizing that justification is given "freely... without a cause" destroy our religious pride?

2. Discuss the concept of "The Great Exchange" (Imputation). Why is it not enough for God to just forgive our debt—why do we also need Christ's righteousness?

3. We talked about how Paul and James do not contradict each other. How do we explain the relationship between faith and good works to a new believer?

Hard Question: Are you terrified of the doctrine of Justification by Faith Alone because it means you get exactly zero credit for your own salvation?

Close

One Sentence Recap: God legally declares us righteous in His courtroom based entirely on the perfect record of Jesus Christ credited to our account.

If You Only Remember One Thing: The trial is over, the verdict is in, and because of Jesus, you never have to exhaust yourself trying to prove your worth again.

Next Week Preview: If Justification is the courtroom, what happens next? Next week we look at Adoption. God doesn't just declare you innocent; He takes you home.

Scripture References Used Romans 3:23–24 Romans 8:1 Romans 8:33–34 2 Corinthians 5:21 Galatians 2:16 Philippians 3:9 James 2:24

My Thoughts & Notes – What Did I Take From This?

WEEK 41 — ADOPTION: FAMILY, NOT TRANSACTION

CORE QUESTION: Is GOD just a judge who legally forgave me, or did He actually invite me into His house?

Why this matters: Because a judge can forgive your crimes and still want nothing to do with you, but a father forgives you and gives you the keys to his house.

At a Glance (One Page)

Big Idea: Justification clears your criminal record, but Adoption is the staggering act of grace where God actually brings you into His family, giving you the exact same rights and privileges as Jesus Christ.

Anchor Text: Romans 8:15–17; Galatians 4:4–7

We believe…: Adoption is an act of God's free grace whereby all who are justified by faith are received into the number, and have a right to all the privileges, of the children of God.

Key Words (3): Adoption - The legal and relational act of God making believers His own children. Abba - An intimate Aramaic word for "Father," equivalent to "Papa" or "Dad." Inheritance - The guaranteed future reality (the new heavens and new earth) promised to us because we are legally God's heirs.

The One Mistake People Make: Treating God like an annoyed boss or a strict parole officer, assuming He tolerates them because of Jesus but doesn't actually like them.

Choose Your Lane: Lane 1 / Lane 2 / Lane 3

This Week's Practice: The "Abba" Pivot.

This Week's Prayer: Father, I confess that I struggle to believe You actually want me around. I understand that Jesus paid my debt, but my mind defaults to thinking of You as a distant, intimidating judge. I live like an employee trying to avoid getting fired, rather than a child living in my Father's house. Thank You for the breathtaking privilege of adoption. Thank You for looking at my broken life and choosing to give me Your name. Teach me how to pray without fear. Help me to rest in the perfect affection You have for me today. Amen.

Lane 1 — Clarity (10 minutes)

The Bottom Line The British theologian J.I. Packer famously wrote that if you want to judge how well a person understands Christianity, find out how much they make of the thought of being God's child. Justification (what we covered last week) is a massive, glorious truth. But it happens in a courtroom. A judge can pardon a criminal, but the judge does not take the criminal home for dinner. God takes us home. Adoption means the Judge stepped down from the bench, took off His robes, put His arm around the guilty defendant, and said, "You are coming home with me, and you get my last name."

Scripture Snapshot Romans 8:15–17: "The Spirit you received does not make you slaves, so that you live in fear again; rather, the Spirit you received brought about your adoption to sonship. And by him we cry, 'Abba, Father.' The Spirit himself testifies with our spirit that we are God's children."

Paul draws a sharp contrast. You have two options for how you relate to God: slavery or sonship. A slave obeys the master out of terror, knowing that one mistake means punishment. A child obeys the father out of love, knowing that a mistake will be met with discipline, but never with rejection. The Holy Spirit's primary job is to convince your anxious, terrified heart that God is actually a perfectly good Father.

Say It Out Loud (One Sentence) God did not just forgive my debt; He gave me His name, His Spirit, and the keys to His house.

Common Confusions Confusion #1: Everyone in the world is a child of God. (All are created by God, but the Bible strictly reserves the title "child of God" for those who have trusted Christ). Confusion #2: God loves Jesus more than He loves us. (Because we are adopted, the Father loves us with the exact same love He has for the Son).

The Tuesday Payoff You make a massive parenting mistake on a Tuesday evening. You lose your temper, yell at your kids, and the house descends into chaos. As you retreat to your room, the shame is suffocating. If your relationship with God is transactional, you won't pray. You will assume God is disgusted with your failure. But if you understand Adoption, you know that God is not a parole officer waiting for you to violate your terms. He is a Father. You can approach Him immediately, confess the failure, and ask for the strength to go apologize to your kids, knowing your place in the family is completely secure.

Lane 2 — Depth (30 minutes)

Define the Terms Sonship - A legal term in the ancient world. Both men and women in Christ are granted "sonship," meaning they receive the full legal inheritance rights (which, in Roman times, typically only went to sons). Slavery - The spiritual state of living under the law, characterized by fear and the constant pressure to perform. Heir - Someone legally entitled to receive the property and wealth of the father.

Build the Doctrine (Scripture-forward)

The Purpose of the Rescue God did not save you just to boost His numbers in heaven. He saved you because He wanted a family. Adoption was the goal from the very beginning.

Key texts: Galatians 4:4–5

Paul explains the entire purpose of the Incarnation: "But when the set time had fully come, God sent his Son, born of a woman, born under the law, to redeem those under the law, that we might receive adoption to sonship." Jesus didn't just come to wipe the slate clean; He came to drag us into the family photo.

The Intimacy of "Abba" The God of the Old Testament was holy and terrifying. The high priest could only enter His presence once a year. But Jesus completely changed the vocabulary of how we address the Creator.

Key texts: Galatians 4:6; Mark 14:36

"Because you are his sons, God sent the Spirit of his Son into our hearts, the Spirit who calls out, 'Abba, Father.'" When Jesus was in agony in Gethsemane, He prayed, "Abba, Father." It is the intimate, completely unpretentious cry of a child. Because you are adopted, you do not have to use flowery, religious language to get God's attention. You have the right to stumble into His presence and simply say, "Dad, help."

The Inheritance In Roman adoption law, an adopted child had the exact same legal rights as a biological child, and the adoption could never be revoked. You could disown a biological child, but you could not disown an adopted one.

Key texts: Romans 8:17

"Now if we are children, then we are heirs—heirs of God and co-heirs with Christ." You are a co-heir with the Creator of the universe. Everything that belongs to Jesus by right, belongs to you by grace. The new earth, the resurrected body, and the eternal joy of heaven are legally secured in your name.

BOX - What This Is NOT Saying We are NOT saying human fathers are perfect representations of God; many human fathers are terrible, but God is the perfect Father we always wanted. We are NOT saying God doesn't discipline His children;

He disciplines us precisely *because* He loves us (Hebrews 12). We are NOT saying women are excluded by the term "sons"; the term grants women the exact same ultimate inheritance rights as men.

BOX - Where Christians Differ Not a major point of disagreement. The doctrine of Adoption is universally celebrated across all orthodox traditions. It is the crowning jewel of the gospel. Some traditions emphasize the legal, inheritance aspect heavily, while others focus on the relational intimacy, but the truth that believers are permanently grafted into God's family is undisputed.

Lane 3 — Deep Dive (Optional)

The Objection You're Already Thinking "I had an abusive, absent, or emotionally distant father. Every time the Bible calls God 'Father,' it just triggers my trauma. How am I supposed to find comfort in this?"

The Best Answer This is a massive, incredibly common pain point. We naturally project the characteristics of our earthly fathers onto our heavenly Father. If your dad was angry, you assume God is angry. If your dad abandoned you, you assume God is distant.

But the Bible reverses this logic. God is not a larger, slightly better version of your flawed human dad. God is the original Father. He is the standard. Every human father is just a flawed, temporary shadow of the real thing. When a human father is cruel or absent, he is not showing you what God is like; he is violating the very definition of fatherhood.

You do not have to map your trauma onto God. Instead, you can let the perfect fatherhood of God slowly heal your trauma. God is the Father who stays. He is the Father who protects. He is the Father who is incredibly strong, yet gentle enough to count the hairs on your head. Adoption means you finally get the Father you deserved all along.

Historical Lens In the first century Greco-Roman world, the *paterfamilias* (the male head of the household) had absolute power. But Roman adoption was a very specific, expensive legal procedure. Wealthy men without an heir would legally adopt a grown man to pass on their estate. Once the papers were signed, all the adopted son's previous debts were completely wiped out, and his new status was legally unshakeable. When Paul used the word "adoption" to his Roman readers, they knew exactly what it meant: debt canceled, status secured, permanently.

Real-Life Translation Most Christians function like the older brother in the Parable of the Prodigal Son (Luke 15). The older brother stayed home, kept all the rules, and worked himself to the bone in the fields. But when his father threw a party, he was furious. He yelled, "All these years I've been slaving for you and never disobeyed your orders!"

Notice his vocabulary: *slaving*. He was a son, but he lived like an employee. He thought his relationship with his father was based on his agricultural output.

We do the exact same thing with God. We serve at church, read our Bibles, and tithe, but we do it with the exhausting mindset of an employee trying to earn a bonus. Adoption tells you to drop the shovel. You cannot earn what you already inherited. Stop slaving in the field and go into the house to enjoy the party.

Midlife Module - This Doctrine at 48 You are 48. If you have kids, they are starting to need you less. If your parents are still living, your relationship with them is shifting as they age. The family dynamics that anchored your identity for decades are heavily in flux. You might be feeling a strange, quiet sense of orphanhood, wondering where you actually belong now that the roles are changing.

The doctrine of Adoption is the ultimate anchor for midlife identity. Your earthly family will always change. People move, age, and pass away. But your position in the family of God is permanently static. You will never age out of being His child. You will never outgrow your need for His fatherhood. When the earthly family shifts, the heavenly family holds firm.

Practice + Prayer

This Week's Practice (3–7 minutes) The "Abba" Pivot. Every time you pray this week, do not start your prayer with "Dear Lord" or "Almighty God." Start every single prayer with the word "Dad" or "Father." Notice how that one simple vocabulary shift completely changes the posture of your heart from religious performance to relational intimacy.

Prayer (100–160 words) Father, it is staggering to think that I have the right to call You that. I know my own heart. I know how often I act like a runaway child, looking for satisfaction in the mud instead of in Your house. Thank You that You did not just forgive my treason; You completely rewrote my identity. Thank You for the Spirit of adoption that kills my fear. I confess that I often fall back into a slavery mindset, trying to earn Your love by working hard. Heal the wounds caused by the flawed human authorities in my life. Help me to stop performing. Let me live today with the quiet, unshakeable confidence of an heir. Amen.

Reflection

Solo (3 prompts)

1. Do you naturally view God more as a judge evaluating your performance, or as a Father delighting in your presence?

2. How has your relationship with your earthly father shaped your view of God (for better or for worse)?

3. Why is it so much easier for us to operate like "slaves" (keeping rules to earn favor) rather than "sons/daughters" (resting in grace)?

Small Group (3 prompts + 1 hard question)

1. Read Romans 8:15. What is the specific difference between a spirit of fear (slavery) and the Spirit of adoption?

2. Discuss the Roman law of adoption (where previous debts were wiped out and the status was permanent). How does this deepen our understanding of what God did for us?

3. We talked about the older brother in the Prodigal Son story. What are the signs that a Christian is living like an "employee" rather than a child?

Hard Question: Are you staying busy doing "things for God" because you are terrified of sitting quietly and simply being "loved by God"?

Close

One Sentence Recap: Adoption is the staggering act of grace where God brings you into His family, giving you the exact same rights and privileges as Jesus Christ.

If You Only Remember One Thing: Stop slaving in the field trying to earn your inheritance; drop the shovel and go into the house to enjoy the Father.

Next Week Preview: If we are adopted into the family, how does God actually change us? Next week we look at Union with Christ: the mechanical engine of the Christian life.

Scripture References Used Mark 14:36 Luke 15:11–32 Romans 8:15–17 Galatians 4:4–7 Hebrews 12

My Thoughts & Notes – What Did I Take From This?

WEEK 42 — UNION WITH CHRIST: THE ENGINE

CORE QUESTION: HOW DOES what Jesus did two thousand years ago actually get applied to my life today?

Why this matters: Because if you try to live the Christian life on your own battery power, you will burn out immediately; you have to understand how you are plugged into the Source.

At a Glance (One Page)

Big Idea: You are not just a follower of Jesus; by faith, you are spiritually welded to Him, meaning everything that is true of Him (His righteous life, His death, and His resurrection) becomes legally and actually true of you.

Anchor Text: John 15:1–5; Ephesians 2:4–6

We believe...: Union with Christ is the central reality of salvation, wherein the Holy Spirit intimately joins the believer to Christ, resulting in shared life, power, and standing before God.

Key Words (3): Union with Christ - The invisible, spiritual reality that believers are connected to Jesus as branches are to a vine, or a body to a head. In Christ - The Apostle Paul's favorite phrase (used over 160 times) to describe the believer's secure identity and location. Imputation - The transfer of our sin to Christ, and His righteousness to us, made possible entirely because we are united to Him.

The One Mistake People Make: Viewing Christianity as a "WWJD" (What Would Jesus Do) copycat religion, trying to imitate Jesus from a distance instead of operating from a shared life with Him.

Choose Your Lane: Lane 1 / Lane 2 / Lane 3

This Week's Practice: The Battery Check.

This Week's Prayer: Father, I spend so much energy trying to be a good Christian on my own. I try to manufacture my own patience, my own purity, and my own faith, and I am constantly exhausted. Forgive me for trying to run on my own battery power. Open my eyes to the staggering reality that I am united to Christ. Teach me what it means to be a branch connected to the Vine. Help me to stop striving and start abiding. Let His life flow through mine today. Amen.

Lane 1 — Clarity (10 minutes)

The Bottom Line Most Christians understand the cross. But they don't understand the mechanics of *how* the cross actually applies to them. They think Jesus is in heaven, we are on earth, and God just beams down grace to us like a Wi-Fi signal. But the Bible gives us a much more mechanical, intimate picture. You are not connected to Jesus via Bluetooth. You are hardwired into Him. The theological term is "Union with Christ." It means that when Jesus died on the cross, because you are united to Him, God counted it as if *you* died. When Jesus rose, you rose. You share His legal record, and you share His living power.

Scripture Snapshot John 15:4–5: "Remain in me, as I also remain in you. No branch can bear fruit by itself; it must remain in the vine. Neither can you bear fruit unless you remain in me. I am the vine; you are the branches."

Jesus gives the disciples the ultimate visual aid for the Christian life. A branch does not have its own independent root system. A branch does not try really hard to manufacture an apple; the apple is just the natural byproduct of the sap flowing from the vine into the branch. Jesus is bluntly clear: severed from Him, you can do absolutely nothing. Connected to Him, life naturally happens.

Say It Out Loud (One Sentence) I am legally and spiritually welded to Jesus, meaning I share His righteous record and operate on His infinite power.

Common Confusions Confusion #1: Union with Christ means we literally become gods. (We share His human/spiritual life, but we remain created beings; we do not absorb His deity). Confusion #2: Christianity is just trying your best to imitate Jesus. (Christianity is Jesus living His life *through* you).

The Tuesday Payoff You are facing a massive conflict at work on Tuesday. You know you are supposed to be patient and kind, but your internal reservoir of patience is completely empty. If Christianity is just a WWJD imitation game, you will clench your jaw, try to act like Jesus, and probably fail by 10:00 AM. But if you understand Union with Christ, your strategy changes. You don't ask God for a "package of patience" to be dropped from heaven. You acknowledge that you are connected to the Vine. You simply ask the Holy Spirit to let the patience of Jesus flow through your branch into that specific meeting.

Lane 2 — Depth (30 minutes)

Define the Terms Mystical Union - The truth that this connection is not just a metaphor; it is a profound, mysterious spiritual reality forged by the Holy Spirit. Federal Headship - The legal side of the union; Jesus acts as our representative (like an ambassador), so what He achieves is credited to us. Abiding - The daily, active practice of resting in our union with Christ through prayer, obedience, and trust.

Build the Doctrine (Scripture-forward)

The Engine of Imputation Last week we talked about Justification—God crediting Christ's righteousness to our account. But *how* is that legal? How can a judge punish one man for another man's crimes? The answer is Union.

Key texts: 2 Corinthians 5:21; Romans 6:5

If a husband gets a speeding ticket, the wife's bank account pays for it because their finances are legally united. When you put your faith in Christ, you are legally married to Him. Therefore, your debt of sin becomes His debt on the cross, and His wealth of righteousness becomes your wealth. Paul says, "For if we have been united with him in a death like his, we will certainly also be united with him in a resurrection like his" (Rom 6:5).

The New Zip Code: "In Christ" If you want to know what the Apostle Paul thought was the most important concept in theology, look at his vocabulary. He rarely uses the word "Christian." Instead, he uses the phrase "in Christ" over 160 times.

Key texts: Ephesians 1:3; Ephesians 2:6

Paul says God has "blessed us in the heavenly realms with every spiritual blessing in Christ" (Eph 1:3). Then he says something mind-bending: God "raised us up with Christ and seated us with him in the heavenly realms in Christ Jesus" (Eph 2:6). Paul writes this to living, breathing people walking around the Roman Empire. But spiritually, their ultimate location—their zip code—is seated in heaven next to the Father, because they are welded to Jesus.

The Source of Sanctification You cannot live a holy life on your own. True spiritual growth is never generated by human willpower; it is always the result of the Holy Spirit transmitting the life of Jesus into your daily actions.

Key texts: Galatians 2:20

"I have been crucified with Christ and I no longer live, but Christ lives in me. The life I now live in the body, I live by faith in the Son of God." Paul views his old, autonomous, self-ruled life as dead. The engine running Paul's life is no longer Paul's ambition; it is the active, pulsing life of the resurrected Jesus operating inside his physical body.

BOX - What This Is NOT Saying We are NOT saying you lose your individual personality; Union with Christ actually frees you to be the unique person God designed you to be. We are NOT saying you are perfectly holy in your actions yet; the sap is flowing, but the branch is still growing. We are NOT saying you can be united to Christ while staying disconnected from His Church (the Body).

BOX - Where Christians Differ There is virtually no disagreement on this doctrine among orthodox Christians. From John Calvin to Eastern Orthodox mystics, Union with Christ is recognized as the beating heart of the New Testament. The only difference is vocabulary (Orthodox traditions often use the term *Theosis*, emphasizing our participation in the divine nature, while Western traditions emphasize the legal and relational aspects of the Union), but the core reality remains identical.

Lane 3 — Deep Dive (Optional)

The Objection You're Already Thinking "This all sounds very mystical and vague. What does it actually mean to 'abide in the vine' on a regular Thursday when I'm just trying to get my kids to school and answer emails?"

The Best Answer "Abiding" sounds like something monks do in a monastery, sitting in silence for hours. But Jesus gave the command to "abide" to blue-collar fishermen who were about to face intense persecution. It is a highly practical command.

Think of a laptop. It has a battery that allows it to operate independently for a few hours. But if you try to run heavy software (like editing a massive video) on battery power, the laptop will drain instantly and die. You have to plug it into the wall to access the grid's unlimited power.

Your human willpower is a battery. It can handle small, daily tasks. But if you try to run the heavy software of the Christian life—loving an enemy, forgiving a betrayal, enduring chronic pain, or conquering an addiction—your battery will drain in ten minutes.

Abiding simply means recognizing your battery is dead, and deliberately plugging into the wall. It is the moment-by-moment mental shift of saying, "Lord, I cannot handle this meeting. I need Your patience." It is bringing your mind back to the reality of His presence through quick prayers, meditating on Scripture, and obeying His promptings throughout the day. It isn't a mystical trance; it is a desperate dependence.

Historical Lens John Calvin, known for his massive intellect, wrote that Union with Christ was the most important doctrine in all of theology. He stated, "As long as Christ remains outside of us, and we are separated from him, all that he has suffered and done for the salvation of the human race remains useless and of no value for us." The cross is the medicine, but Union with Christ is the IV drip that actually gets the medicine into your veins.

Real-Life Translation We suffer from chronic identity crises. We don't know who we are, so we constantly try to define ourselves by our politics, our sexuality, our careers, or our parenting styles. When those things fail, our identity collapses.

The doctrine of Union with Christ provides an indestructible identity. If you are "in Christ," your identity is not tied to your fluctuating performance. Your identity is tied to His flawless performance. When God looks at you, He does not see your failures, your divorce, or your bankruptcy. He sees the absolute perfection of His Son. Because you are welded to Jesus, you are as perfectly secure and loved by the Father as Jesus is.

Midlife Module - This Doctrine at 50 You are 50, and the fatigue is deep. You have been a Christian for a long time, but you feel like you are just going through the motions. The zeal you had in your twenties is gone. You are tired of trying to "be a good Christian," and honestly, you feel a little burned out on religion.

Burnout is the inevitable result of trying to run a branch on its own power. You have been trying to manufacture fruit to impress God. At midlife, the invitation of Union with Christ is an invitation to stop producing and start receiving. You don't have to generate the zeal. You just have to rest in the Vine. The pressure is off. Your only job at 50 is to stay plugged in, and let Him do the work.

Practice + Prayer

This Week's Practice (3–7 minutes) The Battery Check. This week, when you hit a wall of frustration, anger, or exhaustion, stop and visualize a laptop cord being plugged into a wall. Say out loud, "I am out of battery. Jesus, I am resting in my union with You. Please let Your strength operate in my weakness right now."

Prayer (100–160 words) God, I am so exhausted from trying to live the Christian life on my own strength. I confess that I treat You like an example to copy, rather than the Vine that gives me life. Forgive me for relying on my own fragile battery. Thank You for the staggering mystery of Union with Christ. Thank You that I am legally, permanently, and spiritually welded to Jesus. When the enemy accuses me, remind me that my life is hidden with Christ in You. When I am weak, remind me that the same power that raised Jesus from the dead is currently flowing into me. Teach me what it practically means to abide in You today. Amen.

<u>**Reflection**</u>

Solo (3 prompts)

1. In what specific areas of your life are you trying to run on your own "battery power" instead of relying on the Holy Spirit?

2. Why is it so comforting to know that God sees you entirely through the lens of Jesus' perfect record?

3. How does the metaphor of the Vine and the Branches destroy the idea of an independent, "lone wolf" Christian?

Small Group (3 prompts + 1 hard question)

1. Read John 15:4–5. What does the word "abide" (or "remain") actually look like in the context of a busy, modern Tuesday?

2. Discuss Paul's phrase "in Christ." How does changing our mental zip code from our earthly circumstances to our heavenly position change our anxiety levels?

3. We talked about how Union makes Justification (the Great Exchange) legal. How does the analogy of a marriage and a shared bank account help explain this?

Hard Question: Are you currently experiencing spiritual burnout because you are furiously trying to earn God's approval with your works, rather than resting in your union with Jesus?

<u>**Close**</u>

One Sentence Recap: You are spiritually welded to Jesus, meaning everything that is true of Him becomes legally and actually true of you.

If You Only Remember One Thing: You cannot Bluetooth the Holy Spirit; you have to stay plugged into the Vine.

Next Week Preview: If we have a new heart and are plugged into Jesus, why do we still mess up so much? Next week we tackle Sanctification—why growth is so frustratingly slow.

Scripture References Used John 15:1–5 Romans 6:5 2 Corinthians 5:21 Galatians 2:20 Ephesians 1:3 Ephesians 2:4–6

<u>My Thoughts & Notes – What Did I Take From This?</u>

WEEK 43 — SANCTIFICATION: WHY GROWTH IS SLOW

CORE QUESTION: IF GOD gave me a new heart and justified me, why am I still struggling with the exact same sins twenty years later?

Why this matters: Because if you expect instant perfection, you will become deeply discouraged and cynical when you fail; understanding the slow process of growth keeps you in the fight.

At a Glance (One Page)

Big Idea: Sanctification is the slow, messy, lifelong process where the Holy Spirit works with our active cooperation to kill our sin and conform our character to the image of Jesus.

Anchor Text: Philippians 1:6; 1 Thessalonians 4:3

We believe...: Sanctification is a progressive work of God and man that makes us more and more free from sin and like Christ in our actual lives, guaranteed to be completed at glorification.

Key Words (3): Definitive Sanctification - The instant reality that you are perfectly set apart and made holy in God's eyes the moment you are saved. Progressive Sanctification - The lifelong, gradual process of your actual behavior catching up to your new identity. Mortification - The active, daily practice of putting your sinful habits and desires to death.

The One Mistake People Make: Becoming completely paralyzed by shame when they fall back into an old sin, assuming God's patience has run out because they aren't "fixed" yet.

Choose Your Lane: Lane 1 / Lane 2 / Lane 3

This Week's Practice: The 1% Rule.

This Week's Prayer: Father, I am so deeply frustrated with my own lack of progress. I thought I would be a better Christian by now. I thought I would have conquered this anger, this anxiety, and this pride. Forgive me for demanding a quick fix instead of submitting to Your slow process. Thank You that You are patient. Thank You for the promise that You will finish the good work You started in me. Give me the grit to keep fighting my sin today, and the grace to not hate myself when I stumble. Amen.

Lane 1 — Clarity (10 minutes)

The Bottom Line Justification is instant. It happens in a millisecond in the courtroom of God. Sanctification is not instant. It is the agonizing, two-steps-forward, one-step-back process of actually learning how to walk in the new life God gave you. We hate it because we love efficiency. We want Amazon Prime spiritual growth—ordered today, delivered tomorrow. But God is a farmer, not a tech CEO. He grows oaks of righteousness, and oaks take decades. The fact that you are still fighting sin doesn't mean you aren't saved; it proves you are alive. Dead bodies don't fight.

Scripture Snapshot Philippians 1:6: "...being confident of this, that he who began a good work in you will carry it on to completion until the day of Christ Jesus."

Paul writes this to a church that is messy, struggling, and full of friction. He doesn't say, "I am confident in your ability to figure this out." He anchors his confidence entirely in God's follow-through. Notice the timeline. The project isn't completed next Tuesday. It is carried on until "the day of Christ Jesus" (His return). God is operating on a lifelong timeline. He is not going to abandon the construction site just because it is messy.

Say It Out Loud (One Sentence) God accepts me perfectly right now, but He loves me too much to let me stay the way I am.

Common Confusions Confusion #1: Sanctification means trying really hard not to sin so God will love you. (It means killing sin *because* God already loves you). Confusion #2: My effort doesn't matter; "let go and let God." (Sanctification requires extreme, disciplined human effort empowered by the Holy Spirit).

The Tuesday Payoff You lose your temper with your spouse on a Tuesday morning over something incredibly stupid. As you drive to work, you feel a crushing wave of despair: *I've been a Christian for twenty years, and I'm still acting like a toddler.* If you demand instant perfection, you will spiral into shame. But if you understand progressive sanctification, you shift your perspective. You realize that twenty years ago, you wouldn't have even cared that you yelled. The guilt you feel right now is actually proof the Holy Spirit is working. You repent, apologize, and keep moving forward.

Lane 2 — Depth (30 minutes)

Define the Terms Synergism - The theological reality that while *Justification* is God's work alone, *Sanctification* requires the active cooperation of God and man working together. Means of Grace - The ordinary tools God uses to grow us: reading Scripture, prayer, taking the sacraments, and church community. Legalism - Trying to achieve sanctification purely by keeping rules in your own strength.

Build the Doctrine (Scripture-forward)

You Are Already Holy (Definitive) Before we talk about the slow process of growth, we must establish the anchor. The New Testament calls messy, struggling Christians "saints" (holy ones) because in their legal standing, they are already entirely set apart for God.

Key texts: 1 Corinthians 6:11; Hebrews 10:14

Paul writes to the deeply flawed Corinthian church: "But you were washed, you were sanctified, you were justified." He uses the past tense. Hebrews says, "For by one sacrifice he has made perfect forever those who are being made holy." You are already perfect in your standing, while simultaneously "being made holy" in your practice. Your identity is secure before the process even starts.

You Must Sweat (Progressive) While God gives you the new heart, He commands you to do the heavy lifting of walking in it. Sanctification is grueling work. It is war.

Key texts: Philippians 2:12–13; Romans 8:13

"Continue to work out your salvation with fear and trembling, for it is God who works in you." You work it out, because God is working it in. Paul also gives a lethal command in Romans: "If by the Spirit you put to death the misdeeds of the body, you will live." You don't just politely manage your sin; you are commanded to act as its executioner. You must actively kill the pride, the lust, and the greed every single day.

It is a Community Project American Christians try to grow in isolation through private Bible studies and podcasts. But the New Testament knows absolutely nothing of solitary sanctification.

Key texts: Hebrews 10:24–25; Proverbs 27:17

"And let us consider how we may spur one another on toward love and good deeds, not giving up meeting together." Iron sharpens iron (Prov 27:17), and the sharpening process creates friction and sparks. You cannot learn patience alone in a room; you only learn patience by being in a church with annoying people and choosing to love them anyway. Community is the forge of sanctification.

BOX - What This Is NOT Saying We are NOT saying you can reach sinless perfection in this lifetime; that is a heresy called "Perfectionism." We are NOT saying your good works add to your justification; they are the evidence of it. We are NOT saying growth is a straight line upward; it is often jagged, filled with seasons of failure and repentance.

BOX - Where Christians Differ Historically, the Wesleyan/Methodist tradition has sometimes taught forms of "Entire Sanctification" or "Christian Perfection"—the idea that a believer can reach a state in this life where they no longer intentionally sin. Broad Reformed and Evangelical traditions firmly reject this, maintaining that the "flesh" remains a persistent, sabotaging enemy until the day we die (Romans 7), meaning the battle against sin never ends in this lifetime.

Lane 3 — Deep Dive (Optional)

The Objection You're Already Thinking "If God is all-powerful, why doesn't He just instantly remove all my sinful desires the moment I am saved? Why make me fight this exhausting battle for eighty years?"

The Best Answer God absolutely has the power to instantly eradicate your sin. He does exactly that when you die (glorification). So why the delay?

Because God's goal is not just to produce sterile obedience; His goal is to forge a deep, tested, resilient relationship with you. Think of a parent doing a puzzle with a child. The parent could easily complete the puzzle in five minutes. But the parent lets the child struggle, try the wrong pieces, and figure it out slowly. Why? Because the goal isn't just a finished puzzle; the goal is the development of the child and the intimacy of the shared task.

If God instantly made you perfect, you would never have to rely on Him. You would never experience the depths of His patience when you fail. You would never develop the grit of endurance. God leaves the enemies in the land (the lingering sins) to teach your hands how to make war (Judges 3:1-2), forcing you into a daily, desperate reliance on the Holy Spirit.

Historical Lens In the 19th century, a movement called the "Higher Life" or "Keswick" movement swept through Christianity. They taught a two-tier system: you get saved, and then later you completely surrender and achieve a "victorious, struggling-free" Christian life. The motto was "Let go and let God." J.C. Ryle and other orthodox leaders pushed back hard. They argued that "let go and let God" is completely unbiblical. The Christian life is never free from struggle. We are commanded to fight, to run, to wrestle, and to put on armor. There is no lazy path to holiness.

Real-Life Translation We are obsessed with measuring our spiritual growth by our feelings. If we feel **Close** to God, we assume we are growing. If we feel dry, bored, or frustrated, we assume we are backsliding.

But feelings are terrible metrics for sanctification. Often, the seasons where you feel the driest are the seasons where you are growing the most. True sanctification looks incredibly boring. It looks like waking up on a Wednesday, not feeling anything spiritual at all, but choosing to make your kid's lunch without complaining, choosing not to look at pornography, and choosing to read a Psalm. Holiness is built in the mundane, unglamorous, repetitive choices of daily obedience when no one is watching and you don't feel a buzz.

Midlife Module - This Doctrine at 49 You are 49. You look at your life and realize that your deepest character flaws—your need for control, your people-pleasing, your cynicism—are thoroughly baked into your personality. The thought of actually changing feels impossible. You have resigned yourself to saying, "Well, this is just how I am wired."

Sanctification violently rejects the phrase "this is just how I am." You are not stuck. God is not finished with the project. The Holy Spirit is infinitely stronger than your forty years of neural pathways. The change at 49 won't be an overnight, emotional breakthrough like it was at 19. It will be the slow, grinding, glorious work of repenting one day at a time. But the promise of Philippians 1:6 holds: He will finish the job.

Practice + Prayer

This Week's Practice (3–7 minutes) The 1% Rule. Stop trying to completely overhaul your life in one day. Pick exactly one tiny area where you know you are disobeying God (e.g., gossiping at work, looking at your phone during dinner). Commit to 1% improvement this week. Ask the Holy Spirit for the power to say "no" to that one specific thing, once a day.

Prayer (100–160 words) God, I am so easily discouraged by my own weakness. I look in the mirror and I see the same impatience, the same pride, and the same selfishness that I have battled for years. Forgive me for expecting instant perfection, and forgive me for using Your grace as an excuse to be lazy. Thank You that You are a patient Father who does not abandon the construction site of my soul. I ask for the power of the Holy Spirit to put my sin to death today. Give me the endurance to do the boring, daily work of obedience. When I fail, keep me from the arrogance of shame, and help me to run quickly back to the cross. Finish the good work You started in me. Amen.

Reflection

Solo (3 prompts)

1. Have you bought into the lie that sanctification means "let go and let God," instead of realizing it means "sweat and fight by the power of the Spirit"?

2. What is the difference between the guilt that tells you "God hates you" and the conviction that tells you "God is changing you"?

3. What is one specific "weed" (sin) in the garden of your life that you have been managing rather than pulling up by the roots?

Small Group (3 prompts + 1 hard question)

1. Read Philippians 1:6. How does anchoring our growth in God's faithfulness (rather than our own discipline) keep us from quitting when we fail?

2. Discuss the difference between Justification (instant, God's work alone) and Sanctification (slow, cooperative work). What happens if we mix these two up?

3. We discussed how community is the "forge of sanctification." How does hiding our struggles from other Christians actually keep us in bondage?

Hard Question: Are you currently excusing a persistent, ugly sin in your life by shrugging your shoulders and saying, "Well, nobody's perfect"?

Close

One Sentence Recap: Sanctification is the slow, messy, lifelong process where the Holy Spirit works with our active cooperation to kill our sin and make us like Jesus.

If You Only Remember One Thing: The fact that you are still fighting your sin doesn't mean you aren't saved; dead bodies don't fight, so the struggle proves you are alive.

Next Week Preview: If we still mess up so much, how can we be sure we won't eventually lose our salvation? Next week we tackle Assurance and Perseverance.

Scripture References Used Judges 3:1–2 Proverbs 27:17 1 Corinthians 6:11 Philippians 1:6 Philippians 2:12–13 1 Thessalonians 4:3 Hebrews 10:14 Hebrews 10:24–25

My Thoughts & Notes – What Did I Take From This?

Week 44 — Assurance and Perseverance: When You Doubt

Core Question: If I am still struggling with sin and doubt, how can I actually be sure that I am saved and won't eventually lose it?

Why this matters: Because if you live in constant terror of losing your salvation, you will never experience the joy, freedom, and boldness God designed you to have.

At a Glance (One Page)

Big Idea: Your salvation is absolutely secure not because your grip on God is perfectly strong, but because the Father's grip on you is entirely unbreakable.

Anchor Text: 1 John 5:11–13; John 10:27–29

We believe...: All those who are truly born again and united to Christ will be kept by God's power and will persevere in faith until the end, meaning true salvation cannot be lost.

Key Words (3): Assurance - The internal, God-given confidence that you are truly saved and belong to Christ. Perseverance of the Saints - The theological truth that those whom God saves, God keeps; true believers will continue in faith to the end. Apostasy - The act of definitively abandoning and rejecting the Christian faith.

The One Mistake People Make: Looking inward at their own fluctuating emotions and imperfect behavior to find assurance, instead of looking outward at the objective, finished promises of Christ.

Choose Your Lane: Lane 1 / Lane 2 / Lane 3

This Week's Practice: The Promise Anchor.

This Week's Prayer: Father, I confess that my faith is often fragile. When I look at my own heart, I see enough sin and doubt to disqualify me a thousand times over. I am terrified that I might somehow slip out of Your hands. Thank You for the absolute guarantee of Jesus. Thank You that my eternal destiny does not depend on my perfect performance, but on His unbreakable grip. Quiet the accusations of the enemy in my mind. Give me the profound, unshakeable assurance that because I belong to You, nothing can ever snatch me away. Amen.

Lane 1 — Clarity (10 minutes)

The Bottom Line The most miserable place to be in the world is unsure of where you stand with the person who holds your future. If you don't know if your boss is about to fire you, or if your spouse is about to leave you, you live in a state of low-grade panic. Many Christians live this way with God. They think salvation is a tightrope walk—one major slip, and God cuts the safety net. But the Bible violently rejects this anxiety. God does not want His children living in terror of being disowned. He wrote an entire book of the Bible (1 John) specifically so you could know, with absolute certainty, that your eternal future is locked in a vault.

Scripture Snapshot John 10:27–29: "My sheep listen to my voice; I know them, and they follow me. I give them eternal life, and they shall never perish; no one will snatch them out of my hand. My Father, who has given them to me, is greater than all; no one can snatch them out of my Father's hand."

Jesus uses the metaphor of a shepherd protecting his sheep. Notice the double-layered security system. Jesus says you are in His hand. Then He says you are also in the Father's hand. You are en**Close**d in the grip of the Trinity. Jesus makes a definitive, absolute statement: "They shall *never* perish." He does not say they won't perish as long as they try hard. He bases their security entirely on the massive, untouchable power of the Father's grip.

Say It Out Loud (One Sentence) I cannot lose my salvation because my salvation is maintained by God's grip on me, not my grip on God.

Common Confusions Confusion #1: Assurance means I will never have doubts. (Doubt is a normal struggle of the mind; assurance is the bedrock underneath the doubt). Confusion #2: If I can't lose it, I can sin all I want. (If you *want* to live in unrepentant sin, you don't have the Holy Spirit, meaning you were never saved to begin with).

The Tuesday Payoff It's Tuesday, and you commit a sin you swore you would never commit again. The guilt is heavy. The enemy immediately whispers the oldest lie in the book: *If you were really a Christian, you wouldn't have done that. God is done with you.* If you don't have a theology of assurance, you will believe the lie, hide from God, and spiral into despair. But if you know the doctrine of Perseverance, you recognize the lie. You know that a true son can displease his father, but he does not cease to be a son. You run to God for repentance, not out of terror of being fired, but out of the grief of offending the Father who holds you.

Lane 2 — Depth (30 minutes)

Define the Terms Eternal Security - The objective reality that God protects His people from eternal destruction. Subjective Assurance - Our personal, internal realization and confidence in that security. Presumption - A false, dangerous confidence where someone assumes they are going to heaven despite having no desire for Christ and no fruit of the Spirit.

Build the Doctrine (Scripture-forward)

God's Unbreakable Seal When you buy a house, you put down earnest money (a deposit) to legally guarantee you will finish the transaction. God does the exact same thing with your soul.

Key texts: Ephesians 1:13–14

Paul writes, "When you believed, you were marked in him with a seal, the promised Holy Spirit, who is a deposit guaranteeing our inheritance until the redemption of those who are God's possession." The Holy Spirit inside you is God's down payment. If a believer could lose their salvation, it would mean God broke His contract, broke His seal, and forfeited His own deposit. That is a theological impossibility.

The Intercession of Christ Why don't you lose your salvation when you sin? Because Jesus is actively praying that your faith will not fail.

Key texts: Luke 22:31–32; Hebrews 7:25

Before Peter's massive failure, Jesus tells him, "Simon, Simon, Satan has asked to sift all of you as wheat. But I have prayed for you, Simon, that your faith may not fail." Jesus knew Peter was about to completely deny Him, but Jesus' prayer secured Peter's ultimate restoration. Hebrews 7 says Jesus "always lives to intercede" for us. Your faith survives the crushing weight of this world because the Son of God is currently praying for you.

The Proof is Perseverance If salvation is eternally secure, what about the people who walk away from the church, reject Jesus, and die in unbelief? Did they lose their salvation?

Key texts: 1 John 2:19; Philippians 1:6

The biblical answer is devastating but clear: they didn't lose their salvation; they never actually possessed it. John writes about apostates: "They went out from us, but they did not really belong to us. For if they had belonged to us, they would have remained with us; but their going showed that none of them belonged to us." True grace always produces endurance. The proof that you are genuinely saved is that, despite your failures and doubts, you keep coming back to Jesus.

BOX - What This Is NOT Saying We are NOT saying an unrepentant, ungodly person should feel "secure" just because they prayed a prayer at summer camp when they were 12. We are NOT saying believers won't experience seasons of massive failure (like King David). We are NOT saying assurance is automatic; it must be cultivated through prayer and obedience.

BOX - Where Christians Differ This is a major dividing line. The Arminian (and Roman Catholic) tradition teaches that a genuine, born-again Christian can commit apostasy, exercise their free will to reject God, and completely lose their salvation. The Reformed tradition (Calvinism) teaches the "Perseverance of the Saints"—that anyone truly regenerated by the Holy Spirit will be kept by God's power and cannot ultimately fall away. Broad evangelicalism leans heavily toward eternal security, grounding the believer's comfort in the finished work of Christ rather than their own ability to maintain it.

Lane 3 — Deep Dive (Optional)

The Objection You're Already Thinking "But the book of Hebrews warns that it is impossible for those who have 'shared in the Holy Spirit' to be brought back to repentance if they fall away (Hebrews 6). Doesn't that prove you can lose it?"

The Best Answer Hebrews 6 is the most terrifying warning passage in the New Testament. But we have to read it carefully.

The writer is warning people who are sitting in the church, hearing the gospel, seeing the miracles, and tasting the goodness of God's Word, but who are standing on the edge of walking away and returning to Judaism. They have "shared" in the experience of the Holy Spirit the same way a person at a banquet tastes the food without actually swallowing it.

If they walk away from the absolute final revelation of Jesus Christ, there is no "backup" sacrifice waiting for them. The warning is real: if you permanently reject Jesus, you will perish. But the writer immediately shifts his tone in verse 9: "Even though we speak like this, dear friends, we are convinced of better things in your case—the things that have to do with salvation." The terrifying warning is actually the exact tool God uses to keep His true sheep from wandering off the cliff.

Historical Lens The Puritans in the 17th century wrote extensively on the doctrine of Assurance. They recognized a pastoral crisis: many true believers were terrified of hell, while many fake believers were perfectly comfortable. They distinguished between the *root* of faith and the *fruit* of faith. They taught that you should not look deep inside your own messy, fluctuating emotions to find assurance; you should look completely outside yourself to the objective promises of Christ on the cross. Only when you look out, do you find peace within.

Real-Life Translation There is a massive difference between a relationship based on performance and a relationship based on covenant. If your spouse says, "I will stay with you as long as you meet my needs and never make a massive mistake," you will live in constant, exhausting paranoia. You will hide your flaws.

But if your spouse says, "I made a covenant vow. We are going to have hard days, and you are going to frustrate me, but I am never leaving you," the dynamic completely changes. That kind of security doesn't make you want to cheat on them; it makes you want to love them fiercely.

God's absolute guarantee of your salvation operates the same way. Eternal security is not a license to sin; it is the safety required for true intimacy. Knowing God will never leave you is the only thing that gives you the courage to be brutally honest with Him about your failures.

Midlife Module - This Doctrine at 55 You are 55. You have been walking with Jesus for three decades. The fiery passion of your early faith has settled into a quiet, sometimes boring endurance. You have seen ugly hypocrisy in the church, and you have experienced deep disappointment with God. The temptation to just quietly walk away and adopt a secular, cynical lifestyle is surprisingly strong.

This is where the rubber of Perseverance meets the road. At 55, you realize that your continued faith is not a monument to your own willpower. The only reason you are still a Christian today is because the High Priest has been quietly, relentlessly interceding for you. You have not persevered because you are strong; you have persevered because He is faithful. The fact that you still care, that you still repent, and that you still want Jesus is the absolute proof that His grip on you has never slipped.

Practice + Prayer

This Week's Practice (3–7 minutes) The Promise Anchor. When doubt hits you this week, do not try to analyze your own heart to see if your faith is "strong enough." Your heart is a terrible barometer. Look outward. Read John 10:28 out loud. Tell your anxiety: "I might not feel saved today, but Jesus said no one can snatch me out of His hand, and He does not lie."

Prayer (100–160 words) God, I am so grateful that my salvation does not depend on my ability to hold onto You. I know how weak my grip is. I know how quickly I am distracted, and how easily my heart wanders. Thank You for the staggering promise that You will finish the work You started. Thank You for the Holy Spirit, who seals me for the day of redemption. When the enemy tries to use my sin to convince me that I am disqualified, give me the boldness to point to the cross. Help me to rest in the unbreakable grip of the Father and the constant prayers of the Son. Give me the grace to persevere to the very end. Amen.

Reflection

Solo (3 prompts)

1. Do you base your assurance of salvation on how spiritual you feel on a given day, or on the objective promises of God's Word?

2. Why is the idea of "losing your salvation" actually an insult to the power of the Holy Spirit's seal?

3. How does knowing your future is secure change the way you confess your ugliest sins to God today?

Small Group (3 prompts + 1 hard question)

1. Read John 10:27–29. Why does Jesus emphasize the Father's power ("greater than all") when assuring His sheep of their safety?

2. Discuss the difference between a struggling believer who doubts their salvation, and a presumptuous person who lives in sin but claims they are "eternally secure."

3. We talked about how security creates intimacy, not laziness. Have you found this to be true in your own human relationships?

Hard Question: Are you living in constant fear of God's rejection because you have never actually stopped trying to earn your own salvation?

Close

One Sentence Recap: Your salvation is secure not because your grip on God is strong, but because the Father's grip on you is entirely unbreakable.

If You Only Remember One Thing: A true son can deeply displease his father, but he does not cease to be a son; the seal of the Spirit cannot be broken.

Next Week Preview: This brings us to the final chapter of Part 6. If we are perfectly secure, why does God allow us to go through such crushing pain? We tackle Suffering and Endurance.

Scripture References Used Luke 22:31–32 John 10:27–29 Ephesians 1:13–14 Philippians 1:6 Hebrews 6:4–9 Hebrews 7:25 1 John 2:19 1 John 5:11–13

My Thoughts & Notes – What Did I Take From This?

Week 45 — Suffering and Endurance: Faith Under Weight

Core Question: If God loves me and my salvation is secure, why does He allow me to go through seasons of absolutely crushing pain?

Why this matters: Because if you believe the goal of Christianity is a comfortable life, your faith will shatter the first time you experience real tragedy; but if you understand how God uses suffering, your faith can survive the fire.

At a Glance (One Page)

Big Idea: God does not promise to protect us from the fire of suffering in this life, but He promises to walk through it with us, using the intense heat to burn away our idols and forge an unshakeable faith.

Anchor Text: 1 Peter 1:6–7; 2 Corinthians 4:16–18

We believe…: Suffering is an inevitable reality in a fallen world, but for the believer, God sovereignly redeems it to produce endurance, test genuine faith, and prepare us for an eternal weight of glory.

Key Words (3): Endurance - The spiritual grit to remain faithful to God under prolonged, intense pressure. Refining Fire - The biblical metaphor describing how God uses suffering to purify our faith, just as extreme heat burns the impurities out of gold. Glory - The heavy, massive, eternal reality of God's presence and reward that far outweighs our temporary pain.

The One Mistake People Make: Believing the devastating lie of the "prosperity gospel"—that if you have enough faith and live a good life, God is obligated to protect you from sickness, poverty, and grief.

Choose Your Lane: Lane 1 / Lane 2 / Lane 3

This Week's Practice: The Lament Psalm.

This Week's Prayer: Father, I do not like pain. My entire life is built around avoiding discomfort, securing my future, and protecting the people I love. When suffering hits, my immediate reaction is to doubt Your goodness and question Your plan. Forgive my fragile faith. Thank You that You do not waste a single tear. When I am in the furnace, give me the absolute certainty that You are sitting in the fire with me. Keep me from bitterness. Use the weight of this world to forge a faith in me that cannot be broken. Amen.

Lane 1 — Clarity (10 minutes)

The Bottom Line The American dream is the pursuit of comfort. We expect our careers to trend upward, our health to remain stable, and our children to thrive. When the American dream collides with the Christian faith, we accidentally create a theology where God's primary job is to be our personal assistant, guaranteeing our comfort. The New Testament violently destroys this expectation. Peter and Paul do not tell the church *if* they suffer; they tell them *when* they suffer. Christianity is not a bypass around the pain of the human experience. It is the only theology that gives the pain actual meaning, promising that the furnace is not destroying you; it is refining you.

Scripture Snapshot 1 Peter 1:6–7: "In all this you greatly rejoice, though now for a little while you may have had to suffer grief in all kinds of trials. These have come so that the proven genuineness of your faith—of greater worth than gold, which perishes even though refined by fire—may result in praise, glory and honor when Jesus Christ is revealed."

Peter acknowledges that the believers are currently experiencing profound grief. He does not tell them to fake a smile or pretend it doesn't hurt. But he reveals the mechanics of what the pain is doing. He uses the imagery of a goldsmith. You put raw gold into a crucible and turn up the heat so the garbage (the dross) floats to the top and can be scraped off. God uses the heat of trials to burn away our self-reliance, our idols, and our pride, leaving behind a pure, tested faith that will survive judgment day.

Say It Out Loud (One Sentence) God does not waste my pain; He uses the crushing weight of suffering to forge a faith that cannot be destroyed.

Common Confusions Confusion #1: If I am suffering, God must be punishing me for a specific sin. (Sometimes we reap the consequences of our actions, but much suffering is simply the result of living in a fallen world). Confusion #2: A strong Christian shouldn't feel sad when tragedy strikes. (Jesus was a perfect Christian, and He wept openly at the tomb of His friend).

The Tuesday Payoff It's Tuesday, and you are sitting in a sterile hospital room, or staring at divorce papers, or dealing with a child who has walked away. The pain is physical. If your theology says "God rewards good people with easy lives," you will conclude that God has abandoned you. You will become furious and bitter. But if you have a theology of the crucible, your perspective shifts. You don't have to like the pain, but you know it isn't random. The Master Goldsmith has His eye on the thermometer, He has not left the room, and He is doing something in your soul that could not be accomplished in the sunshine.

Lane 2 — Depth (30 minutes)

Define the Terms Trials - The external pressures, tragedies, and difficulties we face in life. Temptations - The internal pull to respond to trials with sin, bitterness, or rebellion against God. Lament - The biblical practice of bringing your raw, unfiltered grief and anger directly to God in prayer.

Build the Doctrine (Scripture-forward)

Suffering is Guaranteed Jesus never used a bait-and-switch. He never promised that following Him would result in an easy, prosperous life. In fact, He guaranteed the exact opposite.

Key texts: John 16:33; 2 Timothy 3:12

Jesus looked at His disciples and said, "In this world you will have trouble. But take heart! I have overcome the world." Paul echoes this reality: "In fact, everyone who wants to live a godly life in Christ Jesus will be persecuted" (2 Tim 3:12). If your theology does not have a massive, sturdy category for unjust suffering, you do not have a biblical theology. Pain is the curriculum of the Christian life.

The Weight Room Why does God allow it? Because the only way to build muscle is through resistance. The only way to build spiritual endurance is to place the faith under heavy weight.

Key texts: Romans 5:3–4; James 1:2–4

Paul writes, "We also glory in our sufferings, because we know that suffering produces perseverance; perseverance, character; and character, hope" (Rom 5:3-4). James tells us to consider it pure joy when we face trials, "because you know that the testing of your faith produces perseverance." You cannot pray for patience and endurance and then be angry when God sends you the exact tribulation required to produce them.

The Future Outweighs the Present The Christian response to suffering is not stoicism (pretending it doesn't hurt). It is perspective. We survive the present agony by aggressively looking at the future glory.

Key texts: 2 Corinthians 4:16–17; Romans 8:18

Paul, a man who was beaten, stoned, and imprisoned, writes: "Therefore we do not lose heart. Though outwardly we are wasting away, yet inwardly we are being renewed day by day. For our light and momentary troubles are achieving for us an eternal glory that far outweighs them all." Paul calls his brutal beatings "light and momentary" not because they didn't hurt, but because he placed them on a scale next to the eternal weight of the resurrection. The future glory makes the present pain mathematically insignificant.

BOX - What This Is NOT Saying We are NOT saying you should seek out suffering or stay in an abusive situation; we avoid pain when possible, but trust God when it is unavoidable. We are NOT saying it is wrong to take medication, go to therapy, or fight a disease; God provides common grace to ease suffering. We are NOT saying you must understand *why* God allowed a specific tragedy; the "why" is often kept secret (Deut 29:29).

BOX - Where Christians Differ The "Prosperity Gospel" (or Word of Faith movement) is a massive, global theological error that teaches God guarantees physical health and financial wealth to those with enough faith. Broad evangelicalism, along with all historic, orthodox Christianity, fiercely rejects this as a heresy that preys on the vulnerable. The true gospel promises that God will save our souls and give us His presence in the fire, not that He will keep us out of the fire.

Lane 3 — Deep Dive (Optional)

The Objection You're Already Thinking "When I am in deep pain, being told that God is 'refining my character' feels incredibly cold and callous. It just makes God sound like a cruel scientist running an experiment on me."

The Best Answer If God were sitting safely in heaven, untouched by pain, running a clinical experiment on your life, that objection would be entirely valid. He would be cruel.

But God is not a scientist in a lab coat; He is the man on the middle cross.

When you are suffering, you are not experiencing anything that God Himself has not already endured. He knows the sting of betrayal. He knows the grief of watching a friend die. He knows the physical agony of a tortured body, and He knows the terror of feeling abandoned by God (Matthew 27:46).

God does not hand you a cup of suffering from a safe distance. He drank the cup of ultimate suffering first. When He allows you to go through the fire, He is not a distant observer; He is the "fourth man in the furnace" (Daniel 3:25). The refinement of your character is not a cold experiment; it is the agonizing, loving discipline of a Father who is actively walking through the flames right beside you.

Historical Lens The book of Job is the oldest book in the Bible, and it is entirely dedicated to the problem of suffering. Job lost his wealth, his children, and his health in a single day. His friends insisted he must have sinned to deserve it (the Karma theology). God ultimately rebukes the friends. The massive theological takeaway of Job is that human suffering is rarely a simple math equation of "sin equals punishment." The universe is vastly more complex, and God's sovereign purposes operate on a level far above our pay grade. Job's comfort did not come from getting an explanation; it came from getting a revelation of the absolute majesty of God.

Real-Life Translation When tragedy strikes, the modern church is often terrible at handling grief. We rush to fix people. We slap a Romans 8:28 bumper sticker on their devastating loss and tell them "God has a plan." We do this because their unresolved pain makes *us* uncomfortable.

But the Bible gives us an entire category for unresolved pain: Lament. A third of the Psalms are laments. The writers scream, cry, and ask God why He is hiding. God canonized their anger in Scripture.

If you are suffering, you do not have to fake a victory you do not feel. You have biblical permission to grieve deeply. You have permission to tell God exactly how angry and exhausted you are. True faith isn't forcing a smile at a funeral; true faith is taking your furious, broken heart and slamming it into the chest of God, trusting that He is big enough to absorb the hit.

Midlife Module - This Doctrine at 52 You are 52. The specific flavor of midlife suffering is often cumulative. It isn't just one thing. It is the compounding weight of a career setback, a terrifying medical diagnosis, the death of a parent, and a struggling marriage, all hitting within a five-year window. You feel like the structure of your life is buckling under the pressure.

This is the crucible. At 52, God is burning away the illusions of your twenties. You thought you were in control; the crucible proves you are not. You thought your career would satisfy you; the crucible proves it can't. The fire is incredibly painful, but it is doing a necessary, beautiful work. It is stripping away everything that is temporary so that you are forced to build the remainder of your life entirely on the Rock that cannot be shaken.

Practice + Prayer

This Week's Practice (3–7 minutes) The Lament Psalm. If you are carrying a heavy burden of grief, anxiety, or frustration, do not try to pray a "polite" prayer today. Read Psalm 13 out loud. Use David's exact words: "How long, Lord? Will you forget me forever?" Give yourself permission to be brutally honest with God about your pain, ending with the stubborn choice to trust Him anyway.

Prayer (100–160 words) God, I do not understand Your ways. When the fire of suffering gets hot, my instinct is to run, to doubt Your love, and to demand an explanation. Forgive me for my lack of trust. Thank You that You are a High Priest who actually understands pain. You wept, You bled, and You suffered unjust agony. I ask You to remove the heavy cup of suffering from me, but if Your answer is no, I ask for the absolute, undeniable reality of Your presence in the fire. Burn away my pride and my self-reliance. Take the things the enemy meant for evil and use them to forge an unshakeable, resilient faith in me. Keep my eyes fixed on the eternal weight of glory. Amen.

Reflection

Solo (3 prompts)

1. Have you unconsciously absorbed the "prosperity gospel," secretly believing that God owes you a comfortable life if you obey Him?

2. What is the difference between complaining *about* God (bitterness) and complaining *to* God (lament)?

3. Look back at a painful season in your past. Can you see now how God used that specific resistance to build spiritual muscle you didn't know you needed?

Small Group (3 prompts + 1 hard question)

1. Read 1 Peter 1:6–7. How does the metaphor of the Goldsmith change the way we view our current trials?

2. Discuss Paul's claim that his brutal beatings were "light and momentary" (2 Cor 4). How does keeping our eyes on the future resurrection literally change how pain feels in the present?

3. We talked about how the church is often terrible at handling grief. How can our group become a safe place for people to lament without us trying to "fix" them with platitudes?

Hard Question: Are you currently allowing a deep wound or tragedy to slowly turn you into a bitter, cynical person, rather than allowing God to use it to make you tender and empathetic?

Close: One Sentence Recap: God uses the intense, inevitable suffering of a fallen world to burn away our idols and forge an unshakeable, enduring faith.

If You Only Remember One Thing: God does not hand you a cup of suffering from a safe distance; He is the fourth man in the furnace, walking through the fire right beside you.

Next Week Preview: This completes Part 6 on Salvation. Next week, we start Part 7 by meeting the most misunderstood Person of the Trinity: The Holy Spirit. Who is He, and what does He actually do?

Scripture References Used Deuteronomy 29:29 Psalm 13 Daniel 3:25 Matthew 27:46 John 16:33 Romans 5:3–4 Romans 8:18 2 Corinthians 4:16–18 2 Timothy 3:12 James 1:2–4 1 Peter 1:6–7

My Thoughts & Notes – What Did I Take From This?

In school, the phrase "group project" struck fear into our hearts because it meant you were going to be tethered to people who either cared way too much or didn't care at all. For many of us, the modern church feels like the ultimate, exhausting group project... messy, hypocritical, and full of politics.

But in Part 7, we discover why you cannot survive this life as a lone wolf. We will look at the actual Person of the Holy Spirit (stripping away the weird 90s televangelist baggage), why He gives us spiritual gifts, and why we desperately need the frustrating, beautiful institution of the local church to keep our faith alive.

WEEK 46 — THE HOLY SPIRIT: PERSON AND PRESENCE

CORE QUESTION: Is THE Holy Spirit an actual person who lives inside me, or just a vague force that makes church services emotional?

Why this matters: Because if the Spirit is just a force, you will exhaust yourself trying to use Him for power; but if the Spirit is a Person, He will transform you through relationship.

At a Glance (One Page)

Big Idea: The Holy Spirit is not a mood, a feeling, or an energy field; He is the fully divine, fully personal third member of the Trinity who takes up permanent residence inside every believer.

Anchor Text: John 14:16–17; Romans 8:9–11

We believe...: The Holy Spirit is a divine Person, co-equal with the Father and the Son, who convicts the world of sin, regenerates the dead heart, and permanently indwells believers to empower them for obedience.

Key Words (3): Indwelling - The reality that God the Holy Spirit literally takes up permanent residence inside the physical body of a believer. Paraclete - The Greek word Jesus used for the Spirit, meaning "Advocate," "Comforter," or "Helper" called alongside us. Blasphemy of the Spirit - The unpardonable sin; an ongoing, hardened, final rejection of the Holy Spirit's conviction regarding Jesus.

The One Mistake People Make: Treating the Holy Spirit like spiritual electricity they need to "plug into" for a better life, rather than submitting to Him as a sovereign Lord.

Choose Your Lane: Lane 1 / Lane 2 / Lane 3

This Week's Practice: The Pronoun Correction.

This Week's Prayer: Father, I confess that I often ignore the Holy Spirit. I am comfortable talking to You, and I am comfortable talking about Jesus, but the Spirit feels mysterious and vague to me. Forgive me for treating Him like a tool or a force. Thank You that You did not leave me as an orphan. Thank You for sending the Comforter to live inside my chest, giving me the power to obey You. Teach me to listen to His quiet conviction and rely on His constant presence. Amen.

Lane 1 — Clarity (10 minutes)

The Bottom Line When Jesus was about to leave the earth, His disciples panicked. They were terrified of being alone. Jesus told them something shocking: "It is for your good that I am going away." How could Jesus leaving possibly be good? Because if Jesus stayed in His physical body, He could only be in one place at one time. By leaving, He could send the Holy Spirit to be present everywhere, living inside the chest of every single believer. The Holy Spirit is not a downgrade from having physical Jesus. He is the exact same presence of God, operating from the inside out.

Scripture Snapshot John 14:16–17: "And I will ask the Father, and he will give you another advocate to help you and be with you forever—the Spirit of truth. The world cannot accept him, because it neither sees him nor knows him. But you know him, for he lives with you and will be in you."

Jesus uses the word "another" (meaning another of the exact same kind). The Holy Spirit isn't a replacement teacher; He is the exact same divine substance as Jesus. Notice the radical shift in location. In the Old Testament, the Spirit was *with* people, coming upon them temporarily for specific tasks. Under the New Covenant, the Spirit is *in* you. The temple of God moved from a stone building in Jerusalem directly into your ribcage.

Say It Out Loud (One Sentence) The Holy Spirit is not an "it" to be used; He is a "He" to be obeyed and trusted.

Common Confusions Confusion #1: The Holy Spirit makes people act out of control. (One of the primary fruits of the Spirit is *self-control*). Confusion #2: Only super-spiritual Christians have the Holy Spirit. (If you do not have the Holy Spirit, you are not a Christian at all).

The Tuesday Payoff You are facing a massive temptation on a Tuesday night. Maybe it is an addiction you are trying to break, or a bitter grudge you are refusing to let go. You feel entirely isolated in the fight. If you don't understand the Holy Spirit, you will just try to grit your teeth and survive the night on your own willpower. But if you know the doctrine of Indwelling, you realize you are not alone in the room. You have the Advocate. You don't have to generate the power to say no; you simply have to yield to the Person inside you who already possesses the power.

Lane 2 — Depth (30 minutes)

Define the Terms Deity of the Spirit - The absolute truth that the Holy Spirit is fully God, sharing the exact same essence as the Father and Son. Conviction - The work of the Spirit exposing our sin and convincing us of our need for Christ. Sealing - The Holy Spirit acting as God's official, unbreakable stamp of ownership on a believer (Eph 1:13).

Build the Doctrine (Scripture-forward)

He is a Person, Not a Power We get confused because the Bible uses metaphors like wind, fire, and water to describe the Spirit. But metaphors describe His *effects*, not His *nature*. The Spirit has a mind, a will, and emotions.

Key texts: Ephesians 4:30; Acts 13:2

Paul commands, "And do not grieve the Holy Spirit of God." You cannot grieve gravity. You cannot hurt the feelings of electricity. You can only grieve a person who loves you. In Acts 13, the Holy Spirit speaks to the church: "Set apart for me Barnabas and Saul for the work to which I have called them." He makes executive decisions. He is a "Who."

He is Fully God The Holy Spirit is not a junior partner in the Trinity or an angel taking orders. He is the uncreated Creator.

Key texts: Acts 5:3–4; 1 Corinthians 2:10–11

When Ananias lies to the early church about his money, Peter confronts him: "Ananias, how is it that Satan has so filled your heart that you have lied to the Holy Spirit?... You have not lied just to human beings but to God." Peter uses "Holy Spirit" and "God" completely interchangeably. Furthermore, Paul states that the Spirit searches the deep things of God and knows the very thoughts of God (1 Cor 2). Only God can fully comprehend God.

He Supplies the Power for Obedience If Justification is the car, the Holy Spirit is the engine. God does not demand you live a holy life and then leave you alone to figure it out.

Key texts: Romans 8:9–11; Galatians 5:22–23

Paul is absolutely ruthless on this point: "And if anyone does not have the Spirit of Christ, they do not belong to Christ" (Rom 8:9). Every true believer receives the Spirit the moment they are saved. And what does He do? He produces fruit. "But the fruit of the Spirit is love, joy, peace, forbearance, kindness, goodness, faithfulness, gentleness and self-control." You don't tape this fruit onto your life; it grows naturally out of you as the Spirit works.

BOX - What This Is NOT Saying We are NOT saying the Holy Spirit only shows up when the music gets emotional at church; He is present when you are quietly doing laundry. We are NOT saying the Holy Spirit will ever tell you to do something that contradicts the Bible; He wrote the Bible. We are NOT saying you have to speak in tongues to prove you have the Holy Spirit.

BOX - Where Christians Differ A major debate among Evangelicals and Pentecostals/Charismatics revolves around the "Baptism of the Holy Spirit."

1. Non-Charismatic Evangelicals believe that Spirit Baptism happens instantly and completely at the moment of conversion (1 Cor 12:13); every believer has the Spirit in full.

2. Pentecostals/Charismatics believe that the "Baptism of the Holy Spirit" is a distinct, second experience that happens *after* conversion, empowering the believer for ministry, often evidenced by speaking in tongues. However, all agree that the indwelling presence of the Spirit is an absolute requirement for salvation.

Lane 3 — Deep Dive (Optional)

The Objection You're Already Thinking "I grew up in churches where the Holy Spirit was used as an excuse for chaotic, weird, and manipulative behavior. It made me incredibly skeptical of anything 'spiritual'."

The Best Answer If you grew up around charismatic abuses—where people were knocked over, manipulated for money, or told that their lack of healing meant they didn't have enough faith—your skepticism is completely justified. That behavior is a violation of God's character.

But we cannot let the abuse of a doctrine rob us of the beauty of the doctrine. When a bank teller encounters a counterfeit hundred-dollar bill, they don't decide that all money is fake. They just learn to spot the counterfeit by studying the real thing.

The real Holy Spirit does not author chaos. Paul says in 1 Corinthians 14:33, "For God is not a God of disorder but of peace." The true mark of the Holy Spirit's presence in a room is not uncontrolled screaming or emotional hysteria. The truest mark of the Holy Spirit is a room full of people deeply convicted of their sin, resting in the grace of Jesus Christ, and demonstrating self-control and love. Do not let the counterfeits steal your Comforter.

Historical Lens In the 4th century, a group called the Pneumatomachi (the "Spirit-fighters") argued that the Holy Spirit was not God, but just an angelic creation of the Son. The Council of Constantinople in 381 AD shut this down entirely, updating the Nicene Creed to declare that the Holy Spirit is "the Lord, the giver of life, who proceeds from the Father, who with the Father and the Son is worshiped and glorified." The church drew a hard line: if you demote the Spirit, you lose the Trinity.

Real-Life Translation We spend a massive amount of time trying to fix our own behavior through podcasts, apps, and scheduling hacks. But behavioral modification without the Holy Spirit is just painting over rot.

You can use sheer willpower to stop yelling at your kids for a week, but you will just replace the yelling with a simmering, quiet resentment. Willpower can change the exterior; only the Holy Spirit can change the interior.

The Christian life requires you to throw up your hands and admit, "I do not have the power to love this difficult person. I do not have the patience to handle this Tuesday." That isn't a failure; it is the starting line. You are finally empty enough for the Holy Spirit to take over the controls.

Midlife Module - This Doctrine at 48 You are 48, and the emotional highs of your youth group days are long gone. You remember a time when your faith felt electric, full of certainty and passion. Now, your faith often feels like a slow, quiet, sometimes boring endurance test. You wonder if the Holy Spirit has left you because you don't "feel" Him anymore.

But emotional highs are not the primary metric of the Spirit. The fact that you are 48, disillusioned with the culture, tired from your career, and yet *still showing up to church and trusting Jesus* is an absolute miracle. That quiet, stubborn endurance is the massive, undeniable work of the Holy Spirit. He isn't just the spark that starts the fire; He is the slow-burning coal that keeps the house warm for decades.

Practice + Prayer

This Week's Practice (3–7 minutes) The Pronoun Correction. This week, pay attention to how you talk about the Holy Spirit in your own mind or in conversations. Every time you catch yourself referring to the Spirit as "it" or an "energy," correct yourself. Say out loud, "He is a Person." Changing your grammar will slowly change your theology.

Prayer (100–160 words) God, thank You for the stunning reality that You did not just save me from a distance. You actually moved into the ruined house of my life. Holy Spirit, I confess that I frequently grieve You. I ignore Your quiet convictions, I rely on my own willpower, and I treat You like a tool to be used rather than a Lord to be worshipped. Forgive me. Thank You for being the ultimate Comforter. Thank You for bearing witness to my spirit that I am a child of God. Fill me today. Produce the fruit of patience, kindness, and self-control in me that I cannot produce myself. Amen.

Reflection

Solo (3 prompts)

1. Why is it so much easier for us to treat the Holy Spirit as an impersonal "force" rather than a Divine Person with feelings and a will?

2. What is the difference between feeling "emotional" at church and actually experiencing the conviction of the Holy Spirit?

3. How does knowing the Holy Spirit is praying for you (Romans 8:26) change how you view your own weak, clumsy prayers?

Small Group (3 prompts + 1 hard question)

1. Read John 14:16–17. Why did Jesus say it was actually *better* for the disciples that He leave so the Spirit could come?

2. Discuss the difference between behavioral modification (trying hard) and spiritual transformation (yielding to the Spirit).

3. We talked about how the abuses of the Holy Spirit make us skeptical. How do we recover a healthy reliance on the Spirit without becoming weird or chaotic?

Hard Question: Are you currently ignoring a clear, nagging conviction from the Holy Spirit about a specific habit, hoping He will just eventually stop bothering you?

Close

One Sentence Recap: The Holy Spirit is the fully divine, fully personal third member of the Trinity who takes up permanent residence inside every believer.

If You Only Remember One Thing: The Holy Spirit is not an "it" you plug into for power; He is a Divine Person you submit to for transformation.

Next Week Preview: If the Spirit is inside us, how does He actually guide us? Next week we tackle God's Will, Spiritual Gifts, and Discernment without the weirdness.

Scripture References Used John 14:16–17 Acts 5:3–4 Acts 13:2 Romans 8:9–11 Romans 8:26 1 Corinthians 2:10–11 1 Corinthians 14:33 Ephesians 1:13 Ephesians 4:30 Galatians 5:22–23

My Thoughts & Notes – What Did I Take From This?

Week 47 — Guidance and Gifts: Discernment Without Weirdness

Core Question: How do I figure out God's will for my life, and are spiritual gifts still a real thing today?

Why this matters: Because chasing "signs" creates paralyzing anxiety, but ignoring the Spirit's guidance leaves you entirely reliant on your own flawed intuition.

At a Glance (One Page)

Big Idea: The Holy Spirit guides us primarily through the clear commands of Scripture and wise counsel, and He gives every believer specific spiritual gifts to serve the local church.

Anchor Text: 1 Corinthians 12:4–7; 1 Thessalonians 4:3

We believe...: The Holy Spirit empowers every believer with spiritual gifts for the building up of the church, and guides believers through the illumination of the written Word of God.

Key Words (3): Spiritual Gifts - Specific abilities given by the Holy Spirit to believers, not for their own benefit, but to serve and build up the local church. Illumination - The work of the Holy Spirit helping us understand and apply the Bible to our specific lives. God's Will of Decree vs. Precept - God's hidden, sovereign plan for the universe (Decree) versus His clearly revealed moral commands in Scripture (Precept).

The One Mistake People Make: Treating God's will like a tightrope where one wrong career move ruins their life, instead of viewing it as a wide pasture fenced in by biblical morality.

Choose Your Lane: Lane 1 / Lane 2 / Lane 3

This Week's Practice: The Tightrope Exit.

This Week's Prayer: Father, I confess that I want You to just give me a blueprint for my life. I want You to tell me exactly what job to take, where to live, and how to avoid pain. I get paralyzed by the fear of making a wrong choice. Forgive me for wanting a crystal ball instead of a relationship with You. Thank You that Your will is not a puzzle I have to solve. Give me the wisdom to obey what You have clearly commanded in Scripture, and the freedom to confidently make choices within those boundaries. Amen.

Lane 1 — Clarity (10 minutes)

The Bottom Line We overcomplicate God's will. We look for signs in the clouds, we over-analyze coincidences, and we freeze when we have to make a decision. We want God to be a magic 8-ball. But God rarely gives us a specific blueprint for our careers or housing choices. He gives us something better: He gives us a renewed mind. The Holy Spirit guides us by deeply anchoring us in the truth of the Bible, so that when we face a complex decision, we have the wisdom to make a choice that honors God. And He gives us spiritual gifts not to make us spiritual superstars, but to give us the tools we need to serve the people sitting in the pew next to us.

Scripture Snapshot 1 Corinthians 12:4–7: "There are different kinds of gifts, but the same Spirit distributes them. There are different kinds of service, but the same Lord... Now to each one the manifestation of the Spirit is given for the common good."

The Corinthian church was obsessed with spiritual gifts. They were using them to show off, rank themselves, and create a chaotic hierarchy. Paul corrects them bluntly. The gifts do not exist to prove how spiritual you are. They are tools in a toolbox given for one specific purpose: "the common good." If your spiritual gift isn't building up the church, you are using the tool backward.

Say It Out Loud (One Sentence) God's primary will for my life is my holiness, and He gives me spiritual gifts to help other people pursue theirs.

Common Confusions Confusion #1: Finding God's will means waiting for a specific, subjective feeling of "peace" before making a decision. (Feelings lie; God's will is found in objective biblical wisdom). Confusion #2: My spiritual gift is just my natural talent or personality type. (Spiritual gifts are supernatural empowerments for ministry, distinct from basic talents).

The Tuesday Payoff You have a massive career decision to make by Tuesday afternoon. Do you take the promotion that pays more but requires more travel, or stay in the current role? You are waiting for a "sign" from God, but the sky is silent. If you treat God's will like a tightrope, the pressure is crushing. But biblical discernment changes the game. Are both jobs legal and ethical? Yes. Does your spouse support the move? Yes. Will it force you to abandon your local church? No. Because both options fall within the moral boundaries of Scripture, you are completely free. You pick the one you want, and you trust God to use it.

Lane 2 — Depth (30 minutes)

Define the Terms Wisdom - The Spirit-given ability to take the truths of Scripture and correctly apply them to complex, real-world situations. Cessationism - The theological belief that the "miraculous" gifts (tongues, prophecy, healing) ceased after the first-century apostles died. Continuationism - The theological belief that all spiritual gifts, including the miraculous ones, continue to operate in the church today.

Build the Doctrine (Scripture-forward)

God's Will is Usually Obvious We spend 90% of our time agonizing over God's "hidden will" (who to marry, what job to take), while entirely ignoring His "revealed will." The Bible is incredibly explicit about what God wants from you today.

Key texts: 1 Thessalonians 4:3; Micah 6:8

Paul writes, "It is God's will that you should be sanctified: that you should avoid sexual immorality." Micah writes, "And what does the Lord require of you? To act justly and to love mercy and to walk humbly with your God." If you are sleeping with someone you aren't married to, or if you are treating your employees unjustly, you do not need to pray about whether you should take a new job. You are already living outside God's clearly revealed will. Obey the obvious things first.

Gifts are for the Body When you become a Christian, the Holy Spirit gives you at least one spiritual gift. It might be teaching, administration, mercy, or hospitality. But the gift is not actually for you.

Key texts: 1 Peter 4:10; Romans 12:6

"Each of you should use whatever gift you have received to serve others, as faithful stewards of God's grace in its various forms" (1 Peter 4:10). If you have the gift of teaching, but you are sitting at home alone listening to podcasts, you are hoarding a gift that belongs to your local church. The church is a body; if the liver decides to stop working, the whole body gets sick.

Test the Spirits Because the spiritual realm is real, not every strong impulse or internal feeling is from the Holy Spirit. We are commanded to be discerning, critical thinkers.

Key texts: 1 John 4:1; 1 Thessalonians 5:19–21

John warns, "Dear friends, do not believe every spirit, but test the spirits to see whether they are from God." Paul adds, "Do not quench the Spirit. Do not treat prophecies with contempt but test them all; hold on to what is good." How do you test it? By the Bible. The Holy Spirit will never, ever lead you to do something that contradicts the Book He inspired. If your "internal peace" tells you to divorce your spouse for someone else, that peace is a lie from hell.

BOX - What This Is NOT Saying We are NOT saying God never prompts us internally; the Spirit does guide, but those promptings always align with Scripture. We are NOT saying you must take a formal personality test to discover your spiritual gift; you usually find it by simply serving where there is a need. We are NOT saying the "boring" gifts (administration, serving) are less important than the public gifts (teaching).

BOX - Where Christians Differ The Cessationist vs. Continuationist debate is massive here. Cessationists believe the dramatic sign gifts (tongues, prophecy, miraculous healing) were the "training wheels" to authenticate the Apostles while the New Testament was being written, and those specific gifts ceased when the Bible was completed. Continuationists believe all gifts are fully active today and should be sought by the church. Despite this sharp divide on *how* the Spirit operates today, both sides fiercely agree that the Spirit's primary job is to illuminate Scripture and build the local church.

Lane 3 — Deep Dive (Optional)

The Objection You're Already Thinking "But didn't God speak directly to people in the Bible and tell them exactly what to do? Why shouldn't I expect God to tell me exactly which house to buy?"

The Best Answer If you read the Bible like a highlight reel, it seems like God is constantly booming directions from the clouds. But look **Close**r. God spoke directly to Abraham, and then hundreds of years of silence passed before He spoke to Moses. The direct, audible guidance of God in Scripture is actually incredibly rare, and it almost always revolves around a massive, redemptive-historical event (like moving a nation or installing a king).

Furthermore, when God *did* speak directly to people like Jonah or Paul, it usually involved sending them into severe suffering or prison. We want direct revelation so we can optimize our comfort; God uses direct revelation to advance His kingdom, usually at the expense of the person's comfort.

Under the New Covenant, we have something the Old Testament saints did not have: the completed, written Word of God and the permanent indwelling of the Holy Spirit. God treats us like adult children. He gives us the moral boundaries, the wisdom of the community, and then trusts us to make decisions. Expecting God to micromanage your housing choices is actually a regression in spiritual maturity.

Historical Lens In the 1980s and 90s, a movement heavily popularized the idea of "hearing the voice of God" in everyday life. Phrases like "God told me to do this" became the ultimate trump card in Christian conversations. The historical danger of this is massive. When a person equates their own internal thoughts with the infallible voice of the Creator, they become immune to correction. If you say, "God told me to quit my job," no one can argue with you. The historic church has always guarded against this by insisting that the phrase "God said" should only be used when quoting a Bible verse.

Real-Life Translation The tightrope view of God's will creates paralyzed Christians. You stand at a crossroads, terrified that if you pick the wrong major, the wrong city, or the wrong spouse, you will fall off the tightrope and ruin "Plan A" for your life, forcing God to relegate you to "Plan B."

God is vastly more competent than that. His will is not a tightrope; it is a pasture. The fences of the pasture are the clear, moral commands of Scripture (do not steal, do not lie, marry a believer). As long as you are inside the fences, you can run wherever you want.

You do not have to live in terror of ruining God's plan. If you make a foolish choice, God is sovereign enough to weave even your foolishness into His ultimate design. Make a decision, execute it with integrity, and go to sleep.

Midlife Module - This Doctrine at 51 You are 51. You are contemplating a major life pivot—a career change, starting a business, or moving to be **Close**r to aging parents. The stakes feel incredibly high, because you know you don't have twenty years to recover if this goes badly. You want absolute certainty from God before you move.

At 51, you must realize that God rarely gives certainty; He requires faith. He isn't going to write the answer in the sky. He has given you decades of accumulated wisdom, the scars of past failures, a Bible full of truth, and a community of friends. Gather the data, seek counsel, check your motives, and then simply choose. Real spiritual maturity at midlife is making a difficult, ambiguous decision and trusting the sovereignty of God to handle the outcome.

Practice + Prayer

This Week's Practice (3–7 minutes) The Tightrope Exit. Identify a decision you have been agonizing over, waiting for a "sign" to give you total peace. Check the decision against Scripture—is it a moral issue? If not, stop agonizing. Pick the option that seems wisest based on the data you have, commit to it, and move forward. Step off the tightrope and into the pasture.

Prayer (100–160 words) God, I confess that I overcomplicate my relationship with You. I ignore the clear things You have commanded me to do, while obsessing over the secret things You have kept hidden. Forgive my paralyzed, anxious faith. Thank You that Your Word is a lamp to my feet. Give me the profound relief of knowing that Your sovereign will cannot be derailed by my imperfect decisions. Holy Spirit, give me the wisdom to apply Scripture to my daily life. Show me the specific spiritual gifts You have placed in me, and give me the humility to actually use them to serve my local church, rather than hoarding them for myself. Amen.

Reflection

Solo (3 prompts)

1. Have you ever used the phrase "God told me" to justify a decision that you just really wanted to make anyway?

2. What is the difference between relying on a subjective "feeling of peace" and relying on biblical wisdom?

3. What is one practical, unglamorous way you could use your time or skills to serve your local church this month?

Small Group (3 prompts + 1 hard question)

1. Read 1 Thessalonians 4:3. Why do we spend so much time worrying about our careers, but so little time worrying about our sanctification?

2. Discuss the metaphor of the tightrope vs. the pasture. How does viewing God's will as a pasture completely change the anxiety of decision-making?

3. We talked about how spiritual gifts are for "the common good." What happens to a church when 80% of the people consume the service, but only 20% use their gifts?

Hard Question: Are you currently withholding your spiritual gifts and your time from your local church because you secretly believe you are too busy or too important to serve?

Close

One Sentence Recap: The Holy Spirit guides us through the clear commands of Scripture, and He empowers every believer with specific gifts to build up the church.

If You Only Remember One Thing: God's will is not a tightrope where one wrong move ruins your life; it is a wide pasture fenced in by biblical truth.

Next Week Preview: If we have the Holy Spirit and the Bible, why do we need other people? Next week we tackle The Church—why we desperately need an institution that has hurt so many of us.

Scripture References Used Micah 6:8 Romans 12:6 1 Corinthians 12:4–7 1 Thessalonians 4:3 1 Thessalonians 5:19–21 1 Peter 4:10 1 John 4:1

My Thoughts & Notes – What Did I Take From This?

Week 48 — The Church: Why It Matters (Even After Hurt)

Core Question: If my salvation is secure and I can read my Bible at home, why do I need to submit to a messy, hypocritical institution?

Why this matters: Because isolated Christians are dead Christians; the church is not a building you occasionally attend, it is a living body you need in order to survive.

At a Glance (One Page)

Big Idea: The local church is God's flawed but glorious "Plan A" for the world; it is the physical gathering of believers commanded by Christ to worship, discipline, and care for one another.

Anchor Text: Acts 2:42–47; Hebrews 10:24–25

We believe...: The universal church consists of all true believers across time, which must be expressed in visible, local congregations gathered for the preaching of the Word, the administration of the sacraments, and mutual discipleship.

Key Words (3): *Ekklesia* - The Greek word for "church," meaning "the called-out assembly." It is a gathered people, not a physical building. Visible/Invisible Church - The Invisible church is all true believers known only to God; the Visible church is the local congregation we can see (which includes both true believers and hypocrites). Church Discipline - The biblical process of confronting unrepentant sin in a believer's life to restore them and protect the church's witness.

The One Mistake People Make: Adopting the modern mantra, "I love Jesus but I hate organized religion," completely ignoring the fact that Jesus explicitly created, organized, and died for the institution of the church.

Choose Your Lane: Lane 1 / Lane 2 / Lane 3

This Week's Practice: The Consumer Pivot.

This Week's Prayer: Father, I confess that my relationship with the church is deeply complicated. I have seen the hypocrisy, the politics, and the egos, and I have frequently wanted to walk away from it all. Forgive my cynicism. Remind me that the church is the Bride of Christ, and You do not take kindly to people insulting Your Bride. Give me the humility to submit to imperfect leaders. Heal the wounds I have received from unhealthy churches, and give me the courage to step back into the mess of a local body. Amen.

Lane 1 — Clarity (10 minutes)

The Bottom Line The most popular spiritual posture of our generation is the "lone wolf" Christian. We download worship music on Spotify, listen to brilliant sermons on podcasts, and consider that our church for the week. It is highly efficient, deeply comfortable, and entirely unbiblical. The New Testament knows absolutely nothing of a Christian who is not intimately, frictionally bound to a local congregation. The church is a hospital for sinners, meaning it is guaranteed to be messy, hypocritical, and frustrating. But Jesus didn't die for a podcast audience. He died for a physical, gathered Bride.

Scripture Snapshot Hebrews 10:24–25: "And let us consider how we may spur one another on toward love and good deeds, not giving up meeting together, as some are in the habit of doing, but encouraging one another—and all the more as you see the Day approaching."

The writer of Hebrews is dealing with people who are tired. They are facing persecution and getting annoyed with each other. They have started "quiet quitting" the church—skipping the gatherings because it is easier to stay home. The command is blunt: stop isolating. You cannot "spur one another on" through a screen. You have to be in the room, dealing with the friction of real human relationships, because that friction is the only thing that keeps your faith awake.

Say It Out Loud (One Sentence) I cannot claim to love Jesus while refusing to commit to the local church He shed His blood to build.

Common Confusions Confusion #1: The church is a building. (The church is the people; the building is just the roof that keeps the rain off them). Confusion #2: Church discipline is abusive and mean. (When done biblically, discipline is the ultimate act of love to save a person from destroying themselves).

The Tuesday Payoff You are completely overwhelmed by a crisis on a Tuesday—a massive financial hit or a sudden diagnosis. If you are a podcast Christian, you have great theology in your head, but you are entirely alone in your living room. A podcast cannot bring you a casserole. A YouTube preacher cannot come sit in the hospital waiting room with you. But if you are a committed, invested member of a local church, Tuesday changes. The body activates. Flawed, awkward, beautiful people show up at your door to carry the weight you cannot carry yourself.

Lane 2 — Depth (30 minutes)

Define the Terms Marks of a True Church - Historically defined as the faithful preaching of the Word and the right administration of the sacraments (Baptism and Communion). Universal Church - Every single person throughout history who has been genuinely saved by Jesus. Polity - The specific structure of church government and leadership (e.g., Elder-led, Congregational, Episcopal).

Build the Doctrine (Scripture-forward)

The Mess is the Point Many people leave the church the moment they discover the leadership is flawed or the people are hypocritical. But the church was never designed to be a museum for perfect people.

Key texts: 1 Corinthians 1:10–11; Ephesians 2:19–22

If you read 1 Corinthians, Paul is writing to a church dealing with lawsuits, sexual immorality, and massive theological division. It was a disaster. Yet Paul still calls them "the church of God in Corinth." The mess does not invalidate the church; the mess is the exact environment where God teaches us how to forgive. You are being built together into a dwelling place for God (Eph 2:22), and construction sites are inherently messy.

Submitting to Imperfect Authority We are a culture that violently rebels against authority. We view any submission to an institution as oppressive. But God explicitly established human authority in the local church for our protection.

Key texts: Hebrews 13:17; 1 Peter 5:2–3

"Have confidence in your leaders and submit to their authority, because they keep watch over you as those who must give an account" (Heb 13:17). Pastors and elders are not CEOs; they are under-shepherds who will literally be judged by God for how they cared for your soul. Submitting to godly (though imperfect) church leadership is the primary way we learn how to submit to the invisible authority of God.

The Necessity of Discipline If a surgeon finds a tumor, the most loving thing they can do is cut it out. If a church finds unrepentant, destructive sin in a member, the most loving thing they can do is confront it.

Key texts: Matthew 18:15–17; 1 Corinthians 5:4–5

Jesus lays out a clear, private, escalating process for confronting sin in Matthew 18. If the person absolutely refuses to repent, Jesus commands the church to treat them "as a pagan or a tax collector"—meaning, remove them from the membership of the church so they realize the gravity of their sin and hopefully return. A church that refuses to practice discipline does not love its members; it only loves its own comfort.

BOX - What This Is NOT Saying We are NOT saying you should stay in a church that covers up abuse or preaches a false gospel; leave abusive systems immediately. We are NOT saying the church replaces Jesus; the church points to Jesus. We are NOT saying a massive megachurch is bad or a tiny house church is good; size does not determine faithfulness.

BOX - Where Christians Differ The main disagreement here revolves around *Polity* (Church Government).

1. Episcopal polity: Hierarchical structure with Bishops overseeing multiple churches (Catholic, Anglican, Methodist).

2. Presbyterian polity: Representative structure where local Elders govern the church and connect to a regional presbytery.

3. Congregational polity: Democratic structure where the final authority rests with the vote of the local congregation (Baptist, non-denominational). While the structures differ wildly, all orthodox traditions agree that a Christian must be submitted to *some* form of local church accountability.

Lane 3 — Deep Dive (Optional)

The Objection You're Already Thinking "I love God, but I have been deeply, profoundly hurt by church leaders. The spiritual abuse and toxic politics I experienced make me physically sick when I walk into a church building. Why should I go back?"

The Best Answer If you have been abused, manipulated, or crushed by the institution of the church, your anger is entirely justified. Spiritual abuse is one of the most horrific crimes possible, because the abuser takes the beautiful, holy name of Jesus and uses it to shield their own narcissism. When a pastor or a church deeply hurts you, it feels like God Himself has betrayed you.

You need to know that Jesus is vastly more angry about that abuse than you are. In Matthew 18, Jesus says that anyone who harms one of His sheep would be better off having a millstone tied around their neck and being drowned in the sea. He does not tolerate wolves in shepherd's clothing.

But the solution to a terrible, toxic church is not isolation; the solution is a healthy, biblical church. If you have a horrible experience with a corrupt doctor, you don't swear off modern medicine forever. You find a better doctor. Take the time you need to heal. Sit in the back row. But do not let a corrupt leader steal the Bride of Christ from you. The enemy wants you isolated because an isolated Christian is an easy target. The bravest thing you can do after being hurt by the church is to slowly, carefully try again.

Historical Lens In the 3rd century, an African bishop named Cyprian wrote a famous and terrifying sentence: "He can no longer have God for his Father, who has not the Church for his mother." While modern evangelicals might find that language too strong, Cyprian was combating a culture of individualists who thought they could define Christianity on their own terms. The historic church universally recognized that the Christian life is an essentially corporate reality. There is no such thing as solitary Christianity in the New Testament.

Real-Life Translation We approach the church like consumers at a restaurant. We sit in the pew and evaluate the music ("Too loud today"), the sermon ("A little dry"), and the children's ministry ("Not enough programs"). If the restaurant stops catering to our specific preferences, we leave a bad Yelp review and drive down the street to a new church.

This consumer mindset is completely destroying our spiritual formation. You cannot be formed by an institution you are constantly judging.

The church is not a restaurant; it is a family. You don't leave your family when the meal is slightly overcooked. You walk into the kitchen and ask how you can help do the dishes. Spiritual maturity begins the exact moment you stop asking, "What is this church doing for me?" and start asking, "Who can I serve in this building today?"

Midlife Module - This Doctrine at 49 You are 49, and your schedule is packed. Between your career, your aging parents, and your kids' traveling sports teams, Sunday morning feels like the only time you actually have to rest. The idea of waking up, getting dressed, and going to sit in a building for two hours feels like an impossible burden. You justify staying home by saying, "We will just watch the livestream; God is everywhere anyway."

The livestream is a great tool for the sick, but it is a lethal poison for the healthy. At 49, you are modeling for your children what you truly value. If you prioritize sports, sleep, and convenience over the physical gathering of the saints, you are explicitly teaching your kids that Jesus is an optional hobby. Dragging your tired body into the pew on a Sunday morning is a massive, weekly declaration that the King is more important than your comfort.

Practice + Prayer

This Week's Practice (3–7 minutes) The Consumer Pivot. This Sunday, consciously refuse to evaluate the service. Don't critique the music or the sermon. Instead, walk into the building with one objective: find one person who looks lonely, look them in the eye, and ask them how their week was. Shift from consumer to contributor.

Prayer (100–160 words) God, I confess that I prefer my faith to be private, neat, and controlled. The church is messy, people are frustrating, and my natural instinct is to stay home where it is safe. Forgive my consumerism. Forgive me for loving the Head of the church while insulting the Body. I pray for my local pastors and elders—give them wisdom, protect them from pride, and give them the courage to preach the truth. Help me to be a joy to lead, rather than a burden. If I am carrying bitterness from past church hurt, please heal that wound and give me the grace to forgive. Wire my heart to love the local church as fiercely as Jesus loves it. Amen.

Reflection: Solo (3 prompts)

1. Do you function like a consumer at your church (evaluating the product) or a contributor (serving the family)?

2. Why is a "podcast sermon" fundamentally unable to replace a local pastor who actually knows your name?

3. Have you allowed a bad experience with a flawed church leader to cause you to quietly pull away from the body of Christ?

Small Group (3 prompts + 1 hard question)

1. Read Hebrews 10:24–25. Why is the physical, gathered presence of other believers so essential for keeping our faith alive?

2. Discuss the concept of Church Discipline. Why does our modern culture view this as abusive, and why does the Bible view it as love?

3. We talked about how the church is a "hospital for sinners." How does this lower our expectations and keep us from becoming cynical when people fail?

Hard Question: If your church was exactly as committed, generous, and forgiving as you are, would your church even survive the year?

Close: One Sentence Recap: The local church is God's physical gathering of believers, commanded by Christ to worship together, discipline one another, and display His love to the world.

If You Only Remember One Thing: A podcast cannot bring you a casserole; you cannot survive the tragedies of life without a local body.

Next Week Preview: If we are part of the church, what are the official badges we wear? Next week we look at Baptism. What is happening in the water?

Scripture References Used Matthew 18:15–17 Acts 2:42–47 1 Corinthians 1:10–11 1 Corinthians 5:4–5 Ephesians 2:19–22 Hebrews 10:24–25 Hebrews 13:17 1 Peter 5:2–3

My Thoughts & Notes – What Did I Take From This?

Week 49 — Baptism: Meaning and Differences Without Fighting

Core Question: What exactly is happening when someone gets baptized, and why do Christians argue about the water so much?

Why this matters: Because if you view baptism as just a meaningless tradition, you ignore a direct command of Jesus; but if you think the water magically saves you, you lose the gospel of grace.

At a Glance (One Page)

Big Idea: Baptism is the physical badge of the Christian faith, commanded by Jesus, to publicly symbolize the believer's spiritual death, burial, and resurrection with Christ.

Anchor Text: Matthew 28:19; Romans 6:3–4

We believe…: Baptism is a holy sacrament/ordinance instituted by Christ, using water to outwardly signify the inward reality of cleansing from sin and union with Jesus.

Key Words (3): Sacrament / Ordinance - A physical, visible sign instituted by Christ that points to a spiritual, invisible reality. Credobaptism - The belief that baptism should only be administered to those who make a credible, personal profession of faith (Believer's Baptism). Paedobaptism - The belief that baptism should be administered to the infant children of believing parents as a sign of entering the covenant community.

The One Mistake People Make: Treating baptism as an optional, extra-credit activity for "super Christians," rather than the basic, mandatory entrance rite into the visible church.

Choose Your Lane: Lane 1 / Lane 2 / Lane 3

This Week's Practice: The Public Milestone.

This Week's Prayer: Father, I confess that I often take the physical acts of worship for granted. I like to keep my faith private, hidden, and entirely in my head. Thank You that You did not design Christianity to be a secret. Thank You for the gift of baptism—a visible, undeniable marker of an invisible reality. Remind me of the day I was buried in the water and raised to new life. Give me the courage to be publicly identified with Jesus Christ, no matter what it costs me in the culture. Amen.

Lane 1 — Clarity (10 minutes)

The Bottom Line The modern world loves a private, internalized spirituality. "My faith is a personal thing between me and God." Jesus completely rejects that idea. He demands that your private faith be made ruthlessly public. How? Through water. Baptism is the official initiation rite into the Christian faith. It is not an option; it is a command from the King. When you are baptized, you are not just getting wet. You are wearing the jersey of the winning team, publicly declaring to the church, the culture, and the demonic realm that you have switched sides and now belong exclusively to Jesus.

Scripture Snapshot Romans 6:3–4: "Or don't you know that all of us who were baptized into Christ Jesus were baptized into his death? We were therefore buried with him through baptism into death in order that, just as Christ was raised from the dead through the glory of the Father, we too may live a new life."

Paul uses baptism as a massive visual aid for Union with Christ (which we covered in Week 42). The physical act tells a spiritual story. When you go under the water, it is a burial. The old, sinful, autonomous version of you is dead and put in a grave. When you come out of the water, it is a resurrection. The water cannot wash away your sins—only the blood of Jesus does that—but the water is the perfect, God-ordained picture of the transaction.

Say It Out Loud (One Sentence) Baptism does not save me, but it is the required public uniform I wear to show the world that Jesus did.

Common Confusions Confusion #1: If I die without being baptized, I will go to hell. (The thief on the cross was saved without baptism; faith alone saves, but true faith leads to obedience). Confusion #2: Getting baptized automatically makes me a Christian. (Baptizing an unbeliever just makes a dry sinner into a wet sinner; faith must be present).

The Tuesday Payoff You are facing intense peer pressure at work or in your neighborhood on a Tuesday to compromise your integrity. You feel the pull to just blend in and be quiet. Remembering your baptism changes your posture. You remember the public vow you made. You remember standing in front of witnesses and declaring that Jesus is Lord. You are not a secret agent; you wear the uniform. Remembering your baptism gives you the spiritual spine to stand out on a Tuesday because you have already publicly crossed the line.

Lane 2 — Depth (30 minutes)

Define the Terms Immersion - The practice of plunging the entire body completely under the water (the standard practice of the early church). Affusion/Sprinkling - The practice of pouring or sprinkling water over the head. Baptismal Regeneration (Heresy for Evangelicals) - The false belief that the physical act of water baptism literally washes away sin and causes the new birth.

Build the Doctrine (Scripture-forward)

The Command of the King Jesus did not offer baptism as a helpful suggestion for spiritual growth. He commanded it as the very first step of discipleship.

Key texts: Matthew 28:19; Acts 2:38

In the Great Commission, Jesus says, "Therefore go and make disciples of all nations, baptizing them in the name of the Father and of the Son and of the Holy Spirit." When Peter preaches the very first sermon of the church in Acts 2, the crowd asks what they must do. Peter replies, "Repent and be baptized, every one of you." In the New Testament, there is absolutely no category for an "unbaptized Christian." If you believed, you were immediately baptized.

The Picture of the Gospel God knows that we are physical creatures who learn through our senses. He gave us a physical ritual to lock the gospel into our memories.

Key texts: Colossians 2:12; Galatians 3:27

"Having been buried with him in baptism, in which you were also raised with him through your faith in the working of God" (Col 2:12). Paul says, "For all of you who were baptized into Christ have clothed yourselves with Christ" (Gal 3:27). When the church watches someone get baptized, they are watching a live-action sermon. It is a visual reenactment of the death and resurrection of Jesus, preached without using any words.

The Badge of Belonging Baptism is not an individualistic, solo event between you and God. You do not baptize yourself in your bathtub. It is an act of the church, officially welcoming you into the family.

Key texts: 1 Corinthians 12:13

"For we were all baptized by one Spirit so as to form one body—whether Jews or Gentiles, slave or free." Baptism is the physical front door to the local church. It marks the boundary line between the watching world and the committed body of Christ. It tells the congregation, "This person is now our responsibility to love and protect," and it tells the person, "You are no longer alone."

BOX - What This Is NOT Saying We are NOT saying you need to be re-baptized every time you sin or backslide. We are NOT saying you have to be baptized in a church building; rivers, lakes, and swimming pools work perfectly fine. We are NOT saying water has magical properties; the power is in the Holy Spirit and the Word, not the H2O.

BOX - Where Christians Differ This is a massive dividing line in Protestantism: Infant Baptism (Paedobaptism) vs. Believer's Baptism (Credobaptism).

1. Presbyterians, Anglicans, and Methodists baptize infants. They view baptism as the New Testament equivalent of Old Testament circumcision—a sign of entering the covenant community. It does not save the infant, but marks them as part of the church family, awaiting their future faith.

2. Baptists and Non-denominational churches baptize only those old enough to make a credible profession of faith. They argue the New Testament only ever shows believers being baptized, insisting the order is always "believe, then be baptized." While the debate is intense, both sides recognize the other as orthodox brothers and sisters in Christ.

Lane 3 — Deep Dive (Optional)

The Objection You're Already Thinking "I was baptized as a baby, but I didn't actually start following Jesus until I was 35. Do I need to get baptized again as an adult?"

The Best Answer This is one of the most common and practical questions in the modern church, and how you answer it depends entirely on your church tradition.

If you are in a Baptist or non-denominational church, the answer is a resounding "Yes." They believe that your infant baptism was a beautiful dedication by your parents, but it was not biblically valid baptism because you did not have personal faith. They will strongly encourage you to be baptized as a believer to publicly declare your own faith.

If you are in a Presbyterian or Anglican church, the answer is a firm "No." They believe the sacrament is based on God's covenant promise, not your performance. To get re-baptized, they argue, is to accidentally imply that God's first promise wasn't good enough. Instead of re-baptism, they will have you "confirm" your baptism through a public profession of faith.

The pastoral key here is humility. Do not let secondary debates cause division. If your conscience convicts you to be baptized as an adult believer, do it joyfully. But do not look down on brothers and sisters who hold deeply to the covenant theology of infant baptism.

Historical Lens During the Reformation in the 1500s, a radical group emerged called the Anabaptists (meaning "re-baptizers"). They read the Bible and concluded that the state-run church's practice of baptizing every infant was unbiblical. They started baptizing adults who actually believed. For this, they were violently persecuted and often drowned by both Catholics and other Protestants. Modern believers who casually put off getting baptized forget that their spiritual ancestors literally paid with their lives for the right to go under the water.

Real-Life Translation We have an epidemic of people who attend a local church for five years, enjoy the music, give a little money, but refuse to ever officially join the church or get baptized. They want the benefits of the community without the commitment of the covenant.

Baptism forces the issue. It forces you to get off the fence. You cannot be a secret admirer of Jesus. He demands that you walk down an aisle, stand in front of a crowd of people, get soaking wet, and state clearly that He is your Lord. It is humiliating to the ego. It is vulnerable. And that is exactly why He commands it. Baptism kills the pride of the uncommitted spectator and turns them into an accountable participant.

Midlife Module - This Doctrine at 45 You are 45. You grew up vaguely religious, walked away for decades, and recently came to true faith in Christ. But you look around your church, and the only people getting baptized are 12-year-olds in the youth group. You feel a massive wave of awkwardness. You think, *I am a grown adult with a mortgage and a career; I am not getting in a tank of water in front of a thousand people.*

That awkwardness is your pride talking. At 45, getting baptized alongside a bunch of middle schoolers is actually the most profound spiritual statement you can make. It proves that the gospel levels the playing field. It proves that a successful

45-year-old is just as desperate for the grace of Jesus as a 12-year-old. Pushing past the awkwardness to obey the command of Christ is a massive victory for your sanctification.

Practice + Prayer

This Week's Practice (3–7 minutes) The Public Milestone. If you have genuinely trusted Christ but have never been baptized, call your pastor this week and schedule it. Stop putting it off. If you have been baptized, take five minutes today to remember that moment. Remember the water. Remember the witnesses. Remind yourself of whose name you bear.

Prayer (100–160 words) God, thank You that You did not leave my faith to be an invisible, abstract concept. Thank You for giving the church the physical, tangible gift of baptism. I praise You for the reality that the water represents: that my old, autonomous, sinful self has been buried in the grave with Jesus, and I have been raised to walk in new life. Forgive me for the times I try to hide my faith and blend into the culture. Give me the courage to wear the uniform proudly. I pray for the unity of Your church. Where we disagree on the mechanics of the water, give us profound charity and grace toward one another, uniting us all under the single banner of the gospel. Amen.

Reflection

Solo (3 prompts)

1. Were you baptized as an infant or a believer? How does your specific experience shape your understanding of the sacrament?

2. Why does the modern mind naturally resist the idea of making a "public declaration" of a private belief?

3. How does the imagery of "burial and resurrection" in baptism change the way you view your old, sinful habits?

Small Group (3 prompts + 1 hard question)

1. Read Romans 6:3–4. How does understanding baptism as a "burial" help us fight temptation on a daily basis?

2. Discuss the historical reality of the Anabaptists who were martyred for their view of baptism. Why do we treat this command so casually today?

3. We talked about how baptism kills the "spectator" mindset. Why is it dangerous to attend a church for years without ever being publicly identified with it?

Hard Question: Are you refusing to get baptized simply because you are too proud to look vulnerable and wet in front of a crowd of people?

Close

One Sentence Recap: Baptism is the physical badge of the Christian faith, commanded by Jesus, to publicly symbolize our spiritual death, burial, and resurrection with Christ.

If You Only Remember One Thing: You cannot be a secret agent for Jesus; baptism is the required public uniform of the Kingdom.

Next Week Preview: This brings us to the second sacrament. Next week we look at The Lord's Supper and Worship. What is actually happening when we eat the bread and drink the cup?

Scripture References Used Matthew 28:19 Acts 2:38 Romans 6:3–4 1 Corinthians 12:13 Galatians 3:27 Colossians 2:12

My Thoughts & Notes – What Did I Take From This?

WEEK 50 — THE LORD'S SUPPER AND WORSHIP: RE-CENTERING

CORE QUESTION: IS TAKING communion just a quiet moment to feel guilty about my sins, or is something deeper actually happening?

Why this matters: Because if worship is just a concert and communion is just a snack, church is a performance; but if they are encounters with the living God, church is a recalibration of your soul.

At a Glance (One Page)

Big Idea: The Lord's Supper is a physical covenant meal given by Jesus to His church to visibly remember His sacrifice, spiritually nourish our faith, and anticipate His promised return.

Anchor Text: 1 Corinthians 11:23–26; John 4:23–24

We believe…: The Lord's Supper (Communion) is a sacrament/ordinance where the gathered church eats bread and drinks the cup, proclaiming the Lord's death and experiencing spiritual communion with Him until He returns.

Key Words (3): Communion / Eucharist - Terms for the Lord's Supper. Eucharist means "thanksgiving," recognizing the meal as a joyful celebration of grace. Worship - Ascribing ultimate value and worth to God, encompassing both our gathered singing and our daily obedience. New Covenant - The unbreakable promise established by Jesus' blood, which we formally renew every time we take the elements.

The One Mistake People Make: Treating communion like an individual, solitary funeral where they sit in isolation feeling terrible about their sins, entirely missing the communal joy of a family meal.

Choose Your Lane: Lane 1 / Lane 2 / Lane 3

This Week's Practice: The Relational Audit.

This Week's Prayer: Father, I confess that I often approach worship like a consumer. I evaluate the music, critique the sermon, and treat communion like a mindless routine. Forgive my casual approach to holy things. Thank You for the gift of the Lord's Supper. Thank You that You know I am forgetful, so You gave me something physical to touch and taste to remind me of the cross. When I take the bread and the cup, feed my soul. Remind me that the debt is paid. Shift my eyes off my own failures and fix them entirely on the finished work of Jesus. Amen.

Lane 1 — Clarity (10 minutes)

The Bottom Line We are incredibly forgetful creatures. We can hear a brilliant sermon on Sunday, and by Tuesday afternoon, we have completely forgotten the grace of God and returned to our anxiety. Jesus knew we would forget. He knew human beings need physical, sensory experiences to lock truth into our brains. So on the night He was betrayed, He didn't just give a theological lecture. He took bread and wine. He gave the church a physical, repeated, communal meal. The Lord's Supper is the ultimate recalibration tool. It forces a wandering, distracted church to physically stop, taste the reality of the gospel, and remember exactly who they belong to.

Scripture Snapshot 1 Corinthians 11:23–26: "For I received from the Lord what I also passed on to you: The Lord Jesus, on the night he was betrayed, took bread, and when he had given thanks, he broke it and said, 'This is my body, which is for you; do this in remembrance of me.' ... For whenever you eat this bread and drink this cup, you proclaim the Lord's death until he comes."

Paul reminds the messy Corinthian church of the original instructions for the meal. Notice the two directions Paul points their eyes. First, they look backward ("in remembrance of me") to the historical, bloody reality of the cross. But then, Paul points them forward. We do this "until he comes." Every time you take communion, you are participating in a countdown. It is a temporary meal we eat in enemy territory, waiting for the King to return and upgrade the snack to a banquet.

Say It Out Loud (One Sentence) Communion is the family meal where we remember the cross, experience Christ's presence, and anticipate His return.

Common Confusions Confusion #1: I have to be completely free from sin this week to take communion. (It is a meal for sick people who need medicine, not a reward for perfect people). Confusion #2: The bread and wine literally turn into human flesh and blood in my stomach. (Evangelicals reject transubstantiation; the elements remain bread and wine, but carry deep spiritual significance).

The Tuesday Payoff You are dealing with a severe lack of motivation and spiritual dryness on a Tuesday. Your faith feels abstract and theoretical. You need something tangible. The memory of Sunday's communion table anchors you. It reminds you that God's love isn't just an idea in a book; it was a physical body broken on a piece of wood. The physical taste of the bread reminds your physical body that grace is real. You don't have to manufacture an emotional high today; you just have to remember the meal.

Lane 2 — Depth (30 minutes)

Define the Terms Transubstantiation - The Catholic belief that the bread and wine miraculously turn into the actual physical body and blood of Christ. Memorialism - The belief (common in Baptist/Bible churches) that the elements are purely symbolic memory aids, with no special spiritual presence of Christ. Spiritual Presence - The Reformed belief that while the elements remain bread and wine, Christ is uniquely and spiritually present to nourish the faith of the believer during the meal.

Build the Doctrine (Scripture-forward)

Looking Back: The Cross The primary function of the Lord's Supper is memory. We have spiritual amnesia, constantly drifting back into self-reliance. The meal stops the drift.

Key texts: Luke 22:19

"And he took bread, gave thanks and broke it, and gave it to them, saying, 'This is my body given for you; do this in remembrance of me.'" We are not re-sacrificing Jesus. The sacrifice was finished once and for all (Heb 10). We are simply dragging the historical reality of Friday into the present moment of Sunday, allowing the truth of the broken body to shatter our current pride.

Looking Around: The Body Communion is not a private ritual. The New Testament knows nothing of taking communion alone in your bedroom. It is deeply corporate. It defines the edges of the family.

Key texts: 1 Corinthians 10:16–17; 1 Corinthians 11:33

Paul writes, "Because there is one loaf, we, who are many, are one body, for we all share the one loaf" (1 Cor 10:17). The Corinthians were eating the meal while divided by class and wealth, and Paul rebuked them fiercely. When you take the cup, you are not just connecting vertically with God; you are connecting horizontally with the person sitting next to you. You cannot take communion with a brother while harboring a bitter, unforgiving grudge against him.

Looking Forward: The Return The Lord's Supper is inherently hopeful. It is an appetizer for the great Marriage Supper of the Lamb at the end of history.

Key texts: Matthew 26:29; Revelation 19:9

Jesus made a striking promise at the Last Supper: "I tell you, I will not drink from this fruit of the vine from now on until that day when I drink it new with you in my Father's kingdom." Jesus is fasting from the wine until we get home. Every time the church takes communion, it is a defiant declaration to a dying world that this age is temporary. The King is coming back, and He is setting a table.

BOX - What This Is NOT Saying We are NOT saying an unbeliever should take communion; it is a covenant meal reserved only for those who have trusted Christ. We are NOT saying communion forgives your sins; only the cross forgives, communion simply remembers. We are NOT saying worship is only singing; worship is the posture of your entire life (Rom 12:1).

BOX - Where Christians Differ The nature of Christ's presence in the meal is a major historical debate.

1. Catholics hold to Transubstantiation (it physically becomes Christ).

2. Lutherans hold to Consubstantiation (Christ is physically "in, with, and under" the bread).

3. Reformed/Presbyterians hold to Spiritual Presence (Christ is truly present, but spiritually, nourishing faith).

4. Baptists/Zwinglians hold to Memorialism (It is a pure symbol to aid human memory). While the mechanics are fiercely debated, all evangelicals agree the meal is a sacred, commanded ordinance that deeply benefits the gathered church.

Lane 3 — Deep Dive (Optional)

The Objection You're Already Thinking "Paul says in 1 Corinthians 11 that whoever eats the bread 'in an unworthy manner' eats judgment on themselves. That terrifies me. I am definitely unworthy, so shouldn't I just skip communion to be safe?"

The Best Answer This is a massive misunderstanding of Paul's warning, and it keeps thousands of sincere Christians away from the table out of fear.

When Paul says "in an unworthy manner," he is not talking about your personal moral perfection. If the table required you to be perfectly worthy, no human being on earth could ever take it. The table is a hospital bed; you don't have to be healthy to get in it.

Paul is addressing the *manner* in which the Corinthians were eating. They were treating it like a frat party. The rich were getting drunk, and the poor were going hungry. They were despising the body of Christ. To eat in a "worthy manner" simply means to recognize the solemnity of what the bread represents, to confess your absolute unworthiness to God, and to make sure you are not actively at war with the church member sitting across the aisle. If you are a broken sinner trusting in Jesus, the table is exactly where you belong.

Historical Lens The word "Eucharist" comes from the Greek word *eucharistia*, which simply means "thanksgiving." In the early church, communion was not a dark, somber, funeral-like ritual where everyone stared at their shoes and felt guilty. It was a joyous celebration. They were celebrating the fact that the war was over and the debt was paid. The shift toward treating communion like a terrifying, miserable guilt-trip happened during the Middle Ages. The Reformers tried to return the table to the people as a meal of joyful grace.

Real-Life Translation We are a generation suffering from profound spiritual ADD. Our lives are fragmented by notifications, sports schedules, and career demands. We are constantly vibrating with low-grade anxiety.

We desperately need recalibration. Think of your car. If the alignment is off, the car naturally drifts into the ditch. You have to constantly fight the steering wheel to keep it on the road. Your soul operates the same way. By Wednesday, your alignment is off. You are drifting into greed, anger, and self-reliance.

Corporate worship and the Lord's Supper are the alignment rack. You walk into the building completely out of alignment, consumed with your own problems. You sing songs that force your eyes up to the majesty of God. You eat bread that forces your eyes back to the sacrifice of the cross. By the time you leave, the drift is corrected. You are re-centered. You cannot survive a secular world without this weekly realignment.

Midlife Module - This Doctrine at 47 You are 47, and you are sitting in a church pew. Three rows ahead of you is a person who deeply annoyed you at a committee meeting, or someone whose political posts infuriate you. Your natural Gen X instinct is cynicism and detachment.

But then the communion trays are passed. You take the bread, and you watch the person three rows ahead take the exact same bread. The theology of the table hits you like a truck: *the ground is completely level at the foot of the cross.* You are both starving beggars. You both require the exact same blood to survive. Communion destroys your midlife cynicism and forces you into a terrifying, beautiful solidarity with the annoying people in your church.

Practice + Prayer

This Week's Practice (3–7 minutes) The Relational Audit. Before you take communion this Sunday, follow Paul's command to "examine yourself" (1 Cor 11). This doesn't just mean looking for private sins. Ask yourself: *Am I harboring bitterness toward anyone in this room?* If you are, go quietly make peace with them before you take the cup. The vertical meal requires horizontal peace.

Prayer (100–160 words) God, thank You for knowing exactly how weak and forgetful I am. Thank You that You did not just give me a book to read, but a physical meal to eat. When I take the bread, remind my soul that the body of Jesus was broken so that my brokenness could be healed. When I drink the cup, remind my soul that the New Covenant is sealed in His blood, and my debt is entirely canceled. Forgive me for the times I have treated Your table casually or taken it while harboring anger toward a brother or sister. Realign my wandering heart. Fix my eyes on the hope of the future, and give me the endurance to wait for the day when the King returns to drink it new with us. Amen.

Reflection

Solo (3 prompts)

1. Do you tend to treat communion as a miserable, guilty funeral, or as a joyful "Eucharist" (thanksgiving) for a paid debt?

2. How does the physical nature of the bread and cup help anchor your faith when your emotions are completely dry?

3. Why is it dangerous to view worship solely as the 20 minutes of singing at the beginning of a church service?

Small Group (3 prompts + 1 hard question)

1. Read 1 Corinthians 11:23–26. Discuss the tension between looking "backward" to the cross and "forward" to the Second Coming.

2. Discuss the misunderstanding of taking communion in an "unworthy manner" from Lane 3. How does clearing this up invite struggling people back to the table?

3. We talked about worship as an "alignment rack." How have you experienced the physical gathering of the church correcting your spiritual drift during a hard week?

Hard Question: Are you currently taking communion every Sunday while actively, stubbornly refusing to forgive someone in your life?

<u>**Close**</u>

One Sentence Recap: The Lord's Supper is a physical covenant meal given to the church to remember Christ's sacrifice, nourish our faith, and anticipate His return.

If You Only Remember One Thing: The communion table is not a reward for perfect people; it is a hospital bed and medicine for broken people who trust Jesus.

Next Week Preview: This completes Part 7. Next week, we start our final section: Last Things. What actually happens the absolute second after you die?

Scripture References Used Matthew 26:29 Luke 22:19 John 4:23–24 Romans 12:1 1 Corinthians 10:16–17 1 Corinthians 11:23–26 1 Corinthians 11:33 Revelation 19:9

<u>**My Thoughts & Notes – What Did I Take From This?**</u>

PART 8 — LAST THINGS

We are the generation that mastered the art of the mixtape, agonizing over the perfect final song to leave a lasting impression. The ending matters. If a brilliant television series has a terrible finale, it ruins the entire show. We need an ending that actually pays off.

In Part 8, we look at God's grand finale. We are moving past the cartoonish pop-culture ideas of floating on clouds with harps to look at the gritty reality of death and the unbending truth of final judgment. Finally, we will look at the breathtaking promise of the New Heavens and New Earth- the ultimate, physical ending that makes all our present suffering actually mean something.

WEEK 51 — DEATH, JUDGMENT, HEAVEN, HELL

CORE QUESTION: WHAT ACTUALLY happens the absolute second after my heart stops beating?

Why this matters: Because if you do not have a robust theology for death, you will spend the second half of your life paralyzed by the fear of it.

At a Glance (One Page)

Big Idea: Death is not the end of your existence; it is the doorway to an immediate, conscious reality where you will face the perfectly just judgment of God, leading to either eternal life or eternal separation.

Anchor Text: Hebrews 9:27; Revelation 20:11–15

We believe...: At death, the souls of believers immediately enter the presence of Christ in heaven, while the souls of the unrepentant enter conscious punishment, awaiting the final bodily resurrection and the ultimate, perfectly just judgment of God.

Key Words (3): Intermediate State - The period between your physical death and the future bodily resurrection, where your soul is consciously in heaven or hell. Final Judgment - The event at the end of history where every human being will stand before Christ to give an account of their life. Hell - The eternal, conscious state of final justice and absolute separation from the goodness of God, chosen by those who reject His grace.

The One Mistake People Make: Relying on pop-culture myths (like playing harps on clouds or partying with friends in hell) instead of the terrifying and glorious realities described in Scripture.

Choose Your Lane: Lane 1 / Lane 2 / Lane 3

This Week's Practice: The Estate Audit.

This Week's Prayer: Father, I confess that I spend most of my time pretending I am not going to die. I obsess over my health, my retirement, and my safety, desperately trying to ignore the expiration date on my physical body. Forgive me for living as if this temporary world is my permanent home. Give me the courage to look at death without flinching, knowing that Jesus has already defeated it. Anchor my hope in the absolute guarantee of heaven, and give me a profound urgency to share the gospel with the people I love. Amen.

Lane 1 — Clarity (10 minutes)

The Bottom Line Modern culture has two ways of dealing with death: we either sanitize it and hide it in hospitals, or we romanticize it by saying things like, "They are just sleeping," or "They are part of the universe now." The Bible refuses to do either. Death is an enemy. It is the unnatural, violent tearing apart of the body and soul. But because of Jesus, death is a defeated enemy. For the Christian, death has lost its sting. It is no longer a permanent vault; it is simply a dark hallway you walk through to get to the immediate, conscious presence of God.

Scripture Snapshot Hebrews 9:27–28: "Just as people are destined to die once, and after that to face judgment, so Christ was sacrificed once to take away the sins of many; and he will appear a second time, not to bear sin, but to bring salvation to those who are waiting for him."

The writer of Hebrews lays out the unbending math of human existence: one life, one death, one judgment. There is no reincarnation. There are no second chances to live a better life. But immediately after stating that terrifying reality, he points directly to the cross. You will face judgment, but if you are in Christ, your sins have already been taken away. The verdict is already secured.

Say It Out Loud (One Sentence) Death is the final enemy, but because Jesus holds the keys, it is only a doorway into the presence of my Father.

Common Confusions Confusion #1: When we die, our souls just sleep until Jesus comes back. (The Bible teaches "soul sleep" is false; to be absent from the body is to be *present* with the Lord). Confusion #2: Hell is where the devil rules and tortures people. (Hell is the place where the devil himself will be punished; God is the one executing justice).

The Tuesday Payoff You are sitting in a lawyer's office on a Tuesday morning, finalizing your will and life insurance. It feels morbid and unsettling. If your theology stops at the grave, this meeting is a grim reminder of your ultimate irrelevance. But with a biblical view of the afterlife, writing a will is an act of quiet defiance. You are managing your earthly assets well, but your peace comes from knowing your ultimate estate is legally secured in heaven. You can plan for your physical death because you know your spiritual life is untouchable.

Lane 2 — Depth (30 minutes)

Define the Terms Purgatory - A Roman Catholic doctrine (rejected by Protestants) claiming there is a temporary place of purifying suffering for believers before entering heaven. Annihilationism - The belief that hell is not eternal conscious punishment, but simply the total destruction of the soul (ceasing to exist). Universalism - The heresy that everyone will eventually be saved and end up in heaven.

Build the Doctrine (Scripture-forward)

The Intermediate State What happens the millisecond after a Christian dies? You do not become a ghost, and you do not go into a state of unconscious sleep. Your body goes into the ground, but your soul goes to Christ.

Key texts: 2 Corinthians 5:8; Luke 23:43

Paul writes, "We are confident, I say, and would prefer to be away from the body and at home with the Lord" (2 Cor 5:8). Jesus told the thief on the cross, "Truly I tell you, today you will be with me in paradise" (Luke 23:43). The intermediate state is a time of conscious joy, worship, and rest in the presence of God, even while we wait for the final resurrection of our physical bodies.

The Final Judgment At the end of human history, Jesus will return, everyone will be physically resurrected, and the books will be opened. No secret will remain hidden. Every injustice will be brought to light.

Key texts: Revelation 20:11–15; 2 Corinthians 5:10

"And I saw the dead, great and small, standing before the throne, and books were opened... The dead were judged according to what they had done as recorded in the books" (Rev 20:12). For the unbeliever, this judgment results in condemnation based on their sins. For the believer, their name is found in the "Book of Life," meaning their sins are covered by Christ. Believers will also face a judgment of their works (2 Cor 5:10) to determine their eternal rewards, but not their eternal destination.

The Reality of Hell Jesus spoke more about hell than He did about heaven. It is a place of absolute, final justice—a terrifying reality of eternal, conscious separation from the goodness of God.

Key texts: Matthew 25:46; 2 Thessalonians 1:9

"They will be punished with everlasting destruction and shut out from the presence of the Lord and from the glory of his might" (2 Thess 1:9). Jesus describes it as a place of "weeping and gnashing of teeth." It is the ultimate consequence of human autonomy. If a person spends eighty years demanding that God leave them alone, God will eventually grant their request permanently. Hell is the terrifying reality of getting exactly what you asked for.

BOX - What This Is NOT Saying We are NOT saying Christians should be arrogant about heaven; we are saved by grace, not merit. We are NOT saying we know exactly what the intermediate state looks like; the Bible gives us comfort, not a detailed map. We are NOT saying God delights in sending people to hell; Ezekiel 33:11 says God takes no pleasure in the death of the wicked.

BOX - Where Christians Differ While historic orthodoxy firmly holds to the reality of eternal conscious punishment, there is a minority view within some evangelical circles called *Conditional Immortality* (or Annihilationism). This view argues that while the fire of hell is eternal, the souls cast into it are eventually consumed and cease to exist, rather than suffering consciously forever. However, the overwhelming majority of broad evangelicalism holds to the historic view of eternal conscious punishment based on Jesus' parallel phrasing in Matthew 25:46 ("eternal punishment" vs. "eternal life").

Lane 3 — Deep Dive (Optional)

The Objection You're Already Thinking "How can a loving God possibly send someone to a place of eternal torment? That seems infinitely disproportionate to the sins committed in a short, eighty-year life."

The Best Answer This is the heaviest objection to the Christian faith. It requires us to completely rethink how we view sin and justice.

First, we misunderstand the severity of sin. As we covered in Week 23, the penalty of a crime is based on the authority of the one offended. Stealing a pen from your brother is a minor offense; stealing national secrets from the government is treason. Because God is infinitely holy, rebelling against Him is an offense of infinite weight, requiring an infinite penalty.

Second, as C.S. Lewis brilliantly argued, God does not violently throw innocent, protesting people into hell against their will. Lewis wrote, "There are only two kinds of people in the end: those who say to God, 'Thy will be done,' and those to whom God says, in the end, 'Thy will be done.'" Hell is the trajectory of a soul that wants to be its own god, locked from the inside.

To demand that God just "forgive everyone anyway" is to demand that God force Himself on people who hate Him. A loving God respects human agency enough to allow people to choose their eternal separation.

Historical Lens During the Middle Ages, the Roman Catholic Church developed the doctrine of Purgatory—a place where Christians go to suffer and pay off the temporal debt for their sins before entering heaven. The Reformers violently rejected this. Why? Because Purgatory implies that the blood of Jesus was not quite enough to cleanse us. By throwing out Purgatory, the Reformation restored the absolute sufficiency of the cross: to die in Christ is to immediately enter the joy of the Lord.

Real-Life Translation We are a culture paralyzed by the fear of death. We spend billions of dollars on medical interventions, diets, and cosmetics just to buy ourselves a few extra years. When someone dies, we quickly move on because lingering on the thought of our own mortality is too terrifying.

For the Christian, you do not have to live in denial. You can look at a casket and admit that it is an ugly, unnatural consequence of sin. But you can also look at it and know it is toothless.

When you fully grasp the doctrine of the afterlife, it fundamentally changes how you live today. If you know that your ultimate future is completely secure in the presence of God, you stop frantically trying to turn this current life into heaven. You can take risks. You can be radically generous with your money. You can endure unfair treatment without demanding revenge, because you know the Final Judge will perfectly balance the scales.

Midlife Module - This Doctrine at 55 You are 55. A friend you have known since college suddenly dies of a heart attack. There was no warning. You attend the funeral, and for the first time, you look around the room and realize that you are the next generation in line. The illusion that you have unlimited time evaporates.

Midlife forces the reality of Hebrews 9:27 onto your calendar. You are destined to die once. This doctrine does not intend to make you depressed; it intends to make you sober. At 55, realizing you have an expiration date is the exact tool God uses to stop you from wasting the next twenty years on petty arguments, accumulating stuff you can't take with you, and holding grudges. The brevity of life clarifies the mission of life.

Practice + Prayer

This Week's Practice (3–7 minutes) The Estate Audit. If you do not have a will or life insurance, start the process this week. Do not ignore it out of fear. Treat it as a profoundly theological act of trusting God with your death and loving your family enough to manage the details. Tell yourself, "My body will die, but my soul is secure."

Prayer (100–160 words) God, You are the Alpha and the Omega, the beginning and the end. I confess that the thought of death terrifies me. The thought of standing before Your judgment seat strips away every excuse I have ever made. If I stand there on my own record, I have no hope. Thank You for Jesus. Thank You that my name is written in the Book of Life entirely because of His blood. When I lose the people I love who know You, give me the supernatural peace of knowing they are immediately in Your presence. Give me a deep, unshakeable confidence in my own future. And give me a heavy, weeping urgency for my neighbors who do not know You. Amen.

Reflection

Solo (3 prompts)

1. What is the most common, unbiblical idea about heaven or hell that you grew up believing?

2. How does the knowledge of the "Intermediate State" (being immediately with Jesus) bring comfort when you think about death?

3. Why is it important to remember that God takes no pleasure in the death of the wicked (Ezekiel 33)?

Small Group (3 prompts + 1 hard question)

1. Read 2 Corinthians 5:8–10. How does Paul balance the comfort of going to be with the Lord with the reality of facing the judgment seat?

2. Discuss C.S. Lewis's quote about hell being "locked from the inside." How does this change the way we view God's justice?

3. We talked about how the fear of death drives our culture. How should a Christian's approach to aging and terminal illness look noticeably different?

Hard Question: Are you living your life as if this temporary world is all there is, quietly refusing to think about the reality of your own inevitable death?

Close

One Sentence Recap: Death is the doorway to an immediate, conscious reality where we will face the perfectly just judgment of God, leading to either eternal life or eternal separation.

If You Only Remember One Thing: Hell is the terrifying reality of getting exactly what you asked for: an eternity completely separate from the authority and goodness of God.

Next Week Preview: If we don't just float as ghosts forever, what is the ultimate endgame? Next week, we finish the book with the New Heavens and the New Earth.

Scripture References Used Ezekiel 33:11 Matthew 25:46 Luke 23:43 2 Corinthians 5:8–10 2 Thessalonians 1:9 Hebrews 9:27–28 Revelation 20:11–15

My Thoughts & Notes – What Did I Take From This?

Week 52 — New Creation: Resurrection Life and Hope That Holds

Core Question: Is the ultimate goal of Christianity just to escape this broken world and float on a cloud forever?

Why this matters: Because if your view of eternity is boring and disembodied, you will desperately cling to this current life; but if your future is a resurrected physical world, you can live with staggering hope.

At a Glance (One Page)

Big Idea: God's ultimate plan is not to throw the physical universe in the trash; He plans to resurrect, purify, and renew it, bringing heaven down to earth so we can live with Him physically forever.

Anchor Text: Revelation 21:1–5; Romans 8:18–25

We believe...: Jesus Christ will return physically and visibly to consummate His kingdom, completely eradicating sin and death, and inaugurating the New Heavens and New Earth where believers will dwell with God forever.

Key Words (3): Consummation - The final completion and perfection of God's redemptive plan for the universe. Shalom - The Hebrew concept of absolute, comprehensive peace, wholeness, and flourishing in every dimension of life. New Heavens and New Earth - The eternal state where the spiritual realm (heaven) and the physical realm (earth) are permanently perfectly united.

The One Mistake People Make: Believing the Greek myth that the spiritual world is good and the physical world is bad, leading them to think heaven is just becoming a ghost playing a harp in the sky.

Choose Your Lane: Lane 1 / Lane 2 / Lane 3

This Week's Practice: The Future Filter.

This Week's Prayer: Father, I confess that my view of eternity is often incredibly small and boring. I have let cultural myths replace the breathtaking promises of Your Word. Thank You that You are not going to abandon the world You made. Thank You that You are going to wipe away every tear, heal every disease, and make all things new. When I am exhausted by the grind of this life, lift my eyes to the horizon. Give me a homesickness for the New Creation that makes me brave, generous, and joyful today. Come quickly, Lord Jesus. Amen.

Lane 1 — Clarity (10 minutes)

The Bottom Line The most damaging lie modern Christians believe about the future is that we are destined to be disembodied spirits sitting on clouds for eternity. That sounds like an unending, boring church service. If that is your theology, it is no wonder you don't actually want to go to heaven yet. But the Bible ends the exact same way it begins: with a physical earth. God does not abandon the material world to Satan. He redeems it. The endgame of Christianity is not humans escaping earth to go up to heaven; it is God bringing heaven down to permanently merge with a resurrected, purified earth.

Scripture Snapshot Revelation 21:1–3: "Then I saw 'a new heaven and a new earth,' for the first heaven and the first earth had passed away... And I heard a loud voice from the throne saying, 'Look! God's dwelling place is now among the people, and he will dwell with them. They will be his people, and God himself will be with them and be their God.'"

John sees the grand finale of human history. Notice the direction of travel. We do not beam up; the holy city comes down. The separation between the spiritual realm and the physical realm is completely eliminated. The curse of Genesis 3 is entirely reversed. God does not restart from scratch; He renews the original design. He takes up physical residence on the earth with His people.

Say It Out Loud (One Sentence) God is not going to trash the physical world; He is going to resurrect it, and we will live with Him in it forever.

Common Confusions Confusion #1: We will be bored in heaven. (We will be ruling, creating, working, and exploring a limitless universe without the frustration of sin). Confusion #2: This world doesn't matter because it's all going to burn anyway. (Because God plans to renew the earth, how we treat it and each other today matters deeply).

The Tuesday Payoff You are completely burned out on a Tuesday afternoon. The grind of paying bills, repairing the house, dealing with health issues, and managing relationships feels like a treadmill that never stops. If you don't have a theology of the New Earth, you will just endure the grind with quiet bitterness. But the promise of the New Creation changes your posture. You know that the treadmill has an end date. You are not destined for exhaustion. You are destined for absolute *Shalom*. The frustration of this Tuesday is temporary; the restoration of the universe is permanent.

Lane 2 — Depth (30 minutes)

Define the Terms Eschatology - The theological study of the "last things" (death, judgment, heaven, hell, and the return of Christ). Second Coming (Parousia) - The promised future event where Jesus returns physically to the earth to judge the living and the dead. Glorified Body - The physical, indestructible body believers will receive at the resurrection, modeled after Christ's resurrected body.

Build the Doctrine (Scripture-forward)

The Return of the King Jesus did not leave the timeline open-ended. He promised a specific, visible return. It will not be a secret spiritual event; it will be an undeniable, global reality.

Key texts: Acts 1:11; Matthew 24:30

As Jesus ascends, the angels tell the disciples, "This same Jesus, who has been taken from you into heaven, will come back in the same way you have seen him go into heaven" (Acts 1:11). Jesus Himself warned, "They will see the Son of Man coming on the clouds of heaven, with power and great glory" (Matt 24:30). The King is coming back to reclaim His territory, judge the wicked, and vindicate His people.

The Groaning of Creation The physical planet is currently broken. It experiences natural disasters, decay, and death. But the planet itself is waiting for salvation.

Key texts: Romans 8:19–22

Paul writes that the creation was subjected to frustration, but it holds a massive hope: "that the creation itself will be liberated from its bondage to decay and brought into the freedom and glory of the children of God." When we receive our resurrected bodies, the earth will receive its own resurrection. The physical universe will be cleansed by fire (2 Peter 3:10) to burn away the corruption, leaving behind a purified, perfect, material world.

The End of Tears The most profound promise of the New Earth is not just what will be there, but what will be completely missing.

Key texts: Revelation 21:4

"He will wipe every tear from their eyes. There will be no more death or mourning or crying or pain, for the old order of things has passed away." In the New Creation, hospitals, cemeteries, and divorce courts will not exist. The crushing weight of anxiety, the trauma of abuse, and the devastation of disease will be entirely eradicated. God will permanently remove the source of all human misery.

BOX - What This Is NOT Saying We are NOT saying we know the exact date or time of Jesus' return; anyone who claims to know the date is a false teacher. We are NOT saying our pets automatically go to heaven; but a redeemed earth will undoubtedly be filled with redeemed animal life. We are NOT saying we become omniscient like God; we will spend eternity continually learning and marveling at His infinite grace.

BOX - Where Christians Differ Eschatology is famous for its massive debates, specifically regarding the "Millennium" (the 1,000-year reign mentioned in Revelation 20).

1. Premillennialism: Jesus returns *before* a literal 1,000-year reign of peace on earth.

2. Amillennialism: The 1,000 years is symbolic of the current church age; Jesus returns at the end.

3. Postmillennialism: The church will successfully Christianize the world over a long period, ushering in a golden age, *after* which Jesus returns. Furthermore, Premillennialists debate the "Rapture" (Pre-tribulation vs. Post-tribulation). Broad evangelicalism permits all these views, uniting instead on the absolute certainty of the visible, physical return of Christ and the final victory of God.

Lane 3 — Deep Dive (Optional)

The Objection You're Already Thinking "Honestly, the idea of floating around forever singing worship songs sounds incredibly boring. Is that really all we are going to do?"

The Best Answer If heaven was just an endless choir practice in the clouds, boredom would be a valid concern. But that is the Gnostic version of heaven, not the biblical one.

When God created the perfect world in Genesis 1 and 2, He didn't tell Adam and Eve to sit around singing all day. He gave them a job. He told them to explore the world, cultivate the garden, and build culture. They were designers, architects, and stewards.

The New Earth is the restoration of that original mandate. We will have physical bodies. We will eat physical food (Isaiah 25:6 promises a feast of rich food and aged wine). We will build, invent, work, and explore an infinite, uncorrupted universe. The only difference is that our work will no longer be cursed by thorns, frustration, or fatigue. It will be an eternity of dynamic, joyful human flourishing in the direct presence of the Creator. You won't be bored; you will finally be fully alive.

Historical Lens In the 19th and early 20th centuries, some Christian movements became so obsessed with predicting the exact timeline of the End Times (creating complex charts and maps) that they completely neglected the actual mission of the church in the present world. They adopted a "lifeboat theology"—the ship is sinking, just save souls and ignore the culture. Historic, robust theology rejects this. Because we know God cares about the physical world enough to resurrect it, we must care about justice, beauty, and human flourishing right now.

Real-Life Translation We all carry a deep, unnamed ache. C.S. Lewis called it *Sehnsucht*—the inconsolable longing in the human heart for we know not what. You buy the house, you get the job, you marry the spouse, and while those things are good, the ache remains. You are homesick for a country you have never visited.

The danger of midlife is that you try to cure that ache by burning your life down—having an affair, buying things you can't afford, or numbing yourself with alcohol. You demand that this temporary world provide the perfect satisfaction that only the New Earth can deliver.

The doctrine of the New Creation tells you to stop demanding perfection from a broken world. You can enjoy the good gifts of this life without crushing them under the weight of your ultimate expectations. You can live with profound joy today because you know your true home is just over the horizon.

Midlife Module - This Doctrine at 59 You are 59. The physical reality of aging is undeniable. Your energy levels are dropping, friends are getting sick, and the cultural relevance you once had is fading. The world tells you that your best days are firmly behind you, and the rest of your life is just managing the decline.

The doctrine of the New Creation violently rejects this. If you are in Christ, your best days are not in your twenties. Your best days haven't even started yet. You are going to be handed a resurrected, indestructible body that makes your 25-year-old self look frail. You are going to experience a level of joy and physical vitality that you cannot currently comprehend. At 59, you are not managing a decline; you are standing on the edge of the ultimate beginning.

Practice + Prayer

This Week's Practice (3–7 minutes) The Future Filter. When you feel a wave of anxiety this week about the economy, a medical issue, or a family conflict, pause and run it through the filter of Revelation 21. Ask yourself: "Will this matter in the New Creation?" Let the massive weight of your secure future shrink the temporary panic of your present problem.

Prayer (100–160 words) Father, we have reached the end of the story, and it is more beautiful than I could have ever imagined. Thank You that You do not abandon the things You love. I confess that my vision of eternity is often small, boring, and inaccurate. Forgive me for trying to find ultimate heaven in this temporary earth. Give me a relentless, joyful homesickness for the New Creation. When my body fails, remind me of the resurrection. When my heart breaks, remind me of the day You will wipe every tear from my eyes. Give me the strength to endure the trials of this life, knowing that the eternal weight of glory far outweighs them all. Come quickly, Lord Jesus. Make all things new. Amen.

<u>Reflection:</u> Solo (3 prompts)

1. How does shifting your view of heaven from "floating spirits" to a "physical new earth" change your excitement about eternity?

2. What is one specific pain, fear, or frustration in your life right now that you are most looking forward to God permanently removing?

3. How does the promise of a future, perfect world free you to endure the disappointments of this current world without becoming bitter?

Small Group (3 prompts + 1 hard question)

1. Read Revelation 21:1–5. Why is it significant that God's dwelling place comes *down* to humanity, rather than us going *up* to Him?

2. Discuss the difference between a "lifeboat theology" (the earth is burning, just escape) and a theology of renewal. How does this affect the way we care for the environment and build culture?

3. We talked about how we try to force this current life to provide the perfect satisfaction of heaven. Where do you see people doing this most often?

Hard Question: Are you so comfortable, wealthy, and insulated in your current life that you secretly aren't really looking forward to Jesus coming back?

<u>Close:</u> One Sentence Recap: Jesus will return to completely eradicate sin and death, inaugurating the New Heavens and New Earth where we will dwell with Him physically forever.

If You Only Remember One Thing: The endgame of Christianity is not humans escaping earth to be ghosts; it is God bringing heaven down to earth so we can finally be fully alive.

Conclusion: You have reached the end of this theology. The ultimate goal of studying God is not a bigger brain; it is a burning heart. Go live boldly in the light of the New Creation.

Scripture References Used Isaiah 25:6 Matthew 24:30 Acts 1:11 Romans 8:18–25 2 Peter 3:10 Revelation 20 Revelation 21:1–5

Conclusion — The House is Built (Now Live in It)

You made it.

Whether you read this book in 52 weeks, binged it in a month, or took three years because life kept interrupting, you reached the end. You didn't do it perfectly, and you probably forgot the difference between justification and sanctification three times. That is entirely okay.

Let's be honest about what just happened.

Learning the mechanics of the Hypostatic Union did not pay off your mortgage. Understanding the difference between justification and sanctification did not make your teenager less moody. Getting a grip on eschatology didn't fix your lower back pain or lower your cholesterol.

If you picked up this book hoping that systematic theology was the ultimate life-hack that would finally make your daily grind easy, you are probably disappointed. Theology does not remove the friction of living in a broken world.

But what theology *does* do is give you a floor that won't collapse when the friction gets heavy.

In the introduction, we talked about how theology is the blueprint for a house. For a long time, you might have been living in a house built on 90s youth group nostalgia, acoustic-guitar emotional highs, and the exhausting pressure to 'change the world for Jesus.' That house was fine when the weather was clear. But midlife brought the storms. You saw marriages fail, you experienced church hurt, you watched your parents age, and you realized that your own willpower had a strict expiration date. The old house couldn't handle the wind.

Over the last 52 chapters, you have been slowly, quietly pouring concrete.

You established that truth exists outside of your own shifting feelings. You anchored your existence in a Creator who actually spoke. You looked at the absolute horror of human sin, and then you looked at the breathtaking, scandalous, one-way grace of God that entirely covers it. You realized that Jesus is not a life-coach you casually consult; He is a resurrected King who demands your life and secures your future.

What does the rest of your life look like?

It looks beautifully, stubbornly ordinary. The pressure is off. You do not have to change the world. You do not have to be the savior of your family, the indispensable hero of your company, or the smartest person in your church. You can officially resign as the general manager of the universe. You have been demoted to 'beloved child and useful servant,' and it is the greatest relief of your life.

You can go to a messy, imperfect local church and just serve the people in front of you. You can do your boring, Tuesday-afternoon job with quiet integrity, knowing the King is watching. You can look at the physical decline of your own body without panicking, because you know a resurrected body is already legally secured in your name.

The adrenaline and the hype of your earlier years are gone. Let them go. Replace them with the deep, quiet grit of a Tuesday-afternoon faithfulness.

The world will continue to be loud, chaotic, and outraged. Let it spin. You know who is sitting at the right hand of the Father. The debt is paid. The tomb is empty. The mission is clear, and the end of the story is an absolute guarantee.

Hold the line. Love your neighbor. And go to sleep tonight knowing you are held by a grip that will never let you go.